W9-DCL-288

3000 800061 77751
St. Louis Community College

WITHDRAWN

BLOCKBUSTERS

A Reference Guide to Film Genres

Mark A. Graves and F. Bruce Engle

GREENWOOD PRESS
Westport, Connecticut • London

Library of Congress Cataloging-in-Publication Data

Graves, Mark A., 1963–
Blockbusters : a reference guide to film genres / Mark A. Graves and F. Bruce Engle.
p. cm.
Includes bibliographical references and index.
ISBN 0-313-33094-8 (alk. paper)
1. Film genres. I. Engle, Frederick Bruce, 1958– II. Title.
PN1995.G663 2006
791.43'6—dc22 2006007914

British Library Cataloguing in Publication Data is available.

Library of Congress Catalog Card Number: 2006007914
ISBN: 0-313-33094-8

First published in 2006

Greenwood Press, 88 Post Road West, Westport, CT 06881
An imprint of Greenwood Publishing Group, Inc.
www.greenwood.com

Printed in the United States of America

The paper used in this book complies with the Permanent Paper Standard issued by the National Information Standards Organization (Z39.48-1984).

10 9 8 7 6 5 4 3 2 1

To Our Families:
John, Marolyn, and Wendell Graves
Fred, Mary, Susan, and Allen Engle
and
fellow movie-lovers
Keith Barnhill and Margaret Muncy Willingham

Photofest

CONTENTS

ACKNOWLEDGMENTS

We would like to thank Carrie Smith for her work compiling the list of films discussed in each chapter and the Graduate College at Morehead State University for providing us her services.

INTRODUCTION

TO MANY FILM VIEWERS, the notion of a *film genre* presents very little difficulty. The managers of most local video stores, or even the Web sites of online rental services, cater to customers looking for simple viewing guidance, dividing up their offerings with labels such as *New Releases* and *Classics* or with broad section titles including *Drama*, *Comedy*, *Action-Adventure*, and *Musicals*. For the majority of viewers, such advice enables us to easily find the types and styles of films we find appealing and would most enjoy watching. Although Hollywood releases are often criticized for their formulaic approaches to telling stories and for their tendency to fall into broad, if not neat, categories as a result, every now and then a film such as *Citizen Kane* (1941) or *American Beauty* (1999) comes along that defies such remedial labeling or that alters and broadens an understanding of its pat categorization. Cases in which films defy expectations for easy categorization are just one of many reasons why an understanding of the characteristics and history of multiple film genres could be helpful. In response to this need for a basic understanding of how films differ in kind from one another, we have composed *Blockbusters: A Reference Guide to Film Genres* to provide the lay viewer as well as the film specialist with easy access to the basic characteristics of each film genre and a basic history of the evolution of each classification.

Most readers and viewers are probably already familiar with the basic term *film genre*, since the tendency to classify favorite books, TV shows, movies, and music begins early in life. The term *film*, of course, refers to the basic artifact subject to categorization, the moving image and all the products of that medium since its inception at the end of the nineteenth century. The notion of *film*—as opposed to *movie* or *cinema*—might suggest distinctions based on artistic appeal or merit or on entertainment value. *Cinema* most commonly refers to a body of "filmic" production overall, and it typically represents high artistic application and advancement of national and international import. On the other hand, *movie* may, in the mind of the typical viewer, simply refer to a form of popular entertainment with attractive performers, formulaic storylines that are often easy to follow, and enjoyable special effects. *Film*, in this context, probably falls somewhere in between, describing literally the material exposed in a camera in the process of recording the moving image (the *film stock*) as well as any one of many different types of motion picture presentations imprinted on this material of varying artistic quality and production. To avoid confusion, and because our goal is to avoid making strenuous aesthetic judgments about the motion pictures discussed, we use these terms synonymously. Moreover, although the term *film* also includes documentaries, news footage, and animation, our principle focus throughout the text is with narrative film, or cinematic presentations that combine all the elements of filmmaking (plot, directing, cinematography, lightning, set design, and costuming) to tell fictional or fictionalized real-life stories visually. An additional qualification involves the original venue or form of presentation, namely feature films versus TV movies versus straight-to-video or DVD releases. We broadly discuss films, both studio and independently produced and largely American, originally intended for viewing on the big screen in places such as neighborhood theaters, art houses, and multiplexes.

To return to the second part of our understanding of the term *film genre*—literally translated from the French to mean *kind*, *genre* is a broad term that can apply to many systems of categorization, such as painting, where landscape paintings are separated from portraits. Both forms rely on the application of pigment to a canvas or surface, but they depict different subjects. *Genre* is perhaps familiar to most of us as applied to the study of literature, where a set of structural and thematic characteristics that may distinguish poetry from fiction, for example, serves as the basic definition of each group of literary works, or *genres*. Just like paintings, films belonging to different genres use the same medium (film stock) and apply nearly the same or similar production techniques, but focus on different stories and different imagery. These differing emphases can make films radically distinct from one another, thus requiring separate categorization.

To most viewers, films fall into separate and readily identifiable categories according to story, setting (both in location and in time), characterization, treatment, and the nature of the conflicts explored as the plot or structure of the film unfolds. These distinctions make up the everyday understanding of film genre, but for film theorists and scholars interested in film as an art form or cultural product, simple changes in terms of character types or storyline may fail to explain inherent differences between genres. The study of these questions collectively may be called *genre criticism*, one of the many methods by which film may be analyzed and interpreted. Scholars engaging in genre criticism often look at factors both within the film itself and outside its boundaries for understanding of genre distinctions. For example, using the Western as a model, Andrew Tudor in his article "Genre" points out that merely looking at films commonly agreed upon as belonging to that genre as a means of extracting the distinguishing features of that categorization is problematic. Instead, the identification of distinguishing features in a genre relies upon a cultural understanding of what constitutes a film in that genre in the first place, particularly in

Photofest

terms of audience expectations for that genre. "Genre notions, . . ." Tudor writes, "are not critics' classifications made for special purposes; they are sets of cultural conventions. Genre is what we collectively believe it to be" (2003, 7).

In attempting to explain the underpinnings of a variety of theories explaining genre, and to fill in holes in each, another critic, Rick Altman, has proposed an approach that classifies films by both semantic features (characteristics such as character types, specific settings, locations, props, and the like) and syntactic features (how these elements are put together to create a structure). To explain his theory, Altman returns to the origins of these terms, using linguistics (2003). Semantic elements are words that hold a place in a sentence, such as nouns, verbs, and prepositions, while syntactic elements describe how those words are put together to form a variety of sentence types. Altman's proposal also attempts to explain why genres change over time, as in the case of the science fiction film, which by the 1970s combined the traditional semantic elements of science fiction with the syntax of the horror film and even the Western.

Steven Neale demonstrates that genres are more than just collections of films that can be classified and labeled; rather, genre represents a dynamic interaction between film texts and viewers in terms of "systems of expectation and hypothesis" that spectators bring to the viewing process. As Neale writes, these specific systems "help render films, and the elements within them, intelligible and therefore explicable. They offer a way of working out the significance of what is happening on the screen" (2003, 161).

What these examples of genre criticism reveal is the dynamic conversation surrounding the notion of something called a *film genre,* and they represent only a few of the many theories and perspectives which continue to be offered and debated in the larger world of film criticism. In this reference guide, we make no claim to solve any of the lingering questions that these theories attempt to address. Rather, it is our purpose to acquaint readers with a working understanding of commonly accepted genres and to point out relevant, significant, or innovative examples of each. To that end, a chapter is devoted to a discussion of each of twelve commonly agreed-upon film genres, with each chapter divided into three principal parts.

The "Defining Characteristics" section of each chapter provides a list of the most recognizable features of films in the genre, such as stock characters, typical plot structures, the principal conflicts or issues examined in the genre, and/or the predominant mood or attitude expressed in films in that category. For genres such as action-adventure, comedy, and musicals, a basic characteristic or approach is often explored in, is applied to, or appears in, a number of contexts or settings, resulting in a variety of subgenres, which offer a more comprehensive definition of the genre than the basic characteristic by itself. In such cases, we have chosen to highlight the subgenres as a means of defining the genre. The identifiability of subgenres such as the musical comedy or romantic comedy points to the fluid boundaries of some genres more than to others, which argues for the importance of the type of concrete descriptions we offer here.

Besides a list of the important features that epitomize each genre, we provide a history of each genre as it has evolved throughout the decades, with an emphasis on influential examples of each film type from the first appearance of the genre to the present. We make no claims that this section in each chapter, labeled "History and Influences," is exhaustive, but when considered together, our historical breakdowns of each genre provide a succinct working history of the American film industry from its point of origin until the present. For some genres such as action-adventure, historical discussions accompany the descriptions of various subgenres rather than appearing as a seamless whole within the chapter. In most cases, however, we end each chapter with this explanation of how genres have been interpreted throughout time. As audiences' tastes have changed, ideological influences have made their mark on each genre, and the art of filmmaking has advanced, considered from a technical standpoint. In some cases, select films such as *Gone With the Wind* (1939) have made such a significant influence on filmmaking in general that they cross genre, so we have discussed them in reference to more than one category. In cases where cross-genre considerations have come to light, we refer readers to other chapters in the text with bold face markers in parenthesis.

The narrative of each chapter is followed by a select bibliography of references and further reading, cataloguing the important scholarly work on each genre. Film studies has become an important and prolific field of academic inquiry, furthered by the appearance in the last fifty years of a number of important film journals, academic presses publishing film scholarship or devoted entirely to it, and academic and professional programs in universities around the world. The ascendancy of the Internet has provided another avenue for information about film, with Web sites such as Tim Dirk's *Film Site* and *The Internet Movie Database* providing film fans and film specialists with an unprecedented amount of information at their fingertips. With the proliferation of information about film, we do not claim our bibliographies are exhaustive. Rather, they represent a starting point for additional study of each genre.

The weighty impact and influence of the moving image in the twentieth century and beyond goes unchallenged by most. Beyond its entertainment value, film has changed the way we look at ourselves, and it has recorded significant historical events as they unfolded. From the perspective of entertainment, film offers viewers the opportunity to travel to exotic lands, meet interesting people, take part in important historical events, suffer the hardships of loss and heartbreak, and elate in the triumph of the human will—all through the lens of a motion picture camera. Because we believe that the movies still have the power to enhance daily life, promote good will, and visualize our hopes for the future, we offer *Blockbusters: A Reference Guide to Film Genres* as a beginning roadmap to the enduring world of the motion picture.

References and Further Reading

Altman, Rick. "A Semantic/Syntactic Approach to Film Genre." In *Film Genre Reader III,* edited by Barry Keith Grant, 27–41. Austin: University of Texas Press, 2003.

Neale, Steve. "Questions of Genre." In *Film Genre Reader III,* edited by Barry Keith Grant, 160–184. Austin: University of Texas Press, 2003.

Tudor, Andrew. "Genre." In *Film Genre Reader III,* edited by Barry Keith Grant, 3–11. Austin: University of Texas Press, 2003.

CHAPTER 1

ACTION-ADVENTURE

ACTION-ADVENTURE, LIKE the woman's picture (see **Woman's Film**), is a clearly gender-identified film genre which deals in gendered fantasy and wish fulfillment. The very things that, traditionally, little boys (or, more specifically, their dreams and fantasies) are made of are the raw materials of action films: speed, gadgetry and vehicles, conquest, physicality, heroics, a buddy or comrades, and escaping the everyday—not to mention crashing and destroying things. Women may enjoy action movies, and occasionally (as in the *Alien* films, *Thelma and Louise*, or *Set It Off*) see female protagonists, but the genre ultimately targets a male audience, offering vicarious thrills and satisfactions unavailable or considered antisocial in the real world.

As the name indicates, the genre is characterized by constant action and movement, this high energy often coming at the expense of logical plotlines or realistic character development. Action-adventure films offer pure escapism, and thus traditionally have not been considered serious film art. Except for *reflectionist* approaches (whereby a genre is examined in terms of its reflection of society), action-adventure films have certainly not received the critical analysis and exploration devoted to other typically male genres such as film noir (see **Film Noir**) or the Western (see **Western**). Action films depend upon exciting visuals, and they have led the industry in terms of the creation and development of special effects (*King Kong*, *Superman*, *The Matrix*, etc.). Unsurprisingly, in recent years the extent and capabilities of computer-generated images (CGI), or special effects, have been most fully realized in action films—often at the cost of story or characterization.

The action-adventure genre originated in the serials that Hollywood churned out from the silent days until the 1950s. These were short films shown before or after the major picture, and, like weekly comic strips, they appeared regularly, featuring recurring heroes and villains in continuing stories. The serials were cheap and quickly-produced dramatizations of derring-do, featuring fast action and inevitable cliffhanger endings to bring back their audiences (made up primarily of boys and young men) the following week. Decades later, utilizing massive budgets and big-name stars, Steven Spielberg and George Lucas would recreate these relentless, roller-coaster plotlines in their Indiana Jones films.

Obviously, action-adventure films can be found within other genres. There are Action Westerns, Action Science Fiction films, Action Thrillers, and so forth. Apart from such hybrids, which can be found in other chapters, action-adventure films themselves fall into discrete categories and subtypes. Before these specific subgenres of action-adventure films are examined, several of the general characteristics, found in all types of the genre, deserve discussion.

DEFINING CHARACTERISTICS

Speed

Action films come by their name honestly, generally placing little emphasis on character development or meaningful dialogue and instead exploiting the excitement generated by fast and constant motion. Many of the plots involve escape and pursuit, and chase scenes typify this most kinetic of all genres. In addition to the bodies, vehicles, and other objects that fly across the screen in all manner of pursuit, escape, and exploration, the films themselves are faster than those of other genres in terms of editing and shot duration. Whereas the average film today is made up of 1000 to 2000 shots (that is, individual cuts of film), action films generally have 3000 or more shots (*Armageddon* [1998] had 3700). While watching action/adventure films, therefore, our eyes are literally moving faster and taking in more and more as the shots themselves extend less and less.

Gadgetry and Vehicles

Fantastic weaponry and fast cars are action film clichés, and they serve as extensions of the hero himself—tangible representations of his dominance and power. Besides their obvious phallic connotations, such technological trappings further remove the hero from the realm of the average man; at the same time, with his superior intellect and physical prowess, the hero himself becomes something of a weapon (see the discussion of physicality, later). Of course, the villain often outfits himself with his own arsenal of mind-boggling weapons of destruction, which sets the scene for an inevitable "mine is bigger than yours" showdown, and highlights the popular theme of the alter-ego confrontation.

A hero and his arch-nemesis are often equals in intellect and cunning, the only difference being their devotion to different causes. Sharing so much, they admire as much as loathe each other, often voicing an "if only" speech in which they marvel at what could be accomplished were they fighting together for the same purpose. In *Raiders of the Lost Ark* (1981), upon gaining the upper hand, the wicked Belloq tells Indiana Jones that they are more than rivals: "Where shall I find a new adversary so close to my own level? . . . You and I are very much alike. . . . I am a shadowy reflection of you. It would take only a nudge to make you like me, to push you out of the light."

For a veritable catalog of cunning gadgets, one need look no farther than the James Bond films: lethal steel-rimmed bowler hats, ejector seats, Jaguars fully equipped with Gatling guns, missiles, and door-mounted rocket launchers, and so forth. As much as for such weaponry, Bond is also known for the stylish cars—Aston Martins, with and without ejector seats, are a particular favorite—in which he tears about the globe. Action heroes' automobiles can be as defining and necessary as were the horses Silver and Trigger for Western heroes such as the Lone Ranger and Roy Rogers; certainly this is true of the detective played by Steve McQueen in *Bullitt* (1968), racing around San Francisco in his mean 1967 Ford Mustang. McQueen plays a relentless cop, out to avenge a fallen comrade. Bullitt's homophonic name says it all, as he is himself a sort of bullet: cold, phallic, and dangerous.

Physicality

As mentioned, a hero's sophisticated and intimidating weaponry reflects his prowess. But an even better indicator of his superiority is his physical appearance and athleticism. On the one hand, there are the impossibly suave superheroes such as James Bond (played first by the impossibly suave Sean Connery and later by Roger Moore, Timothy Dalton, Pierce Brosnan, and Daniel Craig), who look terrific both in and out of their Savile Row suits. Actors such as Douglas Fairbanks, Errol Flynn, and Tyrone Power brought their dashing good looks (and, as a result, attracted hordes of female cinemagoers) to their many swashbuckling adventure films. But these men—particularly Fairbanks, who did most of his own stunt work—were also athletes, jumping from balconies and mastheads and engaging in highly choreographed swordplay. More recently, in the wake of Sylvester Stallone and Arnold Schwarzenegger, action heroes are pumped-up bodybuilder types, never averse to exposing and flexing overdeveloped biceps and pectorals. Before taking on an action-hero role, actors such as Christopher Reeve, Keanu Reeves, Bruce Willis, Tom Cruise, Matt Damon, Will Smith, Tobey McGuire, and Jennifer Garner spend months at the gym, suitably toning and bulking up. In the film itself, the actors (and, especially, their stunt doubles) will demonstrate superhuman physical prowess in all manner of death-defying feats: racing along the roof of a speeding train, jumping from a building onto a moving car or horse, scaling the side of a mountain or skyscraper, or only *just* outjumping the concussive blast of a tremendous explosion. Some films dramatize the misgivings (if not outright trauma) of an Everyman forced by circumstance to rise to heroic levels in order to protect his family or community, but, as in the *Die Hard* and *Spider-Man* series, the audience is certain that the character is up to the task.

Buddies

Action-adventure films occupy male-centered worlds, wherein women may figure as wives, girlfriends, and sexual partners but the deep and meaningful friendships are between men. In some films, such as *The Lost Patrol* (1934), there is not a single female on screen. This total absence of women is not unusual in military, high-seas, or any number of other adventure scenarios (although when a film has no males in its cast, as was the case with *The Women* (1939), the fact is trumpeted in the publicity, and its novelty is exploited). Only the buddy—reliable, predictable, and often the product of the same background and shaping forces as is the protagonist—truly understands the hero. He is an alter ego to whom the protagonist turns for advice and support, to take his place or to hear his last words. The intimacy of the buddy friendship is clearly illustrated in *The Lives of a Bengal Lancer* (1935), where the two young officers bicker and compete with each other in a relationship arc identical to the clichéd boy-meets-girl movie storyline. Resolutely heterosexual, they nevertheless follow the familiar pattern of initial hatred gradually turning into respect and love, complete with a tender and romantically lit shared-cigarette scene. Famous action film buddies include Butch Cassidy and the Sundance Kid and, in recent years, as a nod to racial equality (or, looking at it more cynically, as a ploy to draw a larger audience), the pairings of Sylvester Stallone and Billy Dee Williams in *Nighthawks* (1981), Mel Gibson and Danny Glover in the *Lethal Weapon* films, Bruce Willis and Samuel L. Jackson in *Die Hard with a Vengeance* (1995), and Eddie Murphy and Nick Nolte in the *48 Hours* films. The buddies in these films often start out as opposites, in terms of personality and character, but, in the course of extreme and trying circumstances, they come to depend upon and admire each other. Hollywood has long utilized this plot device, perhaps first adding race to the mix in *The Defiant Ones* (1958), starring Tony Curtis and Sidney Poitier as escaped convicts who are shackled together.

Exotic Locales

In action films, just as character (a hero), props (the gadgets and cars), and behavior (saving the world—or the empire) must be larger than life, so, more often than not, is the setting equally out of the ordinary and therefore escapist for the vicarious needs of the largely male audience. Whereas swashbucklers are set in the past and on the high seas, on the edge of "civilization," colonial-imperial adventures take place on a frontier, at the ever-precarious outposts of empire.

As in epics (see **Epic**), grand heroism and daring seem somehow to fit better in different times and far-flung locales. James Bond and Indiana Jones circle the globe in their various adventures. SWAT members are sent off to the South American jungle in *Predator* (1987); a mob enforcer locates his boss's son in the Amazon in *The Rundown* (2003). Daniel Day-Lewis falls in love and straddles the worlds of Native Americans and eighteenth-century Europeans in *The Last of the Mohicans* (1992), just as Tom Cruise navigates the nineteenth-century collision of East and West in Japan in *The Last Samurai* (2003). These two titles, along with (among others) *The Last Action Hero, The Last Boy Scout, The Last Chase, The Last Hard Men, The Last Man Standing, The Last Outpost*, and *The Last Safari* give an indication of the mythic, nostalgic air surrounding most adventure tales—a lost or vanishing time "when men were men," and fully able to demonstrate true resourcefulness, courage, altruism, and rugged individuality. When the setting of an action-adventure film is closer to prosaic home, both geographically and temporally, a statement is being made, either about the vapidity of modern-day existence or, more usually, about the precariousness of familial and societal structures; an evil or demented person or group can threaten the very fabric of our lives, requiring heroes to step in and reestablish order.

HISTORY OF SUBGENRES

Swashbuckler

The first and greatest swashbuckler hero in the movies is Douglas Fairbanks Sr. In a series of silent adventure films in the 1920s, he set an impossibly high standard for all who were to follow. Combining athleticism, grace, and a knowing, tongue-in-cheek smile, he thrilled early cinemagoers with his stories of derring-do and adventure. Working for United Artists (the studio Fairbanks established with wife Mary Pickford, fellow star Charles Chaplin, and director D. W. Griffith) with some of the best directors of his day, he starred in *The Mark of Zorro* (1920), *The Three Musketeers* (1921), *Robin Hood* (1922), *The Thief of Bagdad* (1924), *Don Q, Son of Zorro* (1925), *The Black Pirate* (1926), *The Gaucho* (1927), and *The Iron Mask* (1929). What captivated audiences was his conflation of Old World mystery and excitement with ultra-American exuberance and extroversion. As a film presence, Fairbanks was a self-made man of the new American century: overcoming obstacles, always optimistic, reaching the heights—and getting the girl. He just did it in the guise and costume of a seventeenth-century musketeer or a medieval robber baron. Whether wielding a rapier or cutlass, scaling a rising drawbridge, leaping from a window or balcony, or sliding down the mast of a tall ship, Fairbanks did most of his own impressive stunts. The latter act, in *The Black Pirate*, became legendary and often imitated: Amid billowing sails, Fairbanks slides precariously down the mast by plunging his dagger into it and literally tearing downward.

Warner Brothers' *The Adventures of Robin Hood* (1938) introduced a thrilling new element to adventure films: Technicolor. The studio had established a gritty house style with gangster films in the early thirties, but, after the enforcement of the censorial Motion Picture Production Code in 1934, it turned elsewhere for projects. In arguably his greatest role, Errol Flynn is both dashing and mischievous as Robin, a Saxon nobleman forced by increasingly rapacious Normans to rally the common folk against their oppressors. All the key elements and characters from the legend are here, in bright vivid colors and accompanied by composer Erich Wolfgang Korngold's sweeping, Oscar-winning score.

Pageboys and men in tights: Errol Flynn strikes a suitably swashbuckling pose as he fends off the swordplay of Basil Rathbone in *The Adventures of Robin Hood* (1938). *Photofest.*

Released in the year that war broke out in Europe, the film—via Robin—calls for justice and freedom for all but particularly champions the trampled little people. He commands his merry men to swear an oath that they will care for the poor, shelter the old and helpless, protect all women, and fight for a free England: "Swear to fight to the death against our oppressors." Explaining his *modus operandi* to Maid Marian (fellow Warner contract player Olivia de Havilland), Robin enthuses, "It's injustice I hate—not Normans." Buckets of Norman blood are shed, nevertheless, in stirring swordfights and bow-and-arrow volleys by the score.

At Nottingham Castle, Robin takes on the entire court, leaping from table to banquet table, and rushing up and down massive stone staircases, his sword slashing to and fro. He also proves a stunning marksman with a bow, shooting arrows behind him from a galloping horse and winning an archery contest by splitting a competitor's arrow in two on a bull's eye target. Basil Rathbone is a wonderfully villainous Sir Guy of Gisbourne (who seems ready at any moment to twirl his moustache malevolently), and de Havilland, not given much to do, is beautiful in a succession of Technicolor-exploiting gowns and wimples. She and Flynn have a Romeo and Juliet–style farewell scene at her precipitous castle balcony (he is adept at ivy-climbing as well), and the two of them succeed in restoring Richard the Lion Heart to the throne, whereupon the king decrees that all his people—Saxon and Norman—must live together peacefully.

Flynn had inherited Fairbanks's swashbuckling crown in 1935 when he appeared in Michael Curtiz's *Captain Blood*, about an Irish surgeon charged with treason, sold into slavery, and transformed into a Caribbean buccaneer. Flynn followed the film at Warner Brothers with *The Charge of the Light Brigade* (1936), *Robin Hood*, *The Sea Hawk* (1940), and *The Adventures of Don Juan* (1949). He soon learned, however, as Fairbanks had learned before him, that swashbuckling is a young man's game. Just as Twentieth Century-Fox always had a younger blonde starlet waiting in the wings to replace its aging female stars, so Warner Brothers groomed new male adventure heroes. In place of an aging Errol Flynn, Warner Brothers cast young, athletic Burt Lancaster in a series of adventure films, including *The Flame and the Arrow* (1950), *The Crimson Pirate* (1952), and *His Majesty O'Keefe* (1954).

Twentieth Century-Fox's answer to Errol Flynn was Tyrone Power, another tall, dark, and handsome actor tailor-made for swashbuckling and high adventure. Power churned out a large number of adventure films for Fox, as well as musicals and contemporary stories. *The Mark of Zorro* (1940) signaled Power's arrival as an adventure hero, masked and ready for daring swordplay to depose villains. In rapid succession came *Blood and Sand* (1941), a gorgeous Technicolor account of a romantic bullfighter; *Son of Fury* (1942), the story of a nobleman's mistreated illegitimate son who goes off to the south seas; *The Black Swan* (1942), about pirates on the Spanish Main; *Captain from Castille* (1947), made after Power's military service in the war, about the adventures of the Conquistadores in Mexico; *Pony Soldiers* (1952), a story about the Royal Canadian Mounted Police; and *King of the Khyber Rifles* (1953), set in India in 1857 with the British Army.

Several classic swashbuckler stories, based on historical or literary characters, have received multiple film treatments. *Mutiny on the Bounty*, filmed in 1935 and 1962, features exciting and vengeful confrontations between the sadistic Captain Bligh and the humane Fletcher Christian. The later version would enjoy the benefits of color and location shooting, but the 1935 film, winner of the Best Picture Academy Award, is much better, with Clark Gable, at the peak of his popularity and charisma, as Christian and a larger-than-life performance by Charles Laughton as Bligh. *The Count of Monte Cristo*, another story of someone abandoned and thought lost reappearing to exact revenge, has been filmed four times (1912, 1834, 1974, and 2002).

The Count's record, however, pales in comparison to the seven film versions of Alexander Dumas's *The Three Musketeers* (1916, 1921, 1935, 1939, 1948, 1974, and 1993). Fairbanks's robust 1921 portrayal of D'Artagnan is endless fun, whereas the 1948 version features an equally acrobatic Gene Kelly (a dancer) and gorgeous Technicolor. The 1939 film is a musical-comedy version, while the director of the 1974 version, Richard Lester (who made his name directing the wild, fast-paced Beatles films in the mid-1960s), brings a youthfully frenetic, slapstick quality to his retelling. Lester's film benefits from European locations and an all-star cast, including Raquel Welch (revealing a gift for physical comedy), Michael York as an innocent, puppy-like D'Artagnan, Richard Chamberlain, Christopher Lee, Faye Dunaway, Geraldine Chaplin, and Charlton Heston.

Filmed simultaneously with the same cast, *The Four Musketeers: Milady's Revenge* was released the following year. Lester (and many of the actors) returned once again to the characters in *The Return of the Musketeers* (which first appeared in America on cable television) (1989), in which an older D'Artagnan attempts to reunite the musketeers twenty years later to save their queen. The most recent *Musketeers* (1993) is a sort of *Young Guns* version, produced by Walt Disney Pictures and targeting a young audience with romantically long-haired Brat Pack actors (Charlie Sheen, Kiefer Sutherland, and Chris O'Donnell), beautiful young actresses (Rebecca De Mornay, Gabrielle Anwar, and Julie Delpy), and an obligatory cloying pop-hit theme song by Bryan Adams.

Robin Hood has enjoyed outings in several films since Flynn's 1938 classic (still the most rewarding of the lot). Disney produced two versions: *The Story of Robin Hood and His Merrie Men* (1952) was shot in England without stars but with excellent actors, and an animated version appeared in 1973, which was not one of the studio's better efforts, substituting animals for the key roles. The story came vaulting back into cinemas with Kevin Costner's big-budget *Robin Hood: Prince of Thieves* (1991), a huge box office success, which discarded much of the fun of the Flynn original in its darker, grittier take on the story, complete with impressive 1990s special effects (most memorable being the point-of-view camera shot from a speeding arrow). Perennial parodist Mel Brooks turned his hand at the legend in the send-up *Robin Hood: Men in Tights* (1993), producing one of his lesser works, although his acting turn as Rabbi Tuchman, a Jewish take on Friar Tuck, is memorable.

Contemporary attempts at pirate swashbucklers have met with wildly varying results. Geena Davis's *Cutthroat Island* (1995) was a disaster at almost every level, and it is considered one of the most costly and damaging vanity projects in recent cinema (it was directed by Davis's husband Renny Harlin), making only $10 million after more than $100 million dollars in expenses. On the other hand, *Pirates of the Caribbean: The Curse of the Black Pearl* (2003), was a huge success with audiences, featuring an outrageously campy performance by Johnny Depp as a pirate out to right wrongs and regain lost treasure, all the while helping a lovelorn young man regain his kidnapped beloved. Balancing pirates and lovers, action and drama, the film features a fine performance by Geoffrey Rush as evil pirate Barbossa and pretty Brits Orlando Bloom and Kiera Knightley as the young lovers.

Exploration

Journeys, an elemental archetype in fairy tales and fable—and therefore in cinema—often involve exploration, whether it be for riches, land, or oneself. Reflecting sociopolitical shifts in perspective, adventure films that focus upon exploration have largely shifted over the years. Where early adventure films tell stories of civilized Europeans or Americans journeying into the wilds of savagery in search of priceless treasure or new worlds, more recent ones highlight clashes in culture that all-too-clearly reveal the savagery of the so-called *civilized*. The racism in many (particularly early) exploration films is shocking in its off-hand presumption, as white culture and humanity are resolutely privileged, while all others are variously infantilized, demonized, or otherwise caricatured.

MGM's *Trader Horn* (1931) was widely discussed for its seven-month on-location filming in Africa, during which the cast was beset by dysentery and other tropical disorders. More than 200,000 feet of film was shot. In fact, long stretches of the film play out like a wildlife travelogue, and much of the African footage is seen in rear projection shots (behind the actors, who were filmed in the studio). There is a great deal of footage of actual big game shoots; the many graphic depictions of shot and speared animals, writhing in their death throes, can be heavy going for modern audiences.

The film is about the lure of Africa—of adventure and the unknown—and it follows the exploits of old trader Horn (Harry Carey) and the young, inexperienced Spaniard Peru (Duncan Renaldo) who accompanies him. The two bond quickly; at one point Horn advises the young man to return to civilization, whereupon the latter replies, "I want very much to go where *you* go." Putting his hand on the young man's shoulder, Horn smiles and says, "Wasn't I the old fool to think you'd feel different?" The two men come upon the legendary young "white goddess" of the jungle, a murdered missionary's abducted daughter who now rules over a jungle tribe. Significantly, even though she has spent most of her life with the Africans, she alone wears clothing that covers her breasts (of course, her get-up is the height of 1931 savage chic). The black women in the (pre-Code) film are clothed only from the waist down. In the old *National Geographic* style of racism, white bodies must be covered, their decency and honor upheld, whereas black bodies are exposed, revealing a mindset of both superiority and indifference. Further evidence of this double standard is seen in *Trader Horn*, as it is in *King Kong* (1933) and *King Solomon's Mines* (1950), when blacks are seen randomly crushed and mutilated by rampaging beasts—a fate which would never have been so graphically depicted were the victims white.

Horn disapproves of Peru's romance with the girl; the older man, dedicated to his trade and unable to settle down, inhabits an all-male world. His closest relationship is with his African gun-bearer and servant Rencharo (Mutia Omoolu), who risks his life to stay with Horn when the natives attack. After Rencharo is speared and dying, Horn takes him on his back and carries him away. "Hold my hand," Horn says, and he keeps repeating the gun-bearer's name and holding him close as he dies.

At the end of the film, the young lovers sail away and back to Europe, entreating Horn to join them on the ship. "Now, what would I be doing away from Africa?" the trader asks. "Why, when you two people are a hum-drum married couple, I'll be trading rivers where no white man ever dared to come before. And I'll still be beholding the wonders of the jungle. It'll never grow old before a man's eyes like a woman does. No, lad, I couldn't live away from them things." Horn proceeds to select a new "gunboy" and marches back towards the jungle, seeing a ghostly image of Rencharo beckoning from beyond the river. Africa is Horn's mistress, and Renchero was his mate.

Most of the 200,000 feet of film shot in Africa never made it into *Trader Horn*. However, much of it was later used in MGM's highly successful series of Tarzan films, which commenced the next year with *Tarzan, the Ape Man* (1932). RKO was readying *King Kong* and MGM studio head Louis B. Mayer decided to go all out with *Tarzan*, planning it all along as a big-budget A-film. The first Tarzan film had appeared in 1918, and there were a few cheap serials in the 1930s. For its major effort, MGM hired *Trader Horn*'s director, W. S. Van Dyke, to direct, and five-time Olympic champion Johnny Weissmuller to play the title role. Edgar Rice Burroughs's basic story of the daughter of an English hunter who is captured (and captivated) by the savage jungle man features a strong sexual element, as Jane (Maureen O'Sullivan) falls for Tarzan over her stuffy English suitors. Audiences were at turns shocked and titillated by the leads' scanty clothing, revealing as much skin as was possible (in later, post-Code films in the series, the costumes were gradually tailored to cover more and more of the beautiful stars' anatomies). As befitted important films, rather than quickly cashing in sequels, MGM took two or three years to turn out new Tarzan films, pairing Weissmuller and O'Sullivan in *Tarzan and His Mate* (1934), generally considered the best of the bunch, featuring a nude underwater swim by Jane and an admiring Tarzan, *Tarzan Escapes* (1936), *Tarzan Finds a Son!* (1939), *Tarzan's Secret Treasure* (1941), and *Tarzan's New York Adventure* (1942). Vine-swinging escapades, comic relief from Cheetah, and Tarzan's immortal cry, capable of terrorizing humans and starting animal stampedes, are all here, although, by the last feature, when Tarzan is put in a suit and he and Jane venture to Manhattan to retrieve their kidnapped Boy, the writers were clearly at a loss for new storylines. O'Sullivan left the series, but Weissmuller moved to RKO studios to make six lesser and increasingly weak films: *Tarzan Triumphs!* (1943), *Tarzan's Desert Mystery* (1943), *Tarzan and the Amazons* (1945), *Tarzan and the Leopard Woman* (1946), *Tarzan and the Huntress* (1947), and *Tarzan and the Mermaids* (1948).

King Kong (1933) is, of course, a milestone of American cinema, an exercise on the *Beauty and the Beast* archetype that has entered our collective consciousness, thanks in part to such iconic images as Kong climbing the Empire State Building while holding a screaming Fay Wray. Unlike the novel-based Tarzan films, *Kong* was an original story of explorers who come upon more than they've bargained for on an unknown jungle isle (where, in addition to the great ape, prehistoric dinosaurs terrorize the local human populace). Even while the film was being made, executives at RKO realized what they were onto, and they poured more money into the project. In addition, before its release, rival studio MGM offered to buy the film for just over a million dollars, but RKO stood firm and went on to see *King Kong* make nearly $2 million at the box office—this in the midst of the Depression. The great ape comes to life via the genius of the sound men, who created Kong's tremendous growls and snarls, and thanks even more to Willis O'Brien's special effects, impressive even today, which were the forerunner of so much stop-action animation. He masterminded the look and movement of the thrilling battles between Kong and the other gigantic island creatures. These and Kong's rampage through the streets of New York, including his final futile attempt to climb to safety up the world's tallest building, thrill audiences today just as they did cinemagoers in 1933. A 1976 remake was a major disappointment. In contrast, the 2005 version, directed by Peter Jackson (flush from the success of his *Lord of the Rings* trilogy), was well received by critics and audiences alike. Many wondered, nevertheless, if the film needed to run three hours, twice as long as the 1933 original.

King Solomon's Mines, an H. Rider Haggard tale of danger and adventure in pursuit of legendary mines of treasure, has been filmed three times. The 1937 version is entertaining; the 1985 film is a weak Indiana Jones imitation; and the 1950 Technicolor treatment is the best. Starring Stewart Granger as Allan Quatermain, the safari leader-for-hire, the film captures the inherent chauvinism of the tale without becoming too heavy-handed. Unlike the greedy or thrill-seeking Britons and Germans who hire his services, Quatermain respects the Africans, the land, and the wildlife ("At times, I prefer them to humans"), even though he has acquired a somewhat jaded and fatalistic view of the world.

Through the course of the film, in a series of physical tests of courage, strength, and endurance, he rethinks his life and falls in love. A sort of *Boy's Own Paper* androcentrism suffuses the film; sex roles are rigidly observed ("A woman on safari? No, thank you!") and codes of living made clear ("The happiest, finest fate a man can have in this world is to be the *best* at something"). There is even a subplot of a deposed young Watusi king who must challenge his usurping rival to combat in order to win back the throne.

With its countless moments of homage to earlier movies and serials, and its gleeful pleasure in simultaneously compiling *and* outdoing as many of those thrilling scenes as is possible, *Raiders of the Lost Ark* (1981) is perhaps the ultimate action-adventure film. The opening sequence has the breathless, extreme excitement of a film climax—and the picture never lets up from there, racing from one cliff-hanger moment to the next, as much a cinematic roller coaster as has ever been created. In this respect, *Raiders* and its progeny might be faulted, in that there is no down time—no respite from the over-the-top thrills and spills. But the film is charming and fun, even as it takes our breath away. It became an immediate hit with audiences, quickly raking in $242 million at the box office.

Explorer-academic-archeologist-adventurer Indiana Jones (Harrison Ford) is a compendium of adventure hero types. Good-looking, debonair, daring, reckless, and boyishly eager, he nevertheless demonstrates endearing weaknesses: a phobia of snakes and bewilderment over the women who throw themselves at him. Set in 1936, the film pits Indy against the Nazis in a race for possession of the ancient Jewish Ark of the Covenant, said to have held the original tablets on which the Ten Commandments were inscribed. The plot is just an excuse for Indy to get into and then out of as many apparently hopeless and deadly scrapes as possible, which actor Ford does with deadpan bravado, complete with leather jacket, jaunty fedora, and lethal bullwhip. Along with various assistants and a former girlfriend, he travels the globe, from South America to Nepal to Egypt; faces an arsenal of arms ranging from poison darts to poisoned dates; escapes

Harrison Ford, as Indiana Jones, combines sensuality and machismo, awaiting his next hair-raising adventure in *Indiana Jones and the Temple of Doom* (1984). *Photofest.*

from deadly tarantulas, cobras, spears, and huge, rolling boulders, not to mention sword-wielding Arabs and gun-toting Nazis; and avoids being set on fire and even buried alive.

The last-minute escapes and evasions are accompanied by an exciting Western-style desert chase sequence, wherein Indy gallops on horseback after the truck carrying the stolen Ark, leaps onto the truck, tosses out the driver and takes the wheel, is overcome and thrown through the windshield, works his way under the rushing vehicle back to the rear axle, is dragged along the ground for a way, manages to get into the truck, overcomes the (second) driver, and again takes the wheel. The nonstop nature of this sequence typifies the film itself, and audiences couldn't get enough.

Director Steven Spielberg and producer George Lucas, masters at creating wildly successful and extremely well-crafted popular films, went on to make two sequels, *Indiana Jones and the Temple of Doom* (1984) and *Indiana Jones and the Last Crusade* (1989), rare cases of top-notch directors, producers, and actors signing on again for multiple action-adventure sequels. The later films were popular, but they did not garner the critical raves and phenomenal box office receipts accorded the first film. A darkness crept in that is largely absent from the original; in fact, because of complaints over violence in *The Temple of Doom*, a new motion-picture rating was created, PG-13, whereby parents of young children are warned of possibly upsetting material. All ages were welcome when the franchise became a television series in the mid-1990s, titled *The Young Indiana Jones Chronicles*, which followed the adventures of Indy at ages ten, seventeen, and even ninety.

Colonialism-Imperialism

Action tales involving conquest and imperialism and marketed for mass consumption date back to the earliest dime novels and, in particular, to the *Boy's Own Paper*-type British periodicals from the last century, which were aimed at a young male readership. The stories involve the perilous but honorable task of creating and maintaining an empire—of carving out and then defending territory (usually British). The far-flung nature of the British Empire ensured exotic locales—the Sahara, the African jungle, the Middle East, high Himalayan passes, Far Eastern jungles, and the antipodes. Such movies deal with regiments and brigades maintaining a peculiarly British code of honor and stiff-upper-lip stoicism amid the most trying and hopeless of circumstances. Honor and duty are trumpeted above all else, as individual cares and desires are subordinated to the greater cause of King and Country.

The Lives of a Bengal Lancer (1935) weds its tale of patrolling the frontier of the British Empire to smaller stories of male rivalry and intergenerational struggle. Two young officers (played by Gary Cooper and Franchot Tone) bicker and compete with each other until a relationship of respect and affection gradually emerges. Simultaneously, the martinet colonel (C. Aubrey Smith) is dismayed when his son, whom he barely knows because of his own lifelong devotion to military service, is posted to the regiment. The colonel explains away his abandonment of wife and infant son with "The Service comes first, something your mother never understood." Even after the son is taken captive by natives, the colonel refuses to rush to his rescue, as it might endanger the regiment.

Such cold devotion to the regiment horrifies the hot-headed, emotional Macgregor (Cooper): "Why can't he be a little less of a soldier and more of a man? Why can't he forget his blasted duty for once?" An old experienced officer counters with a defense of the nationalistic ethos, espousing a creed of British superiority and imperialism: "Man, you *are* blind. Have you never thought how, for generation after generation here, a handful of men have ordered the lives of 300 million people? It's because he's here and a few more like him; men of his breed have *made* British India—men who put their jobs above everything. He wouldn't let death move him from it. Well, he wouldn't let *love* move him from it. When his breed of man dies out, that's the end. And it's a better breed of man than any of us will ever make." The obligatory defense of Queen (most such films are set during the Victorian era) and Country recurs in many imperialist-action films: an old soldier justifies apparent heartlessness or the inexplicable abandonment of familial duties in the name of empire.

John Ford's *Wee Willie Winkie* (1937), an uneasy marriage of action film and Shirley Temple vehicle, is very loosely based upon Kipling's novel (so loosely that the title character has undergone a sex change). Temple's usual screen persona—the cheerful, plucky child who goes about solving all the problems and irascibility of surrounding grown-ups—is simply transferred to north India in 1897, as she and her widowed mother arrive from America to live with the grandfather they hardly know. He is the standard martinet British colonel (again C. Aubrey Smith, who made a career in such roles): blustery, rule-bound, and here largely played for humor. Temple's mother inevitably falls for a handsome young soldier, to whom, after a day of guided horseback riding at the edges of the frontier, the woman cries, "I read about it in school, but you make it sound so thrilling and romantic!"

Of course, such could be said of all these films of empire, which emphasize exoticism, daring rescues, and male bonding over historical accuracy or ethics. Overt racism is played for laughs or menace; indigenous people are either comical and infantile or savage and treacherous. Essentially, the "savage" races need enlightenment, in the form of Christianity and British government and military structure and regulation. The duty speech in *Wee Willie Winkie* is delivered by the colonel to his daughter-in-law, after she accuses him of having a book of army regulations for a heart. "You've never seen a regiment wiped out because of a blunder or laxity in discipline. You've never seen death all around. But I have. . . . Up in those hills there are thousands of savages, all waiting for the chance to sweep down the pass and ravage India. Now, it's England's duty—it's *my* duty, dear—to see that they don't. As long as I live, that duty's going to be done. The only women we want here are those who can understand that and respect it." Women and the natives just don't understand or appreciate what these British men are doing out here, thousands of miles from home.

Kipling is also the basis for perhaps the most famous action-adventure film of the studio era, *Gunga Din* (1939). Inspired by the poem about a brave Indian water bearer who longs to join the British regiment for which he is something of a mascot, the film mixes drama with slapstick humor and schoolboy high jinks. Dashing Douglas Fairbanks, Jr., Cockney Cary Grant, and gruff Victor McLaglen are soldier-comrades, easily outshooting, outfighting, and outdrinking all Indian comers. To escape from one particular scrape, they even take a Butch Cassidy–style leap from a mountainside into a river.

The regiment is currently threatened by "the most fiendish band of killers that ever existed"—the fanatical and murderous cult of Thuggees, who, after fifty years of lying low, have suddenly reappeared. Fairbanks's Ballantine is anxious to marry and leave the military for the tea trade, but he is tricked by his pals into five more days' service, during which time the men are taken captive by the Thuggees and held in their mountain citadel, complete with a fantastic, romantic temple set. Chants of "Kill for the love of killing! Kill! Kill!" whip the cult members into a bloodthirsty frenzy, and the trio is hopelessly outnumbered, but they manage to escape to the mountaintop and fend off armed natives until the regiment arrives to rescue them. Loyal Gunga Din (Sam Jaffe) sacrifices himself, and he wins the undying gratitude and admiration of the English in a suicide mission, climbing high and sounding the trumpet to alert the approaching regiment. Such heroism and the sheer excitement of fighting alongside his mates produces a change of heart in Ballantine ("I hate the blasted army, but friendship—that's something else"), who ultimately chooses the military over a wife.

Other famous tales of colonialism include *The Charge of the Light Brigade* (1936), starring Errol Flynn, set during the Crimean War, and recreating Tennyson's timeless poem of the same name; *Beau Geste* (1929 and 1939), about three devoted brothers serving in the French Foreign Legion and butting heads with the obligatory martinet commander; *The Four Feathers* (1939 and 2002), about a young

British soldier accused of cowardice, who must prove himself—and save his comrades—during the combat in the 1898 Sudan uprising; and *Zulu* (1964) and *Khartoum* (1966), both set in Africa and documenting historical and calamitous British campaigns.

The Disaster Movie

Films have always exploited the cinematic qualities of catastrophes, but the 1970s saw the arrival and vogue of the true disaster film. Earlier movies used disasters to develop or demonstrate a character's mettle, situating the disaster sequence as one self-contained episode within the larger narrative. Thus, in *The Last Days of Pompeii* (1935), *San Francisco* (1936), *In Old Chicago* (1938) and *Titanic* (1953), the disasters of Vesuvius's eruption, the 1906 earthquake, the 1871 fire, and the 1912 sinking, respectively, are isolated, albeit show-stopping, climactic events set within the larger melodramas and romances.

The film that established the modern trend, wherein the disaster and its immediate effects take up most of the movie and are as important as the soap opera storyline, is *Airport* (1970). The combination of snowed-in airport, mad bomber, little old lady stowaway, and a string of famous actors in two-dimensional roles proved box-office gold. The on-board bomb explosion and ensuing cabin decompression and passenger hysteria are still impressive. Helen Hayes (in a comeback role as the stowaway) won the Academy Award, ensuring a parade of out of work, old-Hollywood stars in a succession of new-Hollywood disaster films: Ava Gardner in *Earthquake*, Fred Astaire and Jennifer Jones in *The Towering Inferno*, Gloria Swanson and Myrna Loy in *Airport '75*, and so on. All three of these films were released in 1974, indicating the tremendous popularity of the subgenre. Alongside the old-timers, the studios utilized their big stars (Charlton Heston, Steve McQueen, Paul Newman, Faye Dunaway), as well as media-crossing celebrities (athlete O. J. Simpson, singer Helen Reddy), to draw the biggest audiences possible. As noted, no one was really expected to *act*, but rather to simply hold his or her own amid the tremors, flames, and explosions.

Beyond the big names, disaster films feature human carnage at a level unequaled in any other film genre. There are casts of nameless hundreds, at least, many of whom never make it to the final reel; they are summarily dispatched in scenes of spectacular violence: blown from airplanes, cast from skyscrapers, and swallowed up by the earth or the sea. Probably the best and most entertaining disaster movie (for all the right and the wrong reasons) is *The Poseidon Adventure* (1972). Set on a luxury liner that is capsized by an enormous wave in the Mediterranean on New Year's Eve, the film stars, among others, Gene Hackman, Ernest Borgnine, Red Buttons, and Shelley Winters. It manages to keep viewers in suspense for two hours, wondering "How will they get out of *this* fix?" and "Who will die next?"

The big scene is, of course, the turning over of the ship, which is wonderfully staged, with all the requisite flash, destruction of scenery, and disregard for human life. Thereafter, various stars are burned, scalded in hot water, and drowned as the survivors make their way up to the "bottom" of the ship and rescue. The women are largely helpless, excepting former long-distance swimmer Winters, and they are inevitably shot from below as they climb ladders and enter passageways wearing skintight hot pants (again, excepting the voluminous Winters). The kitsch factor is part of the film's charm, as are the amazing topsy-turvy sets and plot twists. A 2005 television remake was quickly forgotten, but a 2006 remake, *Poseidon*, is nearing theatrical release as this book goes to press.

Audiences eventually burned out on disaster films (as a gimmick, *Earthquake* was even released initially featuring "Sensurround," an effect by which loud, low rumbles on the soundtrack create a vibrating sensation for cinemagoers), but the form reappears periodically. Advances in special effects have made possible the spectacle of such films as *Armageddon* (1998), a hugely expensive blockbuster in which scientists embark on a dangerous mission beyond the planet to divert an asteroid hurling toward Earth, and *The Core* (2003), a not-as-expensive blockbuster wherein scientists embark on an equally dangerous mission to the center of the planet in order to repair a catastrophic problem at the Earth's core. The threat is again extraterrestrial in *Independence Day* (1996), as hostile aliens begin destroying cities, and the president of the United States must join a motley crew of American saviors of the universe. The special effects are impressive, as alien death rays are leveled at, and destroy, the most familiar and photogenic of urban landmarks. Fittingly, in this largely computer-generated disaster film, computer viruses succeed in killing off the aliens. The computer giveth, and the computer taketh away.

Espionage Film

There have always been spy films, but whereas most of these—reflecting the actual profession of secret agents—fall into the genre of suspense-thriller film (see **Suspense**), some occupy a much more cinematic (if inaccurate) realm of action and adventure. Such movie spies circle the globe in all manner of fancy vehicles, are surrounded by fancy women, utilize super-techno-gadgetry, and thwart dastardly and villainous masterminds. The movie spy par excellence is, of course, James Bond, Agent 007. As of this writing, there have been twenty-two Bond films, the most for any series of English-language films and constituting, according to *The Guinness Book of World Records*, the most successful film series of all time. Based upon the novels of Ian Fleming, the cinematic Bond grabbed audiences' attention with *Dr. No* (1962) (introducing himself, unforgettably, as "Bond—James Bond"), and he has never let go.

The first and most rewarding actor to essay the role is Sean Connery, who appeared in *Dr. No*, *From Russia with Love* (1963), *Goldfinger* (1964), *Thunderball* (1965), *Diamonds Are Forever* (1971) and, in a much heralded return to the part, which inspired the film's title, *Never Say Never Again* (1983). The part has also been played by David Niven (*Casino Royale* [1967]), George Lazenby (*On Her Majesty's Secret Service* [1969]), Roger Moore (*Live and Let Die* [1973], *The Man with the Golden Gun* [1974], *The Spy Who Loved Me* [1977], *Moonraker* [1979], *For Your*

Eyes Only [1981], *Octopussy* [1983], and *A View to a Kill* [1985]), Timothy Dalton (*The Living Daylights* [1987], and *License to Kill* [1989]), and Pierce Brosnan (*GoldenEye* [1995], *Tomorrow Never Dies* [1997], *The World Is Not Enough* [1999], and *Die Another Day* [2002]). The actors may change, and there are always new "Bond girls" hanging on their arms, but almost everything else about a Bond film stays the same: tongue-in-cheek dialogue, exotic locales, expensive sports cars, deliciously evil villains, mind-blowing gadgets and weaponry (producing mind-blowing explosions and deaths), fast action sequences, last-minute escapes, chases and wild stunts, and a catchy theme song.

All the components were there in the first Bond film, but most people agree that the next two, *From Russia with Love* and *Goldfinger*, are the best in the series. The villains in Bond films are of the crazed, take-over-the-world megalomaniac variety, with names such as Dr. No, Goldfinger, and Blofeld. The names of the Bond girls are even more outrageously tongue-in-cheek, including Honeychile Ryder, Pussy Galore, Kissy Suzuki, Plenty O'Toole, Holly Goodhead, and Mary Goodnight. The inherent sexism of the series is never oppressive because the films refuse to take themselves seriously. Bond may be saving the world, but he does it with a sense of humor. The early films capitalized on Cold War jitters and neuroses, setting up spy-versus-spy scenarios, whereas more recent Bond pictures tackle computer terrorists, drug kingpins, post-communist Russian saboteurs, and megalomaniacal media magnates.

Regardless of the bad guy du jour, Bond never slows down. The car chase in *On Her Majesty's Secret Service* careens down a mountainside and, inadvertently, into a rough stock car race. Bond steals a car from a Bangkok dealer in *The Man with the Golden Gun* and ends up sailing and spinning it over a fallen bridge, landing safely on the other side of the river. In *GoldenEye*, he leaps off a mountain cliff in pursuit of a plummeting, pilotless airplane, managing to fall on the plane, climb inside, and bring it out of its free fall before flying off to safety. In *Tomorrow Never Dies*, despite being handcuffed together, Bond and a female Chinese agent manage to escape their captors, steal a motorcycle, and ride both the rooftops and busy streets of Saigon to elude pursuing cars and helicopter. *Die Another Day* even has a hovercraft chase sequence. There have been Bond imitators: Michael Caine as Harry Palmer in *The Ipcress File* (1965) and its sequels, James Coburn as Derek Flint in the spy parodies *Our Man Flint* (1966) and *In Like Flint* (1967), and even Mike Myers as Austin Powers in a series of retro-sixties spy spoofs. Accept no imitations.

Cop

Whereas espionage films depict suave spies engaged in thrilling adventures in exotic locales, police action films are located in more familiar milieux in terms of setting (a large U.S. city) and characters (cops). In many cases the police officer is an Everyman with whom the audience identifies: a regular, ordinary Joe, trying to do his job and take care of his family, but forced to rise to the occasion in extraordinary circumstances. In *Die Hard* (1988), New York City cop John McClane (Bruce Willis) just happens to be inside a Los Angeles skyscraper when it is commandeered by terrorists, and its inhabitants are taken hostage. In the sequel, *Die Hard 2* (1990), McClane is picking up his wife at Washington airport when—surprise, surprise—he happens upon another terrorist threat that he alone seems able to take care of. The films aren't logical or particularly believable, but they are fast-paced, loud, violent, and full of coarse language and action that doesn't let up. *Die Hard With a Vengeance* (1995) uses the now-clichéd plot device (seen in *Speed* and elsewhere) of a destructive psychopath who taunts a particular cop, sadistically daring him to figure out the madman's diabolical plans—or else innocent citizens will be killed. The *Die Hard* films are roller-coaster rides, albeit long ones (they all clock in at over two hours), that strain credulity but deliver a succession of hair-raising scenes.

Willis's character is not a superhero, but simply an ordinary guy. Taking things one step farther from the idealized hero cop, the badge-bearing protagonists of police films in recent years have become complex mixtures of benevolence and evil: good cop and bad cop rolled into one. Society is partly blamed—a diseased system that forces well-intentioned officers of the law to resort to dangerous or unethical actions. They must often work outside of the law, which has been rendered impotent by corrupt politicians, meddling special interest groups, and a distrustful public. Clint Eastwood plays iconoclastic rogue cop Harry Callahan in *Dirty Harry* (1971). Determined to capture a serial killer, Harry breaks all the rules (and makes up some of his own). Tapping into society's frustrations and feelings of helplessness, the film is an exercise in gratuitous revenge and vigilante fantasy. Harry, fed up with what he sees as the coddling of criminals, takes the law into his own hands and, no doubt cheered on by audiences, brings down a mad sniper (and a few other criminals) in a "shoot now, ask questions later" approach to urban justice.

In his single-mindedness and his total disregard for social structures and their maxims, Harry is as violent and as ruthless as the serial killer himself; both are products of a broken, inept system. The most famous sequence in the film features Harry leveling a still-smoking Smith and Wesson .44 Magnum at a downed street punk. Grimacing over his non-regulation weapon, Harry taunts, "I know what you're thinking. 'Did he fire six shots or five?' Well, to tell you the truth, in all this excitement, I've kind of lost track myself. But being as this is a .44 Magnum, the most powerful handgun in the world, and would blow your head clean off, you've got to ask yourself one question: 'Do I feel lucky?' Well, do ya, punk?" The scene recurs again at film's end, when Harry, acting as judge and executioner, shoots and kills Scorpio, the serial killer. The film's success led to several Harry sequels: *Magnum Force* (1973), *The Enforcer* (1976), *Sudden Impact* (1983), and *The Dead Pool* (1988).

The *Lethal Weapon* films pair crazy cop Mel Gibson, a suicidal loner in sloppy clothes and long hair, with straight-arrow policeman Danny Glover, conservative family man in suit and tie. In the first film of the series (1987), the men follow the usual buddy pattern of mutual distrust and distaste gradually replaced by respect and love. Gibson plays a problem cop, psychotic and unpredictable, with whom no one wants to work. He is forced upon new partner

Glover, whose cares till now have been bourgeois and domestic: middle age, and adolescent children. Through this and the following films, through car chases, leaps from windows, shoot-outs, and bomb blasts, Glover loosens and lightens up, while Gibson is regenerated by exposure to his partner's close, warm family. The films are equal parts ultraviolence and comedy shtick; unashamedly populist, they court large film audiences (as do most of the films of this type) with their glorification of family, heterosexuality, masculinity, patriotism, and revenge fantasy. Xenophobia is often added to the mix, as in the *Die Hard* films, where *terrorists* equals *foreigners,* and the villains are usually played by European actors (including Alan Rickman and Jeremy Irons).

In the *Lethal Weapon* as in the *Dirty Harry* films, audiences are as surprised as are the bad guys by the cops' unconventional, rule-breaking, even downright illegal methods. Revenge is sweet, however, and we root for the cops the entire time. In *Lethal Weapon 2* (1989), the bad guys, painted in broad strokes of over-the-top villainy, are apartheid-era South African politicos and consuls, racist and murderous, and all the while enjoying diplomatic immunity. They kill the girl—so they are blown to smithereens at the end. The film ends with an injured Gibson cradled in an emotional Glover's arms; Gibson breaks the awkwardness with: "You really are a beautiful man. Give us a kiss before they [the police] come."

The moral ambiguity of the badge-wearing protagonists in *Narc* (2002) is established in the opening, nightmare-like sequence when a Detroit undercover cop (Jason Patric) shoots a fleeing suspect, but also an innocent bystander, a pregnant woman who loses her unborn child. The disgraced narc, dismissed from his job, is offered an assignment to assist another agent (Ray Liotta, in one of his unhinged, maniacal roles) in tracking down a drug kingpin responsible for a popular policeman's death. Patric's cop is a hollow, haunted man—anything but a hero, and suffering violent flashbacks and torturous regrets. Liotta is worse: a brutal live-wire out for revenge. The film is stylishly, if somewhat indulgently, shot in dark, blue tones, with lots of kinetic hand-held camera shots and time/experience fractures by means of flashbacks, flashforwards and split screens (at one point, it is a quadruple screen, showing four simultaneous violent and relentless visitations by the narc agents upon strung-out junkies). The inevitable bloody climax rounds things off.

Other buddy-cop films with an emphasis on nonstop action include *Nighthawks* (1981), another white-black pairing, with Sylvester Stallone and Billy Dee Williams, and *Bad Boys* (1995), another married family man–wild party animal pairing, with Martin Lawrence and Will Smith.

The Chase Film

Many if not most action films involve a chase scene, but occasionally the sequence is so prolonged or memorable that it identifies the film in the public's eyes. In addition, some action films' plotlines consist of nothing but a chase—an extended rush of one character pursuing another in a hurtling dash of forward motion. Perhaps the most cunningly constructed chase film is one of the earliest, Buster Keaton's Civil War comedy, *The General* (1927). The silent film is actually two chases, one a reverse or counterpart of the other, as the meek, unassuming locomotive engineer must travel behind enemy lines after the Northern army has hijacked his beloved train ("the General") and then out again on the General with the Yankees in hot pursuit. Communication lines are cut, tracks and bridges are destroyed, and logs are left upon the tracks to slow one another down, but the chase is relentless. Keaton performed his own stunts aboard the rushing trains, and the audience witnesses the emergence of a hero as the put-upon protagonist defends his three great loves: girlfriend, locomotive, and country. The collapse of a burning bridge over a deep gorge, bearing the Yankees' pursuing train, is reportedly the most expensive scene in all of silent cinema, and it affords a fiery, splashy climax to the film.

Probably the most famous car chase in cinema occurs in William Friedkin's *The French Connection* (1971), the story of two very different NYC cops out to stop a French drug lord from pulling a major international heroin sale in their city. Gene Hackman won an Academy Award for his performance as maverick, bigoted, and hard-headed detective Jimmy "Popeye" Doyle. How much contemporary action films have changed since the 1970s is evident in Hackman's frumpy, sagging demeanor—worlds away from the pumped up glamour of so many action heroes today. "The" chase scene goes from subway cars, where French bad guy Charnier eludes Doyle, to Hackman in an "appropriated" civilian's car, driving frantically, recklessly, and, at ninety miles per hour, far too fast under the elevated train track, swerving to avoid other vehicles, knocking things down, sideswiping a city bus, and only just missing a woman pushing a baby stroller. Despite his faults, audiences identified with and rooted for Doyle, ensuring his reappearance in a sequel, *French Connection II* (1975), which featured an inevitable chase scene finale but was far too long and tedious up to that point.

John Frankenheimer directed *Grand Prix* (1966), a film about multinational race car drivers that mixes exciting split-screen races with silly soap-opera plotlines, and he then incorporated two breathless chase sequences in *Ronin* (1998). Another international cast (including Robert De Niro) plays a motley group of mercenaries sent to retrieve a mysterious briefcase—with the obligatory double-crossing, finger-pointing, and second-guessing that ensues. Despite holes in the plot and too many unanswered questions, the film nevertheless unleashes two spectacular, extended car chases around Paris, one going against traffic and into a tunnel under the river Seine.

Other famous chase films include *Bullitt* (1968) with its ten-minute tear through the narrow, hilly streets of San Francisco as detective Frank Bullitt (Steve McQueen) pursues criminals at 110 miles per hour in his Ford Mustang Fastback. McQueen was at it again in *The Getaway* (1972), in which husband-and-wife bank robbers (he and Ali MacGraw) head out on the lam after a robbery gone wrong. The film becomes an extended chase, including an exciting sequence set on a garbage truck and one of director Sam Peckinpah's obligatory slow-motion shootouts at the end. An unsuccessful remake appeared in 1994, again casting real-life lovers (this time Alec Baldwin and Kim Basinger) in the lead roles. *Gone in 60 Seconds* (1974) devoted a full forty of its 100 minutes to an extended final car chase, once again involving a Mustang. It involves ninety-three car wrecks and is reported to have taken seven months to film. *The Gumball Rally* (1976), *Cannonball* (1976), *The Cannonball Run* (1981), and *Cannonball Run II* (1984) incorporated large, eccentric casting à la TV's *The Love Boat* and *Fantasy Island* (Burt Reynolds, Bianca Jagger, Farrah Fawcett, Shirley MacLaine, Dean Martin, and all manner of 1980s B-listers) in a series of pictures about cross-country road races featuring lots of crashes along the way.

The title of *Runaway Train* (1985) says it all. The pairing of opposites here is an older, hardened criminal and safecracker (Jon Voight) and his young accomplice (Eric Roberts), who escape from prison and stowaway on an Alaskan train, only to discover that there are no brakes and no engineer. Voight is particularly effective, and the film never lets up, with a frozen landscape, police chasing the train in helicopters, bodies run over on the tracks, and a haunting climax. Some critics read the film as Russian director Andrei Konchalovsky's attack on Soviet totalitarianism, but audiences simply enjoyed the breathtaking ride.

The multigenre references and revisions in *Thelma and Louise* (1991) surprised but delighted audiences, and the film struck a chord with female viewers starved for female action heroes. After the women (Susan Sarandon and Geena Davis) shoot a would-be rapist, the film becomes part road-picture, part chase film. Resorting to armed robbery and successfully evading the men who would compromise their freedom (husband, boyfriend, and interstate police), the women, in their pastel Thunderbird convertible, head out into an iconic American West, through Monument Valley, to an eventual date with destiny at the Grand Canyon.

Speed (1994) established Keanu Reeves as an action hero (before he took on the *Matrix* role) and made a star of Sandra Bullock. In a typical cop-action scenario, the young rookie policeman must take on and subvert a crazed villain who has set in motion a plan that would kill innocent citizens. In this case, the bad guy, played by Dennis Hopper, demanding a huge ransom, sabotages a city bus so that, after achieving fifty miles per hour, it and its full capacity of human cargo will explode should the bus fall below that speed. LAPD cop Jack Traven manages to board the moving bus and, after the driver is injured, a young passenger (Bullock) is talked into taking the wheel and keeping the bus moving at a steady speed. The film never lets up and, while it is not exactly a *chase* film (although an LAPD SWAT team shadows the bus as Travis's partner desperately tries to track down the mad bomber), the elements of speed, motion, and impending disaster are all central as the bus tears about Los Angeles. All manner of nail-biting situations lie in the path of the fast, unstoppable, oncoming bus: lots of unsuspecting pedestrians (including a woman pushing a baby carriage, as in *The French Connection*), an obligatory LA traffic jam, a hard right turn, and—gulp—a huge gap in the highway. The film triumphs as much from the chemistry between the earnest Reeves and the protesting but able Bullock characters as from expert and perfectly timed pacing under Jan de Bont's direction. De

Bont and Bullock reteamed in the abysmal sequel *Speed 2: Cruise Control* (1997), which is set on a ship and from which Reeves wisely stayed away.

The Fugitive (1993) is based on the long-running 1960s television serial, in which a doctor, wrongly-accused of killing his wife, must run from and evade approaching police while locating the actual killer. Harrison Ford, as the fugitive, and Tommy Lee Jones, who won an Academy Award as the determined federal marshal, square off and create psychological fireworks on the screen. The real fireworks come in the form of nonstop action, including a tremendous prison bus–train crash (which enables the fugitive to escape), a stolen ambulance, precipitous thrills on a huge dam, and a chase through a crowded, chaotic St. Patrick's Day parade.

"Blaxploitation" Films

After New Hollywood supplanted the old studio system in the late 1960s, the film industry gave new and theretofore unheard of freedom to young directors, and attention to previously ignored audiences. The frustrations, anger, and pride of urban African-Americans were simultaneously illustrated and exploited in more than 200 so-called *blaxploitation* movies. Resentment against whites, set in urban wastelands in which young blacks are either dragged down or empowered by crime, found a release in these cheaply made but extremely successful films. It all started when Melvin Van Peebles produced, directed, financed, wrote, scored, and starred in *Sweet Sweetback's Baad Asssss Song* (1971). X-rated upon its original release, the film is violent and angry wish fulfillment, as a powerful black superstud evades and outwits the racist, relentless LAPD. The advertising cried, "Rated X by an All-White Jury," and it stated that the film is "dedicated to all the Brothers and Sisters who had enough of the Man." In some ways it is an extended chase film, with lots of sex and violence. Years later, Van Peebles's son Mario would write and star in *Baadasssss!* (2004), a depiction of his father's groundbreaking contribution to independent black filmmaking.

While the elder Peebles's film presented a decidedly immoral antihero, 1971 also saw the premier of the first commercially successful crime film with a black hero, Gordon Parks's *Shaft*. Starring Richard Roundtree as ultrahip private eye John Shaft, the film, unlike *Sweet Sweetback's*, crossed over to attract large white as well as black audiences. Tongue-in-cheek but nonetheless graphically violent and sexual, the movie follows Shaft's search for a client's daughter and his run-ins with Harlem mafiosi. Isaac Hayes's theme song, as smooth and as sexy as Shaft himself ("a private dick who's a sex machine to all the chicks," "they say this cat Shaft is a bad mother——"), won an Academy Award, and the film was followed by two sequels, *Shaft's Big Score* (1972), featuring an exciting final chase sequence, and *Shaft Goes to Africa* (1973), wherein the detective takes on a modern-day slave trade. Director Parks's *Superfly* (1972) also produced hit theme songs and large box-office receipts, despite charges that it glorified drug dealers. Cocaine dealer Youngblood Priest (Ron O'Neal) decides to make one last killing deal before quitting the business. If only this had been Priest's last film appearance as well; the two sequels, *Superfly T.N.T.* (1973) and *The Return of Superfly* (1990), have none of the originality and excitement of the first film.

Of the many other blaxploitation films and actors, special mention should be made of Pam Grier, who starred in her own female versions of the subgenre, including *Black Mama, White Mama* (1973), a distaff version of *The Defiant Ones*, as two female criminals, one white, one black, escape—chained together—from a Filipino prison camp; *Coffy* (1973), her biggest hit, as a nurse going after the drug dealers who messed up her sister; and *Foxy Brown* (1974), as another angry nurse, this time out for dealer blood because of a dead lover.

Interest and appreciation for blaxploitation films was revived in the 1990s and inspired several new movies, some of which brought back the subgenre's 1970s stars. *Original Gangstas* (1993) features Roundtree, O'Neal, and Grier, along with others, as old-timers returning to help a bereaved friend kick ass and take down a young gang terrorizing the town. Grier appeared in *Jackie Brown* (1998), made by Quentin Tarantino, a director who has cited his indebtedness to blaxploitation films; likewise, director John Singleton reinterpreted the genre in *Boyz N the Hood* (1991) and then revisited it in his 2000 remake of *Shaft*. Mario Van Peebles's seminal, albeit melodramatic and heavy-handed, *New Jack City* (1991) gave this nineties revisitation of seventies blaxploitation films the name of "New Jack Cinema." Violent and more extreme than their predecessors, these films again explored life in the ghetto and the limited choice of avenues out: education, prison, drugs, violence, or death.

Action Heroes of the 1980s and 1990s

Sylvester Stallone and, particularly, Arnold Schwarzenegger reinvented the action film in the 1980s, becoming huge international superstars in the process. The pumped-up, robotic man of few words who conquers or saves the world stemmed directly from their own cartoonish, over-developed bodies, heavy accents—New York and Austrian, respectively—and limited acting skills (Schwarzenegger seemed to have difficulty with English). Stallone seized the public's heart and imagination in *Rocky* (1976), which he also wrote. The maudlin, albeit compelling, story of a two-bit fighter's million-to-one shot at a comeback won a Best Picture Academy Award and inspired four sequels, as well as countless feel-good movies in the 1980s and 1990s in which the long-shot little guy surmounts all odds (*Rudy, Cool Runnings*, etc.).

Stallone brought his never-give-in machismo to the role of John Rambo, a Vietnam Green Beret veteran falsely accused by the police in *First Blood* (1982). In the follow-up, *Rambo: First Blood II* (1985), the jingoistic testosterone level is pumped even higher (if that is possible), as the protagonist returns to Cambodia in search of American MIAs—a one-man army, dripping sweat and an arsenal of weaponry, who discovers that his own government hasn't been telling the truth. *Rambo III* (1988) saw the title character, sporting a trendy, shaggy mullet hairstyle, head behind Russian lines in war-torn Afghanistan (amid nonstop explosions), out to liberate his former commanding officer. The film was reportedly the most expensive ever made up to that time ($58 million), but the dialogue, plot, and acting are as trashy and fun as the previous Rambo movies. In the nineties, Stallone abandoned Rambo but not action films. *Cliffhanger* (1993) offers spectacular mountain scenery (shot in the Italian Dolomites but set in the Rockies) and nailbiting precipitous stunts (from the opening, in which a hand slips out of a glove holding someone over the edge of a cliff, to a final helicopter explosion) in the predictable story of a mountain rescue expert and the inhabitants of a small town pitted against a villainous gang out to find millions of lost dollars. *Demolition Man* (1993), *The Specialist* (1995), *Assassins* (1995), and *Judge Dredd* (1995)—in which Stallone plays a cop, a CIA agent, a hit man, and a futuristic policeman/judge/executioner, respectively—are fast paced and heavy on the violence but light on story and personality.

Arnold Schwarzenegger's career has been like that of none other, from his early days as a competitive bodybuilder, to his immigration to America, to his residence in the California governor's mansion. In between, he was the ultimate action hero, monolithic and monosyllabic, starring in a series of 1980s and 1990s action-adventure films which were hugely popular, if never really taken seriously. *Conan the Barbarian* (1982) was perfectly suited to Schwarzenegger: a primitive behemoth of a man, using as few words as possible while fighting and having sex. Actually, the bodybuilder star was a bit too developed; he had to lose some bulk in his chest and arms in order to wield a sword, and he had to do his own stunts because no one with a similar body type could be located. The film seems aimed at teen males, with its pillagers on horseback, voluptuous women for the taking, fetishized ancestral phallic swords, and Conan's coming of age in time to defend himself and his people. Complete with a Carl Orff-inspired score, the film is set amid a wintry medieval landscape, but it moves indoors for such scenes as gladiatorial competitions that allow the star to strip down, oil up, and whup all comers.

Schwarzenegger combined action and science fiction as the violent cyborg in *The Terminator* (1984) and its sequels, *Terminator 2: Judgment Day* (1991) and *Terminator 3: Rise of the Machines* (2003). The first two films benefit immeasurably from action master-director James Cameron's sense for pacing and visuals. In the first film, Schwarzenegger is a bad guy: a robot sent back in time to 1984 from 2029 in order to kill a woman (Linda Hamilton) whose future unborn son will lead a rebellion against the evil, powerful cyborgs. Beyond all the technobabble about the Terminator's makeup and engineering specifications, there's endless destruction and mayhem. When the cyborg is refused entry into an LA building, he delivers the film's—and Schwarzenegger's—legendary line: "I'll be back." Indeed, he returns forthwith in a huge tanklike vehicle that he uses to smash into and destroy the place. The second film relies more heavily upon special effects, and the seven years between the movies' releases demonstrate just how far and how quickly computer-generated effects developed in the eighties. The transformations in the 1991 film were completely generated via software, and they're dazzling, particularly the protean android T-1000 (Robert Patrick), apparently indestructible due to its ability to become any shape, form, or appearance, liquid or solid, as necessary. Schwarzenegger here is a good guy, like T-1000 sent back in time from the future, but this time around out to protect rather than destroy the woman (and her now adolescent son). Linda Hamilton grabbed attention for her turn as a female action hero—hard, muscular, and aware of the truth (and, as punishment, locked in a mental institution). Again, the film offers nonstop action and its technical virtuosity earned it several Academy Awards, including Makeup, Special Visual Effects, and Sound.

Between the Terminator films, Schwarzenegger made *Commando* (1986), a generic, pallid actioner about a retired special agent forced back into service after his daughter is kidnapped; *Raw Deal* (1986), an even weaker film about an former federal agent breaking a crime ring; *Predator* (1987), a much more satisfying picture about a mercenary SWAT team sent on a mission in the South American jungle; *Red Heat* (1988), a grim, unappealing look at a Soviet cop tracking Russian drug dealers in Chicago; *True Lies* (1994), proving that Schwarzenegger's best films are those directed by James Cameron, a fun and action-packed story of a super-secret U.S. spy whose wife (Jamie Lee Curtis) thinks he is a boring computer salesman; *End of Days* (1999), a millennial fable about an ex-cop (again!) turned security guard who takes on Satan himself; *The Sixth Day* (2000), a Hitchcockian sci-fi story of a man who discovers that not only has he been cloned, but that, to make way for the clone, assassins are out to get him; and *Collateral Damage* (2002), delayed after the terrorist attacks of September 11, 2001, about a firefighter who seeks out the terrorist responsible for the deaths of his family members.

Comic Book Heroes

The characters played by Stallone and Schwarzenegger are ultimately cartoonish in their exaggeration and lack of dimension. More directly, superheroes taken from DC and Marvel comics inspired several B-picture serials in the 1930s and 1940s and big budget franchises fifty years later. Buster Crabbe appeared as Flash Gordon in a couple of 1936 serials, battling Ming the Merciless in outer space. The fifteen-part Superman serial from 1948 told of his arrival upon earth as an infant and his later battles with the evil Spider Lady. As stated, these are low-budget films with decidedly cheap visual effects. Since the early 1980s, the popularity of cinema action heroes and of sequels has ensured a steady stream of big-budget films about comic book heroes' exploits; these movies offer a textbook on developing ever-more impressive special effects and computer-generated visual possibilities.

The man of steel made a splashy return in *Superman: The Movie* (1978) directed by Richard Donner and making a star of soap-opera actor Christopher Reeve. The film became Warner Brothers' biggest grosser up to that time, which is just as well, because Marlon Brando received $10 million for his four-minute appearance as Jor-El, Superman's doomed father, and millions more were spent on state-of-the-art special effects and sets. "You'll Believe a Man Can Fly!" promised the ads, but the film delivered much more, moving as it did from the early, mythic Americana scenes in the corn fields of Kansas to the fast-paced action sequences and the romantic-comedy scenes between Clark Kent and Lois Lane

(Margot Kidder). Superman's nemesis here is crazed megalomaniac Lex Luthor (Gene Hackman), out to wreak destruction for personal gain. The superhero manages to save California by righting the earthquake-prone San Andreas fault and redirecting a deadly missile off into space. He also flies so quickly against the rotation of the earth on its axis that time is turned back, saving Lois's life and erasing her memory of who Clark Kent really is. Working with seven film units, enough footage was made for a sequel, but when a new director was hired, many reshoots ensued, and *Superman II* appeared in 1980. Many cinemagoers preferred the sequel, in which Superman agrees to give up his super powers in order to marry Lois—only to discover that three villains from his former planet Krypton (who thus enjoy his now-lost powers) have arrived on earth and are doing what arch-villains do.

Flash Gordon (1980) played up the high camp inherent in men-in-tights superhero stories, with an international cast clearly enjoying itself, a flashy soundtrack by the operatic pop band Queen, and such purple lines as "You young hothead! You've brought down destruction on my kingdom!" and "Flash, I love you! But we only have fourteen hours to save the earth!"

Batman has appeared in several films, the first two of which—*Batman* (1989) and *Batman Returns* (1992)—brought director Tim Burton's dark, surrealist vision to the caped crusader's escapades. Impressive production design and effects typify the series. Some viewers felt Jack Nicholson's deliciously over-the-top turn as the Joker in the first film completely overshadowed Michael Keaton's performance as Batman, and stars flocked to participate in the franchise. Keaton took on Catwoman (Michelle Pfeiffer) and the Penguin (Danny DeVito) in the second film; *Batman Forever* (1995) featured Tommy Lee Jones as Harvey Two-Face and Jim Carrey as the Riddler, while Val Kilmer took over the role of Batman; in *Batman and Robin* (1997) the title characters were played by George Clooney and Chris O'Donnell, with Arnold Schwarzenegger (Mr. Freeze), Uma Thurman (Poison Ivy), and Alicia Silverstone, the It girl of that moment (Batgirl). The Caped Crusader's feminine, feline nemesis got a film of her own in *Catwoman* (2004), but despite star Halle Berry, fresh from her Oscar win in *Monster's Ball*, the film was panned by critics and audiences alike. In 2005, a prequel appeared. *Batman Begins* tells the story of young Bruce Wayne (Christian Bale) and the circumstances that lead to his emergence as protector of Gotham City.

The most successful comic-book hero to hit the big screen in recent years is Spiderman. People were surprised by the casting of boyish, introspective Tobey Maguire in the title role, but, after pumping up at the gym, he filled the spandex suit well and brought both intelligence and exuberance to the role in *Spider-Man* (2002) and *Spider-Man 2* (2004). Young (dare one say "mild mannered"?) Peter Parker is bitten by a genetically modified spider, which transforms the high-school nerd into a wall-climbing, thread-swinging arachno-man out to fight evildoers. The love scenes between Maguire and Kirsten Dunst brought in young female audiences, and the spectacular special effects, particularly shots of Spiderman swinging and leaping from skyscraper to skyscraper, are breathtaking. The death of an uncle convinces Parker to devote his powers to combating evil, and he soon encounters the diabolical Green Goblin (Willem Dafoe). In the 2004 sequel, Spiderman's hands are literally full with a new villain, the many-tentacled Doc Octopus (Alfred Molina)—who is Dr. Frankenstein *and* his own monster in one. Many prefer the second film to the first, which again courts young audiences in its combination of ordinary school dramas (romance between the wayward girl and shy boy), combative pyrotechnics when the superhero and villain meet, and Peter Parker's inner struggle as to exactly how—and as whom—he is going to live his life. An aunt's admonition that "Kids . . . need a hero. I believe there's a hero in all of us," helps Peter make up his mind. The film includes an homage to a scene in Donner's *Superman*: as yet another crisis strikes New York, Peter runs toward the camera, tearing open his shirt and jacket to reveal a superhero's outfit underneath.

Hong Kong Martial Arts Influence

In the 1970s, a Hong Kong film studio, Harvest Films, hit the international jackpot with "kung fu" films starring martial artist Bruce Lee. Lee died young, after making only four films, but the world had been introduced to a new kind of cinema, highly stylized and choreographed with nonstop action and violence. In the 1980s, groundbreaking fight films emerged, blending traditional Hong Kong martial arts, Chinese opera's stylized acrobatics and abandonment of reality, and eye-popping special effects. The films also mixed tragedy with low comedy, were shot from all manner of untraditionally juxtaposed camera angles, and borrowed plots from old Hollywood gangster and comedy movies. The energy in these films never wanes, and they are choreographed within an inch of their lives. Actors are suspended from wires in order to twirl and fly through the air, spin in aerial somersaults, and leap atop buildings and over adversaries during their extended fight sequences. Director John Woo, actor-director Jackie Chan and actors Chow Yun-Fat and Jet Li emerged as stars, and, following the economic recession that hit Hong Kong after its return to Chinese sovereignty, they largely reestablished their careers in Hollywood. The greatest choreographer of martial arts films, Yuen Wo Ping, who created the kinetic wonders in the international hit *Crouching Tiger, Hidden Dragon* (2000), also found work in America, designing breathtaking sequences in *The Matrix* (1999) and *Kill Bill* (2003).

Video Game Influence

A unique, symbiotic relationship exists between action films and video and computer games, wherein characters, plots, and scenarios move freely from one form to the other. The games' emphasis upon an individual player's constant movement and activity, revolving around set tasks and achievements that are under continual threat from opposing or malign forces, replicates the plotline of many action films. Realizing the lucrative potential of video game tie-ins, film studios now incorporate appropriate marketing in the overall production of big-budget action films. Thus there are *Spider-Man* and *Star Wars III:*

Revenge of the Sith games released for Game Boy, PlayStation, Xbox, and Nintendo before the release of the films themselves, guaranteeing increased and sustained interest in the motion pictures. Fans of these big-budget action films tend to see them several times, another similarity between the movies and the games, which involve repeated playings. Occasionally the inspiration for a story works in the opposite direction, as evidenced by the production of *Lara Croft: Tomb Raider* (2001), based on the game. In the film, Angelina Jolie plays the kick-ass, pneumatic video adventuress, who is out to retrieve powerful ancient artifacts. Taking her cue from male action heroes, Jolie is somewhat robotic, but given the film's inspiration, such an approach seems fitting.

References and Further Reading

Brode, Douglas. *Boys and Toys: Ultimate Action-Adventure Movies.* New York: Citadel, 2003.
Julius, Marshall. *Action! The Action Movie A-Z.* Bloomington: Indiana University Press, 1996.
Lichtenfeld, Eric. *Actions Speak Louder: Violence, Spectacle, and the American Action Movie.* Westport, CT: Praeger, 2004.
Sobchack, Thomas. "The Adventure Film." In *Handbook of American Film Genres,* edited by Wes D. Gehring, 9–24. Westport, CT: Greenwood, 1988.
Tasker, Yvonne. *Action and Adventure Cinema.* London; New York: Routledge, 2004.
Thomas, Tony. *The Great Adventure Films.* Secaucus, NJ: Citadel, 1976.
Yacowar, Maurice. "The Bug in the Rug: Notes on the Disaster Film." In *Film Genre: Theory and Criticism,* edited by Barry K. Grant. Metuchen, NJ: Scarecrow, 1977.

CHAPTER 2

COMEDY

IN PRESTON STURGES'S 1941 film *Sullivan's Travels,* film director John Sullivan (played by Joel McCrea) has grown disenchanted with directing lightweight, inconsequential, serialized fluff with titles such as *Ants in Your Pants of 1938.* Longing to bring a socially relevant film to the screen, he travels throughout Depression-era America researching his production, ending up in a sweltering Southern work camp for his trouble. When he joins other often brutalized prisoners to watch a cartoon in a black church, "Sully" notices that the room fills with laughter, and once back in Hollywood, he vows to make a comedy. Sturges's character learns here what American filmmakers and audiences have known all along—that humor has the power to raise the spirits and rejuvenate the soul—which explains, in part, the popularity of American film comedies.

DEFINING CHARACTERISTICS

Like the musical, film comedies are best defined by their several variations or subcategories, classifiable, as author and critic Tim Dirks demonstrates, into three broad categories: performance-based, in which the humor results from the physical antics of a versatile performer, such as Charlie Chaplin or Jerry Lewis; context- or situation-based, in which the particulars of the scenario are inherently comic, such as when a character finds him- or herself in an unlikely or alien environment and must adjust); or dialogue-based, in which witty repartee or otherwise uniquely delivered dialogue prevails.

As in other genres, the qualities which distinguish one comedy subgenre from another are most easily discerned by looking at representative films themselves rather than by formulating abstract definitions. Few comedies are pure in the sense that they embody only one type of comedy; different forms of comedy often blend when applied to a variety of narrative situations, creating even more diverse subgenres such as the musical or romantic comedy.

Farce

In the farce, humor often results from mistaken identity, disguise, and other improbable situations. Cross-dressing is a popular theme, as in *Some Like It Hot* (1959), in which Tony Curtis and Jack Lemmon join an all-female dance band to evade mobsters, or *Mrs. Doubtfire* (1993), in which divorced father Robin Williams dresses as a lovable old housekeeper in his ex-wife's household to see his children more. Often dignified individuals are made to appear absurd, such as the society matrons played by perennial Marx Brothers costar Margaret Dumont in *Horse Feathers* (1932) and *Duck Soup* (1933). Fast-paced, physical comedy, slap stick, and sight gags predominate. Serious subjects, such as the Third Reich in *The Producers* (1968), are often recast in wacky or absurd ways.

Gross-Out

Related to farce, this subgenre spares nothing and no one for the sake of a laugh, with no opportunity to violate good taste or courtesy overlooked. "Gross-out" comedies particularly emphasize the comic antics of, and are marketed to, the young. Sexuality, bodily functions, and other excesses often drive the humor, and the awkwardness of coming of age often structures the narrative only in the crudest or crassest terms. Teen comedies overall often fall into this category, but they vary in their degree of explicitness or tastefulness. Not all comedies that explore the confusion of growing up resort to such excesses, but the better known examples of this subgenre often focus on the high school and college years. For example, *National Lampoon's Animal House* (1978) focuses on the antics of a blackballed college fraternity on a fictional college campus during the early 1960s, and *American Pie* (1999) features a group of high school students who seek sexual gratification in some odd ways.

Screwball

These popular lightweight vehicles center on the madcap activities of unconventional characters, quite often female, who get themselves into unconventional situations. The male protagonist is often a staid professional uninterested in or unprepared for love and romance, and in some of the classic versions, the female protagonist hails from a different social class than the male. Because the form's peak in the classical era coincided with the Great Depression, these films often focus on the antics of the idle rich, setting them up for ridicule. Sometimes female lead characters are socialites and heiresses, as in *My Man Godfrey* (1936), with Carole Lombard as a wealthy woman who wins a scavenger hunt by finding a bum at the height of the Depression. On the opposite end of the spectrum, some female leads are gold diggers trying to improve their station through marriage.

The witty, often biting dialogue in screwball comedies usually comes so quickly that the verbal exchange often concludes before the subject perceives an insult. Physical comedy is not as prevalent as in the farce, and when it does occur, it often extends from the characters' verbal sparring. A door is slammed in someone's face, a scheme literally collapses on top of the character, or a swat or a push ends an argument—all in good fun, of course, with no intention to injure and all in the spirit of the battle of the sexes. Zaniness, lunacy, excess, mistaken identity, comic reversals, disguises, and cross-dressing are all common features.

As critic Daniel Shumway notes, the best screwball comedies are really romantic comedies with unconventional characters. Many screwball comedies mystify marriage, while at the same time focusing the narrative toward marriage as a resolution to the couple's verbal and physical sparring. Sometimes the melding of screwball and romantic comedies results in a plot in which a couple separates as a result of a spat or a common misunderstanding, pairing off with other individuals to be reunited by the sudden realization of their love for one another, as in Leo McCarey's *The Awful Truth* (1937). Such screwball comedies might, then, be considered comedies of remarriage.

Romantic Comedy

The typical romantic comedy plot finds two characters brought together by happenstance, mistaken identity, or their differences. The charge or spark between the two may initially manifest itself as hostility or annoyance, and the plot of the film explores how they come together at the end. Love blossoms between some very improbable participants in the most unlikely of circumstances. Contemporary romantic comedies overlap with screwball comedies and woman's film (see **Woman's Film**) in their focus on love and marriage, with a contemporary version now referred to in popular culture as the "chick flick." Classic romantic comedies include *Pillow Talk* (1959), in which Doris Day and Rock Hudson spar over tying up a telephone line, and *Sleepless in Seattle* (1993), in which a widower (Tom Hanks) is brought together with a woman (Meg Ryan) who hears of his plight on a night-time radio call-in program broadcast halfway across the country.

Drawing Room Comedy/Comedy of Manners

These comic examples draw upon many of the elements of the screwball comedy, including double entendre, witty dialogue, and verbal understatement. The setting is normally high society aristocratic circles or some other highly cultured environment in which order and convention reign. The source of humor involves the disruption of that order or the ridiculing of an adherence to convention, normally by the conversion of one of the character to unconventional methods or by the intrusion of an unwelcome or disruptive influence. For example, in *Emma* (1996), a young matchmaker meddles in the affairs of others to her own misfortune; in *Dinner at Eight* (1933), the too obviously sexy trophy wife Jean Harlow exposes her limited social patina and intelligence at a high society dinner party. By his or her mere presence or directly through his or her engagement with establishment figures, such a disruptive character offers a critique on the sterile manners and mores of the upper crust. Faux pas serves as the subject of comedy and identification for audience members in these cases, and the upper classes are often satirized by their harsh rebuke of the "offender" for violating the seemingly arbitrary rules of an insulated and snobbish community. Social criticism takes the form of comic reversals, cases of mistaken identity, disguises, and the entrapment of stuffy social leaders into unflattering circumstances.

Dark Comedy

Many horror films (see **Horror**) and dramas contain passing moments of humor, but this subgenre is meant to be primarily comic even though the fundamental narrative scenario or thematic issue is dark, or the filmmakers bring pessimism, irony, or sarcasm to subjects that are not inherently dark. Dialogue is often sarcastic, dripping with a venom or irony more penetrating than the witty repartee in the drawing room or screwball comedy. The laugher these films elicit is more brittle and unsettling than cathartic because its irreverence often strikes where audiences are most vulnerable: the heart of significant national or international issues, societal taboos, or other sacred cows. Examples include *Arsenic and Old Lace* (1944), in which Cary Grant discovers that his kindly old aunts have been euthanizing lonely old men, and *The War of the Roses* (1989), in which the marriage of Michael Douglas and Kathleen Turner turns into a grudge match to the finish, with the family dog served up as a sacrifice to their dissolving union.

Parody, Satire, Spoof, Lampoon, and Send-Up

Strictly speaking, not all of these comic forms are synonymous, but they share a tendency to use ridicule as a form of commentary. What distinguishes parody or satire from spoof, lampoon, and send-up is the degree of subtlety or exaggeration employed by the commentary. Satire takes a serious approach to the subject in an effort to expose absurdity, self-absorption, extreme or entrenched political ideology, and hypocrisy. Satirical conventions include the use of exaggerated character types, overblown situations, and allegory, as in Charlie Chaplin's swipe at Hitler in the guise of fictional dictator Adenoid Hynkel in *The Great Dictator* (1940). Other films satirize or parody the film or entertainment industry, such as Robert Altman's *The Player* (1992), with its behind-the-scenes look at how motion pictures are pitched and conceived. Some examples parody or spoof film genres or popular film types, such as the popular trend in recent years toward *mockumentaries*: film treatments that adopt an exaggeratedly serious tone and mock documentary film techniques. Christopher Guest's insider's look at the cutthroat world of competitive dog shows in *Best in Show* (2000) and his chronicle of the reunion of a fictional folk group in *A Mighty Wind* (2003) are two examples. Mel Brooks's *Blazing Saddles* and *Young Frankenstein* (1974) parody Westerns (see **Western**) and horror films (see **Horror**), respectively. Neil Simon's *The Cheap Detective* (1978) and *Murder by Death* (1978) spoof Agatha Christie detective thrillers. Carl Reiner's *Dead Men Don't Wear Plaid* (1982), starring Steve Martin, is a send-up of 1940s film noir (see **Film Noir**) detective films. *Airplane!* (1980), *The Naked Gun* (1988), *Hot Shots!* (1991), and *Fatal Instinct* (1993) parody the *Airport* disaster film series, TV cop shows, the Tom Cruise action-adventure film *Top Gun* (1991), and *Fatal Attraction* (1987), respectively.

HISTORY AND INFLUENCES

The Beginning to the 1930s

As Tim Dirks notes, the ability of performers, directors, and scenario writers to make audiences respond to the visual rather than the aural accounts for the special place comedy holds in the development of motion pictures. Film historians point to the formation of Mack Sennett's Keystone Studios in 1912 as the beginning of the American film comedy tradition. Dubbed early on as "the King of Comedy," Sennett wrote, directed, or produced over three hundred motion pictures of various lengths, giving many silent comedy stars such as Charlie Chaplin, Roscoe "Fatty" Arbuckle, and Mabel Normand their start. Sennett's legacy to early comedy includes the Keystone Kops, a group of clumsy policeman who arrive in an overstuffed police car to create havoc; the Bathing Beauties, a group of starlets under contract to Sennett; and the Kid Komedies, a troupe of child performers not unlike Hal Roach's Little Rascals in the *Our Gang* series. Of all Keystone contract players from this period, however, Charlie Chaplin was the first to develop his own comic vision. In his second of thirty-five films for Sennett, *Kid Auto Races in Venice* (1914), Chaplin invented the time-honored Little Tramp, but the character's baggy pants, bowler hat, and identifiable walk did not figure prominently on screen until the Essanay Company's production of *The Little Tramp* (1915). *Tillie's Punctured Romance* (1914) for Keystone cast Chaplin in the unlikely role of a con artist who convinces a country girl, Tillie (Marie Dressler), to take her father's savings and run away with him to the big city.

Chaplin's output in the 1920s rose to the level of art in *The Kid* (1921), his first feature-length production, and *The Gold Rush* (1925), considered by many his best silent film. In *The Kid* (1921), costarring child star Jackie Coogan, an impoverished mother (Edna Purviance) leaves her child in the back seat of a millionaire's limousine, which is eventually stolen by thieves. Hearing the baby crying, the Little Tramp retrieves the child and rears him as if he were his own until a doctor called in to treat the sick child orders the boy to the orphan asylum. The Little Tramp is left out in the cold again when "the kid's" now-wealthy mother eventually reclaims her child. The comic antics of the Little Tramp are transferred to the Yukon in *The Gold Rush* (1925), written and scored by Chaplin, as the little man arrives in the Yukon in search of gold only to fall in love with the lovely Georgia (Georgia Hale). In the process, out of hunger, his cabin mate (Mack Swain) imagines him as a chicken, and the Little Tramp attempts to fill his own stomach by dining on his own boiled leather shoe. The other memorable moment involves the Tramp spearing rolls on forks and doing a high-kick step with his hand.

In his two memorable productions in the 1930s, Chaplin experimented with the notion of a "silent" film in the age of sound in *City Lights* (1931) and *Modern Times* (1936). The film community's high regard for him enabled Chaplin to shoot *City Lights*, his story of the Little Tramp who falls in love with a blind flower seller (Virginia Chervill), entirely without dialogue. His fair-weather friendship with a millionaire provides him with the money to get the girl an operation to restore her vision. Sighted, the girl opens a flower shop, where, by chance, she lays eyes on her benefactor for the first time. The camera fades out on the face of a happy Little Tramp, aware that the object of his affection has been restored to perfection. *Modern Times* casts Paulette Goddard as "the gamin," running from the authorities who seek to place her in an orphan asylum. Chaplin's character—somewhat portrayed as the Little Tramp and somewhat not—is so dehumanized by the monotonous tightening of assembly-line screws that his body involuntarily goes through the motions. When the owner of the company chooses him to test an eating machine designed to eliminate the lunch hour altogether, the experiment goes awry, and he eventually ends up institutionalized. Upon his release and after another series of mishaps, he and the gamin meet up as entertainers in a café, but the authorities recognize the gamin once she takes the dance floor. The pair eventually escapes to the countryside, and the famous final episode finds the two walking arm in arm down the middle of a highway into the sun.

Clearly a satire on the machine age, *Modern Times* has also been suggested to be, in part, a protest against the coming of sound. Although Chaplin may, in fact, have been skeptical of sound in motion pictures, in *The Great Dictator* (1940) he finally gave in to the "talkie" phenomenon in his satire of the Third Reich. Chaplin plays both dictator Adenoid Hynkel and a Jewish barber in a classic prince-and-pauper story. As the "Fooey" of Tourmania, Hynkel dreams of world domination, at one point bouncing and twirling a balloon of the world until it breaks. An argument with Bacterian dictator Napoli (i.e., Mussolini) over Hynkel's plan to invade Osterlitz (presumably Austria) ends up in a comic food fight that reveals the absurdity of the two figures. On a duck hunting trip, Hynkel is mistaken as the barber and vice versa, and the barber finds himself ordering the invasion of Osterlitz to preserve his cover. With the invasion complete, officers serving in Hynkel's regime expect a victorious exaltation in support of dictatorship, but the barber extols the importance of democracy and personal autonomy instead, a clear condemnation of Hitlerian fascism. Chaplin's last American film was *Limelight* (1952), one of the few films in which he appeared without his characteristic mustache. Chaplin plays a music hall performer opposite despondent ballerina Claire Bloom and his silent film contemporary Buster Keaton.

Keaton, nicknamed "stoneface" for his deadpan expression, started in films as a supporting player at Keystone Studios, but the high point of Keaton's career remains the full-length feature films he produced, wrote, or directed himself, including his Civil War–inspired chase film *The General* (1927). Keaton recast the real-life 1862 Union capture of a Confederate locomotive from a Southern perspective, adding a return train chase and a love interest in Annabelle Lee (Marion Mack) (see **Action-Adventure**). In the first of the two train chases that structure the film, Johnny (Keaton) pursues the *General*, his beloved locomotive, captured by Union soldiers with Annabelle on board. In one of the film's memorable scenes, Johnny climbs over the tender of the moving engine (the *Texas*) he has commandeered to reach a flatcar carrying a cannon and then carefully loads the cannon with powder and a shell. He lights the fuse and returns to the locomotive controls in time for the shell to land gently in his own cab; after Johnny pushes it out, it explodes in the bushes. His second attempt hits near the escaping train ahead, and the enemy takes steps to stop Johnny's pursuit. In the return train chase, the now-Union-held *Texas* overtakes the *General* with Johnny at the helm, and a complicated series of thrown switches send the two trains along with a Union supply train, the *Columbia*, toward one another in a probable collision. At the last minute, Johnny brakes his train, throws a switch, and the two Union trains ram into each other, saving the *General*. Keaton ingeniously uses machines, props, and facial expression to enhance the comic mishaps and missteps that befall his character during the train chases.

Another one of Keaton's well-known physical stunts appears in *Steamboat Bill, Jr.* (1928), in which Keaton plays William Canfield Jr., the son of a salty steamboat captain (Ernest Torrence) who intends to train his son as a steamboat captain. Eventually, a fight between land baron John James King (Tom McGuire) and Canfield Sr. lead to the latter's jailing. Access to the jail keys makes breaking out easier for Bill Sr., but he is dismayed when his son hands them back to the Sheriff, getting knocked out for his trouble. Meanwhile, a cyclone sweeps the town away, including the façade of the hospital where Bill Jr. is recuperating—dismayed, but free. As strong winds destroy each form of shelter he seeks, Bill wanders, dazed, until he stands in front of a two-story house, serving as the set-up for one of the most dangerous stunts Keaton performed: as the front façade of the two-story house falls around him, he escapes harm by standing precisely in the space made by an open window.

After the advent of sound, Keaton's popularity waned, with one of his sole remaining film appearances as one of the famous "waxworks" along side Anna Q. Nilsson and H. B. Warner in *Sunset Boulevard* (1950). A similar fate would await the third major film comedian in the silent era, Harold Lloyd, although he would enjoy a more sustained career in the first decade of sound than his counterparts.

Lloyd's "average Joe" character appeared in a number of short films for Keystone and comedy producer Hal Roach from 1915 until 1921. His characteristic "Glasses Character" or "Boy," typically named Harold, debuted in the short *Look Out Below* (1919), but the best film featuring this character type is also Lloyd's best-remembered feature-length film, *Safety Last!* (1923). The film again casts Lloyd as the Boy character, who arrives in the big city seeking fame and fortune for himself and his girl at home (played by Mildred Davis, Lloyd's actual wife). Without the actual prosperity necessary to impress her, he accepts one thousand dollars from his boss to stage a successful publicity stunt for the store. When his roommate's friend, a performer in a human fly act (Bill Strother), runs up the side of the department store higher and higher to elude police, the Boy ends up climbing up floor by floor in pursuit of the man he hired, encountering more and more absurd obstacles on his way. At one point, the still-spectacled Boy dangles from the hands of a clock as it detaches itself from the building, a panoramic view of the elevation in the background (see **Suspense**).

Lloyd made several talking pictures, but he considered his performance as an untalented, accident-prone fellow desperate to get into the movies in *Movie Crazy* (1932) one of his funniest. Lloyd's final screen appearance was in Preston Sturges's *The Sin of Harold Diddlebock* (1947; re-edited and released as *Mad Wednesday*, 1950), about a stable, middle-class clerk who goes on the only rampage of his life twenty years after a solitary football triumph.

The 1930s

The establishment of sound in the 1930s brought forth a whole new crop of comedic performers and even a new subgenre, the screwball comedy. Among the most prolific comedians who brought silent comedy slapstick to the sound era were the Three Stooges (Moe Howard, Larry Fine, and Curly Howard, in the original cast) in a series of short films spanning over thirty-five years of motion picture history. The representative *Punch Drunks* (1934), the only short film entirely written by the group themselves, casts Moe as a down-on-his-luck boxing promoter who discovers that Curly knocks people out cold every time he hears Larry play "Pop Goes the Weasel" on the violin.

Another great comedy team, Laurel and Hardy, met by accident while filming *Lucky Dog* (1917) under the direction of Leo McCarey at Hal Roach Studios. Parlaying the physical differences between them (Stan Laurel as the thin man with a bowler hat and Oliver Hardy as the fat one) and a series of comic gestures (head-scratching, "tie-twiddling," and weeping) into a twenty-year career, the pair made dozens of short films and twenty-seven full-length features from the 1920s until the 1940s, including *The Music Box* (1932), in which the pair try to get a piano up a flight of stairs; *Sons of the Desert* (1933), considered their best film; and the somewhat unfortunate *Babes in Toyland* (1934).

With several films to their name featuring either all or part of the comic quartet, the Marx Brothers (Groucho, Harpo, Chico, and Zeppo) brought their own flair to slapstick, first at Paramount and later at MGM Studios. In *Cocoanuts* (1929), the Brothers play con men initially working against one another to swindle the staff and occupants of a hotel. The film is noted for Groucho and Chico's famous "viaduct"/"Why not a duck?" exchange and for the first use in motion picture history of overhead shots of formations of dancing women. *Animal Crackers* (1930) introduces Groucho's most famous character, Captain Spalding, who delivers his famous African lecture, typified by such one-liners as "One morning I shot an elephant in my pajamas. How he got in my pajamas I don't know." With Groucho starring as an uproarious dictator of Freedonia and brothers Harpo and Chico spying on his political rival, *Duck Soup* (1933) combines political satire with a spoof of thirties Hollywood musicals (see **Musical**).

Margaret Dumont reprises her role as a wealthy society matron and opera patron in *A Night at the Opera* (1935), in which Groucho's outrageous business schemes bring some of Milan's best opera stars to New York. The film's five-minute ocean liner stateroom sequence is one of the most revered in all of comedy history.

With a characteristic comic delivery comparable to the Marx Brothers' style, the much-imitated Mae West is often attributed with saving Paramount Studios from bankruptcy during the earlier 1930s. Her mix of sexual innuendo, over-the-top costuming, sultry strut, and hourglass figure, however, masked a keen artistic and business sense, since West often created her own stories and wrote her own screenplays. In *She Done Him Wrong* (1933), West plays a nightclub owner who has been unfaithful to a criminal about to return to claim his woman. A local temperance league leader (played by a young Cary Grant) must come to her rescue. In *I'm No Angel* (1933), the beautiful Tira (West) drums up a new act as a lion tamer, which propels her to New York, where she experiences heartache and intrigue. In *My Little Chickadee* (1940), Mae West teamed up with another American original, W. C. Fields, known for writing many of the films he acted in, such as *You Can't Cheat an Honest Man* (1939), *The Bank Dick* (1940), and *Never Give a Sucker an Even Break* (1941) for Universal Studios. Fields is known for his exaggerated top hat with a broad band, spats, fastidious and fumbling hand gestures, and for maxims such as "Never work with children or animals." Like West, he cultivated a particular form of comic timing and delivery.

Tough economic times combined with the emergence of directors such as Howard Hawks and Frank Capra and performers such as Carole Lombard, Claudette Colbert, Irene Dunne, and Cary Grant made the 1930s the high point of screwball comedy. The comic antics of the idle rich enabled economically embattled audiences both to laugh at their so-called social superiors and to fantasize about joining their ranks. Perhaps the most versatile screwball performer was Carole Lombard, whose films such as *Twentieth Century* (1934), opposite the legendary John Barrymore as the theatrical impresario who discovered her and is desperate to cast the now-famous Lombard in his new play, routinely make it into critics' top ten lists of the best screwball comedies ever. In terms of critical and popular recognition, Lombard scored her greatest success as Irene Bullock in *My Man Godfrey* (1936), opposite William Powell, a role that earned her an Academy Award nomination for Best Actress. In search of a "forgotten man" to best her sister in a scavenger hunt, Irene Bullock ends up hiring her find, Godfrey, as the family butler. He proves to be a patient, able, and diplomatic member of the household staff, saving the Bullock family fortune and revitalizing the waterfront in the process. Pining for Godfrey throughout much of the film, Irene snags Godfrey in marriage with a reassuring, "Stand still, Godfrey, it'll all be over in a minute."

Irene Dunne demonstrated her versatility throughout the 1930s in a series of screwball comedies that remain, like Lombard's, some of the best known and best loved of the subgenre. Richard Boleslawski's *Theodora Goes Wild* (1936) features Dunne in an Oscar-nominated performance as the prim and proper

Theodora Lynn, who, under a pseudonym, writes a sensational best seller that shocks the community. Bon vivant book jacket illustrator Michael Grant (Melvyn Douglas) sets out to expose Theodora's identity, but a secret of his own ends up turned against him. In Leo McCarey's Oscar-winning *The Awful Truth* (1937), Dunne earned her third Best Actress nomination as Lucy Warriner opposite Cary Grant as husband Jerry, who, after returning from an extramarital rendezvous of his own, has the nerve to suspect his wife of a similar indiscretion. One month later, Lucy finds herself living in an apartment with her Aunt Patsy, in the process of a divorce, and engaged to a wealthy Oklahoma oil baron (Ralph Bellamy). After a series of mishaps, Lucy and Jerry spend the last hours of their marriage together in her aunt's mountain cabin, realizing the mistake they are about to make. Two figures on the cuckoo clock emerge from different doors when the clock strikes, but they return through the same one, suggesting their reunion. Dunne reunited with Grant three years later in Garson Kanin's *My Favorite Wife* (1940), playing Ellen Arden, who returns after being thought dead in a shipwreck to find that her husband Nick (Grant) has remarried. When he discovers that while Ellen was spending years on a deserted island she had the company of a male fellow survivor (Randolph Scott), Nick must know the truth about Ellen's marooning before choosing his "old" wife or his "new" wife.

No discussion of the 1930s screwball comedy would be complete without mentioning Frank Capra's *It Happened One Night* (1934), landmark for its Oscar wins for Best Actor (Clark Gable), Best Actress (Claudette Colbert), Best Director (Frank Capra), and Best Picture of 1934. In the film, rebellious heiress Ellie Andrews (Colbert) remains a prisoner on her father's yacht after he has her marriage to society aviator King Westley (Jameson Thomas) quickly annulled. Andrews escapes by swimming to shore in Miami and she meets a fast-talking reporter Peter Warne (Gable) on a bus to New York. Warne agrees to help her reunite with Westley provided he gets the scoop, but by the time their adventure ends, the two realize they have fallen in love. Two episodes in the film transcend its storyline: the "walls of Jericho" sequence, in which the two share a room divided by a suspended sheet, and the hitchhiking scene, in which Colbert hikes up her skirt to attract passing male motorists. Undershirt sales plummeted after Gable appeared bare-chested in the first sequence.

Along with Irene Dunne and Claudette Colbert, Jean Arthur appeared in a series of comedies produced by Columbia Pictures, with her big break coming in Frank Capra's *Mr. Deeds Goes to Town* (1936), playing a crack reporter seeking an exclusive interview with newly minted millionaire Longfellow Deeds (Cary Grant). Two of Arthur's later comedies are among her best, *The Talk of the Town* (1942) and *The More the Merrier* (1943), both directed by George Stevens. In the former, the Holmes Woolen Mill burns to the ground in Lochester, Massachusetts, and political activist Leopold Dilg (Cary Grant) goes on trial for the crime. His escape from jail after a trial for arson becomes the talk of the town, and unsuspecting high school teacher Nora Shelley (Arthur) discovers Dilg hiding in the attic of her rental property. Convinced that Dilg was framed, Nora finds a way to get her tenant, legal scholar Michael Lightcap (Ronald Colman), on his case, and both men fall in love with her in the process of seeking evidence to exonerate Dilg. For *The More the Merrier* (1943), Arthur would garner her only Oscar nomination, as Best Actress, in the role of Connie Milligan, a woman working in wartime Washington, DC, who rents out part of her apartment in a city suffering from a severe housing shortage. She hopes for a sedate lady tenant, but comedy and romance ensue as she ends up renting to the persuasive elderly Benjamin Dingle (Charles Coburn), who in turn rents half of his own room to a young, good-looking government employee named Joe Carter (Joel McCrea).

Other notable screwball or drawing room comedies of the 1930s and early 1940s era include *Bringing Up Baby* (1938), starring Katharine Hepburn and Cary Grant as opposites whose initial antagonism towards one another turns toward romance. Dr. David Huxley (Grant) is on the verge of three momentous events in his life: marriage to a staid, proper woman who puts their careers in paleontology before connubial bliss, the arrival of the last piece of a brontosaurus Huxley has spent four years reconstructing, and the awarding of one million dollars to the museum where he works. A mistaken golf stroke while Huxley woos the potential donor brings Huxley and heiress Susan Vance (Hepburn) into a collision course with one another, literally. Through a series of madcap adventures with Vance's pet leopard as a catalyst, David learns that the one day he spent with her has been the best of his life. Confusion, cross-dressing, and mistaken identity (both animal and human) result in romance between the pair, but not before Susan winds up in Huxley's arms in the famous last scene.

Hepburn's return to comedy in George Cukor's *The Philadelphia Story* (1940) featured an ex-husband (Cary Grant) determined to disrupt his ex-wife's (Hepburn) new marriage with the help of a skeptical reporter Mike Connor (James Stewart) and photographer Liz Imbrie (Ruth Hussey). Stewart would win an Oscar for Best Actor for his role. Moreover, Cukor's *Dinner at Eight* (1933), a Jean Harlow vehicle, features Billie Burke as hostess Millicent Jordan, convinced by her husband Oliver (Lionel Barrymore) to invite a potential investor (Wallace Beery) in Jordan's failing shipping business and his bubble-headed wife Kitty (Harlow) to her stylish dinner party. With plans for the dinner party in jeopardy, no one knows whether the evening will follow a smooth, charted course or dinner will flounder. The film showcases double takes by Marie Dressler as family friend Carlotta Vance, particularly surrounding Kitty's intellectual stuntedness.

Some comedies of this period crossed genres. For example, *The Thin Man* (1934), the first in the popular *Thin Man* series, starred Dick Powell and Myrna Loy as the happily married verbal duelists Nick and Nora Charles, based upon Dashiell Hammett characters. The film—nominated for Best Picture, Best Actor, Best Director (Woody Van Dyke) and Best Adapted Screenplay—wove comic reversals and snappy dialogue into the story of the mysterious disappearance of an aging inventor, the "thin man" of the title, and the murder of his long-time mistress. Although technically a whodunit, the film's script by Frances Goodrich and Albert Hackett plays up the screwball comedy element to the exclusion of

Cary Grant finds himself becoming ensnared in Katharine Hepburn's charms in the classic screwball comedy *Bringing Up Baby* (1938). *Photofest.*

the detective story. Similarly, comedic mishaps surpass the supernatural elements of the *Topper* series, beginning with Cary Grant and Constance Bennett as George and Marion Kirby, a madcap couple of ghosts, in *Topper* (1937). Roland Young received a Best Supporting Actor Oscar nomination for playing the title character, a henpecked banker whom the ghosts try to rescue from a staid marriage.

Rounding out the 1930s, Cukor assembled an all-female cast in Clare Boothe Luce's play *The Women,* about a securely married woman Mary Haines (Norma Shearer), who, when confronted with the infidelity of her husband, allows her pride and her girlfriends to persuade her to divorce her husband. She gets on a train to Reno, and in time, many of her married friends join her, seeking divorces of their own. A confrontation scene between the soon-to-be past and future Mrs. Haines (Joan Crawford) in a couturier's dressing room results in "the fur flying." A fashion show—the only color sequence in the film—seems clearly intended to draw female viewers in to an otherwise less-than-flattering portrayal of a certain type of female. Rosalind Russell costars as the gossipy Sylvia Fowler, practically stealing the film from an otherwise seasoned cast that includes Paulette Goddard, Marjorie Main, Joan Fontaine, and Lucille Watson.

The 1940s and Early 1950s

A standout in *The Women*, Rosalind Russell portrayed another archetypical fast-talkin' dame in Howard Hawks's *His Girl Friday* (1940), opposite Cary Grant in this remake of Lewis Milestone's *The Front Page* (1931), itself adapted from Ben Hecht's and Charles MacArthur's classic newspaper play *The Front Page*. Famous for lightning fast repartee, sarcastic retorts, and overlapping dialogue, the tale of a managing editor (Grant) who tries to lure his ex-wife back to the newspaper with a front page scoop on the eve of her remarriage to a lackluster fellow (Ralph Bellamy) dissolves into a delightful battle of the sexes. The 1940 version heralded a series of comedic battles of the sexes that would extend into the fifties, with the most famous including the Katharine Hepburn–Spencer Tracy films to be discussed later.

Joining a long list of others in film history, two prominent comedy teams emerging in the 1940s were Bud Abbott and Lou Costello and Bob Hope and Bing Crosby. Abbott and Costello performed in vaudeville and radio for ten years before they got their start in films at Universal in *One Night in the Tropics* (1940). *Buck Privates* (1941) became the first of some twenty-three highly successful films in the 1940s, earning them a position among the top-five box attractions of the decade. They first performed on screen their comic radio sketch "Who's On First," written by John Grant, in *The Naughty Nineties* (1945). Similarly, Bob Hope and Bing Crosby teamed up in the musical comedy genre to star in a series of successful "Road" pictures for Paramount, including *The Road to Singapore* (1940); *The Road to Zanzibar* (1941); *The Road to Morocco* (1942), considered their best; *The Road to Utopia* (1945); *The Road to Rio* (1947); and *The Road to Bali* (1952), their only film in color. By *The Road to Hong Kong* (1962), the magic was over (see **Musical**).

The early 1940s marked the end of the classic screwball comedies, with a new ironic and satirical form of humor gaining prominence in films by writers and directors such as Preston Sturges. His first writing/directorial effort, *The Great McGinty* (1940), featuring Brian Donlevy as a hobo who rises through the corrupt political machine of a major American city, earned high profits for Paramount Studios, and Sturges won the first Academy Award for Best Original Screenplay. Sturges's *The Lady Eve* (1941) pays homage to the classic screwball comedy in a story of father-daughter card sharks (played by Charles Coburn and Barbara Stanwyck) who seek to dupe the scion of a wealthy American brewery family (Henry Fonda)—at least until the daughter falls in love with him. Moreover, in *The Palm Beach Story* (1942), Gerry Jeffers (Claudette Colbert) intends to divorce inventor husband Tom (Joel McCrea) and marry an eccentric millionaire (Rudy Vallee), whom she meets on the train, in exchange for his backing of Tom's next venture. Finally, in Sturges's most financially successful film, *The Miracle of Morgan's Creek* (1944), small-town Trudy Kockenlocker (Betty Hutton) wakes up married to someone after a wild send-off party for troops, but to whom? When she turns up pregnant, her admirer for years, Norval Jones (Eddie Bracken), helps her out of her predicament, and Trudy's delivery of sextuplets—all boys—creates publicity for her home state. Remarkably, the adult nature of the satire on American values, both in the restrictive small town and during wartime, slipped by the censors, and standing-room-only audiences guaranteed the success of the film. The huge success of *The Miracle of Morgan's Creek* contrasted with the failure of Sturges's final notable film, the color *The*

Beautiful Blonde of Bashful Bend (1949). Starring Betty Grable as a saloon singer, this film ostensibly ended Sturges's film career, a victim of changing times.

One manifestation of those changing times and women's changing roles during World War II included the erudite romps featuring Katharine Hepburn and Spencer Tracy, setting a new standard for the he said–she said comedy from the 1940s to the 1950s. In *Woman of the Year* (1942), Hepburn's newspaper woman and Tracy's sports reporter fall in love, but they have trouble learning how to merge their professional and personal lives. Perhaps the best known of the Tracy-Hepburn comedies, *Adam's Rib* (1949), written by husband-wife team Garson Kanin and Ruth Gordon and directed by George Cukor, features the two as a set of married lawyers on the opposite sides of the same criminal case. When Doris Attinger (Judy Holiday) attempts to kill her philandering husband, Adam Bonner (Tracy) prosecutes the case. Irked by the suggestion that the woman should get what she deserves, Amanda Bonner (Hepburn) defends Doris. Unfortunately, the sparring in the courtroom carries over to the personal lives of the two. Judy Holiday's scenes in this legal comedy secured her the lead role of Billie Dawn, a bubble-headed tycoon's girlfriend, in the film version of her Broadway success, *Born Yesterday* (1950), and a surprise Oscar for Best Actress for her efforts. Tracy and Hepburn returned in the sports-related *Pat and Mike* (1952) and *Desk Set* (1957), the latter featuring Tracy as an engineer hired to computerize a television network's research department headed by Hepburn.

The Later 1950s

In the 1950s the fabled blonde comediennes of earlier years, such as Carole Lombard, Jean Harlow, Jean Arthur, and Betty Hutton gave way to a new pair of blonde comedic performers: Marilyn Monroe and Doris Day. Monroe started in films playing a variety of parts as girlfriends and secretaries in A-level films, but when studio executives assigned her larger roles in comedies or musical comedies, she began making her mark. In *Monkey Business* (1952), for example, Monroe plays the secretary of Cary Grant at a chemical company who wears one of his inventions, indestructible hose, over her very shapely legs. Film historians consider it the last true screwball comedy. Monroe starred with Lauren Bacall and Betty Grable in *How to Marry a Millionaire* (1953) as three New York models who set themselves up in a luxurious New York apartment determined to snag three millionaire husbands. Monroe's image as a sultry comedienne unaware of her own sexuality was showcased in Billy Wilder's *The Seven Year Itch* (1955), featuring the famous "fly up" of Monroe's chiffon dress while she straddles a subway grate, and *Some Like It Hot* (1959). In the latter film, Tony Curtis and Jack Lemmon, as witnesses to the St. Valentine's Day Massacre, flee Chicago disguised as members of an all-girl dance band. Along the way, Joe (Curtis) falls for Sugar Kane (Monroe), but he cannot betray his real gender to declare his feelings, lest he risk his safety, and Jerry (Lemmon) catches the eye of an eccentric millionaire (Joe E. Brown). In her final completed comedy, *Let's Make Love* (1960), opposite Yves Montand, drug and alcohol abuse were clearly catching up with Monroe, and she was fired from her last film, *Something's Got to Give* (1962), basically a remake of the Cary Grant–Irene Dunne screwball comedy *My Favorite Wife* with Dean Martin and Cyd Charisse.

Monroe's kittenish sexuality in her comedy roles could not be more strongly offset than by the wholesomeness of Doris Day, revealed in a series of "sex comedies without any sex" that established Day as a gifted comic actress. In *Pillow Talk* (1959), Day earned an Oscar nomination for Best Actress playing an interior designer sharing a two-party telephone line with a songwriter (Rock Hudson), who ties up the phone playing his songs for different women. A split-screen effect highlights the sparring between the two, a technique reproduced in *Down With Love* (2003), director Peyton Reed's homage to Day's romantic comedies, starring Renée Zellweger and Ewan McGregor. In *Move Over, Darling* (1963), Day plays Ellen Arden to James Garner's Nicky Arden in yet another remake of Leo McCarey's story *My Favorite Wife*, with Polly Bergen as Nicky's new wife. And Hudson, Tony Randall, and Paul Lynde join this iconic blonde in *Send Me No Flowers* (1964), in which Hudson plays Day's hypochondriac husband determined to find her a new husband. His wife decides the husband's imagined "illness" is a ruse covering an affair. Day eventually turned to television in the wake of changing tastes, starring in a successful situation comedy for five seasons, but her legacy can clearly be seen in the film work of Meg Ryan and Sandra Bullock, among others.

Although tastes in comedy may change, what does not is the prevalence of important comedy teams throughout history, as shown by the Marx Brothers, Laurel and Hardy, and even Rock Hudson and Doris Day. In the late 1940s and into the 1950s, straight man Dean Martin and physical comedian Jerry Lewis separately played principally secondary roles until they teamed up in *At War With the Army* (1950), pitting Martin against Lewis's Alvin Corwin in this World War II training camp farce. Many critics and fans consider *The Caddy* (1954) the best of the Martin and Lewis pairings and one of the best golf films ever, with real-life golfer Sam Snead featured. The film also included Martin's signature song "That's Amore," a popular standard. The next year, *Artist and Models* (1955), in which Martin and Lewis play an artist and a children's book writer mixed up in a secret government plan involving rocket fuel, features an early performance by Shirley MacLaine.

When the duo broke up in 1957, Jerry Lewis went on to star in several solo comedic ventures, some of which he wrote, directed, or both. In 1958, Lewis reprised the Eddie Bracken role in *Rock-a-Bye Baby*, a remake of Preston Sturges's *The Miracle of Morgan's Creek*. Lewis plays small-town TV repairman Clayton Poole, who agrees to care for the baby of his unrequited love, now a movie star, but he does not bargain for triplets. He marries Carla's younger sister Sandy (Connie Stevens) to adopt the trio, and a series of mishaps send Clayton into hiding. He returns nine months later to discover that Sandy has given birth to quintuplets of her own. *Cinderfella* (1960) is a farcical recasting of the *Cinderella* story complete with a mean stepmother (Judith Anderson), two snobbish stepbrothers (Henry Silva and Robert Hutton), a kindly fairy godfather (Ed Wynn), and a beautiful princess (Anna Maria Alberghetti), whose heart he eventually wins. But *The Nutty Professor* (1963) may be Lewis's most memorable film, remade in 1996 starring Eddie Murphy in the title role. After the football coach humiliates him in front of his most beautiful student, Stella Purdy (Stella Stevens), Professor Julius Kelp (Lewis) sets out to create a potion that turns him into the playboy Buddy Love. Stella falls in love with him, but the potion wears off quickly and he returns to his old self. Although his popularity peaked in the 1960s, Lewis continues to make sporadic film appearances to the present day, and his earlier films are looked at as some of the best examples of physical comedy ever put on celluloid.

The 1960s to Mid-1970s

The 1960s and 1970s saw the emergence of a new rash of comic performers, comic film series, and writers/directors/producers unprecedented since the breakup of the major studios. For example, not since *The Thin Man* series of the 1930s and 1940s had a hybrid of comedy-mystery films captured the public imagination as much as the *Pink Panther* cycle, starring Peter Sellers and directed by Blake Edwards. The origins of the moniker "Pink Panther"—as an illusion perceptible deep inside a flawed but weighty diamond—are explained in the first of the series, *The Pink Panther* (1963), a caper film where the bumbling Inspector Clouseau captures the criminal figure he had been pursuing for years, the illusive Phantom (David Niven). The next year's *A Shot in the Dark* (1964) involves the murder of a man in a country house apparently committed by the maid Maria (Elke Sommer), but Clouseau remains unconvinced. Sellers last appeared as Clouseau in *Revenge of the Pink Panther* (1978), but the Pink Panther series continued after his 1980 death with *The Trail of the Pink Panther* (1982), *Curse of the Pink Panther* (1983), and other variations.

In America, a new comic talent arose from the urban Northeast, writer, director, producer, and actor Woody Allen. Allen remains one of the few filmmakers in the era of the blockbuster still able to snag funding for major feature presentations on the basis of name recognition alone, despite sometimes-meager box office and critical approval. A rarity in the history of motion pictures, Allen's vision largely translates as conceived onto the screen, with little interference from the studios that green-light his projects, but his prolific output has sometimes come at the expense of quality in recent years. But despite flagging box office receipts, Allen continues to have his pick of acting talent, with regulars such as Mia Farrow, Diane Keaton, Dianne Wiest, and Tony Roberts forming a stock company of sorts.

With Bob Hope as an influence, Allen's works reflect an autobiographical bent with a psychoanalytic flair, and the stories often involve Allen-like neurotic protagonists needing to believe in the existence of God and working through their own issues. His earliest comedies, such as *Take the Money and Run* (1969), *Bananas* (1971), and *Sleeper* (1973), rely on Chaplinesque slapstick and sight gags as the source of humor. In his mature phase, beginning with *Annie Hall* (1977), Allen's films turned more serious, with a penchant for literary and high culture references. A mix of stream of consciousness, traditional narrative, and animation in its chronicle of the relationship between the neurotic stand-up comedian Alvy Singer and girlfriend Annie, the film earned Allen Oscars for Best Picture, Best Director, and Best Original Screenplay. Diane Keaton in the title role took home an Academy Award for Best Actress. The comedy *Manhattan* (1979), ironic in its depiction of a recently divorced man's fascination with a high school girl, has been called his love song to New York City, the principal urban environment that becomes like a character in Allen's major works. Shot in black and white, the film is also known for its Gershwin score. A series of eclectic comedy dramas followed, including the mockumentary *Zelig* (1983) and the critical favorites *The Purple Rose of Cairo* (1985) and *Radio Days* (1987). Of the films of this era, *Hannah and Her Sisters* (1986) stands out as the best, with an inventive use of titles as transitional devices and interior monologue. Oscars went to Michael Caine and Dianne Wiest in supporting roles and to Allen for the original screenplay.

Allen's eclecticism has continued in the last two decades with varied looks at life and love and the price we all pay for being human in films such as *Crimes and Misdemeanors* (1989), two separate stories involving adultery. Allen's experiments with a handheld camera and jump cuts in *Husbands and Wives* (1992) adds a documentary feel to his story of an outwardly happily married couple (Judy Davis and Sydney Pollack) whose separation cause their friends (Woody Allen and Mia Farrow) to wonder about the health of their own marriage. The seedy underworld of organized crime in the 1920s meets head-on the idealism of a young writer trying to break into the Broadway scene in *Bullets Over Broadway* (1994). Mira Sorvino took home an Oscar for Best Supporting Actress in Allen's *Mighty Aphrodite* (1995), in which the adoptive father (Allen) of a child genius goes in search of the child's birth mother, convinced that the boy's abilities must be inherited. When he finds her, the mother turns out to be a part-time prostitute and porn star and, what's worse, one of the dumbest women ever. Allen weaves the story of Oedipus into the narrative through the recurring use of a Greek chorus. And *Everybody Says I Love You* (1996) takes on the guise of a 1930s musical, as the events in the lives of a wealthy Upper East Side family provide the excuse for classic musical numbers.

Over the last decade or so, Allen's tendency to churn out a film annually, of varying quality, has been rewarded with decreased box office returns and mixed critical reception. Recent examples include *Deconstructing Harry* (1997), in which an author with writer's block immortalizes events from the lives of his friends in a best seller, to their chagrin; the black-and-white *Celebrity* (1998), casting Kenneth Branagh as a neurotic, Allenesque journalist attempting to become a member of the glitterati with little success; the farcical *Small Time Crooks* (2000), in which petty criminals end up prospering from a cookie business rather than the bank heist they planned; *The Curse of the Jade Scorpion* (2001), which combines a love triangle with hypnotism and petty thievery at an insurance agency; and *Hollywood Ending* (2002), about a has-been film director struck with hysterical blindness during the course of his comeback, perhaps Allen's unwitting statement about his own career. Allen's 2004 *Melinda and Melinda* adopts a typical Allen narrative formula in competing tales of the same female character used by two playwrights to debate whether life is essentially comic or tragic.

Perhaps the only individual of his era able to rival Allen in terms of output is playwright turned screenwriter Neil Simon, largely responsible for a dozen comedy films of varying quality, some based on his own plays. Among the earliest of his comic successes, Walter Matthau stars as Oscar Madison and Jack Lemmon as Felix Ungar, two divorced guys who move in together to save expenses, in Gene Saks's *The Odd Couple* (1968). The film inspired a popular television series starring Jack Klugman and Tony Randall in the Matthau and Lemmon roles. *Plaza Suite* (1971) features three separate stories set in the same New York Plaza hotel room, with Walter Matthau in three roles opposite Maureen Stapleton, Barbara Harris, and Lee Grant. A similar scenario is used in *California Suite* (1978), with Maggie Smith taking home a Best Supporting Actress Oscar for her portrayal of one of the guests. Similarly, *The Sunshine Boys* (1975) earned George Burns a Best Supporting Actor Academy Award as half of a vaudeville team with the opportunity to reunite for a television special.

One of Simon's major successes came with *The Goodbye Girl* (1977), starring Marsha Mason, Simon's then wife, as a divorced dancer who, with her daughter, moves in with an off-off-Broadway actor (Richard Dreyfuss) to cut their expenses. Dreyfuss's performance won the Oscar for Best Actor; Oscar nominations included the film (Best Picture), Quinn Cummings as the daughter (Best Supporting Actress), and Simon (Best Original Screenplay). The last of Simon's major original efforts to appear on screen include the semi-autobiographical *Brighton Beach Memoirs* (1986), with Jonathan Silverman playing the Simonesque role as Eugene Jerome Morris, a character reprised by Matthew Broderick in *Biloxi Blues* (1988). Both films, based on Simon plays, portray different stages in the growing up of a young Jewish man in the middle part of the twentieth century. Simon's nostalgic look at New York during the 1940s continued with *Lost in Yonkers* (1993), starring Richard Dreyfuss, Mercedes Ruehl, and Irene Worth in a story of two boys sent to live with their domineering grandmother and mentally challenged aunt in Yonkers during the summer of 1942.

The Late 1970s to the Present

The creation of a rating system under the Motion Picture Production Code of 1968 enabled a new on-screen permissiveness, demonstrated in, among other comedy subgenres, the "gross-out" and adolescent or teenage comedies. Also called "coming-of-age" or "initiation" comedies, these films portray the foibles endured in a process of self-discovery (sometimes with an emphasis on raunchiness), a process that the adults in these films have either forgotten or never understood. Although growing up has never been easy, not surprisingly, the frank depictions of growing up these films came to the fore in a period of national confusion, the turbulent 1960s and 1970s, and many of them, perhaps in response, hearken back to earlier eras for their setting. Among the first and most important in this subgenre, George Lucas's *American Graffiti* (1973) took an uncharacteristically frank look at the lives of two Northern California high school graduates (Richard Dreyfuss and Ron Howard) on the eve of their departure for college. Drag racers, "Inspiration Point," underage drinking, cigarette packs rolled into shirt sleeves, and ducktail haircuts evoke a pre-Vietnam America, less in political turmoil perhaps, but not any less complex overall. The film launched several other important American stars, such as Cindy Williams, Harrison Ford, and Suzanne Somers (who had a small role), and it inspired the long-running TV series *Happy Days*.

John Landis's *National Lampoon's Animal House* (1978) began the popularization of not only the National Lampoon series of comedies, but also the raunchier "gross-out" variation of growing-up film. Centered on a renegade fraternity that inspires the almost pathological hatred of the buttoned-up Greek-letter organizations and the administration of the fictional Faber College in 1962, the film features an ensemble cast of young actors, including John Belushi as the rather Neanderthal fraternity brother Bluto, whose performance begins a trend toward on-screen scatology in adolescent comedies. The *Porky's* series (*Porky's* [1981], *Porky's: The Next Day* [1983], and *Porky's Revenge* [1985]) immortalizes the exploits of a group of Florida high school students in their quest for sexual titillation. In an early role, Sean Penn plays Jeff Spicoli, a California surfer with a penchant for pot smoking who squares off with high school teacher Mr. Hand (Ray Walston) in Amy Heckerling's *Fast Times at Ridgemont High* (1982). Jennifer Jason Leigh plays a girl searching for love in the same California high school in the 1980s. And *Risky Business* (1983) stars Tom Cruise as a newly sexually experienced youth who lip-synchs Bob Seeger's "Old Time Rock and Roll" in his underwear and sunglasses, an iconic scene from 1980s cinema.

Some of the most recognized coming-of-age films to appear during the 1980s were written, directed, or produced by John Hughes. These films explore not only the typical angst of adolescence but also the often added dimension of social class differences as yet another barrier to connection. *Sixteen Candles* [1984] casts Molly Ringwald as a fifteen-year-old girl on the brink of womanhood with a crush on the most popular boy in school. In Hughes's *The Breakfast Club* (1985), five high school students from diverse backgrounds (Emilio Estevez, Anthony Michael Hall, Judd Nelson, Molly Ringwald, and Ally Sheedy) serve a weekend detention only to make important revelations about what they have in common. Among the most recognized of the teenage rebellion films, *Ferris Bueller's Day Off* (1985) casts Matthew Broderick as a less-than-devoted Chicago high school student determined to skip school, accompanied by two high school friends. Unfortunately, a wily dean of students (Jeffrey Jones) catches on. And in *Some Kind of Wonderful* (1987), the tomboyish Watts (Mary Stuart Masterson) finds her friendship with Keith (Eric Stoltz) turning into something much more important for her. Will he return her affection? Hughes's films developed such an iconic status that they inspired a parody, *Not Another Teen Movie* (2001), set at John Hughes High School with typical coming-of-age fare such as the metamorphosis of the unpopular ugly duckling and the trials of adolescent longing.

The coming-of-age film exploring female development turned decidedly harder-edged with *Heathers* (1989), *Jawbreaker* (1999), and *Clueless* (1995), featuring social ostracism, violence, and even suicide among female social groups. In a related vein, Mark Waters's *Mean Girls* (2004) makes the comparison between female cliques and primitive societies most explicitly, as Cady Heron (Lindsay Lohan), born in Africa, enrolls in an American high school. She survived the jungles in deepest Africa, but how will she fare in a jungle of another kind? *Bring It On* (2000), its sequel *Bring It On Again* (2004), and *Sugar & Spice* (2001) added the variable of competition cheerleading to the already volatile world of young female social interaction. For young men, sexuality continued to be the principal preoccupation in films such as *American Pie* (1999), as four young men (Jason Biggs, Chris Klein, Thomas Ian Nichols, and Seann William Scott) set the goal of losing their virginity before prom night. *American Pie 2* (2001) follows the group the summer after their first year of college, with similar goals on their mind. In combination with *There's Something About Mary* (1998), with Ben Stiller, Cameron Diaz, and Matt Dillon, both films clearly proved that that the popularity of the gross-out comedy was intact.

Closely related to the gross-out comedies in terms of their comic antics, irreverence, and episodic quality is the spoof, parody, or send-up. Among the first, John Landis's low budget *Kentucky Fried Movie* (1977) pushed the limits of good taste and industry censorship in its series of skits that lampooned the news, television commercials, pornography, and kung fu and blaxploitation films, among other recognizable types. Landis and writers Jerry and David Zucker build on the success of this early film in *Airplane!* (1980), a spoof of the *Airport* series of disaster films and others, which included double entendre, deadpan delivery, moments of mock seriousness, and the proverbial send-up of character types such as the singing nun and spunky elderly person characteristic of the Irwin Allen–style of disaster epics. Their later output included *Top Secret!* (1984), a poke at World War II–era espionage films, starring Val Kilmer in an early role; *The Naked Gun* (1988), a spoof of television police dramas; *Hot Shots!* (1986), a tongue-in-cheek homage to 1986's *Top Gun*; and *Hot Shots! Part Deux* (1993), in which Sylvester Stallone's *Rambo*-esque films get the once-over. A related series of films—*Police Academy* (1984) and its six sequels—fall somewhere between gross-out comedy, slapstick, and parody in their comic nod to the police dramas on television.

Writer, producer, director, and actor Mel Brooks wrote and often directed a series of successful parodies of film genres in the 1970s and 1980s. Among the best, *Blazing Saddles* (1974) spoofs the conventions of the Western, with, among other comic performances, Madeline Kahn as the exotic saloon keeper Lili von Schtupp, a clear reference to Marlene Dietrich's role in *Destry Rides Again* (1939). Other "stock" Western characters exposed to comic treatment include a black sheriff (Cleavon Little) hired sight unseen by the desperate Western town, a corrupt political boss called Hedley Lamarr (Harvey Korman), and a wacky but burned-out gunslinger (Gene Wilder). Movie artifice becomes doubly exposed as the set to the Western town bursts open to reveal a musical production number filmed nearby. Filmed the same year as *Blazing Saddles*, Brooks's *Young Frankenstein*, to be pronounced "Fraunken-steen" as the title character (Gene Wilder) asserts, makes the most of Mary Shelley's *Frankenstein* story to comic effect. Like Robert Altman's *The Player* (1992), itself a black comedy, Brooks's *Silent Movie* (1976) comments on the business end of the movie making business, with direct criticism of media giant Gulf & Western (or "Engulf & Devour," as titled in the film) for gobbling up Paramount Studios, among other companies. *High Anxiety* (1977) sends up psychological dramas with episodes that parody Hitchcock's *The Birds, Vertigo,* and *Psycho. Spaceballs* (1987) pokes fun at the rash of science fiction films (see **Science Fiction and Fantasy**) in the 1970s and 1980s, including *Star Wars* (1977). And *Robin Hood: Men in Tights* (1993) looks back at the Errol Flynn classic of the 1930s. Among Brooks's most successful adventures is one of his earliest, *The Producers* (1968), which Brooks turned into a blockbuster Broadway musical.

Starting with Rob Reiner's 1981 film *This Is Spinal Tap*, a new form of comic film has appeared on the horizon, the mockumentary. Itself a spoof of the "rockumentaries" of the 1960s and 1970s, Reiner's film follows a fictional has-been heavy metal band left over from the rock-and-roll era as it makes its comeback. Cowriter Christopher Guest revived the mockumentary format since then to remarkable critical and popular success, forming a stock company of talented performers including Guest himself, Michael McKean (the cowriter of *Spinal Tap*), Eugene Levy, Catherine O'Hara, Fred Willard, Parker Posey, and Bob Balaban among others. *Waiting for Guffman* (1998), for example, portrays a small Missouri town as it puts on a historical pageant without much dramatic talent in the community to draw on. The Guest stock company returned with *Best in Show* (2000), a comic look at the darker side of America's competitive show dog culture. The most recent example of Guest's mockumentary series is *A Mighty Wind* (2003), chronicling the reunion of a 1960s folk trio, The Folksmen, who come together to perform at a memorial concert for a recently departed concert performer influential in folk circles.

Other parodies, send-ups, and films that lampoon include *Monty Python and the Holy Grail* (1975), *Monty Python's Life of Brian* (1979), *Monty Python's The Meaning of Life* (1983), and Mel Brooks's *The History of the World, Part I*, comic looks at Biblical and historical epics and "quest" films of the past; *The Man With Two Brains* (1983), starring Steve Martin in a mad scientist send-up; Keenan Ivory Wayans's take on the blaxploitation films of the 1960s and 1970s, *I'm Gonna Git You Sucka* (1988); Carl Reiner's *Fatal Instinct* (1993), a mock suspense thriller that pokes fun at films such as *Basic Instinct* (1992) and *Fatal Attraction* (1987); *National Lampoon's Loaded Weapon I* (1993), a take on *Lethal Weapon* (1987) and its sequels with Mel Gibson and Danny Glover; and *Scary Movie* (2000) and its sequels, a spoof on teen horror films such as *I Know What You Did Last Summer* (1997).

As any list of comedy films in the 1970s, 1980s, and 1990s reveals, the little screen had a tremendous influence on what appeared on the big screen, particularly in terms of television sketch comedy performers who sought feature film success. NBC's late-night and long-running comedy sketch show *Saturday Night*

Live (*SNL*) has launched the careers of several comedy film performers, including Chevy Chase (*Foul Play* [1978]; *Fletch* [1985], and *Three Amigos!* [1986]); John Belushi (*National Lampoon's Animal House* [1978], *1941* [1979], and *The Blues Brothers* [1980]); Dan Aykroyd (*Trading Places* [1983], *Ghostbusters* [1984], and *Christmas with the Kranks* [2004]); Bill Murray (*Meatballs* [1979], *Tootsie* [1982], and *Groundhog Day* [1993]); Billy Crystal (*Throw Momma from the Train* [1987], and *City Slickers* [1991]); and Eddie Murphy (*Coming to America* [1988], *The Nutty Professor* [1996], and *Dr. Dolittle* [1998]). Most recently, Will Ferrell (*A Night at the Roxbury* [1998], *Elf* [2003], and *Anchorman: The Legend of Ron Burgundy* [2004]), Adam Sandler (*Happy Gilmore* [1996], *The Wedding Singer* [1998], *Anger Management* [2003], and *Spanglish* [2004]) and Mike Myers (*Wayne's World* [1992] and the *Austin Powers* series [1997, 1999, and 2002]) have achieved comic leading man status. In addition, Steve Martin parlayed appearances on the *The Smothers Brothers Variety Show* and frequent guest host spots on *Saturday Night Live* into a varied film career of his own, often in collaboration with actor, writer, and director Carl Reiner, in films such as *The Jerk* (1979), *All of Me* (1984), John Hughes's *Planes, Trains & Automobiles* (1987), and the family comedies *Parenthood* (1989) and *Father of the Bride* (1991). Keenan Ivory Wayans's African American–oriented comedy sketch TV program *In Living Color* brought the comic talents of Jim Carrey to broader public attention, which he expanded with films such as *Ace Ventura: Pet Detective* (1994), *The Mask* (1994), *Dumb & Dumber* (1994), and the family film *How the Grinch Stole Christmas* (2000).

We end this rather lengthy look at a varied genre with the late century romantic comedy, represented by films such as Peter Bogdanovich's *What's Up, Doc?* (1972), which blurs the line between screwball and romantic comedy. Ryan O'Neal plays a Cary Grantesque musical researcher competing for a research grant whose well-ordered life is disturbed by a free-spirited college dropout (Barbra Streisand) hell-bent on shaking up his complacent scholarly world, at one point on the seat of a street vendor's bicycle in the film's screwball action sequence. Morever, the 1980s and 1990s established the reputations of a number of young actresses who performed in a series of highly successful romantic comedies during these decades, creating a new form of woman's film (see **Woman's Film**). Meg Ryan's films alone exemplify the romantic comedy of this period, starting with the ever-popular and much cited *When Harry Met Sally* (1989), directed by Rob Reiner and written by Nora Ephron, with Billy Crystal as Ryan's love interest. The film's central question is best expressed by the tagline used to market it: "Can two friends sleep together and still love each other in the morning?" A debate about a woman's ability to fool an intimate partner at a crucial moment results in one of the most memorably performed scenes in comedy history, or at least the most memorable scene performed in a delicatessen. The quality of the script and the film's marketability set a new standard for romantic comedies to come.

Ryan was joined by Tom Hanks in the Nora Ephron-penned and -directed *Sleepless in Seattle* (1993), another romantic comedy blockbuster. All around America, women such as Annie Reed (Meg Ryan) hear Sam Baldwin's (Hanks)

Meg Ryan proves to Billy Crystal just how fooled some men can be in a memorable scene from Rob Reiner's romantic comedy *When Harry Met Sally* (1989). *Photofest.*

eight-year-old son call a national radio show searching for a partner for his widowed father. Annie travels to Seattle and convinces herself that Sam is not the man for her, but the boy tricks both adults into meeting at the top of the Empire State Building in a scene lifted from the Cary Grant–Deborah Kerr tearjerker *An Affair to Remember* (1957). An Oscar nomination for Best Original Screenplay and multimillion dollar profits make the film among the most memorable romantic comedy of the period. One more Ryan-Hanks-Ephron collaboration, *You've Got Mail* (1998), a remake of the Ernst Lubitsch classic *The Shop Around the Corner* (1940), follows a more conventional romantic comedy plot fueled by romantic antagonism, where two business rivals, unbeknownst to one another, fall in love through the Internet despite tensions face to face. The film would prove to be the most profitable of the three collaborations of the trio.

Along with Meg Ryan, the romantic comedies of Julia Roberts and Sandra Bullock blur the distinction between the romantic sacrifice of the traditional woman's film (see **Woman's Film**) and romantic comedies, with a girl-next-door appeal reminiscent of Doris Day. Representative examples of Roberts's best efforts in this comedy subgenre include the Pygmalion-themed *Pretty Woman* (1990) and the bittersweet *My Best Friend's Wedding* (1997), opposite Dermot Mulroney, as a woman who realizes she's in love with her best friend on the eve of his marriage to another woman. And *Notting Hill* (1999), with Hugh Grant, draws on Roberts's own celebrity as an American actress who stumbles into a British bookshop changing her life forever. In the role that could have easily been performed by her contemporary, Bullock rose to the front ranks of romantic comedy performers with *While You Were Sleeping* (1995), as a ticket seller who witnesses the man of her dreams, Peter (Peter Gallagher), get mugged and lapse into a coma, and then finds herself mistaken for his fiancée at the hospital. And perhaps Bullock's best entry into the romantic comedy subgenre is *Two Weeks Notice* (2002), in which, as a brilliant chief counsel for one of New York's most successful commercial real estate development firms, she spends most of her time and energy as the caretaker to a wealthy yet highly irresponsible corporate executive (Hugh Grant).

Despite the fact that their popularity and profitability lure top-rate talent, few comedies have garnered industry recognition at major awards ceremonies recently. James L. Brooks's *As Good As It Gets* (1997), with Helen Hunt as a struggling waitress and single mother and Jack Nicholson as one of her regular customers, a romance novelist suffering from obsessive compulsive disorder, deserves special mention as one of the few comedies in recent memory to earn Oscars for both lead performers. The next year, Gwyneth Paltrow would win an Oscar for Best Actress in the historical romantic comedy *Shakespeare in Love* (1998). Despite a possible critical bias against comedy among Academy membership, selected films in the new millennium suggest that comedy is as popular as ever among all age groups. The romantic comedy *Something's Got to Give* (2003), with Diane Keaton and Jack Nicholson, took a rare (for motion pictures) look at love in middle age. In *Meet the Parents* (2000), Ben Stiller scored a hit playing male nurse Greg Focker, who hopes to marry his live-in girlfriend, but not before her father (Robert De Niro) makes him earn her hand. Four years later, the sequel reversing the family scenario, *Meet the Fockers* (2004), became the most profitable comedy of all time. As the blockbuster success of *Meet the Fockers*, Nia Vardalos's *My Big Fat Greek Wedding* (2002), and others attest, comedy in all of its forms will continue to be a very healthy part of the American film industry in years to come.

References and Further Reading

Cavell, Stanley. *Pursuits of Happiness: The Hollywood Comedy of Remarriage*. Cambridge, MA: Harvard University Press, 1981.

Dirks, Tim. "Comedy Films." 1996–2005. http://www.filmsite.org/comedyfilms5.html.

Kendall, Elizabeth. *The Runaway Bride: Hollywood Romantic Comedy in the 1930s*. New York: Knopf, 1990.

King, Geoff. *Film Comedy*. London: Wallflower Press, 2002.

Langman, Larry. *Encyclopedia of American Film Comedy*. New York: Garland Press, 1987.

Mast, Gerald. *American Film Comedy*. Niagara University, NY: Film Repertory Center, 1974.

Schatz, Thomas. "The Screwball Comedy." In *Hollywood Genres: Formulas, Filmmaking and the Studio System*, 150–185. Philadelphia: Temple University Press, 1981.

Shumway, Daniel. "Screwball Comedies: Constructing Romance, Mystifying Marriage." In *Film Genre Reader III*, edited by Barry Keith Grant, 396–416. Austin: University of Texas Press, 2003.

Siegel, Scott, and Barbara Siegel. *American Film Comedy.* New York: Prentice Hall, 1994.
Sikov, Ed. *Laughing Hysterically: American Screen Comedies of the 1950s*. New York: Columbia University Press, 1994.
Weales, Gerald Clifford. *Canned Goods as Caviar: American Film Comedy of the 1930s.* Chicago: University of Chicago Press, 1985.

CHAPTER 3

COSTUME FILM

COSTUMES ARE ONE of the many symbolic systems utilized by filmmakers to tell stories. But what, exactly, is a costume film? Clearly, almost all films that concern humans involve costumes of some sort. Trying to define the term, one thinks of historical costumes, but does that mean that *every* period film, by nature of the old-fashioned clothing worn, falls into this genre?

For our purposes, a costume picture is one set in the past in which the costumes are of a lavish nature and play a particular and essential role in the establishment or development of character, theme, or plot. In some cases the clothing of a film's key character places the work in this category; in others the overall look of an entire cast determines the classification. Either way, the clothing draws attention to itself and, in addition to conveying meaning, distances the period characters from us, the audience. Beyond the elaborate nature of the clothes of the period in general, costume films also find any excuse to clothe characters in even finer, more elaborate attire by setting scenes at fancy balls, theatrical productions, military maneuvers, or grand social events such as weddings and funerals. Costume films exploit the extravagant nature of period clothes as well as their manifest difference from contemporary attire. By means of clothing, costume films often aim to comment upon changing mores and standards, with particular regard to women's roles. Thus, pinup girl Betty Grable, famous for showing lots of leg, was frequently cast in films set at the turn of the century, such as *Coney Island* (1943), in order to emphasize that earlier time's disquietude over not only exposed female flesh but female autonomy and freedom. On the other hand, costume films can also strike an ironic note of kinship between the past and present, as seen in the warm response of recognition by audiences on the cusp of the disco era to the frantic, devil-may-care, Charleston-dancing flappers in *The Great Gatsby* (1974). Recent feminist filmmakers have turned to costume films, specifically to reinterpretations of famous literary works such as *Mansfield Park*, *The Portrait of a*

Lady, Washington Square, and *Vanity Fair*, as a means of both commentary and persuasion regarding the inferior social status of women.

Perhaps more so than any other genre here discussed, costume films overlap other film types, particularly the epic (see **Epic**), but also action-adventure (see **Action-Adventure**) and the woman's film (see **Woman's Film**).

DEFINING CHARACTERISTICS/CATEGORIES

Literary Adaptations

Perhaps the majority of costume films are cinematic adaptations of literary works, including novels, short stories, and plays. Since the beginning of cinema, the plays of Shakespeare have been enacted in front of the camera. Shakespeare's works, particularly *Romeo and Juliet, A Midsummer Night's Dream,* and *Hamlet*, have been filmed repeatedly, although, in recent years, American audiences have largely avoided such "serious" films unless the adaptation updates or radically reinterprets the original material.

Like the plays just mentioned, some novels so stir the imagination that succeeding generations of filmmakers feel the periodic need to return to the story in a new film version that will appeal and speak to a new audience. Dumas's *The Three Musketeers*, Alcott's *Little Women*, and Tolstoy's *Anna Karenina* are three such evergreens. In addition to the classics, contemporary historical novels have also received cinematic adaptations; these range from "bodice-rippers"—both trashy, such as Kathleen Winsor's *Forever Amber* (1947), and ambitious, including Margaret Mitchell's *Gone With the Wind* (1939) and A. S. Byatt's *Possession* (2002)—to serious literature, such as Kazuo Ishiguro's *The Remains of the Day* (1993) and Michael Cunningham's *The Hours* (2002).

Historical Films

There are countless films set in the past, but some filmmakers pay particular attention to rich visuals, including costumes. Historical costume films present the past in bold and vivid hues, paying as much attention to the couture and accessories of the characters as to the momentous events these personages enact. Most epics (see **Epic**) fall into this category, as do historical musicals (see **Musical**) and many adventure films (see **Action-Adventure**), such as swashbucklers. Like epics, costume films often are wildly anachronistic, sacrificing historical accuracy for splendor and maximum visual impact. For example, two Twentieth Century-Fox costumers from the early forties dramatize historical events. However, anyone watching *Hudson's Bay* (1940), about trappers in early Canada and the foundation of the Hudson's Bay Company, or *Little Old New York* (1940), about inventor Robert Fulton's arrival in America and the eventual launch of his steamship, will receive utterly skewed and largely fictionalized history lessons. In a similar vein, major stars of the Hollywood studio years inevitably appear beautifully stylish and coiffed, even when playing Russian peasants or Nebraska farm wives.

Biographies

Something of an offshoot of historical films, biographies tackle the life of an historical personage; when period detail and attire are particularly emphasized and examined, they fall into the costume genre. Larger-than-life personalities (and their impossibly ornate clothing) who have filled the screen with finery include Catherine the Great (*The Scarlet Empress* [1934]), *Marie Antoinette* (1938), *Lillian Russell* (1940), *Beau Brummell* (1954), Henry VIII and Anne Boleyn (*Anne of a Thousand Days* [1969]), the Romanovs *Nicholas and Alexandra* (1971), and *Elizabeth* (I) (1998). Again, historical accuracy is usually sacrificed for the sake of visual effects (whether they be the gorgeous costumes or the gorgeous actors wearing them).

Stars

For various reasons, certain actors excelled in or became particularly known for their costume films. Romantic silent stars Douglas Fairbanks and Rudolph Valentino tended to make period films in which they were extravagantly costumed as a gaucho, musketeer, or sheik. Mae West, so startlingly modern and risqué to audiences in the early 1930s, nevertheless tended to make films set forty years earlier. Something about her busty, statuesque stance and demeanor fitted both the costumes and settings of the 1890s, as seen in *She Done Him Wrong* (1933), *Belle of the Nineties* (1934), and *Klondike Annie* (1936). George Arliss, a mature man very much publicized as "the great actor," tended to make biographies of famous personages, including *Disraeli* (1929), for which he won the Best Actor Academy Award; *Alexander Hamilton* (1931); and *Voltaire* (1933). Soprano Jeanette MacDonald appeared in both operettas and "straight" films that, more often than not, were set in the past and opulently costumed. Likewise, Greta Garbo's aura of doomed romanticism particularly suited costume films such as *Queen Christina* (1933), *Anna Karenina* (1935) (of which she had made a silent version in 1927, titled *Love*), and *Camille* (1936).

In the realm of costume dramas, the actors weren't the only stars. Some costume designers became celebrities in their own right. MacDonald and Garbo looked stunning because of the dresses that MGM's chief costumier, Adrian, designed for them. Female stars clamored for his services, aware that Adrian was clever at concealing and correcting an actress's physical "faults"—broad hips, narrow shoulders, or a small bosom. Throughout the 1930s, Adrian was the last word in cinema glamour, dressing all the MGM stars in both period and modern films: MacDonald, Garbo, Joan Crawford, Norma Shearer, and the rest. His white ruffled gown for Crawford in *Letty Lynton* (1932) caused a sensation and was soon imitated and available in stores across the country. He was also responsible for tailoring Crawford's signature squared shoulders, which were imitated through the 1940s. Some of his more successful (if often over-the-top) period costumes can be seen in *Rasputin and the Empress* (1932), *Queen Christina* (1933), *The Barretts of Wimpole Street* (1934), *The Merry Widow* (1934), *Conquest* (1937), and *Marie Antoinette* (1938). Adrian was never afraid of sacrificing historical accuracy in his designs and accessories for the sake of dramatic and visual effect, not to mention the creation and sustenance of individual stars' potent aura. Adrian retired in 1941, supposedly in connection with Garbo's own retirement from film (and, in his eyes, the concurrent demise of such rarified cinematic romanticism). Irene (costumiers, like couturiers, love going by a single name) and Walter Plunkett took over at MGM, the latter specializing in period films such as *Green Dolphin Street* (1947) and *The Three Musketeers* (1948).

Perhaps the most famous costume designer for films is Edith Head, who, in an amazing fifty-four-year career, designed for well over 400 films and most of Hollywood's stars, winning eight Academy Awards (in thirty-four nominations). She was head designer at Paramount from 1938 to 1966, creating costumes for over 1100 films. Unlike Adrian, however, she specialized in modern, contemporary gowns and costumes (*The Great Gatsby* [1949] and *Samson and Delilah* [1949] notwithstanding) and became particularly associated with the films of actress Barbara Stanwyck, the team of Bob Hope and Bing Crosby, and director Alfred Hitchcock.

HISTORY AND INFLUENCES

The Beginning to 1930

Although silent movies were an excitingly new and modern phenomenon, many of them nevertheless dramatized historical stories and events. Popular as well as classic stage plays were filmed—*sans* spoken dialogue, of course—and bygone personages and events were reenacted before the cameras. As noted earlier, some of the most popular early film stars were known for their costume pictures. Swashbucklers such as Douglas Fairbanks churned out tales of pirates, musketeers, and other adventurers (see **Action-Adventure**).

If Fairbanks became a star through gregarious, American physicality, Rudolph Valentino quickened hearts with a smoldering, catlike, European sexuality. Valentino inflamed cinemagoers even when he was smothered under outrageous costumes. In *The Four Horsemen of the Apocalypse* (1921), the film that made him a star, he is decked out as a gaucho—a Spaniard born in Argentina—who becomes a World War I hero. Massive sets, recreating a huge castle and surrounding village as well as Parisian scenes, are peopled by a large cast in fanciful costumes. Valentino's legendary role is that of *The Sheik* (1921). In this and *The Son of the Sheik* (1926), his last film before his sudden, mysterious death, we have the quintessential Valentino: swaggering about the sands and tents as a desert chieftain, swathed in robes, capes, and turban, and quick to subdue fearful Western women with a smoldering glance before whisking them off to his lair—and a fate worse than death. Audiences, particularly women, went crazy for the film, and a new star (as well as a new phenomenon, the Latin Lover) was born. Valentino would appear as a sexy bullfighter in *Blood and Sand* (1922), a nearly naked Indian prince in *The Young Rajah* (1922), and an heroic young Cossack in the court of Catherine the Great in *The Eagle* (1925). In all of these, the star is dressed in magnificent, albeit romantically exaggerated, period costumes and all manner of exotic headgear. What are never covered are Valentino's eyes (those weapons of animal lust) and his flaring nostrils, an arsenal against which no female character stood a chance. Even as Valentino's star rose, however, men came to poke fun at his beauty and passion, characteristics highly suspect in American males.

The ultimate Valentino costume drama, and one that did his reputation no good, is *Monsieur Beaucaire* (1924), about a fop at the court of King Louis XV. Although the film contains a dueling scene and another wherein Valentino is stripped to the waist to reveal a bold musculature, what people remember are the scenes set at a ball and onstage, in which the star wears makeup, a beauty mark, powdered wig, tight silk stockings, and high heels. In her book *Silent Stars*, Jeanine Basinger quotes from the October 1924 issue of the movie fan magazine *Picture-Play*, in which an extra describes "the magnificent Rudolph in gleaming lavender satin embroidered in purple, stitches on the back of his chamois gloves embroidered in heavy, scintillating gold thread studded with small jewels" (1999, 291). The fact that movie magazines ran fashion layouts about a male star—mentioning his pale grey velvet walking costume, pink velvet waistcoat, grey suede breeches and boots, a pale blue taffeta suit with a cape of silver cloth, and so on—only strengthened some filmgoers' distaste for Valentino. What strikes one today is the sheer beauty of the film's costumes, sets, and cinematography and the actor's brash (and boldly ahead of his time) delight in toying with gender issues regarding his strong screen persona.

Other silent stars, particularly some of director D. W. Griffith's actresses, were well suited for period films. The epic *The Birth of a Nation* (1915) recounts the devastating effects, both financial and physical, of the Civil War on a genteel southern family. When the soldier-son returns on leave, his young sister (refreshingly played by Mae Marsh) is desperate to put her best face forward, despite deprivations and once-beautiful clothes now disintegrating into rags. In a touching scene, she tears up bits of cotton, smudges them with soot, and places them strategically about her worn dress, to imitate the dark spots of ermine fur. Griffith's greatest actress was Lillian Gish. In addition to Griffith's epics *The Birth of a Nation* and *Intolerance* (1916), she appeared in his *Orphans of the Storm* (1921), as a twin separated from her blind sister (played by her sister Dorothy) and caught up in the turmoil of the French Revolution; as starving, tubercular Mimi in mid-nineteenth-century Paris in King Vidor's *La Boheme* (1926); and as the stigmatized adulteress Hester Prynne in Victor Sjostrom's film of Hawthorne's *The Scarlet Letter* (1926). Some silent film actresses, such as Louise Brooks and Clara Bow, embodied the modern flapper type, with bobbed hair and revealing, loose dresses; Gish, with her long, flowing hair and prim, child-like face, suited period films and ethereal Victorian ideals. Covered in ribbons, bows, and ruffles, she was the perfect actress for Griffith, who cinematically fetishized these very ideals of childlike female innocence under threat from a violent, masculine world.

The 1930s

In films whose storylines cover a significant passage of time, music is often used to clue the viewer in, quickly and unobtrusively, regarding when something is taking place (such is the case, for example, in *Forrest Gump* [1994]). Costumes are an additional means of indicating time and time's passage. In the film version of Noel Coward's play *Cavalcade* (1933), an episodic account of a well-to-do English family's fortunes from 1899 to 1932, music and costumes, for both the wealthy family upstairs and their servants downstairs, recount the changing eras—from the Boer War, through the death of Queen Victoria and the loss of the *Titanic* to World War I, and finally to the Jazz Age. There were not yet Academy Awards for costumes, but the film did receive a statuette for Art Direction. The striking visuals reinforce the film's nostalgic take on a lost world and the high costs of war.

During the first few decades of motion pictures' history, color was rarely seen on screen because of the laborious nature of hand-tinting individual film frames before the advent of color photography. Gradually, two-strip and, eventually, the more realistic three-strip (including Technicolor) methods of color photography were developed. Color was nevertheless used sparingly and for effect in isolated scenes rather than entire films—splashy scenes of spectacle, such as the masked ball sequence in the silent *The Phantom of the Opera* (1925) and the final dance numbers in several early musicals. The first full-length three-strip Technicolor film is a costume drama: *Becky Sharp* (1935), based upon Thackeray's novel *Vanity Fair,* starred Miriam Hopkins as the single-minded, social-climbing adventuress. Director Rouben Mamoulian's condensation of the long novel to 83 minutes is witty but static, and, despite the film's beauty, it never takes flight. Costume and color are used to denote theme and mood, never more so than in the Duchess' lavish ball sequence, set on the eve of the Battle of Waterloo. *Becky Sharp* is remembered today for its technical breakthrough in color, particularly after a 1985 restoration of the original print revealed the film's true palette. Full-length color films would not become the norm until the 1960s. Before that time, only "big" films—those particularly emphasizing visuals and spectacle—were shot in color.

Louisa May Alcott's *Little Women,* the story of a New England mother and her four daughters' Civil War–era domestic travails and triumphs, has been successfully filmed three times. With the soldier/father and the war in the background, the novel focuses on the bittersweet coming-of-age of young women in nineteenth-century Concord, Massachusetts. For many viewers, the 1933 film version is the best, vividly directed by George Cukor and featuring a brilliant performance by the young Katharine Hepburn as tomboyish Jo. Costumier Walter Plunkett and Art Director Van Nest Polglase create a cozy, feminine world of white gloves, crinoline hoop skirts (Jo's dresses inevitably patched due to burns caused by standing too close to the fireplace), upright pianos, and busy Victorian parlors. Wartime deprivations may lead to the daughters' mortification at not having the new, up-to-date dresses worn by other girls, but their various admirable personality traits—Meg's loyalty, Jo's independence, Beth's compassion, and Amy's vivacity—win them admirers nonetheless. The 1949 version is the weakest of the three but features glossy Technicolor and a superior cast (June Allyson, Mary Astor, Margaret O'Brien, Elizabeth Taylor, and Janet Leigh).

Not as stellar but even more gifted is the cast of 1994's *Little Women*, directed by Gillian Armstrong. Susan Sarandon plays the mother, Marmie, a tower of strength and proto-feminist doctrine, with Winona Ryder, Trini Alvarado, Claire Danes, Kirsten Dunst, and Samantha Mathis (the latter two alternate the role of Amy) as the girls. Danes and Dunst particularly shine in this richly and evocatively produced film, tweaked a bit to suit 1990s sensibilities.

Katharine Hepburn was perfectly cast as the loud, boisterous Jo March. When she burst into films in 1932, the actress looked, sounded, and acted like no other. In her early work she played willfully independent modern girls; perhaps to soften the image of her hoydenish vivacity, RKO Studio also put her in several period costume films. After *Little Women* came *The Little Minister* (1934), based on a play by James Barrie about an 1840s young Scottish lady who likes to dress as a gypsy and fraternize with the poor weavers; *Mary of Scotland* (1936), based on a play by Maxwell Anderson about the sixteenth-century queen; and *A Woman Rebels* (1936), the story of a young woman's struggle for emancipation and independence amidst the strict conventions of the Victorian period. In the latter film, Hepburn wears twenty-two different Walter Plunkett costumes, ranging in styles from 1869 to 1890. The tall actress is striking in period costumes but never loses her trademark verve and strength under the piles of clothes.

Another of Barrie's stage works, *Quality Street*, was filmed twice as vehicles for actresses: in 1927 for Marion Davies and again in 1937 for Hepburn. It tells the story of a woman in the early 1800s who, disappointed in love, passes herself off as her own (nonexistent) young niece in order to win the heart of the soldier/doctor who abandoned her a decade earlier. The later film version creates a female world in which busybody spinsters sit behind their house windows, watching the outside (male) world from behind lace curtains and shutters. They are skittish and repressed, viewing men as another species altogether—one that inappropriately winks at women, thoughtlessly tracks mud upon carpets, and clumsily breaks things in finely appointed parlors. After Dr. Brown, the man she loves, goes off to the Napoleonic wars, Phoebe (Hepburn) and her sister Susan (Fay Bainter) open a school for children, even though they are terrified of "the big boys." With time's passage, Phoebe has "lost all my looks," no longer the young girl whom Dr. Brown (Franchot Tone) compared to the flowers in the garden: "The daisy that stands for innocence, the hyacinth for constancy, the modest violet and the rose." Upon Brown's return, ten years later, the plain, washed-out Phoebe curls her hair and dresses in fancy ballgowns, masquerading as "Livvy," in order to woo him back. The frilly Empire-style dresses and bold military uniforms are vivid demarcations of the often opposing and always unequal gender worlds of the period.

Hepburn's persona was one of female independence and strength. Marlene Dietrich's image was one of impossible glamour and exoticism. Under the direction of her Svengali, Josef von Sternberg, Dietrich became a star as the heartless nightclub singer Lola-Lola in *The Blue Angel* (1930) before sweeping across the ocean from Germany to become fellow European Greta Garbo's only real rival in

Hollywood. In her six Paramount films with von Sternberg, Dietrich doesn't really act; instead, she becomes an iconic image of eroticism and beauty. Von Sternberg put his leading lady in exotic, nocturnal worlds, both historical and contemporary, and master cinematographer Lee Garmes created some of the most stunning chiaroscuro effects in all of cinema, boldly lighting Dietrich's face from above (creating the hollowed cheeks and bow-lips) on sets full of shadow effects and heavy textures. One doesn't watch Dietrich's early films for great acting or coherent plots. They are pure style pieces, charged with a heady erotic atmosphere and bursting the frame with baroque visuals. Whether playing a cabaret singer mixed up with the French Foreign Legion in *Morocco* (1930), a World War I streetwalker-turned-spy in *Dishonored* (1931), an 1890s Spanish *femme fatale* in *The Devil Is a Woman* (1935), or, in her most outrageously opulent and magnificent film, the young Catherine the Great in *The Scarlet Empress* (1934), Dietrich presents a world-weary, disdainful persona, only fully awakened by love. She is surrounded—at times almost smothered—by busy, extravagant sets and draped in equally elaborate costumes, ranging from riotous gowns of feathers, furs and silks to gender-bending tailored men's tuxedos in black or white.

The mid-30s were designer Adrian's peak years at MGM. He never really aimed for historical accuracy in his costumes, preferring visual effects and character disclosure through fabric, style, and cut. In *Queen Christina* (1933), playing the lesbian seventeenth-century Swedish queen who gave up her throne, Garbo spends much of the film swaggering about in pants, saying such things as "I will die a bachelor." Rudolph Besier's play about Robert and Elizabeth Browning, *The Barretts of Wimpole Street*, was filmed in 1934, starring Fredric March, Norma Shearer, and Charles Laughton (as the repellent, incestuous Mr. Barrett). More opulent still is *Anna Karenina* (1935), Garbo's second film of the Tolstoy novel (she made a silent version, *Love*, in 1927). The pre-Revolutionary Russia sets and costumes, featuring lots of fur and uniforms, wonderfully convey the beautiful though rigid world from which Anna tries to escape. The next year saw Leslie Howard and Shearer as somewhat long-in-the-tooth lovers *Romeo and Juliet*. Producer Irving Thalberg brought Oliver Messel over from England to design the sets (with Cedric Gibbons) and costumes, which are magically evocative and romantic. Many critics admired the film, but American audiences, fearful of the name Shakespeare, largely stayed away.

Much better received, all around, was—and is—*Camille* (also 1936), Thalberg's final production before his premature death and Garbo's greatest performance. Gibbons' art direction and Adrian's costumes do wonders in black-and-white at recreating the gorgeous, *louche* world of the 1840s Parisian *demi-monde*—a world of insincere and artificial beauty masking bitter and deadly struggles of class and gender. The overdressed opulence of the courtesans' dresses and boudoirs is perfectly captured, if exaggerated, and serves as an ironic, beautiful surface under which all manner of personal machinations and intrigues take place. Marguerite (Garbo) and her cohorts are much more lavishly dressed and bejeweled than would be courtesans of the period, but Adrian insisted upon the opulence (and real jewels). In his biography of Garbo, Barry Paris notes that her mountains of elaborate costumes "were so heavy that ice-cooled fans were required to keep her from fainting on the set" (1994, 334). Adrian came up with the idea of darkening Garbo's dresses as the film progresses, "from white in the carefree beginning, to grey as the tragedy gathers momentum, to black toward the bitter end." He too arranged for her hairstyles to "evolve from elaborate ringlets and curls at first to simpler, straighter arrangements as she neared death" (1994, 333–34).

MGM's *Marie Antoinette* (1938) is a lavishly opulent biography that never really soars—yet another Hollywood example of What Might Have Been. Producer Irving Thalberg created the property as a showcase both for his wife, actress Norma Shearer, and for the wealth of artistry within MGM's huge costume and set departments. Unfortunately, Thalberg died after spending three years and nearly half a million dollars on the still-unfinished project. The film was ultimately completed, but with a shorter shooting schedule, a faster, less flamboyant director ("one-take Woody" Van Dyke), and, sadly, black-and-white rather than Technicolor film. The film, the kind of prestige picture beloved of studio-head Louis B. Mayer, received a mixed reception from critics and did not do well at the box office. Nevertheless, Cedric Gibbons's sets—particularly those of Versailles's interiors and gardens—are stunning, and the huge cast is meticulously and prodigally costumed by Adrian, who utilized 500 yards of white satin for Marie's wedding gown. Fittingly, in the film the doomed queen's story is told by a costumer.

In the "Fashion and Glamour" chapter of her delightful study *A Woman's View: How Hollywood Spoke to Women 1930–1960*, Jeanine Basinger explores the centrality of clothing in telling women's stories on film. Basinger addresses how clothing may both define a female character's personality and shape the direction—whether good or bad—of her life. Many people saw *Jezebel* (1938), about a scheming, defiant antebellum Southern belle, as Bette Davis's audition for the role of Scarlett O'Hara, filmed shortly thereafter. And just as Scarlett's dresses chronicle changes and developments in her character, the same is true in *Jezebel*. Basinger calls the film "basically the story of four outfits: a riding habit, a red dress, a white dress, and a plain gray cape. These clothes define Davis in four climactic scenes" (1993, 132). Whereas the riding habit (independence), white dress (acquiescent regret for overstepping societal bounds) and cape (sacrifice) are striking, the film is famous for the red dress scene—and suffers tremendously for having been shot in black-and-white. For the Olympus Ball, the highlight of the New Orleans social season, all young unmarried ladies wear white. In a fit of pique at her fiancé Pres (Henry Fonda), Julie Marston (Davis) decides to embarrass him by wearing a shocking scarlet dress. All too soon (but too late) she realizes she has made a fool of herself, and this one fashion *faux pas* leads to a broken engagement, lies, a lethal duel, and Julie's eventual enlightenment and redemption. Until she chooses a life of self-denial and sacrifice, Davis, along with the rest of the cast, is sumptuously dressed in rich satin and lace hoop skirts, at an impressive level of period attention and detail—which nevertheless would be surpassed the following year.

As headstrong Julie Marston, Bette Davis shocks New Orleans high society by wearing scarlet satin instead of the obligatory virginal white in *Jezebel* (1938). *Photofest.*

Academy Awards were not given out for costumes until 1948. Had they done so nine years earlier, Walter Plunkett's designs for *Gone With the Wind* no doubt would have garnered yet another Oscar for that film. In addition to the Civil War uniforms, nearly three thousand costumes were made for the Technicolor extravaganza, to clothe everyone from spoiled young debutantes to prostitutes, from field hands to *nouveau-riche* carpetbaggers. Some of the actresses balked at having to wear corsets and yards of undergarments, insisting that the audience would never see all the fancy but heavy pantaloons and shifts. Realizing the part that costumes play in an actor's assumption of a role, the director simply told them, "But you'll know it is there." At the center of the film is Scarlett O'Hara (Vivien Leigh), whose dresses reflect her dramatically changing circumstances and character. Our first glimpse of her is in a vision of white ruffles and high collar, demurely innocent on the porch of Tara and bored with all the talk of upcoming war. At the charity bazaar, the newly widowed Scarlett is in black mourning, so striking against all the other dresses' bright splashes of color. Scandalizing everyone present (and leveling Aunt Pittypat into a faint), Scarlett agrees to dance with Rhett; the eye-grabbing mass of black silk, emblematic of the blot now on Scarlett's reputation in society's eyes, glides in and out of the other dancers in one of the film's greatest images. In the mad dash to escape the fall of Atlanta, Scarlett has but the dress on her back. Twenty-seven versions of this plain calico dress were made for Leigh to wear, and then (mis)treated by the costume department in order to illustrate cinematically her many months of increasingly straitened circumstances and the gradual decay of the Confederate world. The dress is eventually blood-stained, after Scarlett fends off and shoots a Yankee soldier. In order to weasel money out of Rhett, all the while feigning prosperity, Scarlett wears what is probably the most famous costume in all of film: the green velvet parlor curtains, unceremoniously pulled down and cut into a caprice of a dress by Mammy so as to save the plantation. Scarlett's other important dress is the crimson red "fallen woman" number, complete with plunging *décolletage* and red ostrich plumes and garnets, which Rhett forces her to wear to Melanie's surprise party for Ashley, in whose arms Scarlett was seen that afternoon. "Wear this," commands Rhett. "Nothing modest will do for this occasion. And put on plenty of rouge. I want you to look your part tonight."

The 1940s and 1950s

The decade got off to a grand start with a blockbuster adaptation of Jane Austen's *Pride and Prejudice* (1940). Fresh from his success in *Wuthering Heights* and *Rebecca*, Laurence Olivier stars as Mr. Darcy and, in her first starring role, Greer Garson plays Elizabeth Bennet. Austen's comedy of manners about five sisters and their marriage-obsessed mother was wittily adapted for the screen by Aldous Huxley, and MGM lavished its resources on magnificent sets (which received an Art Direction Academy Award), voluminous costumes, and a large, stylish cast made up of its best character actors. Running-time limitations required that portions of the novel be cut, and the opulence of the sets and clothing are undoubtedly beyond anything that Austen ever imagined, but the film is faithful nevertheless to the original in tone and charm. It captures and exposes the frantic desperation with which a family's hopes and dreams are placed on superficialities such as feminine appearance and deportment.

Pride and Prejudice proved a turning point in Greer Garson's career, and she would return to costume films from time to time. Throughout the decade, several other successful literary adaptations appeared, more often than not as vehicles for established female stars. *Anna Karenina* (1948) and *Madame Bovary* (1949) capitalize on the fragile, porcelain, brunette beauty of Vivien Leigh and Jennifer Jones, respectively. Tolstoy's and Flaubert's classic novels tell of adulterous wives who sacrifice everything for a passionate affair before meeting with tragic ends. Leigh's and Jones's own psychological fragility and edginess add immeasurably to the films' moods, as do large budgets that ensure romantically opulent sets and costumes. *The Heiress* (1949), based upon the Henry James novel *Washington Square*, stars Olivia de Havilland (who won a Best Actress Academy Award) as Catherine Sloper, a plain spinster in late nineteenth-century New York, who is overwhelmed by the sudden attention of a handsome young fortune hunter (Montgomery Clift). Her cruel, emotionally remote father (Ralph Richardson) selfishly enjoys convincing his daughter that her suitor is only after her money. The young man does in fact jilt her, effectively ruining any chance for her happiness—or for escape from the suffocating familial home. Over the course of the film, we see all of Catherine's exuberance and joy, both in her face and in her attire, fade to weary resignation and defeat. "Don't be kind to me," says Catherine to her father at one point. "It doesn't become you." By the end of the film, in defense of her own actions, she can agree, "Yes, I can be very cruel. I have been taught by masters."

Despite having under contract the sexiest and most popular pinup girls of World War II, Twentieth Century-Fox insisted on putting the actresses in period musicals, usually set during the vaudeville age at the turn of the century, and swathing them in yards of silk, satin, and feathers. Of course, as backstage musicals, the films were able to show dressing and undressing backstage, where Rita Hayworth let her hair down and Betty Grable exposed those million-dollar-insured legs. Most of the films are in the eye-popping Technicolor so favored by Fox, and they feature costumes inspired by the Gay Nineties but given an over-the-top Hollywood exaggeration. In addition to their films set in the present, Hayworth starred in *My Gal Sal* (1942), Alice Faye in *Lillian Russell* (1940), *Tin Pan Alley* (1940), and *Hello, Frisco, Hello* (1943), and Betty Grable in *Coney Island* (1943), *Sweet Rosie O'Grady* (1943), *The Dolly Sisters* (1945), *Mother Wore Tights* (1947), *The Shocking Miss Pilgrim* (1947), *That Lady in Ermine* (1948), *When My Baby Smiles at Me* (1948), and *Wabash Avenue* (1950). In a similar manner, Paramount put its two musical comedy stars—Bing Crosby and Bob Hope, both individually and paired—in several splashy period films with songs. The studio even remade a farcical pastiche of Valentino's *Monsieur Beaucaire* (1946), with Hope as a French barber posing as a nobleman in the Spanish court.

Two of the most popular costume films of the period dramatize a woman's desperate climb to the top of the social ladder, using her beauty and sexuality as the means to success. Both are Pygmalion stories, featuring strong, dominating men as the inspiration or manipulators behind the women's rise. In *Kitty* (1945), Paulette Goddard plays an eighteenth-century London guttersnipe transformed into a lady by an impoverished rake (Ray Milland) and dowager (Constance Collier), intent upon replenishing their own diminished fortunes by marrying Kitty off to a nobleman. Despite the avaricious, conniving characters and their selfish goal, true (young) love wins out in the end. Lavishly produced, if somewhat overlong, the film provides a dazzling role for Goddard, who shines, and the picture, based upon Rosamund Marshall's rather trite novel, made lots of money at the box office. *Forever Amber* (1947), based on Kathleen Winsor's spicy, once-scandalous best seller, was an even bigger hit, even though the Hays Office ensured that the novel's earthiness was toned down quite a bit. "This is the story of Amber St. Clare," reads the film's opening title card. "Slave to ambition, stranger to virtue." Starring Linda Darnell, the gargantuan production is nearly two-and-a-half hours long and in splashy Technicolor. Rebelling against her Puritan upbringing, Amber becomes a courtesan in London, sleeping her way up to the position of mistress to King Charles II. All the jewels, fancy dresses, and excitement of court are ultimately meaningless, however, as the one man Amber truly loves leaves England for America with their child. Thus the colorful, rollicking story, which combines intrigue, banditry, warfare, and even the Great Fire of London, is yet another Hollywood cautionary tale for women, reminding them that without a man and a child they are nothing.

The line between costume drama and woman's film (see **Woman's Film**) is often blurred, particularly as costume films regularly deal in female wish fulfillment and escapism: a strong, independent woman, stunningly dressed, defies convention in her search for fulfillment and happiness. Happiness might come in the form of a man or a vocation or, better yet, both. In *Frenchman's Creek* (1944), based upon Daphne du Maurier's best-selling novel, Joan Fontaine plays an English gentlewoman, swathed in Restoration-period gowns, who flees a wicked nobleman (Basil Rathbone, in full treacherous mode) to her estate in Cornwall, where she is wooed by a dashing, swashbuckling pirate (Arturo de Cordova). The film's lush, melodramatic romanticism and luxurious costumes and sets ensured large box office returns. *Anna and the King of Siam* (1946), adapted from Margaret Landon's biography of Anna Leonowens, features Irene Dunne as an adventurous British governess in nineteenth-century Thailand. Hired to instruct the many children (by the many wives) of the King of Siam, Anna embarks upon a strange relationship with her royal employer—part love, part resentment, but imbued with mutual respect. By the end, thanks to Anna's interaction with the King's heir, Thailand is on its way to a greater understanding of and an opening up to the West. Members of the royal court wear luxurious Hollywood transformations of Asian attire, and Dunne wears several grand gowns—looking more like a member of the idle, landed gentry than a busy hired retainer. Ten acres of the Twentieth Century-Fox backlot were used to recreate the Meinam River and surrounding pagodas, temples, and royal palaces, and the film won Academy Awards for art/interior decoration as well as its cinematography. A decade later, Fox produced the musical version of the story, *The King and I* (1956), which is even more lavish and grand, in spectacular Technicolor, with even bigger and more stylized palace sets and luxuriant costumes. The sexual tension between the lead characters, played by Deborah Kerr and Yul Brynner, is also increased, largely by the latter's electric physical presence (which helped Brynner win the Best Actor Oscar).

1957 saw the premiere of what MGM hoped would be another *Gone With the Wind*. Like the earlier film, *Raintree County* is also based upon a lengthy best seller that revolves around a strong-willed Civil War-era heroine. Unfortunately, there are few other similarities between the two projects. The latter story conjures up symbolic nonsense about a mythical "raintree" in its sensationalized account of the heroine's descent into madness, brought on in part by heredity and exacerbated by her fearful obsession with the destructiveness of miscegenation. As Susanna, Elizabeth Taylor has some good moments, indicating the emotional power she would soon demonstrate more fully and convincingly in *Cat on a Hot Tin Roof* (1958) and *Suddenly, Last Summer* (1959). The rest of the cast is fairly wooden, none more so than costar Montgomery Clift, whose weak performance might, in part, be blamed on a near-fatal car accident that he suffered during filming, necessitating extensive plastic surgery that closed down production for six weeks while he recuperated. *Gone With the Wind*'s costume designer, Walter Plunkett, created the beautiful clothes, and location photography took place in Danville, Kentucky. Despite the film's rich visuals, the weak story is insurmountable, and bad reviews ruined any hopes MGM had of box office success.

The film epics (see **Epic**) of the period, with their emphasis upon extravagance in all departments, obviously lavished time, money, and attention on costumes. *Samson and Delilah* (1949), *War and Peace* (1956), *The Buccaneer* (1958), *The Fall of the Roman Empire* (1964), and *Waterloo* (1970), just to name a few, boast embarrassingly rich wardrobes, designed to clothe casts of thousands playing everything from pirates to courtesans, from Napoleonic generals to Roman slaves.

The 1960s and 1970s

With the weakening of the Motion Picture Production Code and a concurrent relaxation of prohibitions regarding film sexual content, the 1960s saw increased bawdiness in costume pictures. Literary adaptations took greater liberties both in recreating sexual elements from the original novels (which, before, would have been omitted) and in emphasizing or introducing sexual scenes or frankness that was not in the original. *Tom Jones* (1963), based upon the Henry Fielding novel, recounts the exploits of a rowdy, randy young man in eighteenth-century England. The film made a star of young Albert Finney in the title role of the naughty, irresistible rake and won Academy Awards for Best Picture, Director (Tony Richardson), and Screenplay Adaptation (John Osborne). All the visuals, from makeup to hair to close-ups, emphasize a general air of carnality. Tom and his many sexual conquests are fairly bursting out of their elaborate, form-fitting clothing, and the atmosphere of youthful, libidinous abandon offsets the strong grittiness of the script. The great critical and popular success of *Tom Jones* sent filmmakers scurrying to the library for other bawdy eighteenth-century novels with a similarly exuberant attitude towards sexual enjoyment. Paramount came up with *The Amorous Adventures of Moll Flanders* (1965), from the novel by Daniel Defoe about a servant girl's rise in society, man by man. Unfortunately, the film in no way matches the fun, skill, or finesse of *Tom Jones*. As Moll, Kim Novak lacks Finney's spark—the wink in the eye of a jolly, irresistible rogue.

As noted earlier, *Romeo and Juliet* has been filmed many times; however, following the lead of stage directors and to ensure star power and acting ability, producers usually cast adults as the star-crossed teenaged lovers. MGM spared no expense on its lavish 1936 production, with huge operatic sets of Juliet's balcony garden and the Capulet ball, splendid costumes by Adrian and big names Leslie Howard and Norma Shearer (aged forty-two and thirty-three, respectively) in the title roles. For his 1968 production of Shakespeare's classic tragedy, Italian director Franco Zeffirelli broke with tradition by casting teenaged unknowns (Leonard Whiting and Olivia Hussey) as Romeo and Juliet. While given to occasional overacting (Hussey in particular), the young actors nevertheless look perfect in the roles. In fact, the film is visually stunning all around, and it won Academy Awards for its cinematography and costumes (designed by Danilo Donati). As famous for what the actors *didn't* wear (there is a brief nude scene as Romeo leaves Juliet's bed early one morning) as for what they did, the film, besides sexual tension, also emphasizes the fight scenes between longhaired young men from the two feuding families and the blind prejudice of the lovers' parents. This sexually defiant, anti-authority angle ensured large audiences in the late 1960s and box-office receipts greater than for any preceding Shakespeare film.

F. Scott Fitzgerald's *The Great Gatsby*, a Jazz Age novel of the idle rich and irretrievable love, has been filmed three times: in 1926, 1949, and, most spectacularly, 1974. Fitzgerald's enigmatic story of the mysterious Jay Gatsby has never really translated to the screen, but the latest version, directed by Jack Clayton, is visually sumptuous, shot among the mansions of Newport, Rhode Island. The entire cast—particularly stars Robert Redford, Mia Farrow, Karen Black, and Sam Waterston (very good in his first important role)—is splendidly dressed in twenties-era clothing that started a mid-1970s fashion trend of flapper-style dresses and pastel men's suits. Especially arresting are the scenes of Gatsby's huge nocturnal parties, held on the lawn and peopled by hordes of inebriated revelers, frantically dancing the Charleston and jumping, fully clothed, into the fountains. As the narrator notes, "in his enchanted gardens, men and girls came and went like moths, among the whispering and the champagne and the stars." The making of the film, which went far over budget, generated mountains of publicity (lots of extras were needed for the crowd scenes), and its visual style helped fuel the nostalgia craze of the 1970s. Straightforward Redford, at the peak of his popularity and beauty, seems a wrong choice as the mysterious Gatsby—a nearly impossible role to cast—but he looks the part. In addition to the colorful costumes (Farrow's dresses had to become ever more flounced and ruffled in order to conceal her advancing pregnancy), Nelson Riddle's lush orchestral score features evocative arrangements of popular Twenties songs.

The same year as *Gatsby,* director Peter Bogdanovich, coming off the tremendous multi-genre successes of *The Last Picture Show* (1971), *What's Up, Doc?* (1972), and *Paper Moon* (1973), tried his hand at costume drama in a film of Henry James's novella about *nouveau-riche* Gilded Age Americans on the Grand Tour, *Daisy Miller.* Like *Gatsby,* it is visually spectacular (shot in Europe at the watering spots of the turn-of-the-century wealthy) with gorgeous costumes, but it never really plumbs the depths of the original book. As Daisy, Cybill Shepherd is not actress enough for the part, but the former model looks wonderful in the elaborate period dresses, as she socializes and scandalizes high society from Switzerland to Rome.

One of the most stunning and evocative period films is Stanley Kubrick's adaptation of the Thackeray novel *Barry Lyndon* (1975). Taking eighteenth-century landscape portraits as his inspiration, the director begins most scenes as a sort of establishing tableau, in long shot, before the camera slowly pulls in to reveal action. Kubrick occasionally reverses this process, moving from close-up to expansive long shot, thereby contextualizing characters. To capture the glow of candlelit rooms unassisted by artificial lights, and recreate the patina of period canvases, special large-aperture lenses (originally built for the space program) were used. It is like looking through a window at a lost world. The ambiance is further enriched through a soundtrack featuring period Baroque music, primarily that of Bach, Handel, and Vivaldi, as well as Irish airs performed by the Chieftains. Kubrick's usual cinematic themes of greed, violence, and ambition play out in this picaresque story of an egotistical Irishman's spectacular rise and fall. In addition to the sets and lighting, much visual attention is paid to the costumes for the large cast; Marisa Berenson, in particular, as Lyndon's abandoned wife, is stunning in (and out of) her extravagant clothes. For a film so concerned with accuracy, the casting of American Ryan O'Neal in the title role was a major mistake—he looks the part but can manage neither the Irish brogue nor the complexities of the role—but it does not destroy a visually arresting work that won Academy Awards for costumes, cinematography, art/set decoration, and musical score.

1980 to the Present

A sort of literary adaptation/costume film industry—which came to dominate the genre by the 1980s—was established by Indian producer Ismail Merchant and American director James Ivory. The team started in the 1960s making small films set in India and then turned to more lavish adaptations of novels by turn-of-the-century writers Henry James (*The Europeans* [1979], *The Bostonians* [1984]) and E. M. Forster (*A Room with a View* [1985], *Maurice* [1987], *Howards End* [1992]). Merchant was a wizard at making small budgets look large on the screen through impressive location shots and meticulous attention to costumes and wardrobe. The fact that Merchant and Ivory were a gay couple no doubt colored their examinations of societal form, expectations, and rejection. Most of the films concern conflict between Victorian ideals of gentility and restraint and more "modern" impulses toward emotionalism and behavioral freedom. Thus, the stern American family in *The Europeans* is shaken to its core by the arrival of two free-spirited European cousins. In *The Bostonians* a young girl is pulled in two directions by her romantic feelings for both a bold suffragette (Vanessa Redgrave) and a young Southern lawyer (Christopher Reeve). *A Room with a View,* the filmmakers' first big success, finds a group of straitlaced English tourists (none more repressed than spinster chaperone Charlotte Bartlett, played by Maggie Smith) responding in various ways to the sensually liberating sights and mores of Italy. In one of her first important roles, Helena Bonham Carter, who would appear in several Merchant/Ivory productions, plays Miss Bartlett's charge, Lucy Honeychurch, giving herself up to love and passion amidst the Renaissance splendor of Florence. In interviews, Carter spoke of how the confining corsets and dresses forced her to move in a stiff, rigid manner, representative of the restrictive existence imposed upon women of the time—an existence her young character longs to escape. Regarding generational struggles, Merchant/Ivory are always on the side of emboldened youth, just as they romanticize intercultural and unconventional relationships. *Maurice,* based upon Forster's unpublished novel about a young man's burgeoning homosexual sensibility, is set amidst the English upper class (as are most Merchant/Ivory films) before the World War I. Two young men fall in love while at university, but one (Hugh Grant) comes to deny both his friend and his own true feelings in order to marry and enter the established and unforgiving social order. Maurice (James Wilby), on the other hand, agonizes over his true nature until finding love in the arms of an affectionate (male) servant. Typically, for the work of both this author and these filmmakers, Maurice is as liberated by his ability to demonstrate physical love as he is by his rejection of a repressive and stifling patriarchy. In contrast to most costume films, the focus here is clearly upon men, who are impeccably dressed in Edwardian suits or college and country attire.

Overcome by the sensuousness of their Italian surroundings, English tourists Julian Sands and Helena Bonham Carter give in to their youthful passion in Merchant/Ivory's *A Room with a View* (1985), based on the E. M. Forster novel. *Photofest.*

The message of *Howards End*, perhaps Merchant/Ivory's greatest film, is "Only Connect." Set in 1910, it presents two families: the convivial, relaxed, and artistic Schlegel sisters, representing Continental emotionalism, and the repressed, rigid Wilcoxes, terribly English, priggish, and stiff-upper-lip. Thrown together by circumstance, Margaret Schlegel (Emma Thompson, in an Academy Award-winning performance) and Henry Wilcox (Anthony Hopkins) fall in love and marry, and the conflicts of the film stem from the clash of two worlds—of emancipated nonconformity butting heads with cruelly conservative traditionalism. A reinforcing subplot concerns the disastrous results of an outsider—a young man from the working class—wandering into the midst of this wealthy group. The dream cast includes Vanessa Redgrave (as Henry's first wife), Helena Bonham Carter (as the second Schlegel sister), Samuel West, and James Wilby. The voluminous Edwardian dresses and sweeping hats are as beautiful as the perfectly decorated townhouse drawing rooms and spacious country estates against which the drama unfolds. The film also won Oscars for Best Art/Set Decoration and Adapted Screenplay.

The Merchant/Ivory *oeuvre* is often categorized as "*Masterpiece Theatre* films," named after the still-running PBS series that made its mark in the 1970s by broadcasting British television serializations of classic novels such as Hardy's *Jude the Obscure*, Thackeray's *Vanity Fair*, and Tolstoy's *Anna Karenina*. These and later blockbuster English series, including *The Barchester Chronicles*, *Fortunes of War*, and *The Jewel in the Crown* (some of which were broadcast in this country on networks other than PBS), bequeathed a legacy of literate sophistication, brilliant ensemble cast acting, and the odd stuffiness to British-made costume films. Many filmmakers got their start in such television projects, including Charles Sturridge, who followed the phenomenal success of his television adaptation of Evelyn Waugh's *Brideshead Revisited* with a film version of E. M. Forster's *Where Angels Fear to Tread* (1991).

As the well of suitable Forster novels began to run dry, filmmakers turned for material to other turn-of-the-century novelists who wrote about the excesses and sufferings of the Gilded Age filthy rich. Particularly popular and photogenic were the works of Henry James (*The Portrait of a Lady* [1996], *Washington Square* [1997], *The Wings of the Dove* [1997], and *The Golden Bowl* [2000]), Edith Wharton (*The Age of Innocence* [1993] and *The House of Mirth* [2000]), and Oscar Wilde (*Wilde* [1997], *An Ideal Husband* [1999], and *The Importance of Being Earnest* [2002]).

Merchant/Ivory worked through the novels of James and Forster, but the biggest literary name in mid-1990s films was Jane Austen, five of whose six novels were filmed for television or the cinema at about this time. Something about the world that Austen described—a controlled, rule-bound society of marriage arrangements and setting up homes in which gender and class roles are strictly prescribed, but one in which true love always seems to win out in the end—was utterly captivating to late twentieth-century filmgoers living in an apparently chaotic world wherein no rules seemed to apply and love appeared all too unpredictably complicated. Austen was a miniaturist, and her perceptive, witty examinations of the often isolated, rural lives of characters confronting love and hate, life and death, and gain and loss, lend themselves to film.

For Austen 1995 was an *annus mirabilis*. *Clueless* (1995) updated the novel *Emma* to a contemporary Beverly Hills high school milieu and made a star of Alicia Silverstone as the meddlesome, clothes-obsessed heroine, bent upon arranging the lives and loves of everyone around her but "clueless" as to her own situation. The same year saw more faithful adaptations of *Persuasion* and *Sense and Sensibility*. The period detail of the former film, financed by British television, seems less romanticized, less "Hollywood" than most of the costume films of this decade, but it is beautiful nonetheless. The film is impeccably acted by performers from the English stage and television whose names seldom figure on American cinema marquees. *Sense and Sensibility*, on the other hand, is clearly a much bigger production, with a greater budget and big-name actors (Emma Thompson, Kate Winslet, Alan Rickman, Hugh Grant). Thompson also wrote the film adaptation of the novel and won an Academy Award for her screenplay. *Sense and Sensibility* is perhaps the most faithful to Austen of all the recent adaptations, finding just the right mixture of comedy and pathos in a story about a family's lost fortune and the search of two sisters—one overly sensible, the other governed by her passions—for love.

Emma (1996) was Gwyneth Paltrow's first major role, the one that made her a star, and she looks stunning in the period Empire costumes, whether engaged in a game of archery or whispering *tête-à-tête* over tea in a drawing room.

Director Patricia Rozema's *Mansfield Park* (1999) is very much Austen by way of Edward Said, the social critic whose work centers on issues of colonialism/

imperialism and class. Following Said's lead, Rozema (who wrote the screenplay) centralizes ideas and situations Austen ignores or marginalizes in her novel, including the treatment of slaves, and adds lesbian undertones. Despite its heavy-handed earnestness and smug political correctness, the basic wit and emotion of the story of a poor relation sent to live among her so-called "betters" is emotionally involving and beautifully filmed.

Austen's most popular novel, *Pride and Prejudice*, was a tremendously popular British television series in the 1990s (making Colin Firth, who portrays Darcy, the intellectual's pinup boy). It was filmed yet again in 2005, starring Keira Knightley, sixty-five years after the Greer Garson-Laurence Olivier version.

There has been a flurry of films based upon Shakespeare's plays in recent years. On the one hand, following the lead of Laurence Olivier in *Henry V* (1944), *Hamlet* (1948), and *Richard III* (1955), some actors have directed themselves in the lead role. Such was the case with Orson Welles in *Othello* (1952) and Kenneth Branagh in *Henry V* (1989), *Hamlet* (1996), *Much Ado About Nothing* (1993), and *Love's Labour's Lost* (2000). Other recent film adaptations of the Bard have featured actors Mel Gibson as *Hamlet* (1990); Laurence Fishburne as *Othello* (1995); Ian McKellen as *Richard III* (1995); Imogen Stubbs and Helena Bonham Carter in *Twelfth Night* (1996); Kevin Kline, Michelle Pfeiffer, and Rupert Everett in *A Midsummer Night's Dream* (1999); and Anthony Hopkins, Jessica Lange, and Alan Cumming in *Titus* (1999). Taking their lead from eclectic stage productions, filmmakers enjoy tremendous freedom in creating unexpected time frames, settings, and costumes for Shakespeare pictures. Some might utilize Elizabethan garb, but many go in inspired and surprising directions as to setting. Thus, Richard Loncraine's *Richard III* (1995) is set in 1930s England during a Fascist coup, whereas Trevor Nunn's *Twelfth Night* (1996) and Michael Hoffman's *A Midsummer Night's Dream* (1999) take place in the 1890s, the latter in Italy.

Recent costume films have proven a boon to actresses "of a certain age," largely because the genre has traditionally appealed primarily to female audiences who enjoy watching middle-aged or older women (with or without men) finding fulfillment—and themselves—in exotic times or locales, while wearing attractive clothes. *Enchanted April* (1992), based upon the novel by Elizabeth von Arnim and filmed earlier in 1935, resembles *A Room with a View* and *Where Angels Fear to Tread* in its depiction of stuffy, repressed English tourists warming to life and love in sunny Italy. Josie Lawrence, Miranda Richardson, and Joan Plowright play the dissatisfied 1920s wives and widow who blossom in the rarified, hothouse atmosphere of a lush Italian villa, shedding dark and restrictive clothing in favor of loose, diaphanous, and colorful dresses. *Tea with Mussolini* (1999), director Franco Zeffirelli's romanticized memories of his youth and the English and American women who molded his appreciation of art and friendship, features a fabulous, dressed-to-the-nines cast, including Maggie Smith, Judi Dench, Cher, Joan Plowright, and Lily Tomlin. Set in 1930s Florence, a colony of English-speaking ladies gradually comes to realize the threat of Fascism to their way of life and the lives of loved ones; they take on the Powers That Be in their struggle to maintain artistic and personal integrity. Finally, *Up at the*

Villa (2000), based upon a Somerset Maugham novella, features Kristin Scott Thomas, Anne Bancroft, Sean Penn, and James Fox in a story of an English widow falling in love with an American playboy in pre–World War II Florence.

With today's more permissive attitudes towards language, violence, nudity, and sexual content in films, costume films seem an odd throwback—bodies completely covered under yards of cloth, rather than fully exposed. However, filmmakers are quite frank about what happens when all those clothes come off, and the *frisson* created by the implication or revelation of a panting, yearning body under the silks and satins galvanizes many recent costume films. Moving away from earlier period films' attitude of "Weren't they pretty?" or "Wasn't it all perfectly civilized?", some films blow the lid off the sexual and perverse desires hidden beneath those pretty, civilized clothes. Director Martin Scorsese, known for graphically violent films about contemporary urbanites, surprised everyone when he took on Edith Wharton's novel of the Gilded Age, *The Age of Innocence* (1993). However, Scorsese brings a brooding, ominous atmosphere to the story of a scandal involving an engaged man who falls under the influence of a beautiful woman with a notorious past. The battlegrounds in the film (which won the Academy Award for Best Costumes) are the opera house and the weekend country estate, the combatants swathed in yards and yards of expensive cloth and feathers, and their arsenal is composed of deadly looks and reputation-destroying remarks. Writer/director Jane Campion won the Oscar for her screenplay to *The Piano* (1993), which has the breadth and scope of a weighty Victorian novel. In the late nineteenth century, a mute Scottish widow (Holly Hunter) travels with her young daughter (Anna Paquin) to New Zealand for an arranged marriage. The woman is buried under her dark and severe "widow's weeds" dresses and clamped-down hair, coming to full emotional life only when pounding out romantic music on her beloved piano. Her adulterous affair with a European who has "gone native" and converted to Maori (Harvey Keitel) leads to the eventual stripping off of clothes, erotic fireworks, and tragedy. Both Hunter and Paquin won Academy Awards for their performances. Hawthorne's *The Scarlet Letter* (1995) has been filmed at least half a dozen times, including a silent version with Lillian Gish. The most recent film is decidedly the worst, universally panned by critics and a disaster at the box office. Demi Moore (hopelessly miscast) plays Hester Prynne, branded with the cloth "A" for committing adultery in Puritan New England. The filmmakers' desperation is evident by their imposition of a happy ending on the story and inclusion of nude love scenes; where Hawthorne's plea for forgiveness and individual freedoms was implied, director Roland Joffe's is heavy-handed and blunt.

Other erotic costume films include *Moll Flanders* (1996), a 1990s take on Defoe's defiant heroine; *Angels and Insects* (1996), based on an A. S. Byatt novella, a story of incest and deception, set in the Victorian period, in which the characters are clad in gowns as colorful and vibrant as the wings of the butterflies and insects collected by an entomologist; *Oscar and Lucinda* (1997), an adaptation of Peter Carey's novel about a pair of social rogues and gambling addicts; *Cousin Bette* (1998), based on a novel by Balzac, with Jessica Lange as a mistreated, put-upon poor relation in 1860s Paris who bides her time before exacting terrible revenge upon her cousins; and the eye-popping *Moulin Rouge* (2001), Baz Luhrmann's outrageous, over-the-top and frenetic musical extravaganza about love and sexual predators in turn-of-the-century Montmartre. *Moulin Rouge* won Oscars for Costume Design and Art Direction.

Finally, although we tend to think of costume films as those whose storylines are set one hundred or more years ago, films set in the more recent past that pay special attention to wardrobe and clothing certainly fall into this genre. This would include, for example, Ang Lee's exploration of 1970s suburban sexual experimentation and familial dysfunction in *The Ice Storm* (1997); Todd Haynes's baroque portrayal of the denizens of the seventies glam and glitter rock scene in *Velvet Goldmine* (1998); and Haynes's homage to Douglas Sirk, the woman's picture and 1950s America, *Far From Heaven* (2002).

References and Further Reading

Basinger, Jeanine. *Silent Stars*. Hanover, NH: Wesleyan University Press, 1999.

———. *A Woman's View: How Hollywood Spoke to Women 1930–1960*. New York: Knopf, 1993.

Gunter, Howard. *Gowns by Adrian: The MGM Years, 1928–1941*. New York: H. N. Abrams, 2001.

Head, Edith, and Paddy Calistro. *Edith Head's Hollywood*. New York: Dutton, 1983.

Landy, Mindy. *The Historical Film: History and Memory in Media*. Brunswick, NJ: Rutgers University Press, 2001.

Leese, Elizabeth. *Costume Design in the Movies: An Illustrated Guide to the Work of 157 Designers*. New York: Dover, 1991.

Maeder, Edward, et al. *Hollywood and History: Costume Design in Film*. London: Thames and Hudson, 1987.

McConathy, Dale, and Diana Vreeland. *Hollywood Costume: Glamour, Glitter, Romance*. New York: H. N. Abrams, 1976.

Moseley, Rachel. *Fashioning Film Stars: Dress, Culture, Identity*. London, BFI, 2005.

Paris, Barry. *Garbo*. Minneapolis: University of Minnesota Press, 1994.

Sharaff, Irene. *Broadway & Hollywood: Costumes Designed by Irene Sharaff*. New York: VanNostrand Reinhold, 1976.

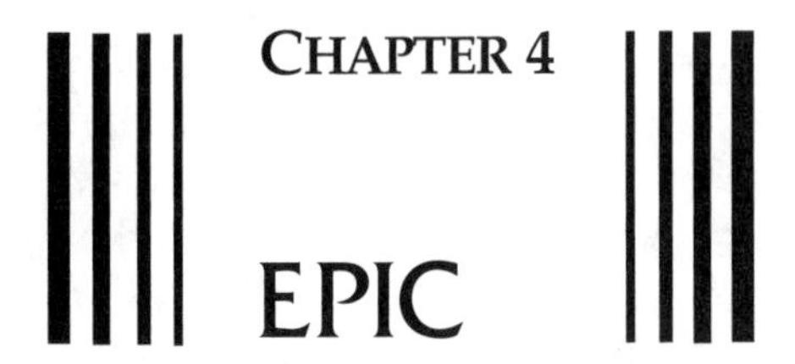

CHAPTER 4

EPIC

ALTHOUGH EPIC FILMS as a genre take their name from classical poetry, they share but few characteristics with the works of Homer, Virgil, and the like. Essentially absent are such narrative features as invoking a muse, cataloguing great men or ships, starting the plot *in medias res*, and journeying to the domain of the dead; nevertheless, epic films mirror their literary namesake in length, extensive cast of characters, general exalted style, grand sweep, depiction of protagonists facing moral tests, and heroic approach to subject matter. Likewise, as the *Aeneid*'s story of Aeneus and the founding of Rome serves as both justification and panegyric of a culture, so epic films often mythologize a people's origins and accomplishments. They tend to explore and extol heroism, often nation-specific (as in *Lawrence of Arabia* [1962], *How the West Was Won* [1962], and *Gandhi* [1982]), or depict the struggle between good and evil (as in the many Biblical films and the *Godfather* trilogy).

Because of the inevitably high costs and demanding logistics of producing epic films, they are generally associated with the studio system, whereby wealthy, extensively staffed motion picture factories could devote seemingly limitless funds and manpower to their creation. And as a result of their sheer size and concomitant massive financial budgets, production of film epics is particularly market-determined and -driven; a studio's economic salvation or destruction has often been linked to the extent of an epic's box office success. Epics are risky business, but when they capture the public's imagination, the sky is the limit. As of this writing, the only films in history to have made a billion dollars are the epics *Titanic* (1997) and *The Lord of the Rings: The Return of the King* (2003).

DEFINING CHARACTERISTICS

Size

The epic's most obvious characteristic—with which the term *epic* has become synonymous—is size or, more specifically, grandiosity. Almost everything about an epic is big and spectacular: the film's length, its cast (the epic term *cast of thousands*, referring to both billed actors and nameless extras, is a cinema cliché), the plotline, the sets, the overwhelming, manipulative musical score, and the general overflow of images upon the screen. With their extended running times and use of wide screens, these films literally take up more time and space than do others. Epics' size promises true escapism, offering eye-filling glimpses into another world, and audiences go to get their money's worth: to gawk at the rich costumes, the towering sets, and the seas of active, embattled humanity. The superlatives that accompanied the making of these films have been used to promote them and ensure their place in the record books: the largest film set (1312 × 745 feet in *The Fall of the Roman Empire* [1964]), the longest commercially made American film (the 4-hour, 3-minute *Cleopatra* [1963]), the most extras used in a film (over 300,000 in *Gandhi* [1982]), the most cameras used in a film sequence (48 for a sea battle in *Ben-Hur* [1925]), the most costumes in a film (32,000 in *Quo Vadis* [1951]), the most horses assembled for a film (8000 in *War and Peace* [1956]), and so on (Robertson).

As in Homer and Tolstoy, the best film epics combine and intersperse grand, overwhelming sequences with perceptive, intimate scenes and details: the big moments and the small. After connecting with the characters at a close, personal level, empathetic audiences thus share the impact and intensity of the huge, encompassing events into which these characters are thrown. In a sense, we see the formation of character and then its testing. Scarlett O'Hara's early competitive, emotional familial and romantic experiences stamp her with the independent, selfish mettle needed to survive the demands and deprivations of war and its aftermath in *Gone With the Wind* (1939). Michael Corleone's troubled, intense, and unresolved relationships with his family and his Catholicism in *The Godfather* (1972) find both release and justification in his violent outbursts against rival mafiosi.

Boastful Publicity

Overblown, hyperbolic publicity, necessary in conveying the sheer magnitude of the epics, is in itself a characteristic of the genre, perhaps more so than with any other film type. What happened behind the scenes in the making of the motion picture—what it took to create the spectacle—is every bit as important as what occurs on screen and is utilized shamelessly to sell tickets. Such claims as "Three Years in the Making!" and "No Expenses Spared!" may mask troubled or even disastrous shooting schedules, but they are trumpeted as tokens of greatness. Epics are considered (and called) "Events," and for three or even four hours audiences are happy to soak in the much-trumpeted spectacle of all that spent time and money. The publicity for the 1948 reissue of *The Crusades*, a film that did poorly at the box office on its initial 1935 release, used sheer numbers to draw in audiences. "Spectacle and pageantry storm the screen! Legions of knights battling their way to the Holy Land! Thousands of horses in one mighty charge! In all history, no love story so inspired! No spectacle so *gripping*!" If spectacle *and* a love story can be promised, as is the case not only here but in such films as *War and Peace* (1956), *Doctor Zhivago* (1965), *Reds* (1981), and *Titanic*, all the better. And while we may smile at such advertising hyperbole, writing it off as naïve exclamations for a less jaded time, the written copy on the cover of the 2001 DVD release of *Ben-Hur* (originally released in 1959) proves that Hollywood's macho insistence that bigger is better is alive and well: "The numbers speak volumes: 100,000 costumes, 8,000 extras, 300 sets and a staggering budget in its day the largest in movie history. *Ben-Hur*'s creators made it the best, the greatest Biblical-era epic ever."

The 1948 publicity for *The Crusades* also tied that film's Holy Land battles to contemporary struggles, specifically the creation of the Israeli state. An interesting aspect of film epics' promotion is the conflation of subject matter with the film production experience itself. In this way, the laborious, trailblazing efforts toward emancipation or greatness that are the stuff of an epic plotline are compared to the filmmakers' own efforts to translate that very story onto the screen. Moses surmounted untold hardships to lead his people to freedom; the makers of *The Ten Commandments* (1956) overcame unprecedented difficulties in bringing the epic to the screen. Press book materials accompanying the premiere of *How the West Was Won*, the saga of settlers in nineteenth-century America, depict those filmmakers and technicians involved in the project as every bit the pioneers their homesteading forebears were. The movie's groundbreaking widescreen Cinerama process is said to inaugurate a new era in filmmaking. Just as countless pioneers gave their all to make this country what it is, so "thousands of creative men and women and skilled technicians combined their talents to make this motion picture a reality." The future promise of American westward expansion ("they came by the thousands from everywhere") is likened to the new era of widescreen film entertainment (Sobchack 2003, 288).

Setting in the Past

In addition to sheer spectacle, another mark of epics is their usual setting in a distant time (in the past or, occasionally, in the future, placing them also in the domain of science fiction [see **Science Fiction and Fantasy**]) in which such outsized events and images, removed from the present, somehow fit. Perhaps appealing to a postmodern viewpoint whereby our age is a post-heroic one in which significant individual acts are nearly impossible, audiences look to historical or Biblical stories of revolution, exodus, or survival for extreme examples and proof of human potential. On the other hand, part of the reason for these films taking place long ago may also be the popular belief that things really were worse—in terms of human depravity and general standards of living—in the past. For cinemagoers, those were indeed the best of times and the worst of times. Yet, although much is made of the idiosyncrasies or peculiarities of life in ancient Rome or during the Civil War, epics ultimately reinforce a sense of shared human experience that bridges time and space. We may never face Roman centurions or an invading Yankee army, but we can identify with the basic emotions, hopes, and longings that bind us to our predecessors on the screen, and we can cheer on their determination and desire for a better life.

Inevitably, much is made of a film epic's painstaking attention to historical detail and accuracy, yet it is very much a product of its own time, imprinting its era's social and cultural ideals upon the age in which the story is set and resulting in some amazing anachronisms. In a famous short subject film (released, along with countless others, in the years before the mid-1960s to accompany newsreels, cartoons, and previews between feature films), shot on the set of *The Crusades* (1935), director Cecil B. DeMille, clearly scripted, demonstrates his attention to detail by berating an extra—one of the four thousand people on the set that day—for showing up in a 1930s hairstyle: "We spend thousands and thousands of dollars on research. We comb the museums of the world. We scour every library there is, to get accurate and authentic detail . . . And they give me a girl who looks like she just walked out of a beauty salon." Hollywood prided itself on the truthfulness of its historical epics, or at least its attempt to convince Middle America of this veracity. Nevertheless, one of the joys of watching historical epics is in locating the frequent and audacious historically inaccurate howlers. "This isn't fantasy, this is reality," DeMille cries in the short; but, of course, these films are total fantasies: glossy, beautiful, and escapist. We learn much more about the desires, standards, and aspirations of the time at which the epic was made than about those of, say, the Civil War or the Middle Ages. There is always a high kitsch value to the film epic, as the most modern and populist of art forms turns its hand at recreating ancient history, and actors we have recently seen portraying bank robbers or bank managers are now suddenly pharaohs or knights. Despite DeMille's protestations, most of his actresses *do* appear to have just emerged from a contemporary beauty parlor. Likewise, in *Doctor Zhivago*, set in Russia at the time of the revolution, actors Julie Christie and Geraldine Chaplin wear makeup and hairstyles that are the height of mid-1960s swinging London fashion. *Titanic*'s headstrong Rose (Kate Winslet) speaks and moves like a 1990s liberated woman, bearing little resemblance to an actual, traditionally raised 1912 heiress. To his role as overlord Dathan in *The Ten Commandments*, Edward G. Robinson brought the same urban swagger and accent he had used in all his films as a gangster.

Morality Plays

At heart, epics are morality plays in which good and evil struggle both within individual characters and also upon grand, sweeping stages, whether they be the Holy Land, the American West, or the streets of Little Italy. Speaking as they do for and about groups of people, epics flourish when audiences for the most part share moral outlooks and societal expectations. From the 1930s through the 1950s, facing the Depression, World War II, and the Cold War, Americans largely shared common enemies and a sense of national identity and purpose—even religious faith. Hollywood responded with unequivocal morality tales told from a decidedly traditional and conservative perspective. The social upheavals in 1960s and 1970s America had a major impact upon the public's tastes; after various civil rights movements, Vietnam, and Watergate, filmmakers could locate no common ground among cinemagoers where right and wrong was concerned, and therefore no clear indicators of what was indeed the common good or the shared evil threat. Whereas earlier epics often pitted the individual against the system, the individual himself usually represented a group of some sort—often one with which the audience was expected to identify, such as Christians in *The Sign of the Cross* (1932) or *Ben-Hur.* Many post-1970 films offered no such clear-cut divisions or empathetic characters. Epics largely disappeared from the screen or underwent significant revision.

The Director as Driving Force

Unlike some other film genres, such as the woman's picture (see **Woman's Film**) or the musical (see **Musical**), which are largely star/performer-driven, the epic is essentially identified with the director or producer. With the exception of Charlton Heston, there really are no "epic film stars" as far as actors are concerned. Rather, epics are known as DeMille, Lean, or Coppola films, wherein the director's vision is paramount. The epic's emphasis upon immensity, the size of the sets and sheer number of bodies on screen, call for studio backing but also a strong overriding vision. Epics tend to dwarf individual actors. This is not to say that fine acting cannot be found in the films: simply observe Laurence Olivier in *Spartacus* (1960), Rex Harrison in *Cleopatra*, or Marlon Brando in *The Godfather.* Nevertheless, stars are not really called on (or hired) to *act* in epics; they must simply hold their own amidst the multitudes and not get lost in the sheer size and richness of the production. Stars are hired for their larger-than-life personae and established character types. Like the personified human virtues and sins in the medieval morality plays, an actor in an epic must project a strong universal idea: lust, piety, injustice, authority, and so on. Rita Hayworth is Rita Hayworth-sex goddess in *Salome* (1953); Charles Laughton is Charles Laughton-effete emperor in *The Sign of the Cross.* In some epics, such as *The Greatest Story Ever Told*, featuring the clichéd "all-star cast," the celebrities are just another spoke in the huge publicity wheel, spinning hyperbole, selling tickets, and emphasizing magnitude. They become part of the scenery, familiar (though very expensive) national wonders set amidst the equally monumental sets. More recently, the centerpieces of epics have been brawny, gym-toned actors such as Russell Crowe, Brad Pitt, and Colin Farrell, hired to match physically the impressive visual spectacle that surrounds them.

HISTORY AND INFLUENCES

The Beginning to the 1930s

With its dependency upon various manifestations of immensity—its *raison d'être*—the film epic is closely connected to technological advances that have had an impact on the length and actual size of movies. The earliest commercial films are regularly referred to as "shorts," as befits both length and, in many cases, aspiration. A comic did a *shtick*, a couple fell in love, a villain was thwarted: time as much as technological restrictions dictated film content. The earliest kinetoscopes (showing at the nickelodeons of the 1890s) were but a 50-foot film loop, containing less than 20 seconds of action. By the teens, films were quite a bit longer, but they had to "fit" on a single reel, lasting about fifteen minutes, because distributors were convinced that audiences (many if not most of whom did not attend live theater) would not sit still for longer movies. In 1913, after five years of turning out one-reelers, director D. W. Griffith felt constrained by their brevity and started making two- and three-reel films, some of which distributors insisted upon releasing in two parts. But even three reels were insufficient to contain Griffith's grand, pioneering visions of the battle between good and evil. The success at this time of some Italian feature-length film spectacles (*Quo Vadis?* [1912] at eight reels and *Cabiria* [1914] at twelve), which played in "legitimate" theaters rather than nickelodeon halls, spurred on Griffith to unheard-of expansiveness and the creation of the first American film epics, the greatest of which are *The Birth of a Nation* (1915; thirteen reels long and lasting three hours) and *Intolerance* (1916; fourteen reels).

Like the Thomas Dixon novel (*The Clansman*) upon which it is based, *The Birth of a Nation* was controversial from the start. Set in the American South and covering the years from just before the Civil War through the period of Reconstruction, the film (much as *Gone With the Wind*, another novel and film epic, would do twenty-four years later) eulogized what it saw as a lost golden age. Griffith's father died in 1885, when his son was ten, of wounds received during the war, and the boy had grown up among romanticized and nostalgic stories of a lost Southern world of honor and gentility. The film presents the Ku Klux Klan's arrival on the scene after the war as an effort to preserve white civilization; the "nation" that is born is what today would be called an Aryan one, decidedly putting down threats of black autonomy and, even worse in Griffith's eyes, miscegenation. Despite President Wilson's excited comment that the film is "like history written with lightning," the true thunderbolt was the film's inevitable divisiveness. Demonstrations (both for and against the film), condemnations, and even angry mobs have surrounded *The Birth of a Nation* since its release in 1915, and its blatant racism haunts and diminishes Griffith's artistic reputation to this day. The film is filtered not only through the prism of its director's racism but also his Dickensian view of True Womanhood as being childlike, virtuously moral, and under constant threat as well as decidedly Caucasian. Despite the protests, audiences flocked to see the film.

Running to thirteen reels, costing $110,000, and featuring, literally, a cast of thousands, *The Birth of a Nation* was certainly bigger than anything yet attempted in America. At a time when most films were rehearsed (if at all—many were not), shot, and edited in a week, Griffith's massive work was rehearsed for six weeks and shot in nine. The large set pieces—great battle sequences, a recreation of Lincoln's assassination in Ford's Theater, the peace signing at Appomattox, political meetings, and dances—are woven into the story of two families, one from the North and the other from the South. The eventual Romeo and Juliet-styled marriage of representatives from each family is the film's version of national reconciliation, overcoming the violence and disruption brought about by both war and the perceived menace of mixing the races. On the one hand the film contains intimate, domestic scenes, perhaps the most moving of which is the return of the "little Colonel" (the Southern son) home from battle, walking down the deserted street, standing on the dirty, neglected front porch, and finally, in profile, being embraced and drawn into the house by the thin, trembling arms of his mother, standing just inside the front door and out of sight except for her arms. The simplicity yet universality of such scenes make all the more powerful the large-scale battle sequences, which Griffith directed and edited to stunning effect. The catalog of cinematic devices, which Griffith may not have invented but which he is known for perfecting—iris shots, integrated multidistance shots, masking shots, rhythmic and stimulating editing, and so forth—are fully exploited in the battle scenes, as when a tight iris shot zeroes in on the worried, sorrowful face of a mother, gradually opening and revealing her superimposition over a massed army of countless mothers' sons, or in the famous sequence of the little Colonel grabbing up a fallen Confederate flag, rushing across no man's land and into the heart of the Yankees' line and ramming the flagpole down the throat of a Union cannon. The film's Victorian sentimentality is leavened with such grand action sequences; it is Dickens-meets-P. T. Barnum.

Griffith seemed honestly shocked at the negative reactions to *The Birth of a Nation,* and—partly to justify his art and partly to chasten his detractors—he immediately commenced work on *Intolerance.* If *Nation* is big, then *Intolerance* is colossal. At $1.9 million, it cost fifteen times the money spent on the earlier film (Mast and Kawin 2003, 73). The film intertwines four separate stories to illustrate mankind's prejudice and inhumanity towards others, set in ancient Babylon, the Judea of Christ, Renaissance France, and contemporary America. *Intolerance* is famous today for two things. One is Griffith's audacious, groundbreaking splicing together of four apparently disparate storylines. The scenes run fairly long until late in the film, when, as tension builds, they become shorter and the jumping from one era to another more frequent, all building towards a climax—well, four climaxes, actually. The juxtaposition of these storylines is not entirely successful. What is unquestionably impressive—legendary, in fact—and for which the film is primarily known is the sequence in which the camera pulls back and upward to reveal the massive Babylon set, probably the most famous in history. For sheer size and audacity it has never

The most famous set in all epics, if not all film: Babylon and a cast of thousands, as recreated by D. W. Griffith in *Intolerance* (1916). *Photofest.*

been equaled, and perfectly illustrates our collective view of what is "epic": teeming with grand stairways, gargantuan columns, and statues of rampant elephants, with countless choreographed, costumed actors scattered as far as the eye can see. The scene has never been equaled on film.

The other great director of American silent film epics, one who would go on to even greater heights in sound films, his name synonymous with all things epic, is Cecil B. DeMille. The name DeMille is still famous not only because of his amazing longevity in the business but because he was a master showman and publicist. DeMille gave the public what they wanted—sex and spectacle—and took full advantage of flamboyant advertising and promotion, both of his films and of himself (he appeared as himself in *Sunset Boulevard* [1950], in which Norma Desmond's line, "I'm ready for my close-up, Mr. DeMille," immediately became a classic). Whereas Griffith had decidedly Victorian moral sensibilities and, in his scenes of child/woman heroines and dastardly, often non-Caucasian male villains, avoided overt sexual content, not so DeMille. He has been called a "master of depravity and spectacle" (Eames 1985, 26), and his favorite theme is the wages of sin, the battle between flesh and the spirit. The spirit always wins, but only after the majority of the film has wallowed in titillating, highly sexual scenes; his are erotic films disguised as morality plays.

DeMille was working in films in New York but ended up in Southern California in 1914, after location shooting in Arizona proved futile. His *The Squaw Man*, produced that year, was Hollywood's first full-length film (running an hour); he would remake this title in 1918 and 1931. DeMille's predilection for historical spectacle first appeared in *Joan the Woman* (1916) and *The Woman God Forgot* (1917), both starring opera star Geraldine Farrar (whose manner suited DeMille's larger-than-life, operatic production style) as Joan of Arc and Montezuma's daughter, respectively. About the earlier movie, a publicity department made perhaps the first claim of filming a cast of a thousand. On the one hand, DeMille produced a string of romantic comedies and dramas (often starring Gloria Swanson), set in the world of the extremely wealthy and exposing (but all the while reveling in) their adulterous and amoral ways. On the other hand, he began turning out the epics for which he would become so well known. Some of these have plotlines in contemporary settings with flashbacks to ancient, decadent times. *Male and Female* (1919) voyeuristically shows a modern, aristocratic Gloria Swanson taking a bath but contains a totally unconnected sequence set in ancient Babylon in which slave-girl Swanson, in a sexy fur outfit, is cast to the lions. His first *The Ten Commandments* (1923) falls into two parts, the first of which ran double over its initial budget of $600,000 (the second half is set in the present and is exaggerated family melodrama).

Of course, Griffith's and DeMille's are not the only silent film epics. Perhaps the most spectacular, considered by some to be Hollywood's greatest epic, is 1925's *Ben-Hur*. Based on the best-selling novel by Lew Wallace, this "tale of the Christ" had already been turned into a stage spectacular in the first two decades of the twentieth century; on stage the chariots raced on treadmills while a backdrop of Roman architecture rolled behind them. Goldwyn Pictures bought the rights to the novel in 1923, but an historic studio merger the next year resulted in the newly formed Metro-Goldwyn-Mayer inheriting the troubled property. Goldwyn had sent a film crew to Egypt and Italy, but political and language problems as much as profligate shooting had burned up most of the allotted budget. MGM hired a new director (Fred Niblo), star (Ramon Navarro), and writers and sent them off to Italy on a rescue mission, but ultimately called the entire operation back to California, where things could be managed more easily. A huge financial investment had been lost, but producer Irving Thalberg, in an attempt to add luster and prestige to the new film company's image, defied advice and decided to spend more money in order to make (or at least save) money. On a lot the size of three football fields, $300,000 was spent to recreate the Circus Maximus, site of the massive chariot race that is the film's centerpiece. The shoot was the talk of the film industry: Forty-two cameras (several borrowed from other studios) were positioned throughout the set to film the spectacle from every conceivable angle (including from ground level as the chariots raced over the camera); more than three thousand extras (including three hundred curious bystanders whom the director scooped up at the last minute) crowded the stands, dressed in Roman finery and cheering wildly. Actors Navarro and Francis X. Bushman manned two of the four-horse chariots, which were actually driven by cowboy stuntmen. The final effect, as several chariots hurl round the colossal oval track, framed by a veritable mass of humanity, is truly awe-inspiring. An unplanned crash produced a chariot pileup that, miraculously, killed no one and was used in the film. The sheer numbers involved in the filmmaking were fully exploited in the movie's publicity, as ads screamed, "Cost a fortune and worth it!", and the publicity booklet sent to distributors urged, "By all means—get over [convey] the BIGNESS of the picture." *Ben-Hur* opened on December 30, 1925, to huge critical and worldwide box office success.

The 1930s and 1940s

DeMille made his first sound epic in 1932 and remained a defining force within the genre until 1956, churning out yet another historical extravaganza every three or four years. The most memorable of these feature biblical or other ancient settings. *The Sign of the Cross* (1932) has all the DeMille sex and violence (much of it edited out for a 1944 re-release) as early Christians face persecution and hungry lions in Nero's Rome. A Paramount publicist exclaimed, "Rome burns again! The sets are marvelous and the costumes spell sex" (Doherty 122). It's not just the costumes: everything about the film is riotously sensual and over the top. Claudette Colbert plays the wicked Empress Poppaea, wearing seductive gowns she readily sheds for the leering camera, in order to bathe, only *just* up to her nipples, in asses' milk. When a friend rushes to the palace for some good gossip, Colbert quips, "Take off your clothes, get in here, and tell me all about it." Charles Laughton overacts wonderfully as a depraved Nero. Supine after an all-night orgy, he declares, "My head is splitting. The wine last night, the music, the delicious debauchery!" The virtuous tranquility of the Christians is contrasted to such sensual profligacy of their Roman oppressors in the first half of the film. The Roman Prefect Marcus (Fredric March) falls for the Christian girl Mercia—"that baby-faced Christian girl," the jealous Poppaea cries; "I find I am sick of patrician women who haven't heard of virtue," he replies—and takes her to his house, where she is ridiculed by the partying orgiasts. Much to their delectation, bad-girl Ancaria (played by an actress named simply Joyzelle!), described as "the most wicked and . . . um . . . *talented* woman in Rome," tries to single-handedly arouse and debauch Mercia by lap dancing all over the unresponsive girl. Amazing as this scene is, which was not restored to the film until 1993, the true spectacle comes in the latter part of the film, set in the Colosseum and filled with countless sadistic and bloodthirsty Romans, demanding satisfaction. The camera swoops and scans impressively from level to level, revealing the various strata of Roman society, before focusing upon the unbelievable games taking place within the arena. In quick succession, we see armed gladiators goring one another, elephants stepping upon and crushing men's heads before dragging corpses about, men boxing with gloves fitted with razor-sharp spikes, tigers devouring women, crocodiles and then gorillas set upon half-naked women who are tied to stakes, and, finally, tall Amazonian women battling male midgets with swords and pitchforks. Nero sits entranced upon his throne, his nearly naked and pin-curled catamite pouting campily at his side. As the Christians are brought out to meet their deaths in the jaws of the lions, Marcus undergoes a conversion, sacrificing himself and walking into the arena with the doomed Mercia. Within him, good has won the battle against evil, and a beatific smile reflects his assurance of immanent transportation to heaven with his lady love. In typical DeMillean hypocrisy, the Christians may win Marcus' soul, but the pagans are a lot more fun, their escapades and all that exposed flesh—both male and female—infinitely more photogenic.

DeMille's *The Crusades* (1935) was not as successful as the preceding films but, like *The Sign of the Cross*, pits violent infidels (in this case, the Muslims occupying Jerusalem) against zealous Christians and ends with a man's conversion at the urging of a devout woman, as the nonbeliever English King Richard the Lionheart (Henry Wilcoxon) weds and comes under the pious influence of Berengaria of Navarre (Loretta Young). Their initial scenes together play out like so many other boy-meets-but-doesn't-yet-understand-girl 1930s movies, but by the end of the film Richard casts off his rash, violent nature and, inspired by Berengaria's selfless example, sues for peace rather than pursuing a costly but assured victory over Saladin. The final shots are of ecstatic Christians entering the now-open Jerusalem to view relics of the Holy Cross, but the scenes that stick in the mind and which thrilled audiences are the grand spectacles of the combined Christian forces setting off on the crusade and, even more so, the attack upon the Muslim fortress of Acre. Using a huge catapult, hoisting fireballs of flaming oil, and wielding swords and arrows, the Crusaders pummel, burn, hack at, and puncture acres of infidel flesh. Unfortunately, the majority of the film is slow-moving, the leads Wilcoxon and Young are unengaging, and all the twentieth-century clichés of the Middle Ages—falcons, jousting, troubadours, revelry, merry men, damsels' tokens, and town criers—never quite come together. Other than a salacious sequence wherein statuesque Christian females are sold off to drooling Arabs ("Look at this gold Christian hair!"), there is little of DeMille's usual sexual vulgarity to enjoy.

DeMille made some films on a grand scale that are set in more recent history. *Union Pacific* (1939) depicts the building of the first transcontinental railroad, spicing up a plot involving a good guy, a villain, and a female love interest with dramatic action scenes of a train wreck, a Native American attack, and a rousing rescue by the cavalry. *Reap the Wild Wind* (1942) won an Oscar for its underwater special effects, integral to its story of nineteenth-century shipwreck salvagers and scavengers in Florida. *The Greatest Show on Earth* (1952) is indeed great entertainment, exploring the entangled lives of performers in the Ringling Brothers-Barnum and Bailey circus. With such stars as Charlton Heston, James Stewart, Betty Hutton, and Dorothy Lamour as manager, clown, trapeze artist, and aerialist, respectively, and featuring a spectacular circus train crash as the climax, with wild animals on the loose, the film became Paramount's biggest money-maker up to that time and won the Academy Award as best picture. More familiarly DeMillean are his returns to Biblical stories in *Samson and Delilah* (1949), with the equally voluptuous Victor Mature and Hedy Lamarr in the title roles, and *The Ten Commandments* (1956).

Gone With the Wind (1939) is essentially an epic, although it lacks one of the genre's key components: a huge set piece involving crowds of people. Unlike *The*

Birth of a Nation, the film remains on the home front, offering no battle scenes. What we see are civilians, dancing to raise money for the cause, hurrying to collect the names of the war dead, and rushing about in panic as Sherman's army approaches the city. The one Big Scene takes place at the Atlanta railroad terminal, where Scarlett walks among hundreds of recumbent wounded and dying soldiers (many of whom are costumed dummies), laid out upon the dusty city streets because the hospitals are full. A building crane was borrowed with which to raise the camera high above street level, as the shot grows ever wider, revealing wounded men as far as the eye can see and a tattered Confederate flag flapping over what has become of her army. The film's epic nature lies in its length, sweeping story, cost, and overall opulent production values; its indestructible popularity stems from a brilliant cast, a long story that never drags, a highly romanticized portrait of both the South and male-female relationships, and Scarlett's resolute, inextinguishable pluck and courage, qualities that appeal to today's audiences as much as they did to 1939 filmgoers on the brink of world war.

The 1950s and 1960s

Particular social and film industry circumstances led to a rush of technological innovations in the early 1950s and produced a sort of golden age of screen spectacles lasting roughly a decade from the mid-fifties on. In the years after the war, and for the first time, cinema audience numbers fell drastically. Weekly movie attendance in 1953 fell to about a quarter of the 1948 figure. By 1955, weekly average attendance dropped to 45.8 million, the lowest since 1923. Americans were leaving the cities for the suburbs, which as yet lacked anything like a movieplex. Collegiate and professional sports enjoyed a swell in popularity. But the true culprit and competitor, regarding lower box office receipts, was the explosion of television upon the culture. People could—and did—stay home and be entertained. In 1949, there were one million TVs in American homes; that number grew tenfold by 1952 and, by the end of the decade, had skyrocketed to 50 million (Mast and Kawin 2003, 284–85). The movie studios knew that something had to be done to recapture the audience, and they set about supplying a competitive, distinctive product, one that could not be found in one's living room. As the 1950s televisions featured smallish screens, mediocre speakers, and broadcast exclusively in black and white, the movies would develop the technology to create an alternative entertainment world: huge, wide screens, stereophonic sound, and splashy, exaggerated color. Whereas TV was intimate and still technologically crude, Hollywood would exploit slick and overwhelming spectacle. Cinemagoers were suddenly confronted with a multitude of baffling but highly impressive names, coined to justify that trip to the theater: Cinerama, CinemaScope, Todd-AO, Super Technirama, Super- and Ultra-Panavision, Vistavision, and even 3-D.*

*The ratio of film width to film height is called the *aspect ratio*. Up until the mid-1950s, the standard aspect ratio for American films was 1.33 to 1; since then, various widescreen ratios have prevailed, the most common today being 1.85:1. However, the CinemaScope ratio, for example, was a whopping 2.35:1.

Clearly, these new expansive screens needed to be filled, and spectacular epics fitted the bill. The 1950s saw a run of historical spectacles, involving legendary characters from history and the Bible, and ranging widely in terms of spectacle and quality: *Salome* (1952), *The Serpent of the Nile* (1953, about Cleopatra and using the same sets as *Salome*), *The Silver Chalice* (1954), *Land of the Pharaohs* (1955), *Helen of Troy* (1956), and so on. CinemaScope was first used in 1953's *The Robe*, based on the Lloyd C. Douglas novel about the presiding Roman centurion at Christ's crucifixion who undergoes a religious conversion. Stating the obvious, a trailer for the Twentieth Century-Fox film and its new widescreen technique pronounced, "You see more because there is more on the film to see." Visually, there is indeed a great deal to see, but dramatically the film is weak. Richard Burton stars as Marcellus, but, although the actor can be effective when playing complex characters who recognize their weaknesses, here is very much the Serious Shakespearean Thespian, wooden and lifeless.

DeMille's second version of *The Ten Commandments* (1956) takes itself very seriously, both as history and morality play. The opening credits promise that "Those who see this motion picture—produced and directed by Cecil B. DeMille—will make a pilgrimage over the very ground that Moses trod more than 3,000 years ago—in accordance with the ancient texts of Philo, Josephus, Eusebius, The Midrash and The Holy Scriptures." In its first run showings, a filmed prologue featured DeMille in front of a large theater curtain describing the film as "the story of the birth of freedom," its theme "whether men are to be ruled by God's law or whether they are to be ruled by the whims of a dictator like Rameses." *The Ten Commandments* was the most expensive film of its time, with a 308-page shooting script containing over seventy speaking parts. Filmed over the course of a year, in Egypt and on the Paramount lot in Los Angeles, the picture shines in Technicolor VistaVision. While the special effects, such as the burning bush, look dated today, the legendary parting of the Red Sea sequence (reverse photography of two strong currents rushing together) was used for years as the movie's selling point. Seventy-five years old at the time of the film's completion, DeMille suffered a severe heart attack while filming in the Sinai peninsula (only missing three days' work), but his showmanship, eye for spectacle, and storytelling abilities never fail. No one else mastered the epic genre as he did, pulling off intimate scenes of Pharaoh's daughter and her handmaidens as well as the gigantic in every sense sequence of the departure of the Israelites from the pharaonic gates. Entire Egyptian villages were hired as extras, swelling the screen to 20,000 people, all rushing forth from huge gates along an avenue of massive carved sphinxes. In the lead role, Charlton Heston is a bit stiff, particularly as the older, stentorian Moses, but as Rameses Yul Brynner delivers a delicious performance in the best tradition of crafty cinema villains.

One of the greatest of epics, often seen as the last gasp of both MGM and the studio system itself, is *Ben-Hur* (1959). As noted earlier, MGM had acquired the rights and finished the silent film version upon its merger with Goldwyn Studios in 1924–25. The two filmed versions of the story, thirty-five years apart, are thus bookends that mark MGM's auspicious beginning and unhappy end. William

Wyler, famous for trying his hand at all film genres, was coaxed into directing the sound version with a million-dollar paycheck—the highest salary ever for a director up to that point—and the desire to "make a Cecil B. DeMille film." At $15 million, the film cost more than had any motion picture in history, but it fairly quickly made $80 million in profit and won eleven Academy Awards, the most given to any picture. (Two other film spectacles would later equal this Oscar haul, with eleven statuettes each: *Titanic* and *The Lord of the Rings: The Return of the King*.) As in the earlier version, the most spectacular sequences in *Ben-Hur* are the sea battle and the Circus Maximus chariot race; nevertheless, though unquestionably impressive in color and splashed across a wide Panavision screen, they but do not quite match the sheer insane audacity and grandeur of their silent predecessors. Much of the sea battle uses miniature models, and it shows, but the chariot race is masterfully choreographed and edited. The story's battle between good and evil is situated in the persons of boyhood friends Judah Ben-Hur (Charleton Heston) and Messala (Stephen Boyd), Jew and Roman but nearly the same person, who fall out after the latter goes away and is corrupted by the heartless and greedy machinations of Roman imperialism. Even after Messala has condemned Ben-Hur to a life of slavery and imprisoned his mother and sister, Judah knows the true source of evil. "I knew [Messala]—well—before the cruelty of Rome spread in his blood. Rome destroyed Messala, as surely as Rome is destroying my family." The incredible hardships and losses he endures threaten to harden Judah into a violent and vengeful man. His wife, a recent convert to the teachings of local holy man Jesus, points out to her husband, "You seem to be the very thing you set out to destroy, giving evil for evil. Hatred is turning you into stone. It's as though *you* had become Messala." The film ends with another conversion, sort of, as Judah witnesses the Crucifixion and an accompanying healing rain cures his family of leprosy. In a nod toward audience diversity, considered unnecessary for DeMille's 1930s films, the Jews' embrace of Christ is understood, not spelled out.

Another epic, another mind-boggling set, and a few thousand more extras. Somewhere in there Charlton Heston steers his chariot to victory in *Ben-Hur* (1959). *Photofest*.

Like Wyler, other established directors have tried their hands at producing epics. George Stevens' *Giant* (1956) lives up to its title: a sprawling, three-and-one-half hour Texan family saga, based on the Edna Ferber best seller, of oil fortunes replacing cattle fortunes amid jealousies, one-upmanship, and racial prejudice. The Benedict clan, a prototype for the Ewings on the *Dynasty* television series, must hold on to their family tradition of scrappy survival while rejecting that of anti-Mexican racism. Stevens topped his career with *Giant;* Stanley Kubrick established his with *Spartacus* (1960), featuring an all-star cast (Kirk Douglas, Laurence Olivier, Jean Simmons, Tony Curtis, Charles Laughton, Peter Ustinov) in the story of a rebellious slave who fronts a war for freedom against imperial Roman forces. In addition to huge battle sequences, there are entertaining scenes—both serious and campy—for the actors, including the initially cut but now restored scene in which master Olivier propositions servant Curtis in a bath. John Ford's western epic *How the West Was Won* (1962) covers fifty years of westward expansion as seen through the experiences of two pioneering families. Although the film breaks into sections, according to time and place (some of which were directed by Henry Hathaway), the overarching story is compelling and, unlike, say, *The Robe*, never drags or lets up.

Nicholas Ray tackled the DeMillean *King of Kings* (1961), but, despite its subject matter, the film's relentlessly serious and awed tone makes one long for some of DeMille's sexy vulgarity. Orson Welles intones a weighty narration, sharing soundtrack space with several common epic film aural effects: the Romans speak with British accents, not so their slaves or non-Romans, and a large choir of heavenly voices ensures that the audience knows when they are watching an Important Scene of particular religious consequence. Likewise, and common to many religious films, rays of light represent the unfilmable Holy Spirit. Director Ray studied architecture under Frank Lloyd Wright, and the film features interesting, multi-angled shots of palace interiors, in addition to some beautiful outdoor scenes.

The life of Christ was filmed again four years later, when George Stevens turned from family saga to full-blown religious epic in *The Greatest Story Ever Told* (1965). The film is rather static, often relying upon tableau instead of action; uses very few close-ups (perhaps in an attempt to fill the widescreen with as much detail as possible); and suffers from the jarring effect of countless Hollywood stars popping up in cameo roles. Look, there's Sal Mineo as the healed cripple! It's Shelley Winters as a cured sinner! And that's John Wayne as a Roman centurion! The very Nordic Max von Sydow plays the Semitic Jesus Christ (*King of Kings* featured a similarly blue-eyed Jesus in the person of Jeffrey Hunter), with Charlton Heston his John the Baptist. As in *King of Kings*, angelic voices clue us in to the presence or activities of divinity, culminating in a round of Handel's "Hallelujah Chorus" at the raising of Lazarus. There are some big, crowded sequences, such as the Massacre of the Innocents and the Entry into Jerusalem, but the film never soars.

King of Kings was one of several films made in Spain in the early 1960s, where producer Samuel Bronston had established a vast studio outside Madrid in order to create a series of monumental epics, lavish in scale and production values and featuring international all-star casts. *El Cid* (1961) tells the story of the legendary eleventh-century hero who drove the Moors from Spain, with Charlton Heston as the warrior and Sophia Loren as his love interest. *Circus World* (1964) is a rather pale rehash of *The Greatest Show on Earth*, with Rita Hayworth, Claudia Cardinale, and John Wayne as a Big Top boss leading his three-ring Wild West show (not to mention his three-ring domestic affairs) on a tumultuous European tour, climaxing with a spectacular fire. That same year saw the $20 million *The Fall of the Roman Empire*, with Loren, Alec Guinness, James Mason, Christopher Plummer, and Omar Sharif. Despite the cast and overall magnificent production, the film received decidedly mixed reviews and failed at the box office, whereupon Bronston closed down his Spanish epic factory.

David Lean's *Lawrence of Arabia* (1962) has been called "the thinking man's epic" and is the yardstick by which all visual epics are measured. Starting with T. E. Lawrence's death in a motorcycling accident on a quiet English lane, the film in flashback tells the story of his adventures in the Arabian desert, leading various Arab tribes in revolt against the Turks during the World War I. Lawrence was a baffling man in life—at once horrified by death yet ultimately excited by it, first courting fame and hero-worship but eventually desperate for obscurity—and he remains an enigma in the film. Worshipped by his Arab followers and a worldwide newspaper audience (as well as by Lean's camera), Lawrence for a time believes his own press. "Do you think I am just *anybody?*" he asks Ali (Omar Sharif), his companion and moral conscience. "I'm going to give [their freedom] to them." Like most of Lean's films, *Lawrence of Arabia* investigates the moral questions facing individuals placed under extreme pressure. The film's themes expand from that of personal to national or cultural identity and crisis, specifically European-Middle Eastern clashes, ending with Lawrence's feelings of guilt at having sold out the Arabs to English and French imperialists. In the star-making title role, Peter O'Toole commands the center of a huge, sprawling film of unrivaled visual opulence. Shot in Jordan, Morocco, and Spain in unforgiving desert locales (the film stock actually began to melt and had to be refrigerated for shipment out), the "Super Panavision 70" Technicolor footage of vast, endless sand hills, shimmering mirages, and distant fleets of camels on the horizon are designed by Lean's expert eye and filmed by photographer Fred Young to stunning effect. In a famous sequence, as Lawrence decides to leave his lowly posting in Cairo and venture into the desert, a close-up of O'Toole holding and suddenly blowing out a lit match cuts immediately to a wide shot of the red desert at dawn, the match's flame replaced by the first glimmer of the rising sun. Part of the film's success is its ability to pull off both quiet, intimate scenes of Lawrence and his associates and also huge set pieces, perhaps the most powerful of which is the blowing up and derailment of a Turkish train. It is the moment of Lawrence's apotheosis, as he stands atop his prey, an overturned railway carriage, twirling about victoriously in blinding white Arab robes, the sun streaming through them from behind.

Lean followed up *Lawrence* with a film version of Boris Pasternak's *Doctor Zhivago* in 1965. Omar Sharif plays the title character, a decent, compassionate man devoted to medicine and his family during the cataclysm of the Russian Revolution. Somewhat heavy-handedly, death and destruction are thus pitted against life and love. Love triumphs, of course: greater than war, death, and time. Politics is kept in the background, while the love story takes center stage, veering the film into soap opera territory; in fact, the first hour and a quarter is straightforward domestic drama, dealing with family and romantic relationships, before world war and the Bolsheviks supply the spectacle. Vast, overwhelming landscape shots almost rival those found in *Lawrence*, the desert here replaced by expansive snowscapes. In telling Russia's story, Lean realized the importance of scale. As in the earlier film, *Zhivago* is told in flashback, with a framing sequence at the beginning in which people debate the true identity of the film's title character. There is then a startling cut from the cramped Soviet bureaucrat's office to a wide shot of the steppes—Zhivago's birthplace—over which the Ural Mountains loom in the distance. Lean's two films were tremendous successes, appealing as they did to audiences' sense of nostalgia (simultaneously sparking dramatic fashion trends, first toward Middle Eastern and then Russian clothing), but also the mid-sixties obsession with the search for self and personal identity.

The film often singled out as responsible for the end of the 1950s epic boom is *Cleopatra* (1963), a textbook in profligacy even by Hollywood standards. Elizabeth Taylor, the top box office star at the time, has said that she didn't want to play the role of Cleopatra and that, when the telephone call came, offering her the part, she facetiously cried out, "Tell them I'll only do it for a million dollars." Twentieth Century-Fox quickly agreed to this then-unheard-of salary and gave Taylor a percentage of the gross as well, setting the scene for several years' worth of indiscriminate and prodigal spending. Fox had been losing money consistently in recent years, so, when costs for *Cleopatra* started to skyrocket, they plowed ahead, desperate for a box office winner. Nearly nine acres of sets were built in England, but very un-Egyptian weather eventually called for shooting in Rome. Taylor was chronically ill and repeatedly postponed filming, as did replacements in director, costars, and script. Eventual director and scriptwriter Joseph L. Mankiewicz (who replaced Rouben Mamoulian) tried to focus on Cleopatra's dichotomous nature, torn between fierce ambition to rule the world and an emotional weakness for strong men. The film has some literate scenes, at times indebted to Shakespeare, but at four hours it is far too long and static in stretches. When not overwhelmed by gaudy sets or some trite dialogue, Richard Burton and Rex Harrison, as Mark Antony and Julius Caesar, are able to shine. Likewise, Taylor rises to some of her dramatic scenes but is often shrill and always beset by excessive and heavy early 1960s hair and makeup. Splashy sequences—the film features forty-seven interiors and thirty-two exteriors—include a banquet aboard Cleopatra's fabled barge and a reconstructed Roman Forum actually larger than the original, but they are all dwarfed by Cleopatra's arrival in Rome, a quarter-million-dollar movie scene nearly as spectacular as

Griffith's Babylon shots in *Intolerance*. The Egyptian queen and her young son by Julius Caesar enter the Imperial capital in an attempt to dazzle and win over Roman citizens—to persuade them to accept Caesarion as Caesar's rightful heir. Decked out as the Goddess Isis, Taylor wears a gown spun from twenty-four-karat gold cloth and sits beside the boy between the paws of a massive sphinx, pulled toward Caesar's throne by 300 slaves. The sphinx is but the *end* of a long riotous procession featuring countless archers, acrobats, trumpeters, dancing girls, guards, slaves, horses, zebras, and elephants and surrounded by thousands of ecstatic, cheering Romans, who throw streamers and confetti. The Todd-AO widescreen overwhelms the viewer with color and spectacle, in a scene unequaled in cinema history. Twentieth Century-Fox ended up paying nearly $40 million on the film (before distribution and publicity costs), but they hoped that hype and a worldwide tabloid love affair scandal involving Taylor and Burton (both of whom were married to others) would sell tickets. Alas, the film was blasted by critics, audiences were underwhelmed, and the picture was regularly whittled down in length to suit exhibitors complaining about its excessive running time. *Cleopatra* ultimately cost and lost more money than had any film in history, and Fox ended up in the red for years.

The 1970s and 1980s

This golden age of widescreen epics died with the studio system. After roughly a decade of historical spectacles, audiences grew tired of the genre, and it proved impossible to make back in profit what these ever-more-expensive films cost to produce. As the old studios themselves either closed down (as did MGM in the early 1970s) or drastically reduced costs, the first projects to go were expensive epics and musicals. All this coincided with a societal shift in demographics and, resultantly, in outlook. The big epic morality stories, emphasizing tradition and the triumph of a supposedly shared view of what is good and right, did not go down well with young filmgoing audiences of the 1960s. The "New Hollywood" that emerged at this time, in such films as *Easy Rider* (1969) and *Five Easy Pieces* (1970), questioned—and, more often than not, rejected—all of the authorities and proscribed morals which the historical epics extolled. The epic heroes now seemed out of date ("your parents' heroes"), hopelessly misogynistic, hypocritically violent, and rule-bound. Young audiences identified with the antiheroes in such films as *Bonnie and Clyde* (1967) and *Midnight Cowboy* (1969), trapped within a corrupt, exploitative society where there is no escape or possibility of heroism but simply defiant rebellion or crime. All political, religious, and social authorities were suspect. The tremendous financial success of these youth-oriented films, which were produced on extremely low budgets, only hastened the studios' abandonment of epics.

When the odd epic was made after this shift in the film industry, it often subverted the genre, darkening the moral landscape, complicating protagonists' motivations and characters, and refusing to reduce things to a simple good-winning-over-evil framework. Francis Ford Coppola's *Godfather* Mafia trilogy explores the favored epic theme of good-vs.-evil but is unusual in its depiction (in the first two films, at least) of evil triumphant. *The Godfather* (1972), based on the Mario Puzo novel, exploded onto the American consciousness, coining expressions ("Make him an offer he can't refuse"), winning numerous awards and becoming one of the biggest moneymaking films of its time. Shot in rich sepia tones, the film's thematic moral contrasts are emphasized by an interplay of bright, sunny domestic scenes of family celebration (weddings, confirmations) and dark, claustrophobic rooms in which the men plan and carry out the mob's various misdeeds. This ironic placement of horror amidst the everyday—of heartless murderers within a loving family—provides much of the film's impact, and Coppola was in fact criticized for making such despicable characters so charismatic. And so there are scenes of Don Vito Corleone (Marlon Brando, winning an Academy Award he would refuse) affectionately stroking a kitten as he plans mortal revenge, or playing with his young grandson in the tomato garden and lovingly scooping the boy into his arms after he has unintentionally frightened him. Evil triumphs in the person of Michael (Al Pacino), the Don's youngest son, an educated war hero who is nevertheless corrupted by his father's world, to the extent that, in the film's final, bravura sequence, he intones "I reject Satan" at his nephew's christening, while the audience is subjected to a stylishly edited and choreographed bloodbath as the heads of various rival Mafia families—at Michael's behest—are violently murdered.

The Godfather, Part 2 (1974) is a directorial *tour de force*, intercutting Michael's further corruption as head of the family in the 1950s with the story of his father Vito's (Robert De Niro) arrival in America as a child at the turn of the century (fleeing Mafia vengeance in Sicily) and his criminal path to becoming a Don. Successfully interweaving these two storylines, director Coppola has come into his own by *Part 2*; the film is even more vibrant and operatic than its predecessor (the late-night cries of "Any family who hides the boy Vito Andolini will regret it!" in the Sicilian village are like something out of Puccini's *Turandot*) and the cinematography (by Gordon Willis) even more daring in its willingness to darken the frame to near-total blackness in appropriate scenes. The family "business" ("we're bigger than US Steel") is in the hands of the next generation, as they spread their influence and power from New York to Miami and Las Vegas. Michael lies under oath, strong-arms a senator, slams the door shut on his wife and marriage, and eventually has his own brother killed. By the film's final shot, sitting all alone in the desolate wintry grounds of his garrisoned family estate, Michael is a cold, heartless despot. "If anything in this life is certain . . . if history has taught us anything," he has said, "it's that you can kill anyone." These films subvert the totemic, oft-mythicized story of American enrichment whereby poor immigrant families come to this country and fulfill their dreams of success by adopting the national ideals of hard work and fair play. Instead, murder begets murder as, over a couple of generations, more and more people are sucked into a world of greed, lies, and deadly grudges.

After the praises and awards showered upon the first two films, *The Godfather, Part 3* (1990) was something of a disappointment, with scenes and sequences (and certainly the musical score) that strike one as all too familiar. Coppola received particular criticism for casting his daughter Sophia in the pivotal role of Michael's daughter Mary, a part that was beyond her abilities as an actress. Catholicism, whose rites and ritual so imbue the Corleones' lives, moves center stage, as the family has direct (albeit questionable) dealings with the Vatican and a repentant Michael tries to disentangle himself from the world of crime—only to be sucked back in, with devastating results.

The comparatively few post-1960s epics depicted individuals as victims of political and economic graft or as pawns caught up in social revolution and upheaval. Michael Cimino's *Heaven's Gate* (1980) achieved infamy as *the* example of an obsessive, uncompromising director nearly bankrupting his studio. The film tells an important story of nineteenth-century immigrant settlers in Wyoming and the money-hungry empire builders who annihilate them, and it includes breath-taking photography and impressive period detail. However, Cimino's devotion to visuals was not matched by attention to storytelling or character development, and the prodigal expenses (the entire crew flew to Oxford because Princeton was not available; costumes for thousands of extras included period undergarments that were never seen), gleefully reported in the media, ensured a major financial loss. The effect of amazing set pieces, including a "dance" by homesteaders on roller skates in a huge prairie hall, are undercut by long stretches of film wherein dialogue is unintelligible and character motivation nonexistent. Warren Beatty's *Reds* (1981), for which he was producer, director (winning an Academy Award) and star, tells the story of John Reed, author of *Ten Days that Shook the World*, journalist and idealistic social reformer, who became captivated from afar with the revolution in Russia, eventually traveling there as witness, newspaper correspondent, and Communist martyr. The love story is rather heavy-handed at times (his lover Louise Bryant, played by Diane Keaton, overcomes everything—including a Russian winter—to achieve a miraculous reunion with Reed), but the tone remains bittersweet, as Reed becomes disillusioned with the very system he has championed. Bernardo Bertolucci's *The Last Emperor* (1987) is a biography of Pu Yi, last emperor of China, and his passive endurance of circumstances utterly beyond his control—whether they be the familial machinations that put him on the throne or the revolution that toppled his empire. Bertolucci's was the first Western film to be shot in Beijing's Forbidden City, actual fortress of the emperors, and the spectacle and grandeur of these sequences is unsurpassed. The film won nine Academy Awards, including those for Best Picture, Director, and Cinematography, the latter going to Vittorio Storaro for his stunning photography. Color, particularly red and the yellow reserved for the imperial family, is masterfully utilized. Despite its huge canvas, however, the film never loses sight of its human drama, of the quiet, shy man brought up to rule millions but eventually under house arrest in a bleak, desolate outpost, pressured to function as a pawn of the invading Japanese.

1990 to the Present

Like the widescreen phenomenon of the 1950s, another technological revolution in cinema in the 1980s and 1990s spurred a small but incredibly profitable resurgence in spectacular film epics. Computers and digital effects allow for endless visual possibilities, so that almost any image the mind conjures can be realistically depicted on screen. George Lucas, the force behind (and frequent director of) the *Star Wars* films, created his own special-effects company, Industrial Light and Magic (ILM), which has been at the forefront of innovation in both film image and sound. ILM provided the effects for most of Steven Spielberg's spectaculars, such as Neverland derring-do in *Hook* (1991), the dinosaurs in *Jurassic Park* (1993), and the dazzling world of the future in *Minority Report* (2002). Computer-generated imagery (CGI) has been used in all manner of films, from *Forrest Gump* (1994) to *The Mask* (1994). Of particular use in spectacle films is the optical effect called the "composite," which combines into one frame elements that were photographed or created at different times, such as background, sets, and actors. Composites have long been used in Hollywood; *Gone With the Wind* combined foreground photography and background painted mattes, as well as superimposition of several filmed shots, such as in Scarlett and Rhett's escape from a burning Atlanta. But the image capabilities of computers are truly revolutionary. What these effects mean for filmmakers is that a background or setting such as a desert can simply be computer-generated instead of requiring a David Lean to swelter and lose film stock in the heat. A few hundred extras can be hired and filmed, instead of thousands, and then those numbers can be visually enhanced tenfold. Countless costumes needn't be created, for they too can be done on the computer. To cite just one example, some sequences in *Star Wars: Episode I—The Phantom Menace* (1999) are entirely computer creations—no photography was done. In other sequences, the sky was photographed, a model city was filmed, various separate landscapes were filmed and reassembled as one, and then computers created action within the scene, which is a composite of all the several parts. The climactic battle scene, involving thousand of computer-generated (CG) warriors, required no hiring of extras or making of costumes; these were created by the computer and set within a digitally modified filmed landscape (Mast and Kawin 2003, 599). The *Star Wars* films take place in the future, combining generic epic elements with those of science fiction (see **Science Fiction and Fantasy**), Saturday afternoon film serials, and the Western (see **Western**).

The new age of epics truly arrived with the production of J. R. R. Tolkien's *Lord of the Rings*. Like the fantasy novels on which they are based, the films constitute a trilogy: *The Fellowship of the Ring* (2001), *The Two Towers* (2002), and *The Return of the King* (2003). The three films were shot all at once in New Zealand under the direction of Peter Jackson, and the "numbers" are indeed impressive: a fifteen-month shooting schedule; budgets of roughly $120 million per film; a worldwide gross—for all three films—of $3 billion just a year after the final installment was released; six million feet of film shot; 19,000 costumes, seventeen Academy Awards in total (eleven for the third part), and so on. Tolkien was a language and literature professor at Oxford, steeped in medieval epic tales of monsters, treasure hoards, warrior knights, and elves, and he wove a twisting, three-book story set in a world, Middle-earth, that he had been painstakingly constructing in his own imagination for decades. The creatures of Middle-earth range from the Ents (like walking trees), to the beautiful and immortal Elves, to the orcs (goblin soldiers of the evil powers), to the small, hairy-footed (but otherwise thoroughly human) hobbits. All these creatures have their own languages in the books, and new dialogue and songs were composed in those languages for the films. The trilogy is an epic struggle between good and evil, revolving around a magical Ring with a nearly irresistible allure of power. Hobbit-underdog Frodo (Elijah Wood) is entrusted with undertaking a treacherous journey to destroy the Ring in the fires of Mount Doom and thereby shatter its power to give the resurrected dark lord Sauron dominion over the whole world. He is assisted by various traveling companions and champions, including warrior-king Aragorn (Viggo Mortensen), warrior-elf Legolas (Orlando Bloom), and wizard sage Gandalf (Ian McKellen), while threatened and hindered in his expedition by all manner of wickedness, such as good-wizard-gone-bad Saruman (Christopher Lee) and Ring-coveting Gollum (a computer-generated creature, modeled after the movements and expressions of actor Andy Serkis). Each film has its own huge set piece, usually a battle sequence, which is seemingly limitless in scope. In *The Two Towers*, 10,000 wicked Uruk-hai—über-orcs who can endure sunlight—storm the good guys' fortress of Helm's Deep. The number of baddies is upped to 200,000 in *The Return of the King* as that many orcs lay siege to our heroes at Minas Tirith. These sequences involved weeks of filming several hundred extras and horses in vast New Zealand sets, and then the real work began: many more weeks of CG manipulation and enhancement to add a fantasy element to the settings and increase the number of combatants many times over. By the end of the final film, after many risks, loyalties, and hardships, the ring and its inherent evil are destroyed. Goodness triumphs, the king gets the girl, the hobbit gets eternal life, and quite a few people made lots and lots of money.

Clearly, audiences still flock to "big" pictures, happy to lose themselves for a few hours in the sweep and computer-aided spectacle of a recreated past that inevitably reinforces contemporary mores and standards. Once again "bigger is better," as proven by the millions who turned up to see James Cameron's *Titanic* (1997), a marriage of spectacle and social commentary in which bureaucracy and the system kill the little man but, as Celine Dion sings, "our love will go on and on . . ." Publicity surrounding the making of the film, which took years to complete and spiraled uncontrollably over budget, predicted a box office disaster along the lines of *Heaven's Gate*, but audiences, particularly women (many of whom became repeat viewers), embraced the splashy sets, costumes, and hyper-romantic love story; ignored the bad writing; and made it the most financially successful film of its time. It won eleven Academy Awards, including those for best film and director. *Titanic* and *Gone With the Wind* are rare among epics in that they feature female protagonists. Otherwise, the genre is decidedly masculine, emphasizing action and size (pun intended) over—although not necessarily in place of—characterization and human relationships.

More recently, a spate of ancient historical "sword and sandal" epics, bringing the genre full circle, has proven popular. Current cinema-going audiences—

those who determine huge box-office success (*Titanic* notwithstanding)—are decidedly young and predominantly male, and these films shy away from too much moral ambiguity (the good guy beats the bad system) in favor of rough and tumble action, brawny heroes, and spectacular CG effects. Proof of the testosterone-laden epics' potency was the tremendous financial success of *Gladiator* (2000), which also managed to win Academy Awards as best picture and for its star, Russell Crowe. Like the rebellious slave in *Spartacus* who takes on the Roman Empire, gladiator Maximus Meridas uses his martial prowess to gain fame and sufficient power to take on the Emperor's son (who managed to have Maximus, a Roman general, sold into slavery and gladiator-hood in the first place).

A banner year for the genre was 2004, which saw three sprawling historical epics that, at a time when the United States was at war, unsurprisingly emphasize military conflict and clan loyalty. Wolfgang Peterson, inspired by David Lean, cast the latter's Lawrence of Arabia, Peter O'Toole, as King Priam in *Troy,* a take on *The Iliad.* To ensure young audiences, Peterson also cast heartthrobs Orlando Bloom (Paris), Eric Bana (Hector), and Brad Pitt (Achilles). The gods and their manipulation of men and battles were jettisoned, as was nuance, from the story, while spectacle, battles large and small, and gym-toned male biceps and chests are emphasized. *King Arthur* angered historians and purists with its version of a Russian warrior Arthur, brought by the Romans to control their imperial outpost in Briton against Saxon hordes, but does feature a good-versus-evil storyline, lots of combat, and a bow and arrow-toting, leather bikini-clad Guinevere (Keira Knightley). Finally, Oliver Stone's independently financed *Alexander* stars Irish bad boy Colin Farrell, in a blond wig, as the fourth-century B.C. conqueror of the world. Farrell hasn't the power or charisma to carry the monumental film, nor does Stone adequately establish the hero's character and mythic status, thus creating a hole at the picture's center. Two battle sequences, the first against the Persians and the second in the Indian forest, are wonders of computer digitization and effects, but these techniques have become the norm in big-budget films. Farrell's nude scene and Alexander's apparent bisexuality were slightly toned down to court male audiences; perhaps that was also the rationale in hiring the voluptuous Angelina Jolie, one year Farrell's senior, to play his mother in the film. Her over-the-top, bizarrely accented performance supplies a bit of fun in the at times tedious three-hour movie.

In the same year the Biblical epic made its reappearance, more or less, in Mel Gibson's *The Passion of the Christ*. Envisioned as a work of religious art rather than entertainment by the devoutly Catholic Gibson, the film offers no DeMillean eroticism. Instead, the pains of the (seemingly interminable) scourging and crucifixion of Jesus (played by Jim Caviezel) are shown in terrifyingly vivid detail. For Christian viewers, the film is a heartbreaking reminder of the price of their redemption. Perhaps taking a leaf from Tolkien, Gibson put all the dialogue in Latin and ancient Aramaic, only some of which is translated in subtitles. In retrospect, Gibson's *Braveheart* (1995), about the fourteenth-century Scottish patriot William Wallace, can be seen as a dry run for *The Passion*, as the hero is put to death by torture, on Good Friday, on a cross-shaped stone slab, while the ghost of his wife is a loving presence amid the jeering crowd just as is the Virgin Mary in *The Passion.*

The financial success of recent epics, driven by a preponderance of young male cinemagoers, ensures their continued production. As this genre reinvents itself upon the arrival of various new technologies, one can but wonder what directions await the film epic after today's exploitation of computer-generated images—and steroids.

References and Further Reading

Doherty, Thomas. *Pre-Code Hollywood: Sex, Immorality, and Insurrection in American Cinema 1930–1934.* New York: Columbia University Press, 1999.

Eames, John Douglas. *The Paramount Story.* New York: Crown, 1985.

Elley, Derek. *The Epic Film: Myth and History.* London: Routledge and Kegan Paul, 1984.

Mast, Gerald, and Bruce Kawin. *A Short History of the Movies.* 8th ed. New York: Longman, 2003.

Munn, Michael. *The Stories Behind the Scenes of the Great Film Epics.* Walford, England: Illustrated Pub. Co. Ltd., 1982.

Robertson, Patrick. *Guinness Film Facts and Feats.* New York: Sterling/Guinness, 1985.

Smith, Gary A. *Epic Films: Casts, Credits and Commentary on Over 350 Historical Spectacle Movies.* 2nd ed. Jefferson, NC: McFarland, 1991.

Sobchack, Vivian. "'Surge and Splendor': A Phenomenology of the Hollywood Historical Epic." In *Film Genre Reader III,* edited by Barry Keith Grant, 296–323. Austin: University of Texas Press, 2003.

CHAPTER 5

FILM NOIR

OUT OF THE DARK, a car comes screeching around a corner onto the rain-soaked pavement. Streetlights cast slanted shadows, with the oblique lines of a dark city silhouetted in the background as the car whizzes by. Inside, a woman in a long coat, scarf, and sunglasses and a man in a fedora careen down the dimly illuminated street ahead of them to an unknown destination, symbolic of their uncertain fate. The generic scene just described is reminiscent of any number of films now classified by film critics and historians as film noir, a collection of American motion pictures produced in their heyday, roughly 1941 through 1959. Characterized by a prevailing sense of alienation and doom, the film noir impulse can be seen in many contemporary films, even though its golden era ended when color processes became the mainstay in popular American cinema and the concerns of the American public turned from post–World War II alienation to Cold War angst.

DEFINING CHARACTERISTICS

Literally translated, film noir means *black film*, a reference predominantly to the prevailing mood and subject matter of this group of films rather than their cinematography and lighting, with its contrasting uses of darkness and shadows. Coined in 1946 by French critic Nino Frank based on a series of American films shown in post–World War II France, the term itself is somewhat of a misnomer, since no films would by definition be considered "white films" by contrast, at least not in the sense of a predominant lighter mood or tone. Films with more upbeat or optimistic themes might better be considered varieties of comedies. Rather, the term *black* comes to mean an overwhelming sense of uncertainty, moral ambiguity, anxiety, questionable motives, and violence that typifies these films. Although not all films that explore these themes would be considered films noir, some of these themes must be present in some form for the example to be classified within this category.

Ambiguity about the term *film noir* spotlights questions about the notion of the genre itself. The individuals making these films with regularity throughout the 1940s and 1950s would not have called them films noir; instead, they might use expressions such as *crime dramas*, *crime thrillers*, or *suspense stories* to describe the meshing of certain narrative and visual elements. Although they recognize and can agree upon most of the elements commonly identified as film noir, not all film critics or historians agree that the films containing most of these elements really belong to a separate genre. Some see these films as too diverse narratively to constitute separate categorization, whereas others consider films noir as a subgenre of crime films. As a result, no discussion of film noir would be complete without some understanding of the debate as it currently stands. In the first significant book-length examination of American film noir to appear, the 1955 *Panorama du film noir américain*, authors Raymond Borde and Étienne Chaumeton argue that the films embodying noir characteristics should be best considered a series rather than a genre. They define *series* as a collection of films from one country with "essential traits" such as style, atmosphere, and subject matter that indelibly mark them and give them a distinctive character over time, usually derived from earlier and recognizable features from prior films. A series lasts for varying periods of time, largely determined by audience appeal, and it normally peaks once the most representative or "purest expression" of the form has been achieved. Attempting to account for why films with many variations in plots and settings can be considered noir, the authors note that films in series often respond to a particular moment in history; once that initial historical impulse reaches the peak described, the defining features of the series filter out into sequels and films in other genres.

Echoing the work of Raymond Durgnat, a pioneer in the classification of film noir cycles and motifs, American writer, director, and producer Paul Schrader (*Taxi Driver* [1976], *Raging Bull* [1980], and *Affliction* [1997]) claims that films noir are disqualified as a genre because they cannot be categorized by their conflicts and settings (as are Westerns [see **Western**], for example), but rather by a more subtle emphasis on mood and tone. In contrast, Foster Hirsch, in *The Dark Side of the Screen: Film noir*, argues that all genres operate within visual and narrative conventions, which film noir demonstrates in abundance, and audiences in the 1940s, when these films were produced most prevalently in America, quickly caught on to the repetition of these visual and narrative patterns sufficiently for filmmakers to target such films to audiences. This "shared acknowledgment," as Hirsch calls it, qualifies film noir for genre status, resulting in films with visual and narrative codes as significantly embedded as in Westerns.

Whether film noir is a genre, a subgenre of crime films, a series, or something else, its critical history is self-defining; that is, the defining features originally identified in groundbreaking films in this category have been gleaned from the repetition of elements in film after film, rather than defined beforehand and consciously translated into the classic examples of "black cinema" by filmmakers. As with most artistic or cultural impulses, as the trend toward films noir continued, conventions and features evolved and were added to, but the following list outlines several defining characteristics of the classic film noir. It is important to note, then, that not all films classifiable as film noir will contain all of these elements, but many films in this genre will contain more than a few. Similarly, a prevailing mood of tension or melancholy or a creative use of lighting does not by itself make a film noir. The inclusion of a film in this category requires a stylized use of these elements in combination with the pervading mood associated with films noir. For ease of understanding, we have divided the characteristic elements into two categories: narrative and visual.

Narrative Elements

Mood

Films in this genre contain an overwhelming, stifling air of anxiety, tension, confusion, alienation, deception, duplicity, contradiction, entrapment, abandonment, and melancholy, a result more of complicated plots than of violence. Characters often possess shifting, mysterious personalities and operate according to hidden agendas that rapidly change, throwing off the viewers' moral compass and shrouding the events and circumstances depicted in the plot in moral ambiguity. The individuals who populate these films can trust no one, and viewers often experience this same absence of moral and emotional certitude. The film noir world is a moral and psychological minefield that can explode into crisis and chaos at any time.

Plot

The tension and alienation that viewers experience often results from convoluted plots purposely intended to confuse and twist them in narrative knots. Although film noir relies on an almost documentary-style realism to suture the audience into the narrative, audience members can only momentarily rest on any secure narrative ground in this contradictory, shifting world. The result is a disorienting, nightmarish, surreal quality in these films. A classic example can be found in Howard Hawks's 1946 version of Raymond Chandler's novel *The Big Sleep,* starring Humphrey Bogart as Philip Marlowe. By the end of this tale of murder, blackmail, sexual intrigue, infidelity, and family loyalty, audiences never discover who murdered Sean Regan, the Sternwood family chauffeur, or his real link to the missing wife of gambler Eddie Mars. Audiences are drawn into the plot by stylistic elements, sexual innuendo, and the suggestion that all points in the narrative will be resolved, but the payoff, to use a hard-boiled term, often never comes.

Violence

Violence is a significant feature, resulting from murder and other criminal behavior, revenge, payback, coercion, car crashes, accidental deaths, pistol whipping, fixed prize fights, domestic humiliation and abuse, and alcoholic blackouts. As Borde and Chaumeton point out, characters in films noir are denied a fair fight. Violent impulses are unrestrained, erupt spontaneously, and originate from any corner, rather than following the intricate and implicit code understood in the depiction of Old West shootouts or crime movies, a "code of thieves" of sorts.

Crime

Films noir can explore any theme, but most thematic variations can be boiled down to one: crime. Of the eleven film noir subvariations identified by Durgnat, nearly all of them involve crime in some way: crime dramas that offer social criticism, films in which gangsterism becomes a heroic counterforce against Nazism and communism and then later becomes the subject of governmental crime probes; chase films; private eye capers; murderous melodramas among the respectable middle classes; presentations that focus on the paranoia of doubling and the mystification and allure of portraits; and exposés of sexual pathology and the psychopathic personality.

Unlike the gangster film of the late 1920s and 1930s, in which the fate of the criminal is sealed from the outset and events are depicted from the outside, and the detective story or whodunit, where the narrative focuses on solving the crime, the film noir focuses on the psychology of the criminal and where it takes him or her or how it accounts for the chaos that erupts as a result. Audiences are often made to identify with these lawbreakers and often root for them, although they know the characters' downfall is inevitable. As a result, the moral compass of the film is disrupted, calling into question the innocence of the alleged victims of this criminal behavior. Ambiguity surrounds these so-called victims because they usually contribute to their own victimization in some way by getting mixed up with the wrong individuals, letting down their moral guard to indulge in one-time seemingly harmless behavior that proves to be potentially deadly, or succumbing to greed or frustration and the temptation of advancement. If the police are present to stem the seeming tide of criminal activity, even they are suspect and corruptible. The private detective, then, becomes the police surrogate, with only his own moral and mortal destiny in peril in the upside-down ethical world of film noir.

Setting

Usually an American urban or urban-type environment is the norm, although films noir have been set or partially set in small towns (*Beyond the Forest* [1949]; *Shadow of a Doubt* [1943]; *The Strange Love of Martha Ivers* [1946]), rural environments (*Leave Her to Heaven* [1945]; *Impact* [1949]), along highways (*The Postman Always Rings Twice* [1946]; *Detour* [1947]), along the sea coast (*Mildred Pierce* [1945]), and in foreign cities (*The Third Man* [1949]; *Night and the City* [1950]; *Man on the Eiffel Tower* [1949]). Desert settings also reveal the aridness and alienation of the noir universe, as in *Touch of Evil* (1958) and *Detour* (1945). When included, the countryside often provides the noir "hero" with solace and a sense of release, but the ominous often intrudes (as in *Impact*). The anonymity of the city increases the alienation and claustrophobia indicative of the vintage film noir, emphasized by the oblique lines of nondescript urban structures, flashing neon signs that interrupt the darkness, and the air of menace and lure of sexual excess that lurks in every corner and down every alley. Of the noir city, Andrew Dickos writes in *Street With No Name: A History of the Classic American Film Noir*, "The criminality and passions driving many noir characters stem from the premise that the insecurity of existence here promises little in rectitude, and so pursuing one's obsessions becomes acceptable, even desirable, in the face of an unclear future" (2002, 63).

Characters

These films are populated by a variety of character types whose prominence often dictates the film's narrative structure and narrative progression. Private investigators, gamblers, businessmen, con men, three-time losers, murderers and petty criminals, rum runners, bartenders, hitchhikers, police officers and their surrogates such as government agents, prison wardens, psychopaths, newspaper reporters, prison inmates, call girls or "hostesses," nightclub singers, boxers, adulterers, writers, drifters—in short, all figures who represent the broad sociological and psychological panorama of life in postwar America and its detachment and the uncertainty of the Cold War can be players in film noir games. While multiple film noir character types may appear in the same film, normally one or two come to the fore and become the predominant personas the film centers on or explores.

Some character types, in particular, figure prominently again and again in films in this genre. The first, the private eye or "private dick," is often hired to solve a murder or find a missing person, but events spiral out of control and the investigator fights hard to preserve the cool observational powers on which his success on the case and his survival so depend. In John Huston's *The Maltese Falcon* (1941), for example, Sam Spade, played by Humphrey Bogart, is initially hired by Brigid O'Shaughnessy (Mary Astor) to find her missing sister, but this task is really a cover for tracking the whereabouts of her competitors for the fabled bird of the title. Similarly, Mark McPherson (Dana Andrews) in Otto Preminger's *Laura* (1944) becomes entranced by the portrait of a woman whose murder he is supposed to be solving, and he is sent on a wild goose chase by the bon vivant and radio announcer (Clifton Webb) who actually murdered Laura's look-alike by mistake out of a jealous rage.

In plots in which victims commit a one-time crime, engage in a one-time moral transgression, or are accused or drawn into crimes they did not commit, films often chronicle the progressive downfall of the individual, as in Edgar Ulmer's *Detour*, in which an unwitting nightclub pianist en route to a reunion with his fiancée becomes involved in the accidental death of a man giving him a ride. Certain that he will be accused of a crime, he assumes the man's identity and falls victim to the blackmail scheme of a woman from the man's most recent past, leaving him literally stumbling along down an abandoned road to an uncertain future. Similarly, successful insurance agent Dick Powell, in *Pitfall* (1948), compromises his happy home and forever alters the status of his marriage to his high school sweetheart in a jealous rivalry for a mobster's girlfriend. And Edmond O'Brien in *D.O.A.* (1950) steps out on his small-town girlfriend in a bar, giving a murderer a chance to spike his drink with a slow-acting poison and ultimately preventing O'Brien from supplying evidence in a murder case he doesn't even know he's involved in yet.

These males often lose their detachment and become victims through the seductive charms of a femme fatale, an alluring woman with sexual and

Dick Powell's Philip Marlowe looks warily at shady Clare Trevor in a scene from Edward Dmytryk's *Murder, My Sweet* (1941). *Photofest.*

manipulative powers far stronger than they can withstand. The damsel-in-distress-cum-black-widow preys on the protagonist's weakness while she ensnares him in her net of violence and eroticism, a game he often goes along with in an arrogant belief that he is in control. In other cases, the appeal and agendas of these women often serve as a catalyst for devious plans or temptations the man already fantasizes about but hasn't the courage to put into play by himself. By the time he realizes just how little he is pulling the strings of his own destiny, his fate is sealed with hers as both ride a downward spiral of lawbreaking, violence, and eventual death or its equivalent. Classic examples of the devouring film noir femme fatale include Barbara Stanwyck in Billy Wilder's *Double Indemnity* (1944), who convinces "bored" insurance agent Fred MacMurray to murder her husband; Jane Greer's murderous Kathie Moffett in *Out of the Past* (1947); Yvonne DeCarlo in Robert Siodmak's *Criss Cross* (1949); and Lizabeth Scott in *Dead Reckoning* (1947).

Moreover, narratives that focus on the obsessed, the maniacal, or the psychologically afflicted often replace the typical detachment of the film noir private eye or his surrogate with the distorted perspective or heightened psychology of the troubled individual. In *Spellbound* (1945), for example, Hitchcock blends Salvador Dali's surrealist imagery with traditional Freudian elements to create the nightmarish world of Gregory Peck's amnesia. In other cases, doubling, or the appearance of the "evil twin," offers filmmakers a method to examine obsessive or aberrant psychology, as in Robert Siodmak's *The Dark Mirror* (1946), starring Olivia de Havilland in a dual role.

Chronology

A traditional sense of time and chronology is disrupted, often accomplished through the use of flashback and voice-over. Many films noir make significant use of flashbacks, and sometimes flashbacks within flashbacks, furthering the disorientation of these films and creating a sense of chaos and dissociation from viewers. Often, the narrative structure of these films is nothing but flashbacks, sometimes under the guise of police questioning—a distancing feature that enhances the cool detachment and assessment indicative of the film noir world view. In Michael Curtiz's *Mildred Pierce*, for example, Joan Crawford narrates the events that lead to the dissolution of her first marriage, the roots of her restaurant empire, and the betrayal of her daughter and death of her second husband, and in *D.O.A.*, Edmond O'Brien reports to authorities the events that make him a living murder victim. An early example anticipating further development and skillful use of the technique is *The Letter* (1940), directed by William Wyler. In the opening long shot, the camera follows a defiant but determined Bette Davis firing shot after shot at a fleeing figure, with the rest of the film chronicling the investigation of the distinctively noir shooting, often flashing back to Davis's explanations of the events, which do not always jibe with the evidence.

Voice-Over

Voice-over narration performs many functions in film noir. Characters enmeshed in the intricacies of the plot narrate, discuss, lament, comment on, or otherwise describe the twists and turns of the events as they occur. Events are told as if in retrospect and the viewer is being taken back through the circumstances leading up to and contributing to the anxiety of the present moment. In this topsy-turvy, anything-goes-world, voice-over often serves as the only link to stability, normalcy, and the verifiable, but at the same time it creates distancing and emphasizes detachment, particularly when the events narrated do not always match the images presented on screen. Sometimes it is spoken by the criminal himself (Waldo Lydecker in *Laura*), sometimes by the hapless individual drawn into committing a crime or drawn into a crime he did not commit (Walter Neff in *Double Indemnity*; Frank Chambers in *The Postman Always Rings Twice*; Johnny Farrell in *Gilda* [1946]; Al Roberts in *Detour*), sometimes by an individual pinning his or her hopes on the safe outcome of a mishap or seeking to redress a miscarriage of justice (Pat Cameron in *Raw Deal* [1948]), sometimes by an individual later killed (Joe Gilles in *Sunset Boulevard* [1950]), and sometimes by the "voice of God," an unnamed, unidentified individual not implicated in the events in the narrative, as in Anthony Mann's *T-Men* (1947), in which an announcer provides context for the story about to be unfolded for viewers, or in *Impact* (1949), in which a disembodied voice defines the word of the title. In some cases, voice-over narrators are essential to the narrative progression of the story through framing devices but appear infrequently or never directly on screen themselves, as in *The Lady in the Lake* (1947), in which Robert Montgomery, playing Philip Marlowe, is often photographed in a mirror, wryly telling the events in the mystery, and in *A Letter to Three Wives* (1949), in which actress Celeste Home is never even credited for her role even though her character tells the story and precipitates the events of the film. Closely aligned with flashback, voice-over often allows viewers to recognize the difference between what is spoken or narrated and events as they are actually portrayed on screen. In this capacity, first-person voice-over often reveals more about the character and his or her perspective from what he or she fails to disclose than from what the speaker's actual words betray.

Stylistic or Visual Elements

Lighting

By far, chiaroscuro, or contrastive lighting, is the dominant visual element in film noir. More than in typical black-and-white photography, film noir cinematographers adopt the full spectrum of black-and-white tonality, from the hazy, soft texture suggesting the stifling heat of Southern California in *Double Indemnity* to the almost blue-black harshness of the cold city streets surrounding Dennis O'Keefe's prison in Anthony Mann's *Raw Deal*, and everywhere in between. Muted streetlights cast elongated, oval shadows against an inky black backdrop in urban environments, with the shapes of the urban settings barely protruding through the darkness. Flashing neon signs, car radio dials, single lit matches, cigarette lighters, and car headlights pierce the darkness and become the focus of the frame. Shafts of light wrap around corners, creating fractured lines. Highlights ripple across murky rivers, and shallow mud puddles sparkle on rain-soaked streets. Characters are often silhouetted against backdrops whose boundaries are indefinable in the darkness by the human eye, as in the much featured still from *The Big Combo* (1955), directed by Joseph Lewis, in which the backlighting used by cinematographer John Alton turns Jean Wallace, her back to the camera, and Cornel Wilde, facing forward, into stark outlines against a rising cloud of almost silvery smoke and an irregularly circling light. In scenes such as this, the darkness, literal and metaphorical, threatens to swallow up characters rather than set them apart.

Low key lighting distorts faces, recognizable objects, and usually-inviting places, filling the frame with indeterminate, disorienting images and sharpening shadows, turning ordinary spaces into amusement park funhouses. At other times, these lighting techniques emphasize the seediness or claustrophobic atmospheres of settings such as the backrooms of bars, smoke-filled gin joints, roadhouses, boxing arenas, all-night diners, and dimly lit gambling casinos. Faces in this lighting take on a particularly hard or lacquered appearance suggestive of film noir's cool detachment and the femme fatale's icy beauty. In other cases, faces are often obscured or blacked out or presented in half-lighting to suggest the characters' sinister qualities, the uncertainty of their agendas, or the obliteration of individual identify.

In the film noir world, transcendental virtues of truth, honesty, trust, hope, and fidelity no longer survive very long, and the abandonment of traditional high-key and backfill lighting, used to illuminate scenes fully, reflects this shift in attitude and mood. Interior sets, for example, are lit as if at night, with drawn shades, shafts of light invading the darkness from adjoining rooms, or table lights or wall sconces casting low, enclosed puddles of light on objects and characters near by. Often, subdued beams of light are broken into grids by shutters, Venetian blinds, gates, fences, divided windows, the ropes of boxing arenas, or screens, suggesting the entrapment and prison-like atmosphere in which characters often find themselves. In John Huston's *The Maltese Falcon,* for example, as Mary Astor is being lead away by police detectives and turns around in the elevator in one of the last shots of the film, the crisscrossed metallic doors close in front of her face, suggesting the prison sentence that awaits her. Similarly, in Billy Wilder's *Double Indemnity* (1944), in the showdown between the murderous lovers in the Dietrichson living room, the heavy velvet drapes are momentarily pulled back, with the light seeping in between the blinds casting horizontal lines on the room. Director of photography Joseph LaShelle uses similar imagery in *Laura* not only to emphasize the cavernous quality of Laura's empty apartment as a result of her death, but also to highlight her antique grandfather clock containing the murder weapon.

Line

The comforting horizontal lines the human eye has grown to find so appealing are replaced with slanted, vertical, fractured, and otherwise oblique lines and camera angles, enhanced and emphasized by lighting techniques, creating a sense of menace, doom, disorientation, and fragmentation. Gone are the panoramic views of cities stretched out across the horizon as points of reference. Instead, the elongated shapes of big city buildings threaten to crush the bystander below. Dutch angles—shots taken oblique to the vertical and horizontal orientation of the structures in the shot—suggest cut-off escape routes and a topsy-turvy world, as in Orson Welles's *The Third Man* (1949). In addition, in Jules Dassin's *Night and the City*, obliquely photographed city buildings whiz by and threaten to overtake Richard Widmark as he runs for his life from the London docks and through the streets of the British capital, certain that he has been betrayed by the woman he loves. Moreover, in *The Maltese Falcon*, the words *Archer and Spade* painted on the outside window are projected and inverted on the floor of the detective agency in a gray trapezoid, symbolic of the skewed moral landscape lurking out the window as it intrudes to the office environment within.

Focus

Depth of field in all shots remains consistent. That is, elements in the background remain in as clear focus as elements directly in front of the camera's eye. An example occurs in the often-uncategorizable *Citizen Kane* (1940) when Charles Foster Kane is confronted in the ballroom of Xanadu with the loss of his business empire and he paces away from the camera, with his business advisors in the foreground, and then back toward them again. The effect of this noir deep focus, Janey Place and Lowell Petersen write, is such that "the world of the film is thus made a closed universe, with each character seen as just another facet of an unheeding environment that will exist unchanged long after his death; and the interaction between man and the forces represented by that noir environment is always clearly visible" (1999, 67). The method used to achieve this effect was the creative use of wide angles and their tendency to distort images. Place and Petersen cite the first shot of Hank Quinlan in *Touch of Evil* as an extreme example.

Framing

Film noir framing and composition are tight, emphasizing claustrophobia, entrapment, and chaos. Action maintains less importance than the framing of characters within the densely arranged sets. The sharp lines of furniture, curved edges of lampshades, and similar objects within each frame cut across or interfere in the camera's clear point of view. Rather than creating a harmonious, balanced composition, the effect instead suggests enclosure, obstruction, a lack of balance, and a lack of free access.

Symbolic Objects

The repetition of elements of set decoration such as portraits, reflective surfaces, clocks, telephones, neon signs, staircases, gates, street lights, cigarettes, or cars makes them assume symbolic significance beyond their functional purpose. These elements suggest the passage of time, an obsession with appearances or self-disclosure, clouded or obstructed vision, self-delusion, opportunities for self-reflection and examining motives, or dual personalities as well as serving as icons of everyday life in modern, urban societies. For example, as part of his introduction to the police detective in *Laura,* director Otto Preminger photographs Dana Andrews through a glass curio cabinet full of carefully arranged and reflective objets d'art. Later, his character, Mark McPherson, falls in love with the portrait of Laura Hunt hanging over her fireplace, a woman whose murder he is responsible for solving. Edward G. Robinson in *Woman in the Window* (1945) and *Scarlet Street* (1945), both directed by Fritz Lang, is brought to a tragic end by women in portraits—one with whom he becomes obsessed in a window next to his men's club and the other whose portrait he actually paints from life, a portrait that she and her ne'er-do-well boyfriend pass off as her own work. In *The Night Has a Thousand Eyes* (1948), Robinson (as mentalist John Triton) sees premonitions of his own death in a hallway mirror. *The Lady from Shanghai* (1948) features the famous hall-of-mirrors confrontation scene. Moreover, Alfred Hitchcock reflects the murder of Miriam Haines in *Strangers on a Train* (1951) in the victim's own eyeglasses, discarded in the grass at her feet. And in the famous opening sequence from *Sunset Boulevard,* Billy Wilder photographs William Holden, face down in the swimming pool, from a fish's perspective at the bottom.

Clocks figure prominently in Anthony Mann's *Raw Deal* as Claire Trevor patiently ticks off the moments until she and Dennis O'Keefe can make a safe escape from a police dragnet. In John Farrow's *The Big Clock* (1948), a large timepiece in the lobby of business mogul Charles Laughton's office building, synchronizing all of his worldwide enterprise, comes to symbolize his megalomania as well as serving as a hiding place for his editor Ray Milland once Milland has discovered that his boss is a murderer. A characteristic cigarette lighter with crossed tennis rackets becomes a key part of Robert Walker's blackmail scheme in *Strangers on a Train* (1951). The telephone becomes an instrument of psychological torture in Anatole Litvak's *Sorry, Wrong Number* (1948), and the telephone cord becomes a means of accidental death in *Detour.*

Water

Water takes on almost primal or elemental importance, often photographed as gushing out of a downspout, lying in puddles on darkened streets, or softly falling against windowpanes. Film noir settings are often photographed as if it has just rained, but not the benign rain of baptism and rebirth. Rather, the rain comes to symbolize psychological burdens, physical obstruction, alienation, despair, loss, cold, decay, and foreboding doom. In *Scarlet Street*, for example, Chris Cross (Edward G. Robinson) uses an umbrella to fend off a would-be attacker of femme fatale Kitty March (Joan Bennett) in the rain-soaked streets of Greenwich Village, a pivotal event that starts him on a road to murder and insanity. Barbara Stanwyck and Fred MacMurray drive through rain-drenched streets in executing their plot to kill her husband in Wilder's *Double Indemnity.* And it's pouring down rain when Barbara Stanwyck clubs her hated aunt, drawing Van Heflin and Kirk Douglas into a web of blackmail and wasted lives in *The Strange Love of Martha Ivers*.

HISTORY AND INFLUENCES

As a term, *film noir* refers to an era in American, if not Western, filmmaking as much as it does a mood or style. As with most aesthetic styles, no single moment in film history can probably be unequivocally identified as the birth of "black film." Not surprisingly, film historians and critics disagree on when exactly the film noir impulse can said to have started. Some critics believe the first examples of noir filmmaking began as early as 1939, with Columbia's *Let Us Live* and *Blind Alley* and Universal's *Rio*. Others point to RKO's *Strangers on the Third Floor* (1940) (Lyons 2002, 35). Still others cite John Huston's adaptation of Dashiell Hammett's *The Maltese Falcon* as the most likely first unified cinematic presentation of narrative and visual elements later identified or associated with film noir, although some believe that the one-dimensional nature of the characters in the adaptation, as well as the evidence of moral imperative in the narrative (Sam Spade's commitment to discovering the murder of his business partner and avenging it), make the film more an anticipation of later films noir rather than a fully realized example. The Betty Grable vehicle *I Wake Up Screaming* (1942) also gets mentioned as the first American film that fully represents the moral ambiguity and alienated nature that typifies the films in this genre.

Similarly, not everyone agrees on when film noir in its classic phrase ended. Some cite 1953 as the year when a new emphasis on political suspense began supplanting the postwar alienation of the genre. Others cite 1958, the year Orson Welles's *Touch of Evil* was released, as the last year of film noir's classic phase. After that, the depiction of noir-like conventions and stylistics were generally considered to be, in the words of Foster Hirsch, a "self-consciously resurrected form," referred to as either "noirish," "neo-noir," or "revisionist noir" (1981, 202, 204).

Regardless of when the genre truly began, the majority of film historians clearly acknowledge that by 1946 a new attitude was being explored in the American crime film and crime-related thriller. In his important "Notes on Film Noir," Paul Schrader breaks down the classic era into three discernable subperiods, some of which overlap:

Orson Welles stars as corrupt police captain Hank Quinlan in *Touch of Evil* (1958), a film regarded as marking the end of film noir's classic phase. *Photofest.*

> *1941–1946:* The private eye, or "the lone wolf," predominates as film noir protagonist. These films benefited from the significant resources of the major studios in terms of production design and sets, and A-film directors signed on to shoot these productions. "Talk" supplanted "action" as the source of narrative interest.
>
> *1945–1949:* More hard-edged protagonists supplant the romanticism of the private eye on a mission to solve a mystery. This postwar realistic period focuses on crime as a problem erupting in the streets, political corruption, and the nature of "police routine." Proletarian directors create a more realistic urban look.
>
> *1948–1953:* Schrader calls this period the era of "psychotic action" and "suicidal impulses." He writes, "The psychotic killers, who in the first period [had] been a subject worthy of study, in the second a fringe threat, now became the active protagonist" (59). This period, the least romantic phase and, in Schrader's mind, the best, also saw the creation of the B-movie noir and the "psychoanalytically inclined" director. (1999, 58–61)

The film noir mood and attitude probably result from several conditions, and the resulting filmmaking style and technique have been influenced by earlier craftsmanship and cinematic styles and exemplars, both from America and abroad. The prevailing mood of alienation and disillusionment, experienced by returning servicemen who had defeated fascism abroad as well as by the individuals who had sacrificed for the war effort at home, was reflected in a desire for a grittier, realistic portrayal of the fluctuating world. After over a decade of pumping out films serving as an escape from the dire economic circumstances of the Great Depression and boosting morale for the struggle for international political, economic, and social equilibrium in World War II, filmmakers found themselves free to express the mounting anxiety and disillusionment experienced in the post-war period. Documentary and newsreel photographic techniques contributed to the reality-based and hard-edged look of many films in this genre, as well as their narratives. The earliest examples in the noir vein, films such as *The Maltese Falcon* and *Laura,* embodied most of the principal mood and style epitomized by the genre, but films appearing after the war contained a harder edge and more sardonic character, as Schrader confirms.

In addition to lessons and techniques learned from documentary-style filmmaking during World War II, film noir lighting owes much to Expressionist painting, German Expressionist cinema from the 1920s, Italian Neo-Realism, and the emerging noir atmosphere of 1930s French cinema. It is no accident that many of the most significant film noir directors learned their craft in the studios of Germany and Austria, including such greats as Fritz Lang (*The Woman in the Window; Scarlet Street; The Big Heat* [1953]), Robert Siodmak (*Phantom Lady* [1944]; *The Killers* [1944]; *The Dark Mirror; Criss Cross* [1949]; and *The File on Thelma Jordan* [1950]), and Billy Wilder (*Double Indemnity; Sunset Boulevard;* and *Ace in the Hole* [1951]). The 1920s and 1930s saw an influx of these directors, among others, familiar with the Expressionist technique of lighting artificial sets to create a nightmarish quality, fractured space, disruption of time, chaos, and an overwhelming emphasis on death and loss—all distortions of reality particularly apparent in Robert Wiene's *The Cabinet of Dr. Caligari* (1920), with its skewed sets, oblique lines, and stark shadows. Fritz Lang's *M* (1931) and later Expressionist films begin anticipating the film noir protagonist's attempts to survive in a hyper-real and often difficult world where danger lurks in the shadows. Other Expressionist motifs include an emphasis on subjective reality, such as sequences in which the camera replicates the fevered consciousness or perspective of an individual in crisis or when a character's point of view stands in for the camera's eye (Hirsch 1981, 57).

Moreover, Italian Neo-Realism—embodied by the work of directors Rossellini, De Sica, and Visconti, to name a few—offered a semi-documentary perspective, both visually and in terms of narration, and placed an emphasis on location shooting, but it shifted "crime into the real world and away from the tormented victims" of early years and highlighted law enforcement officials and "protectors of the status quo" rather than the more psychologically marginalized characters emphasized by Expressionism (Hirsch 1999, 67). French cinema of the 1930s, particularly the films of Marcel Carné, Julien Duvivier, Jean Renoir, and Jacques Prévert, contributed more than the mere melancholy and pathos of a preordained, uncaring world. Rather, they portrayed characters succumbing to romantic desire in an effort to rebel against plan. Andrew Dickos describes their link to American noir as follows: "Theirs is the death knell sounding the impossibility of passion fulfilled, and in that failure arrives the noir disposition that leads to personal destruction" (2002, 43–44). Between-the-wars and postwar French films of the noir variety drew particularly from B-movie crime dramas rather than the more prestigious A variety, forging another link to American examples of the same period.

Although European models offered much to the noir sensibility and style and benefited from it as well, American cultural influences cannot be underestimated as having a significant impact on the evolution of "black film," including the American gangster film and the American plastic arts. Although the cultural conditions that made gangster films so appealing during the Depression had disappeared by the classic noir era, they shared with film noir an emphasis on crime; an urban, although interchangeable setting; claustrophobic, smoke-filled interiors settings; and occasional uses of chiaroscuro lighting—in short, all the ingredients or language that would be combined and heightened in the postwar period. Although the protagonists in both types of films ultimately meet their fate (often in the very streets where they lurked), distinct differences in mood, emphasis, and visual effects set films noir separate from conventional crime dramas. Gangsters often take on heroic proportions and are admired for their bravo and self-assertion, whereas film noir protagonists rarely take on a larger-than-life persona, suffering internally in dimly lit corners and alleyways. The film noir hero is a misfit or an introvert; the gangster, a somewhat slow-witted psychotic. Cinematographers during the gangster era made creative uses of black-and-white photography, but it does not resemble the richer, more tonally varied darkness of the film noir world. The crime-infested city of 1930s gangster films such as Howard Hawks' *Scarface: The Shame of the Nation* (1932) or Mervyn LeRoy's *Little Caesar* (1931) does not become a character in the film as does the film noir metropolis. Even the art works of Edward Hopper (*Nighthawks* [1942]; *New York Movie* [1939]) and Reginald Marsh have been mentioned as likely source material for film noir frame composition, cinematography, and prevailing mood of alienation and isolation or at least as emerging simultaneously with the film noir perspective (Hirsch 1999, 82–83).

Visually, film noir traces its roots back to the chiaroscuro lighting and oblique lines and shadows indicative of European cinematic models. Narratively, the genre owes much to America's own tradition or school of hard-boiled detective fiction, pulp magazines, and the introduction of the paperback novel in 1939. Novelists and short story writers such as Dashiell Hammett (*The Thin Man, The Maltese Falcon, The Glass Key*), Cornell Woolrich (*Black Curtain, Black Alibi, Black Angel,* and *The Black Path of Fear*), James M. Cain (*Double Indemnity, Mildred Pierce,* and *The Postman Always Rings Twice*), Raymond Chandler (*Farewell, My Lovely, The Big Sleep,* and *The High Window*), Horace McCoy (*Kiss Tomorrow Goodbye*), and even Ernest Hemingway ("The Killers"), created characters and situations embodying a tough, no-nonsense, earthy sensibility with a devil-may-care lingo to match, features readily translatable to the screen in noir terms. Unlike the genteel whodunits and mystery stories of Edgar Allan Poe, Dorothy Sayers, Sir Arthur Conan Doyle, and Agatha Christie, which emphasized well-reasoned detection of a criminal, American crime stories appearing from the end of the nineteenth century to the 1920s—the pulp fiction of publications like *The Black Mask* and *The Dime Detective*—were gritty, realistic, of the streets, and often written from the perspective of a streetwise hoodlum skirting the law himself or a detective not above using violence to uphold the law. Hemingway was perhaps the only writer of the group to achieve high art status, but Hammett wrote almost exclusively in this style and was the master at perfecting the first-person, tough-talking detective figure. Woolrich's novels and stories were adapted and readapted into films over and over again over a period of several decades, and Chandler's Philip Marlowe is a time-honored character played by no fewer than eight actors in feature films (most famously by Humphrey Bogart in 1946's *The Big Sleep*) and others on TV. In Cain's novels, the criminals often serve as the narrators with little doubt in terms of who committed the crime. Rather, Cain places emphasis on the psychology of the criminal and how they came to be in their present predicament, a detachment perfect for film noir's use of voice-over.

Stylistically, film noir stretched the boundaries of black-and-white cinematgraphic and narrative filmmaking, but the genre also had an impact on various aspects of motion picture making as an industry. With their gritty, realistic emphasis on previously taboo subjects, these films began the progressive loosening of narrative restraints by the Hays Office (later the Breen Office), the enforcer of the 1930s Motion Picture Production Code, which regulated onscreen content. The example of Billy Wilder's *Double Indemnity*—originally optioned in the 1930s and approved for production only after several script rewrites almost ten years later—represents the degree to which motion picture censors dictated the artistic content of motion pictures. The combination of writers and producers with the interest in and ability to produce harder-edged films on more realistic subject matter, in combination with an audience anxious for films that departed from the escapism and morale boosting of the previous decades, forced censors to reconsider the tastes and morals of a society hardened by four years of war and fearing for national security during the Cold War.

No branch of motion picture production was more ready for or more revitalized by the shift to more realistic, documentary-style film noir than B-movie units, so called because of a film's position as the second presentation in a double-featured bill and because of its cut-rate budget. In an effort to lure audiences to the theater during the Depression, theater owners strove to provide three-hour showings of quality entertainment, about the maximum length a film showing could run and be repeated over and over during a day. Few owners could afford to rent two A, or higher budget, features, because rental fees were charged as a percentage of gross rather than a flat fee, and studios charged more for long, high-quality films. A program of one A film and a shorter, and thus more economical to rent, B-movie enabled theater proprietors both to bring in quality entertainment at an affordable price and to get their money's worth out of daily rentals (Lyons 2002, 29–30). The demand for B-movie features became so great that the major studios could not churn them out fast enough, so a number of independent companies such as Monogram, Republic, and Eagle Lion sprung up to meet the clamoring for such films. In *Death on the Cheap: The Lost B Movies of Film Noir,* Arthur Lyons demonstrates how, by the late 1930s, B movies were gaining in status in the industry and each major studio had B-movie units, most of which granted their writers, producers, and directors tremendous autonomy to experiment and develop effective techniques for no additional cost. During this same era, the film noir impulse began emerging, and it seemed only natural that the lessons learned in B-movie production overall would be effectively applied to create many significant and artistic films in the genre. The shorter running time of the B-movie format, dark noir lighting (which camouflaged the repeated use of film sets), and the more character-driven story lines enabled studios to make noir films using fewer resources during wartime. After the war, innovative filming techniques and the documentary style emerging from the war enabled B-movie units to shoot on location and create artistically significant shots for even less cost. The result was a cadre of films noir that rival the best of the genre, such as *Detour, D.O.A.*, and *Raw Deal*.

Although most critics and historians commonly identify the term film noir with its classic phase, films with the noir sensibility continued to be made since the classic phase ended and are still made today. Clearly, the immediate cultural conditions that contributed to the rise of noir mood have changed from alienation to more outright cynicism—perhaps explaining why few exemplars of the noir sensibility emerged in the 1960s and early 1970s. In America, although color photography has replaced the shadows and oblique lines of the classic noir city, neo-noir, as these films might best be labeled, still speaks to viewers, possibly either nostalgically to admirers of Hollywood's golden age or to a new audience of suspense-thriller or action-adventure fans. In France, for example, New Wave directors such as Jean-Luc Godard, Francois Truffaut, and Jean-Pierre Melville, according to Andrew Dickos, ". . . took from American noir cinema [. . .] nothing less than the terrifying glamour of social isolation with its insouciant arrogance, ideological annulment, and rejection of convention [. . .]" (2002, 226–227). Film noir's link to the French New Wave is perhaps most obviously portrayed in *À bout de souffle (Breathless* [1959]*)*, when Godard's Michel Poiccard (Jean Paul Belmondo) stands in front of a poster of his idol Humphrey Bogart and whispers his name as if it had sacred significance.

With crime as a constant, new investigative techniques and new stars add a dimension to this time-honored genre, although more recent noir films are typically conscious attempts on the part of filmmakers to pay homage to an earlier feeling or mood in classic Hollywood cinema while containing violence not possible in the Code era. Neo-noirs have seen the return of old favorites and old story lines, such as political corruption and murder in *Chinatown* (1974) and its sequel *The Two Jakes* (1990) and in Curtis Hanson's *L. A. Confidential* (1997). Detective dramas in the noir vein have even made it into futuristic settings in films such as Ridley Scott's *Blade Runner* (1982). Famous remakes of earlier film noir classics have included *Farewell, My Lovely* (1975) with Robert Mitchum as Philip Marlowe (originally filmed as *Murder, My Sweet* [1944]), *The Postman Always Rings Twice* (1981), *Body Heat* (1981) (following closely the plot line of *Double Indemnity), Against All Odds* (1984) (*Out of the Past* [1947]), and *No Way Out* (1987) (*The Big Clock*). Sam Peckinpah's *The Getaway* (1972; itself remade in 1994), Terence Malik's *Badlands* (1973), and Oliver Stone's *Natural Born Killers* (1994) harken back to the great on-the-run films such as John Stahl's *Deadly Is the Female* (1949; rereleased as *Gun Crazy*). The influence of the hard-boiled school of writing reemerged with the filming of *The Getaway; After Dark, My Sweet* (1990); and *The Grifters* (1990), all based on Jim Thompson novels. Sidney Lumet's *The Morning After* (1986) and Adrian Lyne's *Fatal Attraction* (1986) seem to fall clearly into the noir narrative structure of bystander-turned-victim, such as *Detour* and *D.O.A.*. The neo-noir era has seen the rise of new femmes fatales

Kathleen Turner (*Body Heat*), Sharon Stone (*Basic Instinct* [1992]), Linda Fiorentino (*The Last Seduction* [1994]), and Nicole Kidman (*To Die For* [1995]). David Lynch's *Blue Velvet* (1986) and *Mulholland Drive* (2001), Quentin Tarantino's *Reservoir Dogs* (1992) and *Pulp Fiction* (1994), and Martin Scorsese's *Mean Streets* (1973) and *Cape Fear* (1991) contain a rich mixture of neo-noir narrative elements, visual techniques, and character types.

The classification of film noir as a genre separate from crime or suspense films or the all-encompassing category *drama* will continue to be debated by film scholars and historians. Regardless of its categorization as a genre, series, or cycle, without question, the impulse toward "black cinema" has influenced many films, not just crime films, since the 1940s. Many recent examples suggest that the tendency toward a dark cinema, although perhaps photographed in different ways from the classic era, is not likely to disappear any time soon.

References and Further Reading

Borde, Raymond, and Étienne Chaumeton. "Towards a Definition of Film Noir." In *Film Noir Reader*, 5th ed., edited by Alain Silver and James Ursini, 17–25. New York: Limelight, 1999.

Borde, Raymond, and Étienne Chaumeton. *A Panorama of Film Noir: 1941–1953*. Trans. Paul Hammond. San Francisco: City Light, 2002.

Christopher, Nicholas. *Somewhere in the Night: Film Noir and the American City*. New York: The Free Press, 1997.

Dickos, Andrew. *Street With No Name: A History of the Classic American Film Noir*. Lexington: University of Kentucky Press, 2002.

Durgnat, Raymond. "Paint It Black: The Family Tree of the Film Noir. In *Film Noir Reader*, 5th ed., edited by Alain Silver and James Ursini, 37–51. New York: Limelight, 1999.

Hirsch, Foster. *The Dark Side of the Screen: Film Noir*. New York: Da Capo Press, 1981.

——. *Detours and Lost Highways: A Map of Neo-Noir*. New York: Limelight, 1989.

Kaplan, E. Ann, ed. *Women in Film Noir*. London: BFI, 1998.

Lyons, Arthur. *Death on the Cheap: The Lost B Movies of Film Noir!* New York: Da Capo Press, 2002.

Martin, Richard. *Mean Streets and Raging Bulls: The Legacy of Film Noir in Contemporary American Cinema*. Landham, MD and London: Scarecrow Press, 1999.

Naremore, James. *More Than Night: Film Noir In Its Contexts*. Berkeley: University of California Press, 1998.

Place, Janey, and Lowell Peterson. "Some Visual Motifs of Film Noir." In *Film Noir Reader*, 5th ed., edited by Alain Silver and James Ursini, 65–75. New York: Limelight, 1999.

Schatz, Thomas. "The Hard-Boiled Detective Film." In *Hollywood Genres: Formulas, Filmmaking, and the Studio System*, 111–149. Philadelphia: Temple University Press, 1981.

Schrader, Paul. "Notes on Film Noir." In *Film Noir Reader*, 5th ed., edited by Alain Silver and James Ursini, 53–63. New York: Limelight, 1999.

CHAPTER 6

HORROR

WHAT IS A HORROR FILM? Most film genres are defined by content, but horror is equally identified by its purpose: to frighten. Yet there are all kinds of scary movies. Some jump out at us and cry "Boo!" Others create an ever-increasing sensation of uneasiness and foreboding. Horror comes from all manner of sources, but for our purposes we shall concentrate on movies involving monsters or nonhuman entities. Human sources of fear, whether vicious children, escaped madmen, or serial killers, ground the narrative squarely in the known and familiar world. The twisted little girl in *The Bad Seed*, the ruthless drug dealer in *Wait Until Dark*, and the sick cannibal in *The Silence of the Lambs*—frightening as they might be—are torn from the headlines and, more often than not, inhabit what could be called thriller or suspense films (see **Suspense**). The events could, or do, actually happen. Films properly placed within the horror genre occupy a fantasy world or, even more effectively, demonstrate what might occur were the fantastic and horrible to intrude upon the real world. Our horror comes from knowing it could never happen to us, even as we identify with the hapless characters and the situations within which they find themselves. It's a matter of semantics, of course, but we will say that frightful things that *could* happen to us are terrifying, while scary things that could *never* happen are horrifying.

As is the case with westerns and epics, the horror genre pivots upon a struggle between good and evil. Owing to their origins in Central European folklore and nineteenth-century literature, horror films often incorporate strong religious—specifically, Roman Catholic—iconography and ritual. The arsenal of goodness used to vanquish monstrous movie evil comes directly from the church: crucifixions, holy water, exorcism, crossing oneself, wayside shrines, priestly absolution, and the last rites. Such devices maintain the rightful division between two worlds, ensuring that the dead stay dead and the living alive. It's when the monstrous and the human collide that we're in trouble.

Besides their raison d'être—to frighten audiences—horror films explore transformation. Nature and the established order are tricked or outraged to produce deadly results. All that is expected and familiar becomes transformed into its frightening opposite. With horror, we enter an alternate world in which the normal is turned abnormal. Light into dark, day into night, life into death (or the reverse), man into animal, goodness into evil, sanity into madness—the list of dreadful metamorphoses found in horror films goes on and on. This subversion of the normal outrages our sensibilities and demands restoration of the common order. The components and results of this frightening transformation of the familiar largely constitute the basic features of the horror film.

DEFINING CHARACTERISTICS

Exotic Setting

The initial source for horror films was largely Gothic fiction, from which filmmakers inherited established settings of Romantic isolation and antiquity. The crenellated and multi-towered castle, perched on a remote mountain, is a given, as is the dark and stormy night in which it is introduced. This building often becomes a character in itself, redolent of aristocratic decay and untold evils, a defiant bulwark against the outside world. The mere mention of Castles Frankenstein or Dracula sends villagers into a frenzy of crossing themselves. Evoking Poe in its asymmetrical, illogical design and setting, the castle comes to represent the distorted and perverse world of its inhabitants—establishing and reflecting their unsettled and exaggerated psychological states. Unsurprisingly, the castle becomes a focus of outsiders' fear and hatred and is regularly stormed, attacked, and set afire in attempts to root out its evil. An additional influence upon the distorted, menacing sets is the stylization of German Expressionist silent films, many of whose makers eventually came to work in Hollywood. *The Cabinet of Dr. Caligari* (1919) and *Nosferatu* (1922) create nightmarish worlds of claustrophobic menace through confined, angular, and highly artificial sets and lighting.

Roman Polanski's *Rosemary's Baby* (1968) takes place in contemporary New York City, but is set in the suitably Gothic and then-rundown Dakota building (infamous, years later, as the site of John Lennon's murder). Similarly, large haunted houses figure in countless films; such titles as *The Old Dark House* (1932), *House of Frankenstein* (1944), *House of Dracula* (1945), *The House of Usher* (1960), and *The Haunting* (1963) clearly identify the locus of fear. Like castles, these houses are primary characters in the films, their winding corridors, locked rooms, and vacant windows bespeaking a troubled, secretive past.

To emphasize this sense of the unfamiliar, horror films are often set in the Old World, usually Europe or Egypt and the Middle East; likewise, they may take place in the past and in a remote part of the countryside—the moors, the desert, a swamp, the mountains—to cut the action off from the rest of the world.

The ever-present threat of death or dying is underscored by many scenes set in graveyards, mausoleums, and tombs.

Deformity and Makeup

Just as the grotesque and decaying castle and graveyard sets represent psychic imbalance and corruption, fantastic makeup is used to delineate depravity. Horror films abound in physical deformities. A mangled or horrible physiognomy clues the audience to the malevolent personality within. Frankenstein's monster's patchwork face of sewn-together skins, the wolfman's hirsute countenance, the zombie's hollow stare, the mummy's disintegrating swathe of dusty wrappings, the vampire's sallow, waxy face offset by bloodshot eyes and dirty fangs—evil incarnate is not pretty. Upon long-suffering Boris Karloff, makeup wizard Jack Pierce created the iconic, universally recognized visage of Frankenstein's monster, considered by some to be the most powerful character makeup ever created for the movies, as well as that of the wrinkled, desiccated mummy of high priest Im-ho-tep in *The Mummy* (1932). For Lon Chaney Jr. in *The Wolf Man* (1941), Pierce fashioned the on-camera transformation of mannered aristocrat into furred, fanged werewolf. In addition to monstrous faces, misshapen bodies populate these films: hunchbacks, amputees, circus freaks, and half-man beasts. In order to emphasize the monsters' ugliness, horror films inevitably feature comely young women, paragons of human beauty, who are threatened and hurt but strongly desired by their physical opposites. A recurring theme running through horror films, and voiced at the end of *King Kong* (1933), is that of Beauty and the Beast.

Pity

Even as we recoil from these monsters, we cannot help but pity them at times. Forced by death or by another's will to perform unspeakable deeds, they are the evil Other, shunned by the world, inhabiting the night and forever longing for what they have lost. Unsurprisingly, émigré filmmakers such as James Whale and Karl Freund, transplanted to Hollywood from Europe for political, financial, or personal reasons, evoked emotional poignancy with these stories of ultimate outsiders. In several cases, fearful physiognomy is used ironically: in *Frankenstein* (1931), only the blind hermit interacts with and comes to recognize the worth and childlike innocence of the hideous monster; in *The Wolf Man* (1941), after being killed for helplessly metamorphosing into a savage canine, the werewolf transforms back into gentle, well-bred Larry Talbot; in Tod Browning's *Freaks* (1932), the misshapen circus performers share a camaraderie and compassion largely absent in their "normal" counterparts. Recent writers and critics have had a field day applying queer theory and the like to these "monsters," who are ostracized and shunned because of their perceived abnormalities and difference.

Beauty and the Beast

The transformations that occur within an individual, from man to wolf, living to dead, Jekyll to Hyde, make manifest humans' dual nature of good and evil—we are all potential monsters, trying desperately to hang on to our better nature. This inner turmoil is partly manifested by the monsters' attraction to and desire for beauty (whether for redemption or sexual gratification). King King longs for Fay Wray, and Quasimodo for Esmerelda; Erik, the Phantom of the Opera, kidnaps Christine; Frankenstein's monster demands a bride; *The Creature from the Black Lagoon* (1954) performs a sort of underwater ballet courtship with an oblivious female swimmer; Dracula is enflamed by a miniature painting of Jonathan Harker's fiancée (well, by her throat, at least); *The Mummy* Im-ho-tep risks it all—again, 2,000 years later—in stalking the young woman who is the reincarnation of his lost love. A defining image from countless classic horror films is that of the monster carrying off the limp body of an unconscious beautiful woman to a fate worse than death. These women are almost invariably victims—virgin fiancées and brides, servants and schoolgirls—who scream and faint and suffer until the hero rescues them. Theirs is a passive power over men: beauty that inflames monstrous passions and goodness that redeems wayward heroes (such as overambitious mad scientists) and calls them back to the straight and narrow path. In the slasher films of the 1980s we at last have autonomous, sexual women, but they are made to pay for this carnal independence with their lives.

Outraged Populace

Turning as they do on the theme of good versus evil, horror films dichotomize their casts of characters. Opposing the evildoer is an outraged populace, most predictably the angry villagers, erstwhile happy country folk pushed into overcoming their fear, taking up torches and pitchforks, and storming the evildoer's castle or place of refuge. These might be family members of victims (the father of the drowned girl in *Frankenstein* [1931] spurs the folk-dancing villagers into action) or simply prospective victims themselves, taking out their anger and fear on an individual or family that has destroyed rural felicity. In other instances, friends and family of the evildoer himself try to avert disaster. When Dr. Frankenstein defies natural law and sets his sights on restoring cadavers to life, former school friends ("At University, they called me mad . . ."), a worried father, and a baffled fiancée all try to dissuade him from following this destructive path.

Horror Laws

Despite all the breaking of natural laws, horror films and their inhabitants largely abide by set rules, specific to the particular monster and determining the course of its creation, behavior, and ultimate destruction. A vampire cannot cross running water or abide the presence of garlic or crucifixes, and can only be killed by a stake through the heart or the rays of the sun; a man is transformed into a werewolf when the wolfbane blooms under a full moon and must be killed by a silver bullet, preferably one discharged by the hand of a loved one; specific incantations and tanna leaves revive ancient mummies; a magic word in a Star of David amulet brings the Golem back to life; and so on. Many of these laws come from folk legends, but Hollywood altered and adapted them for maximum cinematic effect. Box office potential played a part as well, as successful film series necessitated killing off popular monsters at the end of one film and bringing them back at the start of the next. Universal burned the monster in its first Frankenstein film, but wait . . . the next film in the series reveals that, in fact, he fell through the floor into a water-filled basement. The second picture ends with the monster pulling a lever and destroying the laboratory, his newly created "bride," and himself. But the follow-up shows how the hunchback Igor rescued the monster from the wreckage and has kept him alive in the ruined cellars. He eventually falls to his death in a vat of boiling sulfur, only to be exhumed again.

Stars

Horror films are proven star makers and star vehicles. Over the years, certain actors created successful careers out of the genre; Lon Chaney, Boris Karloff, Bela Lugosi, Lon Chaney, Jr., Vincent Price, and Christopher Lee all made non-horror films, yet in the public's mind their names are synonymous with monsters and horror. In silent films, Chaney Sr. was "the man of a thousand faces," most of them horrible enough to inspire the novelty musical number "Lon Chaney's Going to Get You, If You Don't Watch Out" in *The Hollywood Revue of 1929*, an all-star MGM film in which Chaney himself refused to appear. With sound came the unmistakable voices—often buried but never lost under fantastic makeup—of Karloff, Lugosi, and later Vincent Price. The acting is often hammy and over the top, perhaps a nod to horror films' roots in stage and silent cinema. Nevertheless, Karloff, at least, managed nuance and authenticity, even in nonspeaking roles.

Comedy

Shakespeare realized the necessity of comic relief to break tragedy's unbearable tension. Likewise, horror filmmakers place comic characters and touches in the most frightening movies. As in Elizabethan drama, comic duty often falls to lower-class servants. At Universal Studios, actress Una O'Connor was the resident Cockney crone, playing the innkeeper's wife in *The Invisible Man* (1933) and, even more outrageously, a servant to the Frankensteins in *Bride of Frankenstein* (1935). A pooh-poohing busybody and general know-it-all, she pops her eyes, jumps up and down, screeches like a banshee, and throws her apron over her head when confronted with monsters. In the Universal films of the 1940s, the humor appears more frequently, such as the competitive one-upmanship of the men involved in the archaeological expedition in *The Mummy's Hand* (1940) or the skeptical American college students in *The Mummy's Tomb* (1942). The conventions and dialogue of horror films became so familiar to cinemagoers that parodies were inevitable. In a series of Universal films, over a seven-year span, the comic duo Bud Abbott and Lou Costello had run-ins with Frankenstein's monster, the Invisible Man, Dr. Jekyll and Mr. Hyde, and the Mummy. In 1967, director Roman Polanski made *The Fearless Vampire Killers or Pardon Me, But Your Teeth Are in My Neck*, costarring as a bumbling assistant vampire exterminator. The film is beautifully shot, set in a snow-bound Transylvanian mountain village, and, in a twist on the heterosexual norm, features a lisping, campy gay vampire who chases attractive young men. Mel Brooks offered a loving spoof of the old black-and-white mad scientist monster films in his equally monochromatic *Young Frankenstein* (1974). All the clichés are there, as demanded by horror film aficionados, but this time around the young doctor (Gene Wilder) ineffectually denies his family background ("That's 'Fronkensteen!'") and his monster (Peter Boyle) does a song-and-dance routine before eventually bedding the doctor's fiancée (Madeline Kahn).

HISTORY AND INFLUENCES

The Beginning to the 1930s

From its inception, cinema—as its parent form, photography, had done—sought to reveal the unreal and the supernatural: ghosts appearing and disappearing, human transformations, and a folkloric catalog of goblins and bogeymen. With their emphasis upon the visual, scary movies became a staple, and several such German and American films, coming late in the history of silent cinema, are essential to any discussion of the horror genre.

Robert Wiene's 1919 *The Cabinet of Dr. Caligari* is considered the first great horror film and certainly the prototype for all that followed. It and F. W. Murnau's *Nosferatu* (1922) characterize an Expressionist period in German silent films, emerging from the theatre, in which highly stylized and unnatural sets with painted shadows and exaggerated angles and perspectives play as large a part in establishing theme and meaning as do plot and character. At a time when Hollywood films were shot with strong, flat lighting, the Germans explored much more atmospheric interplays of light and darkness.

Nosferatu is the Dracula story (names changed because of copyright prohibitions) and features a creeping, insect-like Count Orlok (Max Schreck) emerging from the shadows to inhabit a "Symphony of Horrors," the film's subtitle. From the opening sunny, idyllic scenes of domestic happiness, we watch young real-estate agent Hutter travel to Transylvania, "the country of thieves and ghosts." Omens and warnings accumulate as the locales become increasingly dark and remote. Orlok, all bulging eyes and elongated ears, nose, and fingers, is a sort of messianic death figure, bringing the plague with him as he travels back to Hutter's home town to recruit disciples and destroy Hutter's wife. The sanctity of marriage, the source of life itself, is threatened, but goodness triumphs through the intervention of the self-sacrificing young wife and the rays of "the living sun," which vaporize the Count.

In *Caligari*, the eponymous doctor is a sideshow hypnotist, later revealed to be the director of an insane asylum, who commands his sleepwalking slave Cesare (Conrad Veidt) to commit a series of nocturnal murders. The unreal city

Beauty and the Beast revisited, in the quintessential monster pose: stiffly carrying away the lifeless form of a beautiful woman. Conrad Veidt and Lil Dagover in *The Cabinet of Dr. Caligari* (1919). *Photofest.*

in which these horrors are committed is an Expressionist nightmare of painted shadows, precipitous alleys and buildings, and dark, threatening corners. The shot of Cesare carrying the limp body of an abducted woman across jagged rooftops is one that would find echoes in countless later horror films. In a framing sequence, the hallucinatory nature of this vision is eventually explained to be the paranoid ramblings of an inmate of the asylum (although this framing device seems to have been chosen against the writers' wishes). Along with Paul Wegener's *The Golem* (two versions, 1914 and 1920), about a man-made monster of clay called to life to protect Jews in the Prague ghetto, images and situations from these German films would resonate through sound horror films for decades to come.

In mid-1920s Hollywood, Lon Chaney created a set of silent horror classics whose impact stems from the star's fantastic makeup rather than stylized sets. His vampire film, *London after Midnight* (1927), has been lost. What remain are *The Hunchback of Notre Dame* (1923) and *The Phantom of the Opera* (1925), portraits of deformed men whose frightful appearance has made them embittered social outcasts. *Phantom* is famous primarily for its delayed unmasking scene, in which Mary Philbin snatches the mask from Erik's face, finally revealing—in a still-startling close-up that sent audiences into paroxysms of shock—his fiendish, skull-like visage. Chaney endured hours of painful makeup application for his films, earning the nickname "the Man of a Thousand Faces." As the hunchback Quasimodo, he wore seventy pounds of weighted padding, as well as a wig, false teeth, and facial putty, to become a sort of cathedral gargoyle in the flesh.

The 1930s and 1940s

Shortly after the introduction of sound films, Universal Studios, responsible for both *Hunchback* and *Phantom*, turned its hand to creating horror films with the new synchronized sound technology. Naturally they wanted Chaney, but the star was dying of cancer. *Dracula* (1931), *Frankenstein* (1931), and *The Mummy* (1932) made new stars of Bela Lugosi and Boris Karloff and became a sort of unholy trinity—establishing archetypal images, language, and situations that would remain in the minds of all future audiences and horror filmmakers. This is not to say the films did not look back to what had come before. Before directing the beautifully atmospheric *The Mummy*, Karl Freund had established himself as one of the most brilliant and original cinematographers of German silent films (*The Golem* [1920], *The Last Laugh* [1924], and *Metropolis* [1926]) and, as cameraman, brought the German visual style to Universal's *Dracula*, itself essentially a silent film. Perhaps the most memorable scene in *The Mummy*, in which the wizened, dusty mummy's eyelids slowly open, revealing a glimmer of light reflected upon the moist eye within, is strikingly similar to sleepwalking Cesare's coming to life in Robert Wiene's *Cabinet of Dr. Caligari*. The German influence is even greater in James Whale's *Frankenstein* (1931) and *Bride of Frankenstein* (1935): bold, almost expressionistic sets and, just as in Paul Wegener's *The Golem*, mad scientists, angry villagers, and a monster brought to life who connects with a child, longs for a woman, and would like to be a man. In typical Hollywood fashion, the Universal movies jettisoned much of the metaphysical questioning of the German films in favor of slick escapist entertainment.

Bela Lugosi had played the part of Dracula on Broadway before signing to do the film, and his slick, suave Count, debonair and somewhat sexy—so different from the dry stick-figure created by Schreck in *Nosferatu*—remains the public's ideal Dracula. The early sound film is primitive by today's standards, silent for long stretches with no musical score except for Tchaikovsky's *Swan Lake* over the titles, and featuring humorously artificial bats jerking about on strings and no vampiric transformations onscreen. The large castle set, however, is stunning, featuring cavernous Gothic dungeons and an impressive, seemingly endless cobwebbed staircase. Lugosi gets to deliver some legendary lines in his theatrical, heavily Hungarian-accented manner: his initial greeting, "I am *Dracula*."; responding to wolves howling out-of-doors with "children of the night . . . what *music* they make"; and, turning down an offered beverage, "I never drink . . . wine."

Before *Frankenstein*, English actor Boris Karloff had worked ten years in Hollywood, largely unnoticed, but with the advent of sound films he was able to use his unique, mellifluous voice (which made such an impact years later in the animated *How the Grinch Stole Christmas* but remained silent in his greatest monster roles). Whereas Lugosi created a memorable character through stylization, Karloff, despite all the makeup, pulled off a remarkable acting coup, communicating and evoking powerful emotions and a core of childlike innocence without the assistance of dialogue. Like Cesare in *Caligari*, Frankenstein's monster is a mute, passive figure created by a madman ("It's alive! It's *alive*!!"). Karloff manages to

"I am Dracula." In the role with which he would forever be identified, Bela Lugosi welcomes the unsuspecting to his castle in *Dracula* (1931). *Photofest.*

convey a pathos and vulnerability with which audiences strongly empathize, even as the monster is driven to murderous acts. In one scene, the monster, in a deep dungeon, is first exposed to sunlight, raising his face and stretching his arms upward in an almost religious wonderment, as if to grasp this elusive source of life and goodness. The work's "man playing God" theme is played to the hilt, though later censors required the removal of Dr. Frankenstein's (Colin Clive) line "In the name of God, now I know what it feels like to *be* God!" Another notorious sequence, censored in some areas of distribution, is of the monster innocently playing with a young girl by the side of a lake. The two of them toss flowers into the water to watch them float on the surface; when the flowers are all gone, the monster naively throws in the only other beautiful object at hand: the child—who does *not* float.

Visually, the film surpasses *Dracula*. Enduring transformations similar to those visited upon Lon Chaney, Karloff suffered through nearly four hours of makeup application each morning (it took nearly as long to remove). Visual effects made him 18 inches taller and 65 pounds heavier, and he owed his stiff walk to steel rods strapped to his legs. Dr. Frankenstein's castle laboratory is a marvelous set influenced by German films, particularly *Metropolis*. This is the mad scientist lab *par excellence*, soaring up to the heavens (and to lightning, the source of the monster's animation) and containing all manner of fantastic machinery, electric sparks, boiling liquids, and furiously active wheels, pulleys, and levers. A Los Angeles inventor created most of the props for the set, many of which were reused in countless later mad scientist films (including Mel Brooks's 1974 parody, *Young Frankenstein*).

Four years later, Karloff reprised his role in the sequel *The Bride of Frankenstein*. By 1935, the actor had made quite an impression upon the public, so that the screen simply flashes a single word: KARLOFF. Director James Whale is here even more theatrical and baroque, introducing a witty sense of humor and emphasizing the fine line between seriousness and camp. With a bigger budget than its predecessor, *Bride*'s sets and overall art direction are even more expressionistic and striking, with swirling painted skyscapes, large forests, ruined graveyards, and, of course, a lavish scientific laboratory. One of the greatest film composers, Franz Waxman, supplied a richly evocative orchestral score (how far things had come from the largely silent *Dracula*!), and cinematographer John Mescall worked wonders with varied lighting techniques and effects. Most critics consider the resulting film superior to the original. The monster is *not* dead after all, and, as the publicity posters screamed, "The monster demands a mate!" A prologue, set in nineteenth-century Switzerland, dramatizes the genesis of Mary Shelley's original story and novel. Elsa Lanchester plays both Shelley and the monstrous bride of the title, in her famous shroud-like wedding dress and upright Nefertiti-inspired fright wig with white streaks at the temples. The Bride is perhaps the sole female monster from cinema whose image has achieved iconic significance—courtesy, yet again, of the wizardry of makeup man Jack Pierce. In addition to Dr. Frankenstein and the monster, the film introduces the outrageous, Mephistophelean Dr. Praetorius (Ernest Thesiger), himself a mad scientist suffering a God complex, who convinces his fellow scientist to create a female and start "a new world of gods and monsters."

In this film, Karloff's monster is able to speak. His vocabulary is rudimentary, but his musings on the nature of life and humanity are tellingly profound: he progresses from the morbid ("I love dead . . . hate living") to the affirmative ("Alone . . . bad. Friend . . . good.") after being taken in and shown kindness by a blind hermit. Whale mixes such scenes of pathos with others of horror and even comedy. Praetorius' prissy, ironic tone has been read by recent critics as gay camp but Whale biographer James Curtis maintains that such revisionist criticism, based largely on the revelation of the director's homosexuality in the 1970s and 80s, exaggerates any gay subtext to the film's exploration of "unnatural" outsiders and outcasts (1998, 143).

Depression-era audiences, reeling from economic, social, and agricultural catastrophes, flocked to these films as an escape from the bewildering modern world into one in which the enemies have identifiable faces and the heroes always win in the end. This was Universal's decade of great horror films; the first few, generally considered the best, were followed by *Murders in the Rue Morgue* (1932), *The Invisible Man* (1933), *The Black Cat* (1934), *The Werewolf of London* (1935), *Dracula's Daughter* (1936), and *Son of Frankenstein* (1939). The latter two titles indicate the repetitive direction in which things were headed. The 1940s saw a second crop of Universal monster films, unoriginal but entertaining; "image without art," as Ethan Mordden puts it (1988, 350). These sequels generally employed lesser actors, directors, and budgets and featured a bizarre marriage of nineteenth-century monsters to 1940s American culture—complete with slang, contemporary fashion, and a string of buxom young sweater girls hired for their girl-next-door looks and ability to scream on cue. Screenwriters stretched to find new ways to resurrect destroyed monsters for series of their own: *The Mummy* spawned *The Mummy's Hand* (1940), *The Mummy's Tomb* (1942), *The Mummy's Ghost* (1944), and *The Mummy's Curse* (1945); *The Invisible Man* was followed by *The Invisible Man Returns* (1940); and the most famous series continued with *Ghost of Frankenstein* (1942) and *Son of Dracula* (1943). *Frankenstein Meets the Wolf Man* (1943) was an attempt to recharge the worn formula with a two-for-one enterprise, leading to the inevitable addition of Dracula to the mix in *House of Frankenstein* (1944) and *House of Dracula* (1945). As if advertising some bizarre family reunion, posters for the latter two films read, "All Together! The Wolf Man. Frankenstein's Monster. Dracula. The Hunchback. The Mad Doctor." The three great monsters would show up together one last time, fully tamed and played for laughs, in *Abbott and Costello Meet Frankenstein* (1948).

Universal was not the only studio to produce horror films, especially after its initial successes proved the popularity of the genre. The ultimate Beauty and the Beast fable is *King Kong* (1933), important for Willis O'Brien's pioneering use of stop-motion animation, which created a living, breathing Kong, at once terrifying and pitiful, as well as the iconic images of the great ape climbing (and eventually falling to his death from) the Empire State Building. The showmen who drag Kong from his far-off island in order to reap financial gain are exposed as ecocriminals, doomed for tampering with nature, and Fay Wray's translucent beauty has won over generations of fans as effortlessly as it captivated Kong himself. The great ape serves as the embodiment of any number of the audience's fears and aspirations: nature, the unknown, masculinity, brute force, Eden, and so on.

Favoring psychological drama and the power of suggestion, producer Val Lewton and director Jacques Tourneur eschewed the blatant stereotypical trappings of the genre in creating two horror masterpieces for RKO Studio. *Cat People* (1942) and *I Walked with a Zombie* (1943) are B-pictures in terms of cast and budget, but both films brought in huge box office returns, and they equal—if not surpass—any A-picture in effectively creating suspense and an atmosphere of menace. The former film (unsuccessfully remade by Paul Schrader in 1982), suffers some plot holes, but it contains effective, stylized sequences and an ominous atmosphere of unseen horror. It tells the story of a young Serbian woman (Simone Simon) in New York who is cursed to change into a black panther and kill anyone who arouses her passions. No transformations or violence appear onscreen. Instead of utilizing revelation, Lewton and Touneur build suspense and play with the audience's imagination by means of clever editing and chiaroscuro lighting effects. A woman walks through a deserted Central Park in the dead of night, the panther following her silently; the same woman is later stalked as she floats alone in a swimming pool, the surrounding walls alive with fluid shadows and reflections, the camera locating unique angles, and the soundtrack full of strange sound effects and the hiss of an angry feline.

Even more atmospheric is *I Walked with a Zombie*, set in the West Indies and, amazingly, loosely based upon *Jane Eyre*. A young nurse is sent to the islands to care for a planter's comatose wife, who turns out to be one of the walking dead. Again, horror is indirect: native drums heard in the distance, diaphanous shadows cast on every conceivable surface, and an ongoing storyline that hints at family violence, voodoo, and murder. There are ruminations upon the danger of beauty and the power of love, but these films are important not so much for ideas as for their creators' powerful grasp of cinematic visuals and style.

The 1950s and 1960s

Political, technological, and social changes in the 1950s helped usher in a horror film renaissance. Cold War paranoia, specifically the fear of atomic weaponry, accompanied curiosity about life in outer space, as Russian and American rocket rivalry began. At the same time, the phenomenon of the teenager and teenage lifestyle first emerged, accompanied by rock and roll music and the new television set. With its hand ever at the pulse of the country's lifeline, Hollywood wedded these phenomena in a spate of science fiction and horror films (see **Science Fiction and Fantasy**). Fear of the Bomb and accompanying fallout produced mutation films such as *Them!* (1954), featuring giant ants wreaking havoc in the Southwest. In reaction to the threat of television entertainment, the movies offered what audiences *couldn't* get from the TV set: widescreens and "living color." One gimmick that—temporarily—drew in audiences was 3-D, featured in *House of Wax* (1954), a remake of *Mystery of the Wax Museum* (1933), wherein a vengeful sculptor (Vincent Price, in the role that crowned him the new King of Horror) creates wax statues from human corpses. Wearing colored, Polaroid spectacles to view the 3-D effects, audiences jumped and gasped as all manner of objects appeared to be flung at them, including knives and, most effectively, a paddle-ball.

Drive-in theaters, another attempt to lure Americans away from the television set, proved the perfect vehicle for Hollywood's new teenager horror movies, many of which connected monstrous transformations to adolescent sexual drives. The unpopular high school student in *Blood of Dracula* (1957) is hypnotized into vampirism by her sinister chemistry teacher. That same year, science—or its practitioner—was again the bogeyman and a teenager the victim in *I Was a Teenage Werewolf*. This time, an insane psychiatrist, who believes that humanity's return to a primitive, bestial state is the only way to subvert total atomic war, injects a young man (Michael Landon) with a serum that produces the titular werewolf. Actor Whit Bissell reprised the role of the mad doctor in the following year's *I Was a Teenage Frankenstein*, moving from psychiatry to surgery as he assembles parts from various cadavers to form a monster. The face is taken from a boy killed in an automobile accident, and when the monster turns on its maker, the doctor addresses it as he would any teenager: "Answer me! You have a civil tongue in your head! I know—I sewed it in there!" Paranoia about science and world domination returned in *Teenage Zombies* (1958), in which a mad female doctor kidnaps a group of waterskiing teenagers to serve as guinea pigs for testing a nerve gas that turns people into mindless slaves.

The year 1957 was something of an *annus mirabilis* for horror films. Universal released its old horror catalogue to television for Friday and Saturday night broadcasts, simultaneously introducing a new generation to the genre and whetting its appetite for more. *I Was a Teenage Werewolf* appeared that year, as did Hammer Studio's *The Curse of Frankenstein*, considered by some to be "*the* breakthrough movie, not only for Hammer but for the entire genre in the post–war era" (Milne, Willemen, and Hardy 1986, 107). The English studio had tried its hand at science fiction, but when it filmed the unbeatable combination of horror and sex in vivid Eastmancolor, everything changed. The use of color was revelatory and, coupled with Hammer's use of European locations and lavish sets, produced operatic results. Hammer eventually bought out the rights to the old Universal horror films and, through the 1950s and 1960s, rereleased the entire catalogue of monsters upon an insatiable public. Specific images from the Universal films—namely, Jack Pierce's makeup for Karloff's turn as the monster—were guardedly under copyright, which bothered some filmgoers (although Christopher Lee's monster is probably closer to Mary Shelley's description than is Karloff's). What was new to the Hammer series, besides vivid color and fresh visual takes on familiar monsters, was the blatant sexual content, as the ghouls share the screen with a succession of buxom young women spilling out of low-cut blouses (the lead actress in *Frankenstein Created Woman* [1966] was a *Playboy* model). One thing the Hammer films have in common with their Universal predecessors is the curse of popularity and the disappointing fact that initial treatments of each monster are undeniably effective and memorable while the sequels become increasingly silly and mechanical, with infrequent flashes of originality and inspiration.

The first two Hammer horror films, *The Curse of Frankenstein* (1957) and *Horror of Dracula* (1958), breathed new life into the genre, the former announcing its colorful arrival with a blood-red title sequence—revelatory to audiences weaned on old black-and-white Universal films. The story follows the basics of Mary Shelley's novel, but it is told in flashback by an imprisoned Victor Frankenstein (Peter Cushing). After the young Victor and his tutor restore a dead puppy to life ("It's alive!"), he shocks the older man with blasphemous audacity: "We've restored life, when life was extinct. It is no longer sufficient to bring the dead back to life. We must create from the beginning. We must build up our own creature . . . build it up from nothing." Despite the tutor's warning that "this can never end in anything but evil," Victor's ego—the mad scientist's insatiable thirst for power and the conquest of new worlds—has been unleashed. A twist on Victor's character is the film's depiction of him as womanizer, lying to and impregnating a servant girl and then locking her in a room with the monster (Christopher Lee) to face both a fate worse than death *and* death itself. Color is used effectively in the richly appointed sets, with particular attention to strategically-placed reds: a silk dressing gown, a rose set in a woman's plunging *décolletage*. Audiences particularly enjoyed seeing colorful gore: decapitated heads, pickled eyeballs, the laboratory's boiling blood-red liquids, the monster's scarred and putrid visage, and so forth. Another of the film's revolutions in horror movie visuals is the inclusion of several outdoor sequences, breaking away from the studio set. Nor was innovation restricted to visual elements. The old Universal horror films had contained odd mixtures of nationality and dialect—nobility spoke with upper-class English or cultured stage accents, servants were often Cockneys, and the villagers sounded American but had German names and attire. In the Hammer films, for a change, the primary characters all sounded alike, while servants often had continental accents.

The next year's *Horror of Dracula*, shot in widescreen Cinemascope and Technicolor, features even more outdoor photography and blatant sex. Jonathan Harker (who is not the ignorant innocent in this version, but actually comes to Transylvania to destroy Dracula) is met at the castle by a vampiric femme fatale baring fangs as well as breasts as she spills out of a tight, low-cut dressing gown. The sets are a bit grander than in the Frankenstein film (although Castle Dracula is perhaps too clean and tidy, suffering in comparison to the evocative ruin of the 1931 version), and color is again integral to the picture's effectiveness. Christopher Lee, fresh from his role as Frankenstein's monster, here assays the part with which he would forever be associated: Count Dracula, complete with blood-shot eyes and red fangs. Whereas Lugosi was debonair and seductive, Lee is much younger and more vital—both sexually and physically threatening.

Hammer ran with this lucrative franchise, producing *The Revenge of Frankenstein* (1958), *The Mummy* (1959), *Brides of Dracula* (1960), *The Two Faces of Dr. Jekyll* (1960), *The Curse of the Werewolf* (1961), *The Phantom of the Opera* (1962), *The Evil of Frankenstein* (1964), *The Curse of the Mummy's Tomb* (1964), *Dracula, Prince of Darkness* (1965), *Plague of the Zombies* (1966), *Frankenstein Created Woman* (1967), *The Mummy's Shroud* (1967), *Dracula Has Risen from the Grave* (1968), *Frankenstein Must Be Destroyed* (1969), *Taste the Blood of Dracula* (1969), *Scars of Dracula* (1970), *The Vampire Lovers*, (1970), *Countess Dracula* (1971), *Lust for a Vampire* (1971), *Dr. Jekyll and Sister Hyde* (1971), and *Dracula A.D. 1972* (1972). The last few titles indicate the desperate directions in which the studio was moving to attract audiences: lesbianism, vampires infiltrating girls' schools, sex changes, and retelling the story in the present were blatant potboiling tactics that, predictably, brought box office rewards. Interestingly, while Hammer, like Universal before it, killed then revived both Dracula and the mummy in numerous film sequels, the studio saw no need to restore Frankenstein's monster for later movies. Instead, Baron Frankenstein (Peter Cushing) links the films, as he creates a variety of creatures (including *Playboy* centerfolds) "from nothing."

Alongside the Hammer pictures, other horror films continued to flourish through the 1960s, although the majority of them dealt with insanity rather than with actual monsters. Producer/director Roger Corman, in association with American International Pictures, turned from westerns to film adaptations of Edgar Allan Poe stories, many of which featured theatrical performances by Vincent Price. These included *The House of Usher* (1960), the first and possibly best of the bunch, *The Pit and the Pendulum* (1961), *The Premature Burial* (1961), *The Raven* (1962), *The Masque of the Red Death* (1964), and *The Tomb of Ligeia* (1964). Like the stories on which they are based, terror comes not from threatening monsters but from inventive sadists and incapacitating guilt. The presence of actor Price and the familiar haunted house milieu emphasize these films' horror roots.

So-called splatter movies, cheaply made, highly sexual in a manner prohibited up to this time, and heavily, explicitly gory, originated with *Blood Feast* (1963), directed and photographed by Herschell Gordon Lewis. Shot in nine days on a miniscule budget, the film was critically damned but tremendously successful commercially. Part mummy film (a madman attempts to bring an Egyptian goddess to life), part Frankenstein (he must do so with the body parts of young women), the film broke new ground in terms of gruesomely explicit violence, but this was just the beginning of a trend that would push the boundaries further and further in attempts to satisfy an insatiable audience. Increasing public acceptance of extreme film content, coupled with a general relaxation of censorship (sped by the institution of the less-restrictive motion picture ratings system in 1968), opened the bloody floodgates. The body parts piled up in Lewis's two 1964 follow-ups, *Two Thousand Maniacs* (a sort of gore version of *Brigadoon*) and *Color Me Blood Red*, as well as in his later films: *The Gruesome Twosome* (1966), *The Wizard of Gore* (1968) and *The Gore Gore Girls* (1971). Obviously, the self-parodic element of such exploitation films was never masked.

The 1970s and 1980s

These monsterless splatter movies begat the late 1970s and 1980s "slasher films," variations upon a woman-in-peril scenario that reached their zenith in John Carpenter's *Halloween* (1978). The tremendous success of this film ensured careers for both director Carpenter and his star, Jamie Lee Curtis, and triggered a long succession of stalk-and-slash movies in which demented psychopaths terrorize suburban youths, with particular homicidal aggression aimed at sexually active teenage girls. Such films include six *Halloween* sequels, *The Toolbox Murders* (1979; the name says it all), *Terror Train* (1979), *Friday the 13th* (1980) and its *eight* sequels, *Prom Night* (1980), *He Knows You're Alone* (1980), *Hell Night* (1981), *The Slumber Party Massacre* (1982), and *A Nightmare on Elm Street* (1985) and its sequels. With titles like these, audiences knew what they were in for. Teenage-massacre films enjoyed a renaissance in the 1990s with *Scream* (1996) and *I Know What You Did Last Summer* (1997) and their inevitable progeny.

True monster films were still occasionally made. Excepting the earliest Universal films, horror movies are often made by lesser studios and neophyte directors and actors. Radiation fears and zombies proved a winning combination in George Romero's directorial debut, *Night of the Living Dead* (1968). Shot on a nonexistent budget over several weekends outside Pittsburgh, the film barricades seven hapless people in an abandoned farmhouse while cannibalistic zombies swarm outside. The movie rejects clichéd heroics and a happy ending, as the victims crumble and bicker under pressure and the sole survivor is mistakenly shot by the police. Such anti-heroism and exposure of bureaucratic ineptitude securely position the film alongside other countercultural motion pictures from the late 1960s.

As the Hammer films ground out their last vestiges of originality in the late 1960s and early 1970s, two best-selling novels inspired major studios and directors to take on the biggest monster of them all: Satan. Paramount's *Rosemary's Baby*

(1968), based on the book by Ira Levin, places horror squarely in the modern, everyday world—specifically, Central Park West. Set in the Gothic, spooky Dakota Building, the film slowly and masterfully builds suspense and horror as newlywed Rosemary (and the audience) realizes that she is carrying the devil's child in her womb. Every expectant mother's terror and paranoia take on infernal dimensions as Rosemary's worst suspicions about those eccentric old neighbors and her increasingly distant husband—all members of a coven—are realized. Actress Mia Farrow's fragile vulnerability adds immeasurably to the film's effectiveness, as does Polanski's refusal to show us anything more than, ever so quickly, the shadowy demonic figure that rapes Rosemary. The child of the title is never seen—only its mother's terrified reaction to it and her accusatory scream, "What have you done to its *eyes*?" thus forcing the audience to conjure its own dreadful images of the baby. Witches and demons, more often associated with seventeenth-century Boston, become convincingly real in contemporary New York, where struggling actors sell their souls for success and the cover of *Time* magazine asks, "Is God Dead?"

Four years later, William Friedkin directed *The Exorcist* (1973) for Warner Brothers. William Peter Blatty produced and wrote the screenplay based on his own novel about a twelve-year-old girl possessed by a millennium-old demon. Whereas *Rosemary's Baby* shocked cinemagoers with what it *didn't* show them, Friedkin and Blatty went in the opposite direction, staging all manner of explicit and gory sequences. The most horrific of these (the girl's head revolving 360 degrees, laceration and tearing of the skin, green projectile vomit, and the girl violently masturbating with a crucifix), coupled with a volatile battle to the death between Catholic priests and the Devil himself, worried the censors, offended many people, triggered countless copycat claims of demonic possession, and made the picture a phenomenal success. As in the earlier film, an innocent female is emotionally and sexually abused by satanic forces but, here, a terrified albeit determined mother (Ellen Burstyn) and two priests manage to win the girl back and send the demon packing—at least until the sequel four years later.

The 1990s to the Present

The surprise hit of 1999 was the low-budget, independent *The Blair Witch Project*, which borrowed Lewton and Tourneur's style of horror filmmaking by largely refusing to show the audience the source of menace and destruction, focusing instead upon frightened innocents and cinemagoers' darkest fears and imagination. The film is framed and styled as the homemade documentary of a group of young adventurers who set off to discover the truth about a rural New England haunting. In an update on nineteenth-century epistolary Gothic novels (such as *Dracula*), the movie is a jerky, handheld video of personal confessions, daily updates, and the record of things going terribly—and fatally—wrong. The film's immediacy stems from its random, disjointed, documentary style, as well as the claustrophobic close-ups of terrified expressions and frantic references to off-camera events. *The Blair Witch Project* is a case, as was *Night of the Living Dead*, of a film's low budget actually increasing the work's power.

The titles of *Bram Stoker's Dracula* (1992) and *Mary Shelley's Frankenstein* (1994) announce their intention of faithfulness to the twin paragons of horror literature, but the films are of uneven quality. Although not a complete success, the earlier movie is by far the better, as director Francis Ford Coppola uses every cinematic trick in the book to create an atmosphere of sexual tension and dread. Overlong, this version of Dracula nevertheless boasts a high-voltage cast (Brits Gary Oldman, Anthony Hopkins, and Richard E. Grant are more convincing in a period piece—and with their accents—than are the young Americans Winona Ryder and Keanu Reeves), Academy Award-winning costumes, special effects and makeup, and a director adept at cinematic explorations of treachery and evil (as evidenced in his *Godfather* films). The Frankenstein film, directed by and starring Kenneth Branagh, is a disappointment, not just in Robert De Niro's monster (who seems to be doing a De Niro impression), but also in the frenetic camerawork, intended to create atmosphere but ultimately just distracting.

The Stoker and Shelley books are now in the public domain and their 1990s film versions were made by Columbia and Tristar, respectively. To counter them, Universal periodically unleashes its own strictly guarded monsters (in new and "improved" versions) upon the cinemagoing public—and critics, whose knives invariably are out. *The Mummy* (1999) brought back the high priest mummy of the 1932 version and his thousand-year longing for a lost princess, but the interminable film (nearly twice as long as the classic 1932 version) is mostly interested in showing off computer-generated effects and telling an Indiana Jones–type tongue-in-cheek adventure story than in creating atmospheric horror. The 1999 version's Imhotep is able to assume different guises, including that of a massive sandstorm, and wreaks vengeance upon tomb desecrators—and anyone else who gets in the way.

As it had done repeatedly in the 1940s, Universal threw all its monsters (and $148 million dollars) in one basket in *Van Helsing* (2004), lambasted by critics and topping many Worst Films lists in its year of release. Again, the amazing but rather antiseptic computer effects take over, robbing the film of life and personality. Director Stephen Sommers (who helmed *The Mummy* and its 2001 sequel), builds the film around Van Helsing (Hugh Jackman), the vampire stalker from the Dracula story, who here takes on not only the vampire count but also werewolves and Frankenstein's monster. The film grinds to a halt whenever people start conversations and batters the audience senseless in action sequences and special effects run riot. Van Helsing produces and wields all manner of outrageous weaponry, and monsters undergo gory transformation after transformation, more to show off special effects than to provide story coherence or atmosphere.

Unlike some other genres, such as the musical and the western, horror films have never fallen out of favor; instead, over time, they focus on different dark corners of the human psyche, depending upon the tenor of the day as much as upon contemporary standards and film censorship. And just as audiences have always flocked to the cinema to bask in the glow of impossibly beautiful film stars, so they seem equally drawn to the hideous and misshapen monsters that have paraded across the screen since the medium's inception.

References and Further Reading

Curtis, James. *James Whale: A New World of Gods and Monsters*. Minneapolis: University of Minnesota Press, 1998.

Douglas, Drake. *Horrors!* Woodstock, NY: Overlook, 1991.

Jancovitch, Mark. *Horror: The Film Reader*. London; New York: Routledge, 2002.

Kawin, Bruce. "Children of the Light." In *Film Genre Reader III*, edited by Barry Keith Grant, 324–345. Austin: University of Texas Press, 2003.

Marrero, Robert. *Horrors of Hammer*. Key West, FL: RGM, 1984.

Milne, Tom, Paul Willemen, and Phil Hardy. *Encyclopedia of Horror Movies*. New York: Harper and Row, 1986.

Mordden, Ethan. *The Hollywood Studios: House Style in the Golden Age of the Movies*. New York: Knopf, 1988.

Silver, Alain, and James Ursini. *The Horror Film Reader*. New York: Limelight, 2001.

Wells, Paul. *The Horror Genre: From Beelszebub to Blair Witch (Short Cuts)*. London: Wallflower, 2000.

CHAPTER 7

MUSICAL

OF ALL FILM GENRES, the musical would seem perhaps the most easily defined: if people sing, it must be a musical. However, things are more complicated than this. If a woman climbs a mountain (*The Sound of Music*) or rides a streetcar (*Meet Me in St. Louis*) and her emotions impel her to break into song, *that's* a musical. But what about when the singing in a film only occurs as an onstage performance (*Cabaret*, *Nashville*), not in everyday places or situations, and actually interrupts the narrative? *The Sound of Music* and *Meet Me in St. Louis* are examples of "integrated" musicals, in which songs are a natural outgrowth of the plot and serve to advance the narrative—nearly always a love story—as well as to express emotion, thereby delineating and developing character. Songs thus function as monologue or dialogue that exists on a higher emotional plane, formalized as they are in structure, rhyme, and melody and triggered by extreme personal experiences. Integrated film musicals have their roots in operetta (where, unlike in grand opera, dialogue is spoken rather than sung) and in the more populist Broadway book musical. Whereas some critics hold that the only true musicals are integrated ones, we shall throw our net a bit wider, to embrace other types of musical films, in all of which music and dance figure prominently and are bound inextricably to the films' themes and purpose.

For forty years, musicals were among the most popular films produced in Hollywood, until changing tastes and the demise of the studio system nearly killed them off. And yet, at that very time, many American directors turned their attention to the musical, as a sort of generic proving ground: Woody Allen (*Everyone Says I Love You* [1996]), Robert Altman (*Nashville* [1975], and *Popeye* [1980]), Peter Bogdanovich (*At Long Last Love* [1975]), Francis Ford Coppola (*Finian's Rainbow* [1968], and *One from the Heart* [1982]), Blake Edwards (*Victor/Victoria* [1982]), Milos Forman (*Hair* [1979]), and Martin Scorsese (*New York, New York* [1977]). Although it is too soon to determine whether the recent popularity of a couple of musicals heralds a renaissance, it is clear that successive generations of filmmakers continue to be drawn to updating and reinterpreting the genre.

DEFINING CHARACTERISTICS AND CATEGORIES

The variety and breadth of the musical can be illustrated by examining its subgenres:

The Backstage Musical

The hardiest of musicals, backstagers inhabit the world of show business and chronicle the vagaries of performers' lives. Such films are set in theaters, as well as in radio, recording, and film studios, with songs that occur in both rehearsal and performance, charting the rise or fall of singers' and dancers' careers. More often than not, songs are strictly performed for audiences and are not integrated into the straight storyline. The earliest musicals were of this type, the quintessential backstage musical being *42nd Street* (1932) in which a jaded, temperamental Broadway star twists her ankle and is replaced at the last moment by a reticent, naïve chorus girl, shoved onstage with the immortal admonition, "You're going out a youngster . . . but you've *got* to come back a star"—which, of course, she does.

This parallel plotting of rising star/falling star has been extremely popular, as seen in *A Star is Born* (1954 and 1976 versions), wherein a boozing established male star kills himself, rather than allow jealousies and his fading career jeopardize the blossoming success of his talented, hardworking, singing wife. Another recurring backstage musical storyline centers on the breakup of a musical group, family, or friendship concurrent with the emergence into stardom of one of its members. Americans love a success story and the dedication and single-mindedness required for show-business ascendance has ensured the popularity of backstage musicals among audiences nurtured on the mythology of the self-made man or woman. In *Ziegfeld Girl* (1941), three young women bond as they try to make it into the Ziegfeld Follies: one (Hedy Lamarr) marries (which means abandoning a show-business career to focus her energies on husband and home); one (Judy Garland) makes it, through perseverance, sacrifice, and talent; and the third (Lana Turner) fails, owing to indolence and lack of focus. In *Gypsy* (1962), frustrated performer and ultimate stage mother Mama Rose (Ethel Merman) focuses all her hopes, dreams, and overpowering personality on the vaudeville career of daughter June, who balks at the pressure and runs off with one of the boys in the act, while the neglected and overlooked elder daughter, Louise (Natalie Wood), also defies her mother to become the most famous stripper of the day, Gypsy Rose Lee. Many more backstagers focus on the rags-to-riches (or reverse) journey of an individual entertainer, perhaps unencumbered by show-business partners. These serve as cautionary tales (the rock singer in *The Rose* [1979] performed by Bette Midler and based on the life of Janis Joplin, who self-destructs on drugs, alcohol, and bad relationships that stem predictably from neglectful parents and a miserable childhood) or as celebrations of ability and drive (*The Great Ziegfeld* [1936] charts the rise and rise of the great showman [William Powell], whose sky's-the-limit attitude of "bigger is better" is perfectly shared and captured in one of MGM's most visually opulent films of the time, with its huge, revolving wedding-cake staging of "A Pretty Girl Is Like a Melody").

This type of film—the biography of an actual singer, dancer, or composer—is called the *biopic*, almost a subgenre in itself. *Yankee Doodle Dandy* (1942) is one of the best, with an electrifying performance by James Cagney as George M. Cohan and some attempt at fidelity to the facts of Cohan's life. More often than not, however, Hollywood abandons historical fact for the sake of the story, sometimes to ludicrous effect. In *Night and Day* (1946), for example, the short, crippled, homely homosexual Cole Porter is transformed into the impossibly debonair heterosexual Cary Grant, and in *Lady Sings the Blues* (1972), despite references to Billie Holiday's connections to prostitution and heroin use, the storyline is equally inaccurate regarding Holiday's disastrous love affairs and lost battle with drugs. The latter film stars singer Diana Ross, who was allowed to sing Holiday's songs on the soundtrack, a privilege also allowed Barbra Streisand when portraying Fanny Brice in *Funny Girl* (1968), and even allowed nonsingers Gary Busey (in *The Buddy Holly Story* [1978]), Sissy Spacek (as Loretta Lynn, in *Coal Miner's Daughter* [1980]), and Joaquin Phoenix and Reese Witherspoon (as Johnny and June Carter Cash in *Walk the Line* [2005]). Playing it safe, in *The Jolson Story* (1946), Larry Parks lip-synchs to recordings of Al Jolson, as Jessica Lange does to recordings of Patsy Cline in *Sweet Dreams* (1985). More complicated is *Your Cheatin' Heart* (1964), about the career of Hank Williams, for which actor George Hamilton lip-synchs to recordings made by the country singer's *son*, Hank Williams Jr.

The Revue

The revue, like its stage antecedent, is an assemblage of sketches, songs, and dances, usually with a thin storyline to link the otherwise unconnected sequences but often lacking any sort of narrative. Revues often serve as a showcase for the stars of a particular studio, and tend to appear at particular historic moments. To satisfy curious filmgoers in the earliest days of sound motion pictures, every major studio produced a musical revue in 1929 and 1930. In MGM's *The Hollywood Revue of 1929*, there is no narrative—just Jack Benny introducing thirty acts that range from Joan Crawford singing and dancing a Charleston, to the assembled company standing before Noah's ark dressed in raincoats, mugging through "Singin' in the Rain." On the other hand, Fox's *Happy Days* (1930) precedes its production numbers with the slight story of a down-on-his-luck showboat owner whose many entertainer pals band together to put on a show and restore him to solvency. In revues, stories are secondary to stars.

Revue musicals fell out of popularity until World War II, when soldiers and civilians alike needed big, flashy entertainment that only Hollywood could provide. Once again, most of the studios produced narrative-weak, showstopper-heavy revues, with an upbeat emphasis on exhortative affirmation. *Star Spangled Rhythm* (1942) has the thinnest of plots, about a gatekeeper at a film studio who has told his sailor son that he is actually an executive. This musical is really an excuse for Paramount to cheer on the boys in uniform and parade its stars in a series of patriotic numbers, with such song titles as "I'm Doing It for Defense" and "He Loved Me till the All-Clear Came." It culminates in a blazing finale with Bing Crosby singing "Old Glory" before a Mount Rushmore backdrop.

The Showcase or Star Vehicle

Often a backstage musical in form, the star vehicle's purpose is to showcase the talent of a musical personality whose success has already been achieved in radio or through recordings. Movies are thus the next step in this star's multi-faceted career. After Barbra Streisand had conquered the recording industry, appeared on Broadway, and won awards for her television specials, her next move was inevitable: appearing as Fanny Brice in the biopic *Funny Girl*. Many if not most of the successful singing stars of the twentieth century made films, including the three most popular singers of all. Soon after his success on the radio in the late 1920s, Bing Crosby started making movies in 1930, appearing initially in cameo spots or in his own short musical films. Crosby's relaxed, natural style of acting (much like his singing) and a flair for comedy soon propelled him into starring roles in feature-length films wherein, as far as the audience was concerned, he essentially played himself. Crosby's film career, spent primarily at Paramount, spanned three decades, from his first starring role in *The Big Broadcast* (1932) as—what else?—a radio crooner, through such hits as *Holiday Inn* (1942), the six *Road to —* pictures (1940–62) with Bob Hope, *Going My Way* (1944, for which he won an Academy Award), *White Christmas* (1954), and *High Society* (1956). The latter film costars Frank Sinatra, who overtook Crosby in popularity as a singer in the 1940s and made the same successful transition into movies. His early MGM musicals tap an appealing vulnerability behind the brash Italian American machismo, casting him as a sailor on shore leave in *Anchors Aweigh* (1945) and *On the Town* (1949), a ballplayer in *Take Me Out to the Ball Game* (1949), and a gambler in *Guys and Dolls* (1955).

By the time of this last film, rock and roll had appeared on the scene. With the crowning of a new "king" of popular music came the inevitable film career of Elvis Presley. More so than the films of Crosby and Sinatra, Presley's are true showcases: they rarely feature important costars and are not preexisting stage musicals. The half-dozen songs that Presley sings in each movie are largely forgettable, as are the plots, which managed to cast the star as, among other things, a farm boy in *Love Me Tender* (1956), a jailbird in *Jailhouse Rock* (1957), and a soldier in *G.I. Blues* (1960), and send him to all manner of exotic locales (*Blue Hawaii* [1962], *Fun in Acapulco* [1964], *Viva Las Vegas* [1964]). Presley cranked out an amazing number of films (27 in his first 11 years of moviemaking) and he proved as successful at the box office as on vinyl: between 1957 and 1965, his films made over 175 million dollars (Hirschhorn 1981, 384).

Singers have continued to more or less play themselves on screen, to mixed results: for every infectious *A Hard Day's Night* (1964), with the Beatles as beleaguered pop stars, there are far too many miscalculations, including vanity projects such as Mariah Carey's disastrous *Glitter* (2001), and the dead-on-arrival assembly-line spin-off from the *American Idol* television series, *From Justin to Kelly* (2003). Madonna's stillborn film career (granted, she has chosen to appear primarily in nonmusicals) stands as proof that even tremendous recording and concert success does not guarantee cinematic triumph.

The Screen Adaptation

Whereas many film musicals are written and composed directly for the screen, a large number are filmic adaptations of successful stage musicals and operettas. However, a stage success does not ensure a film hit. What works on Broadway or in an opera house cannot always be captured on or translated effectively to the screen, and filmmakers often completely overhaul the score or book of a stage musical for its cinematic adaptation. For example, *Cabaret* was a very successful integrated Broadway musical in which most of the cast members performed a featured song. In his 1972 film version, director Bob Fosse decided to restrict almost all the musical numbers to the smoky stage of the pre–war Berlin Kit Kat Klub, thereby eliminating the songs performed by the protagonist and his landlady in the apartment building and allowing only the stage performers—Sally Bowles and the cabaret's MC, played by Liza Minnelli and Joel Grey, in Oscar-winning performances—to sing. Composers Kander and Ebb agreed to cut some songs, and were hired to write a couple more for performance in the cabaret. Likewise, in the filming of Rodgers and Hammerstein's *The Sound of Music* (1965), a few songs performed by lesser characters in the stage version were dropped and new ones written for the screen. For example, on Broadway, the scene in which Maria travels from the abbey to the Von Trapp family home was omitted. With all of photogenic Salzburg at their disposal, however, the filmmakers decided to make this a major bridging sequence in the movie, and commissioned Richard Rodgers (Oscar Hammerstein had died in 1960) to compose "I Have Confidence" for the episode. Ironically, in recent theatrical revivals of both *Cabaret* and *The Sound of Music*, songs absent from the original shows and written for the screen have been worked into the revised stage versions. Audiences are more familiar with the film versions than with the originals, and would be disappointed if some of their favorite songs were missing.

More bizarre but quite common in the 1930s, a studio would buy the rights to a popular Broadway musical and then drop *all* of the songs. In their stead, they would substitute songs whose copyright (and, therefore, whose sheet music and record sales) belonged to the studio. In the late 1920s, with the introduction of sound films, movie companies not only rushed to hire the services of composers, but several major studios actually purchased music publishing houses in order to have their vast catalogs of songs at their own (exclusive) disposal. *No, No, Nanette* was a big hit on Broadway, but when it was filmed in 1930, only one of its songs was used while several others were written for the film by studio composers. Even established composers got the axe: the Astaire/Rogers film *The Gay Divorcee* (1934), based on the stage success of *The Gay Divorce*, retained only one of the original Cole Porter songs ("Night and Day"), while RKO commissioned (and therefore owned the sales rights to) several new songs for the film.

Later, Broadway show scores remained more or less intact upon their translation to the screen, and film adaptations of popular stage musicals continued to appear through the 1970s and 1980s, as the popularity of the musical genre itself faded: *Fiddler on the Roof* (1971), *Man of La Mancha* (1972), *Mame* (1974), *A Little Night Music* (1977), *The Wiz* (1978), *Hair* (1979), *Annie* (1982), and *A Chorus Line* (1985). In recent years, the few film musicals to be produced are largely adaptations of Broadway successes, including *Chicago* (2002) and *Rent* (2005).

Although the stage book musical is an American achievement, more often than not set in and celebrating things American (*Show Boat* and *Oklahoma!*), its roots lie in the European operetta, whose own origin is in grand opera. Rather than tackling life-and-death plots of betrayal and fatal passions, operetta is escapist and comedic. The works of Austrian composers such as Strauss and Lehar are set among the palaces, great houses, and watering holes of the aristocracy, while the English Gilbert and Sullivan tell of love among well-behaved pirates, Chinese maids, and gondoliers. Operettas are perceived as somewhat more highbrow than stage musicals and therefore have smaller audiences, but the filmed operetta has enjoyed occasional bursts of popularity. In the early 1930s, Paramount produced several newly-composed operettas, directed by the German Rouben Mamoulian (*Love Me Tonight* [1932]) and the Russian Ernst Lubitsch (*The Love Parade* [1929], *Monte Carlo* [1930], *The Smiling Lieutenant* [1931], and *One Hour With You* [1932]), mostly starring Jeanette MacDonald and Maurice Chevalier and set among the absurdly wealthy, stylish, and libidinous upper classes of Europe. A few years later, MGM produced a series of adaptations, based on established European and American operetta successes, starting with *The Merry Widow* (1934) with both MacDonald and Chevalier. The next year, the tremendous success of *Naughty Marietta* ensured this new string of operettas and established the popular pairing of MacDonald with Nelson Eddy, who would love and sing together in *Rose Marie* (1936), *Maytime* (1937), *Sweethearts* and *The Girl of the Golden West* (1938), and *New Moon* and *Bitter Sweet* (1940). In contrast to the earlier (pre-Code) Paramount films, the MGM operettas are more romantic than sexual, and are set in America, albeit with European exiles as frequent characters. MGM would produce a couple more operettas in the 1950s, as vehicles for such "highbrow" singers as Howard Keel, Kathryn Grayson, and Mario Lanza (*Rose Marie* and *The Student Prince*, 1954). However, with but few exceptions (such as the film version of the successful but extensively reworked and pop-influenced Broadway version of Gilbert and Sullivan's *The Pirates of Penzance* [1983], and Mike Leigh's biopic of Gilbert and Sullivan, *Topsy-Turvy* [1999]), the operetta has fallen out of favor.

The Dance Musical

In the dance musical, dance rather than song is the means of delineating character and furthering narrative. Songs are often involved, but choreography assumes primacy as the film's medium. In the Fred Astaire/Ginger Rogers films at RKO, songs give way to dance routines in which emotions and desires are played out—love is found, lost, or rediscovered, in lieu of and transcending mere words. Most musicals involve some degree of choreography, but dance musicals privilege it over the lyrics to the songs.

Fred Astaire championed a breezy, sophisticated manner of dance, always light, every movement precisely controlled and graceful, and often involving props (the tuxedo in the title song to *Top Hat* [1935], a hat stand in "Sunday Jumps" [*Royal Wedding*, 1951], and the walls and ceiling of a hotel room on which, defying gravity, he dances, in "You're All the World to Me" [*Royal Wedding*, 1951]).

The other great Hollywood performer in dance musicals is Gene Kelly. Much more athletic and physical than Astaire, and more plebian in persona (and believable as a romantic lead), Kelly helped revolutionize the musical in the 1940s, primarily through his insistence upon the centrality of dance in the exposition of narrative and character and on the ability of dance to replace dialogue. His exuberant dance-in-the-rain number in *Singin' in the Rain* (1952) is perhaps the single most famous musical sequence in all of film. Even more important in the realm of dance musicals are his choreography and performance in *An American in Paris* (1951), which won him a special Academy Award and culminates in a twenty-minute ballet sequence whose bold, abstract conception and design make it the most innovative dance number of its time, fully utilizing movement, color, and characterization. Cinemagoers enjoyed Kelly's extended dance numbers, such as "Slaughter on Tenth Avenue" in *Words and Music* (1948) and "The Broadway Melody" in *Singin' in the Rain* (1952). However, when Kelly directed, choreographed, and starred in an ambitious film that told three separate stories entirely through dance (*Invitation to the Dance* [1956]), audiences and critics were put off.

The disco craze of the 1970s saw a revival of dance musicals, the most notable of which is *Saturday Night Fever* (1977). Just as Astaire/Rogers films of the 1930s had sent entranced filmgoers—would-be Freds and Gingers—off to dance studios to learn the Continental and the Piccolino, so John Travolta inspired millions to "Do the Hustle." A decade later, *Dirty Dancing* (1987) and *Lambada* (1990) did the same for close-body, highly suggestive dance moves.

An odd offshoot of the dance musical is that in which an athlete-turned-performer "dances" in another medium. After winning three Olympic gold medals in figure skating, Sonia Henie was snatched up by Twentieth Century-Fox and starred in several immensely popular films (including *One in a Million* [1937], *Thin Ice* [1937], and *Happy Landing* [1938]) in which the nonactress was called upon to do little more than smile prettily and skate spectacularly, while bringing in a quarter of a million dollars in ticket sales. A few years later, champion swimmer Esther Williams was put under contract at MGM. In such films as *Neptune's Daughter* (1949) and *Million Dollar Mermaid* (1952), she turned the water ballet film into a box office bonanza.

The Animated Musical

The one type of musical whose popularity has never waned is the animated film. Animated musicals were once the exclusive domain of Walt Disney who, against everyone's advice, decided to move from producing short musical "Silly Symphonies" to feature-length animated films with songs. Disney pioneered the form with *Snow White and the Seven Dwarfs* (1937), named by the *New York Times* the best film of its year. For years, it was the most financially successful of all films. An integrated musical, *Snow White* is groundbreaking in many ways and in a single stroke, established animation as a vibrant new art form. Disney's team spent four painstaking years in production, but the fabulous, richly-detailed Old World sets, fully developed and realistic characters, exciting treatment of a fairy tale, and classic score (including immediate hits "Some Day My Prince Will Come," "Heigh-Ho," and "Whistle While You Work") silenced the naysayers. Disney's team was off to a tremendous start and would go on to produce such classics as *Fantasia* and *Pinocchio* in 1940 (the latter perhaps Disney's greatest film, technically and artistically, with the Oscar-winning song "When You Wish Upon a Star"), *Dumbo* in 1941, *Bambi* in 1942, *Cinderella* in 1950, *Alice in Wonderland* in 1951, and *Peter Pan* in 1953 for RKO. For his own Buena Vista studio, the Disney team made *Lady and the Tramp* in 1955, *Sleeping Beauty* in 1959, *The Sword in the Stone* in 1963, *The Jungle Book* in 1967, and *The Aristocats* in 1970. Buena Vista also experimented with musicals that mix animation and live action, producing the immensely popular *Mary Poppins* in 1964 and *Bedknobs and Broomsticks* in 1971. By the 1970s, Disney's glory days seemed over. A revival began with *The Little Mermaid* (1989), based on Hans Christian Anderson's story but adopting contemporary gender attitudes. Perhaps in penance for so many earlier animated heroines waiting to be rescued by princes, *The Little Mermaid* features an empowered, independent female lead. Girl power is in even greater evidence in the follow-up musical *Beauty and the Beast* (1991), considered the best of Disney's recent films and the only animated film at that point to be nominated for a Best Picture Academy Award. Although the film did not win this award, it did garner trophies for Best Song (for the title song, which also became a huge pop hit) and Best Score for composers Howard Ashman and Alan Menken, the best film songwriting team in recent years. Their songs, as much as the genius of Disney's animators, are what bring these cartoon characters, whether they be beast or teapot, to vibrant life, and rejuvenate the long tradition of the integrated musical. Convinced that audiences were there, Disney produced such films as *The Lion King* in 1994 (which won the Oscars for Best Song, "Can You Feel the Love Tonight," and for Score), *Pocahontas* in 1995 (which also won the awards for Song, "Colors of the Wind," and for Score), *Hercules* in 1997, *Mulan* in 1998, and *Tarzan* in 1999 (winning the award for Best Song, "You'll Be in My Heart"). These movies introduced new animation techniques—specifically, computer generation—but maintained such stock Disney components as orphans, slapstick comedy, cute animal sidekicks, unashamed sentimentality, and uplifting life lessons of empathy and understanding. The movies' subject matter and settings are increasingly far-flung from the America that first enjoyed animated film in the 1930s, now embracing women and Native American, African, Asian, and classical mythologies and philosophies more in line with politically correct multiculturalism and diversity.

In an unusual reversal of the norm, Disney translated *Beauty and the Beast* and *The Lion King* into successful Broadway and touring musical shows, pulling off the twin feat of satisfying audiences familiar with the films and bringing the animated characters to life onstage with imaginatively costumed actors. Recently, Disney's dominance of the field has been challenged by other makers of animated films, including Stephen Spielberg, who produced *An American Tale* in 1986 (made by former Disney animators). The array of Academy Awards bestowed upon these animated musicals indicates the industry's recognition of their having assumed the mantle once worn by the classic Hollywood musicals.

HISTORY AND INFLUENCES

The Beginning to the 1930s

Unlike most film genres, the musical owes its existence to a specific change in film technology, namely the introduction of sound. By 1927, silent films had become a true art form, combining a stylized manner of acting, endless editing and montage capabilities, and a highly mobile and sensitive camera. All of this was forced to change or reinvent itself with the introduction of sound. Silent films had always involved music, in the form of piano, organ and, in large cities, orchestral accompaniment. In fact, many silent films were made of famous operas and operettas, taking advantage of melodramatic plots and allowing accompanists to play the familiar arias and songs during the appropriate scenes.

By the mid-1920s, several different cinematic sound technologies had appeared. The initial system used for "talkies" involved a sound-on-disc device: sound and image were recorded simultaneously but on separate devices, which required both turntable and projector for reproduction. Inevitable problems of synchronization plagued the system, which was eventually replaced by the sound-on-film technology used to this day. Convinced that sound was merely a fad—and a laborious and expensive one at that—all the major studios but one turned down Western Electric's pioneer Vitaphone sound-on-disc process. Warner Brothers, a small studio desperate (and able) to try new things, took a chance and, in 1926, started producing short plotless sound (music) films, featuring performing orchestras, opera singers, and vaudeville acts. The films were immediately popular—at those few cinemas with sound equipment—and the Warners' efforts culminated on October 6, 1927, with the premiere of *The Jazz Singer*, the first full-length feature film to use sound.

The shamelessly sentimental story of a cantor's son who, despite his father's wishes, finds a musical outlet in singing popular African-American songs rather than in the synagogue, *The Jazz Singer* is primarily a silent film (in fact, an all-silent version was released simultaneously), with five short sound sequences, featuring seven popular songs and a few minutes of ad-libbed dialogue. Broadway star Al Jolson uttered the prophetic and legendary lines, "Wait a minute! You ain't heard nothin' yet. Wait a minute, I tell ya, you ain't heard nothin'!" before launching into an exuberant rendition of "Toot Toot Tootsie."

The film featured such Jolson standards as "Blue Skies" and "My Mammy," as well as "Mother (of Mine), I Still Have You," the first song written expressly for a sound film. Establishing the still-practiced pattern of multimedia synergy, the film's songs were released as records, which became hits, as did the film itself, grossing millions of dollars worldwide. Jolson was rushed into *The Singing Fool* (1928), another talkie-silent, in which he again hammed it up, emoted broadly (this time over a dying son, rather than a put-upon mother), sang his heart out, and proceeded to sell even more records and break worldwide cinema box office records that would stand for a decade. All of Hollywood—then as now, loathe to take a chance but impetuous to imitate and capitalize on a success—rushed to embrace talkies.

The hybrid part-silent, part-talkie films were quickly supplanted by all-talking, all-singing, all-dancing efforts, one of the earliest and best of which is MGM's first all-talkie, *The Broadway Melody* (1929), which won an Academy Award for Best Picture. Like most of the earliest musicals, it featured uninspiringly choreographed numbers, filmed with a camera rooted to a single vantage point in the orchestra seats. Its backstage story of both members of a sister act falling for the same song-and-dance man was old in 1929. Yet *The Broadway Melody* was groundbreaking in several ways. For one, most of its songs were newly written, specifically for the film. In addition, whereas all of the musical numbers were filmed and recorded live, one of them, "The Wedding of the Painted Doll," required a reshoot several days later. Rather than calling back the orchestra and setting up the microphones, the sound director simply replayed the prerecorded track, and the singers and dancers mimed to it. This would soon become common practice in all musicals, allowing for greater camera flexibility as well as total but separate visual and musical manufacture. A final innovation is the introduction of the film musical's first "integrated" song—a song that springs from the plot, furthers the storyline, and delineates character. While integrated songs existed in Broadway shows, where the artificial theatricality of the production is unavoidable, filmmakers assumed that audiences would balk or laugh at the unreality of a film character suddenly bursting into song in a living room or sidewalk cafe. Thus, songs in the earliest musicals were introduced into the narrative in the context of a show: sung by a performer as a performance, on a stage or at a piano, with seldom anything to say or do with the plot itself. However, at one point in *The Broadway Melody*, Eddie (Charles King) can no longer hide his feelings for Queenie (Anita Page). As they sit together in her hotel room, the music suddenly rises and he sings "You Were Meant for Me." As an integrated song, it advances and is part of the plot, functioning as dialogue, but suiting Eddie's heightened emotional state.

The integrated film musical was being created but studios—uncertain of how audiences would react to the unexpected singing by characters in everyday places and situations—initially avoided them, preferring the safety of the backstage musical with its straight, all-spoken storyline, occasionally interrupted by a musical number in a rehearsal situation or onstage performance. In fact, of the twenty-two film musicals that opened in the first half of 1929, seventeen were situated in the world of show business, with such titles as *Queen of the Night Clubs*, *On with the Show!*, *Broadway Babies*, *Broadway Scandals*, and *Gold Diggers of Broadway* (Bradley 1996, 25). Many of these were vehicles for popular stage performers who, lured by large paychecks and the possibility of reaching a huge new audience that never made it to Broadway, stepped off the stage and in front of the camera. George Jessel, Texas Guinan, Sophie Tucker, the Marx Brothers, Marilyn Miller, Beatrice Lillie, George Burns and Gracie Allen, and radio stars Fred Waring, Ted Lewis, Rudy Vallee, and Bing Crosby were just some of the names and voices to which Middle America could now connect a face.

Many people went to these new talking films out of sheer curiosity at the novelty of a cinema screen that, so recently silent, now burst with music (and, in many cases, primitive color). Like the earliest film audiences that sat entranced before short plotless "flickers" (as they were called) of a train leaving a station or a busy city street, 1929 filmgoers couldn't get enough song and dance—so why even bother with a storyline? In a running time of roughly ninety minutes, the all-star musical revue packed in as many unrelated musical and stunt numbers, by a wide variety of performers, as was possible. All the major studios rushed to produce a revue that would showcase the abilities and personalities of their stable of performers—new acquisitions from the stage as well as established stars whose future careers depended on passing the microphone test. The Fox studio was first, with *William Fox Movietone Follies of 1929.* That same year saw *Hollywood Revue of 1929* (MGM) and *The Show of Shows* (Warner Brothers), followed in 1930 by *Paramount on Parade* and *King of Jazz* (Universal).

There is nothing remarkable or important about these or most of the other early musicals. Cinemas were being wired for sound and audiences demanded more and more pictures, which Hollywood gladly produced. The same tried and true plots and situations appeared over and over. Only a few films of this period demonstrate originality or continue to hold our interest. Those musicals that do accomplish this are the creation of innovative and maverick directors who created new film aesthetics and broke from their stage roots. King Vidor's *Hallelujah!* (MGM) was one of two African American musicals of 1929. Although its condescending racial and sexual stereotypes are undeniable, it is a noble effort and one of very few works of the studio age with an all-black cast. Vidor put up his own money to produce what MGM considered a potential box office disaster, especially in the South, and the film had separate, segregated New York premieres. Among its claims to fame is the inclusion of Irving Berlin's first song written for a film, "Waiting at the End of the Road."

Film writer David Thomson has characterized director Rouben Mamoulian's film work as an effort "to blend movement, dancing, action, music, singing, décor, and lighting into one seething entity" (1995, 474). Mamoulian's *Applause* (1929) does this in spades, and has been called "the first artistically successful American talking film" (Bradley 1996, 249). The story of a self-destructive, alcoholic burlesque queen (played by the similarly hard-living Broadway star Helen Morgan), fatally ill-used by men but redeemed by her love for her daughter, *Applause* combines grim realism with astonishing stylistic methods of movement and continuity and innovations in sound. Frustrated by the sound camera's immobility, Mamoulian shot long, sweeping tracking shots with a silent machine and dubbed in the soundtrack later. For one sequence involving simultaneous actions, as the mother sings a lullaby while her daughter prays aloud, the director defied the Paramount sound crew and set up two microphones instead of one, capturing both performers in the first instance of multichannel sound recording. Inventively, *Applause* uses music and images for continuity and transition, as when a handbill advertising the burlesque queen's act is snatched from the sidewalk by a dog that runs down the street and eventually passes the carriage in which the very performer is riding into town. In another scene, a shot of the mother fondling a necklace fades into a scene of her daughter clutching a rosary at convent school.

The 1930s

The third and perhaps most innovative director of early musicals was Ernst Lubitsch. The famed "Lubitsch touch" that animates his films (including nonmusicals such as *Trouble in Paradise* [1932], *Design for Living* [1933], *Ninotchka* [1939], and *The Shop Around the Corner* [1940]) is a stylish, sophisticated, and worldly treatment of sex and relationships, wherein love and fidelity are applauded but not generally practiced. In an endearing, nonjudgmental way, Lubitsch delights in exposing his characters' human foibles: they constitute an in-joke to which the audience is privy and deflate all the tired, theatrical clichés of grand passion. *The Love Parade* (1929), *Monte Carlo* (1930), *The Smiling Lieutenant* (1931), and *One Hour With You* (1932) are witty operettas set in a Ruritanian Europe, peopled by wayward counts and countesses pushing societal mores (and their marital vows) to the limit but always, albeit somewhat jadedly, restored to happiness in the end. The imaginative fluidity with which Lubitsch stages the song "Beyond the Blue Horizon" in *Monte Carlo* is justifiably famous. Jeanette MacDonald has abandoned her nobleman husband at the altar, fleeing to Monte Carlo for adventure and, inspired by the rhythmic clicking of the train upon its tracks, she sings of a future full of the promise of romance. The camera pans to happy peasants in the fields who, inspired by her rapturous message, burst out in song to accompany her in the second verse, as the music and train rush breathlessly forward.

Unfortunately, for every groundbreaking Vidor, Mamoulian, and Lubitsch, there were countless hack directors, turning out uninspired, imitative musicals. The problem with all these revues and films made of stage shows was that, although they are an interesting record of musical theater of the day, they represent a setback in cinematic art. Most of them were simply filmed plays, unnecessarily aping the necessities and conventions of the theater. Technology was another problem. The sound recording quality was often poor. Because the early cameras were extremely loud, they had to be kept far from the action (and microphones) or were encased in heavy soundproof boxes. Either way, the camera became immobile, and the amazing tracking shots and camera movement that typify late silent films were impossible. In addition, actors and singers had to stand near stationary microphones in order to be heard, further restricting movement. Mamoulian was unique in his attempts to escape these limitations. A glut of stagy, inconsistently audible, and numbingly similar musicals soon wearied cinemagoers who, by 1931, were staying away. The backlash against the musical is measurable: in 1929, sixty were produced and in 1930, more than eighty were produced, but in 1931 and again in 1932, only eleven were made. By then, horror and gangster films were the new rage. Before it could recapture the public's imagination, the musical would have to reinvent itself for the screen.

Starting in 1933, RKO and Warner Brothers began producing two series of films whose original, audacious dance numbers revolutionized the musical and restored its popularity with audiences. RKO's *Flying Down to Rio* suffers a flimsy plot and wooden performances by its stars Dolores Del Rio and Gene Raymond. Besides a bizarre but fun sequence in which chorus girls dance upon and then parachute from the wings of biplanes, the film is remembered as the first pairing of dancers Fred Astaire—another Broadway transplant—and Ginger Rogers. Realizing what it was on to, the studio ended the film with a shot of this couple—supporting players—rather than of the film's two purported stars, and rushed Astaire and Rogers into their own starring vehicle. Thus began a series of frothy dance musicals, filmed in sparkling black and white, in which boy meets girl, boy loses girl, and boy gets girl, amid stylized art deco sets, fabulous gowns, and tailored tuxedos: *The Gay Divorcee* (1934), *Roberta* (1935), *Top Hat* (1935), *Follow the Fleet* (1936), *Swing Time* (1936), *Shall We Dance* (1937), *Carefree* (1938), and *The Story of Vernon and Irene Castle* (1939). The pair played off each other well: he softened her somewhat hard, driven persona, while she vitalized his distanced, sexless manner. For their numbers, Astaire and choreographer Hermes Pan created totally original dance routines (to newly composed—and immediately classic—songs commissioned from Jerome Kern, Irving Berlin, and the Gershwins). Like integrated songs, these routines function as character and narrative development, and spring organically from the plot. Most musicals of the time utilized preexisting songs, but the written-for-the-screen Astaire/Rogers songs are integral, narrative-driven components. In *The American Film Musical*, Rick Altman demonstrates how traditional New Comedy (as seen in Shakespeare and Moliere), in which a generational conflict is resolved when young lovers overcome the machinations and thwarting efforts of disapproving parents and are allowed to marry, is supplanted in many musicals by a romantic comedy that pits the lovers against *each other*, wherein pride or vanity on one or both sides engenders plot complications (1987, 143–44). Thus, in the Lubitsch films, Maurice Chevalier and Jeanette MacDonald fall in love, quarrel, suffer misunderstandings, and are inevitably reunited, all in song. Astaire and Rogers do the same, but in dance numbers, which become true mating rituals. In *Roberta*, Astaire says to Rogers, "People in love are always quarreling with each other." In their films, song and dance titles such as "I'll Be Hard to Handle," "Let's Call the Whole Thing Off," and "Never Gonna Dance" sum up the bumps encountered on the road to reunion and love. These RKO films let the dancing speak for itself; the imaginative, slick choreography is filmed in lengthy medium shots, with few cuts or self-evident angles. Elsewhere, another—equally entertaining—kind of dance film emerged.

Warner Brothers' contribution to the watershed year 1933 was the reinvigoration of the backstage musical, by means of three astonishing films: *42nd Street*, *Footlight Parade*, and *Gold Diggers of 1933*. These and their successors—*Wonder Bar* and *Dames* (1934), *Gold Diggers of 1935*, and *Gold Diggers of 1937*—featured a rotating set of actors (Dick Powell, Ruby Keeler, Joan Blondell, Ginger Rogers, Guy Kibbee), songwriters (Al Dubin and Harry Warren), and, most important, the visionary dance sequence director Busby Berkeley. When Broadway sensation Eddie Cantor came to Hollywood in 1930 to film his stage sensation *Whoopee!*, he insisted that dance director Berkeley accompany him and choreograph the film. *Whoopee!* features cinema's first extended use of an overhead camera in a dance number, introducing audiences to Berkeley's signature kaleidoscopic effects. Over the next few years, he would indulge in increasingly audacious and visually stunning production numbers, utilizing large numbers of chorus girls arranged in angular, geometric configurations and shot from every conceivable perspective. Berkeley had worked on Broadway but, unlike most early film choreographers who simply filmed staged numbers, he realized that a new spatial approach was needed for the cinema. Unlike stationary theatergoers with their single vantage point, Berkeley's camera revolves and zooms in and out and up and down—choreographed every bit as much as are the dancers themselves. In addition, Berkeley's cinematic license demolished the simulation of a theater stage. His numbers were shot in huge studio soundstages, featuring sequences and sets that no real theater stage could hold: waterfalls ("By a Waterfall"), city streets ("42nd Street"), trains ("Shuffle Off to Buffalo"), subway cars ("I Only Have Eyes for You"), waterfront dives ("Shanghai Lil"), and exclusive nightclubs ("Lullaby of Broadway"), as well as endless open spaces for large numbers of dancers to assume all manner of geometric patterns and configurations. A song and dance number may begin and end with a curtain going up and down, but within the routine, we are off on a flight of fancy into pure cinematic visual imagination.

The Warner Bothers/Berkeley films are backstage, not integrated musicals. In fact, the first few pile up all their big musical numbers at the very end of the film, following a straightforward story of the hard-knock life in the theater. The studio was aware of cinemagoers' dissatisfaction with musicals and, if need be, was prepared to remove the numbers altogether, releasing a nonmusical. As it was, the films were enormously successful with Depression-weary audiences. Warner Brothers was known for its harsh gangster films, and a gritty, cynical mood imbues these musicals, which are, as Ethen Mordden puts it, "suffused with Depression panic" (1981, 236). The title song of *42nd Street* proclaims, this is "Where the underworld can meet the elite," and a subplot in the film involves a gangster hired to threaten or even kill a boyfriend who is distracting the leading lady of the new show. The gold diggers, chorus girls desperate for work in a hard-hit profession, speak in a jaded and abrasive urban slang, have such nicknames as "Anytime Annie" ("She only said 'no' once and, then, she didn't hear the question.") and will do literally anything to further their careers.

The gold diggers are put through their paces. Chorus girls Ginger Rogers, Ruby Keeler, and Una Merkel help put on a show in *42nd Street* (1933). *Photofest.*

Musicals were extremely popular during the Depression, but not necessarily because they offered hope (cinemagoers flocked to saccharine, goodness-affirming Shirley Temple vehicles, but also to the hard, cynical *Gold Diggers* films). Rather, audiences sought a much-needed escape from reality—a penthouse and a yacht, or the Big House and the streets. Either extreme offered cinemagoers a glimpse into other worlds and an hour or two in which to forget their own.

The 1940s and 1950s

By the late 1930s, the Berkeley and Astaire/Rogers films had spent themselves, and Warner Brothers and RKO were replaced as the primary musical-producing studios by Twentieth Century-Fox and MGM, which would jointly rule this genre for the next twenty years, until its demise. Each studio devoted vast amounts of time and money toward discovering, training, grooming, and displaying musical talent. The 1940s and 1950s, the great age of the studio system, is also the great age of the movie musical. Fox had survived the Depression through the tremendous success of its Shirley Temple films. (Temple, like such stars as Paramount's Mae West and Marlene Dietrich, was not known primarily as a singer—indeed, she was a more gifted dancer, yet their films almost always cast them as performers and contained some musical numbers.) Alice Faye emerged from the Temple vehicles as Fox's first great musical star and appeared in several films set at the turn of or early in the century: *In Old Chicago* (1938), *Alexander's Ragtime Band* (1938), *Lillian Russell* (1940), *Tin Pan Alley* (1940), and *Hello, Frisco, Hello* (1943). Fox always seemed to have a new blond female star waiting in the wings, and a collection of tall, dark, and handsome (nonsinging) men with whom to pair her, including Don Ameche, Tyrone Power, Cesare Romero, Victor Mature, and John Payne. By the early 1940s, Faye's career was running out of steam, but she had been paired with and was now supplanted by Betty Grable, who quickly became the No. 1 pin-up girl of World War II and a top-ten box office star from 1942 to 1951. Grable had more sex appeal than Faye, and her nonthreatening, all-American, girl-next-door persona (she acted, sang, and danced but was not extraordinarily gifted at any of these) was perfectly suited to the times: *Down Argentine Way* (1940), *Tin Pan Alley* (1940), *Moon Over Miami* (1941), *Song of the Islands* (1942), *Coney Island* (1943), *Sweet Rosie O'Grady* (1943), *Pin Up Girl* (1944), *Diamond Horseshoe* (1945), *The Dolly Sisters* (1945), *The Shocking Miss Pilgrim* (1947), *Mother Wore Tights* (1947), and so on. Grable was paired in *The Dolly Sisters* with blond June Haver, groomed by the studio to be her successor, but whose personality was not as strong and whose success was only moderate. Fox would do much better with its 1950s blonde, Marilyn Monroe, who starred in a couple of musicals whose titles could be used to describe the raison d'etre of these women's careers: *Gentlemen Prefer Blondes* (1953) and *There's No Business Like Show Business* (1954).

MGM was known for stars and glamour, and its musicals certainly maintained this reputation. While Fox had its blonde du jour, MGM had a large roster of musical and dance talent, both female and—unlike Fox—male. Fox almost exclusively produced backstage musicals, their songs performed in rehearsals or on stages, and often in low-brow or working class settings (*Tin Pan Alley*, *Coney Island*). MGM, on the other hand, had highbrow aspirations, employing opera singers such as Lawrence Tibbett, Jeanette MacDonald, Kathryn Grayson, and Mario Lanza, and favoring the integrated musical. Producer Joseph Pasternak in particular favored such highbrow fare. While at Universal, he had produced several films starring Deanna Durbin, a young singer with a light operatic voice, surrounding her with classical musicians and incorporating "serious" music in such films as *One Hundred Men and a Girl* (1937) and *Mad About Music* (1938). At MGM, Pasternak worked orchestra conductor Jose Iturbi and classical music into the plots and soundtracks of several films, including *Music for Millions* (1944) and *Anchors Aweigh* (1945), coaxing to Hollywood other stars of the classical music world, such as Wagnerian tenor Lauritz Melchior in *The Thrill of a Romance* (1945). One of the studio's great successes was the pairing of MacDonald with baritone Nelson Eddy in a series of operettas, including *Naughty Marietta* (1935), *Rose Marie* (1936), *Maytime* (1937), and *Sweethearts* (1938). Whereas MacDonald had been relaxed, sexual, and teasing in her early (pre-Code) films with Chevalier at Paramount, at MGM she was a dignified if somewhat aloof "great lady." Her tongue-in-cheek Paramount films are about sex, while the schmaltzy MGM operettas—with or without Eddy—are about romance. In the 1950s, MGM's operetta lovers were Kathryn Grayson and Mario Lanza, in *That Midnight Kiss* (1949) and *The Toast of New Orleans* (1950), and Grayson and Howard Keel, in *Show Boat* (1951), *Lovely to Look At* (1952), and *Kiss Me, Kate* (1953).

The greatest star of MGM—if not of all—musicals was Judy Garland. Brought to the studio as a child, she was groomed (completely irresponsibly and unhealthily, it would later be revealed) for greatness. At fifteen, she stopped the show in *The Broadway Melody of 1938* (1937), singing "You Made Me Love You" to a photograph of the "king of the MGM lot," Clark Gable, in her astonishingly mature voice. Two years later, she herself became a star, playing Dorothy in the legendary *The Wizard of Oz* and winning a special Academy Award. Garland possessed a startlingly emotional intensity—even a rawness—in both her singing and acting. While never exotic or a great beauty, she excelled portraying characters with whom the audience could relate. MGM rushed her into a string of films, at times paired with Mickey Rooney in such "let's put on a show!" juvenile backstage musicals as *Babes in Arms* (1939), *Strike Up the Band* (1940), and *Babes on Broadway* (1941), all directed by Busby Berkeley in the second stage of his film career, working as director as well as choreographer, away from Warner Brothers and not as obsessed with overhead geometric shots but still creating complex and imaginative stagings for large groups of dancers. (He would work at Twentieth Century-Fox as well, creating, among other sequences, the completely over-the-top campiness of Carmen Miranda's "The Lady with the Tutti-Frutti Hat" number in *The Gang's All Here*, 1943.) Even better are Garland's later MGM films, *Ziegfeld Girl* (1941), *For Me and My Gal* (1942), *Meet Me in St. Louis* (1944), *The Harvey Girls* (1946), *Easter Parade* (1948), and *In the Good Old Summertime* (1949). Blockbusters all, they enjoyed the budgets, sets, scoring, and high production values ensured in a premium MGM project and performed by Garland in her prime, before years of problems with weight, drug use, and emotional breakdown made her unreliable and forced the studio to let her go.

While Fox musicals may have employed as fillers such novelty dance acts as the Nicholas Brothers, MGM was known for showcasing its choreographers and dancers, including Eleanor Powell, Ann Miller, Donald O'Connor, Cyd Charisse, and, greatest of all, Gene Kelly and Fred Astaire (after Astaire left RKO and Ginger Rogers). As discussed earlier, Astaire and Kelly (especially Kelly) brought the dance musical to new heights.

Musicals were very much of their time but seldom ready to offer up social or political commentary. So although the early 1930s *Gold Diggers* films painted a caustic portrait of economic hard times, the big production numbers such as "Pettin' in the Park" and "I Only Have Eyes for You" are pure escapist froth, filling the screen with scantily clad chorines and the love-starved young men who desire them. Only once did a Busby Berkeley production number utilize men exclusively—"Remember My Forgotten Man," from *Gold Diggers of 1933*. This number, featuring marching hordes of World War I ex-soldiers, erstwhile heroes now out of work because of the Depression, attempts (noncontroversial) social criticism. With the approach of another world war, however, musicals were more than ready to parade their patriotism. First came the "good neighbor" policy films that mirrored and fueled a rage for Latin American music. Using just one studio as an example, Twentieth Century-Fox's *Down Argentine Way* (1940),

Judy Garland, the greatest star of the film musical. The seventeen-year-old sings "Over the Rainbow" in *The Wizard of Oz* (1939), and a legend is born. *Photofest.*

That Night in Rio (1941), and *Weekend in Havana* (1941) take place in a sunny, peaceful, southern hemisphere of racetracks and nightclubs, and come alive to the inimitable and infectious sounds of congas, rhumbas, and fruit-topped, platform-shod Carmen Miranda. After the bombing of Pearl Harbor, all of Hollywood set about producing patriotic projects to fulfill its unquestionably important role in the war effort. Doing "their bit," musicals sought to entertain both the boys at the front and their anxious friends and relatives back home, all the while reminding them of what they were fighting for.

Some musicals conveyed their patriotic messages in films set in the past. Warner Brothers' *Yankee Doodle Dandy* (1942) uses a framing device of legendary showman George M. Cohan ("born on the fourth of July") in consultation with President Roosevelt, from which unfolds a flashback retelling the tumultuous career of the singer-dancer-composer (played by James Cagney, who won an Academy Award in his greatest role). In it rags-to-riches plot and theatrical razzle-dazzle, the film is a paean to both show business and America itself, coalescing in such splashy production numbers as "Yankee Doodle Boy" and "You're a Grand Old Flag." Cohen simultaneously demonstrates his devoted sense of duty to both the stage and his country. Indeed, during the war, according to Hollywood, the two could not often be separated. That same year, the protagonist of MGM's *For Me and My Gal* struggles between his egotistical, selfish desire to become a success in vaudeville and his patriotic, selfless duty to fight in World War I. In his film debut that would make him a star, Gene Kelly sets his sights upon "playing the Palace" (Theater). Despite the disapproval of stage partner—and eventual girlfriend—Judy Garland, he initially dismisses the war as an avoidable obstruction to his career plans. She does her duty, performing for the troops, while he shuns his, injuring his hand to avoid military service. Of course, Kelly eventually sees the error of his ways, goes off and fights, becomes a hero in the process, and returns to triumphantly play the Palace with his proud and adoring partner. Audiences in 1942 ate it up.

Another MGM period piece, unconnected in plot to war or show business, is *Meet Me in St. Louis* (1944), which chronicles a year in the lives of the Smith family of St. Louis, around the time of the 1903 World's Fair. The film is very much a reminder of "what we are fighting for," a Norman Rockwell Americana painting come to life, as the Smiths go about their ordinary, everyday business of growing up, falling in love with the boy next door, making ketchup, throwing parties, and generally looking out for each other. Such integrated musical numbers as "The Boy Next Door," "The Trolley Song," and "Have Yourself a Merry Little Christmas" reminded audiences of the simple joys of a peacetime existence. A crisis arises when the father, to the family's dismay, accepts a job transfer to New York City, an emergency that brings to a head the film's wartime theme of outward threats to tradition and the sacrosanct American home. This threat is subverted, and the film ends, as had *The Wizard of Oz*, with Judy Garland proudly extolling the wonder and virtue of home.

A defining aspect of the wartime musical is the reintroduction and success of the revue film. While the USO and various entertainment committees toured military bases at home and overseas and opened canteens in the larger cities to divert and amuse soldiers on leave, Hollywood jumped at the chance to join in the effort, and created all-star extravaganzas for both soldiers and civilians. These efforts resemble Depression-era escapist movies, but the message is now one of affirmation. Set in the world of show business, revue films exploit the "show must go on" mantra of the entertainer, easily conflating it with the wartime mentality. Performers' struggles and successes are thus set within a broader context of patriots' duty to work together and produce their best. The musical revue films thus extol the glory of both show business and the Allied cause, as seen in *Stage Door Canteen* (1943) and *Hollywood Canteen* (1944), which simultaneously apotheosize Hollywood stars *and* American G.I.s.

After the war, MGM reigned supreme in the field of prestige musicals, with a string of artistic and popular successes. In addition to the Kathryn Grayson/Mario Lanza and Judy Garland films mentioned above, MGM produced the revue *Ziegfeld Follies* (1946), the college musical *Good News* (1947), a musical version of Eugene O'Neill's stage play *Ah Wilderness*, titled *Summer Holiday* (1948), the baseball musical *Take Me Out to the Ball Game* (1949), a re-teaming of Rogers and Astaire in *The Barkleys of Broadway* (1949), the glorious sailors-on-leave musical *On the Town* (1949), the Broadway version of Annie Oakley's story, *Annie Get Your Gun* (1950), Fred Astaire dancing on the ceiling in *Royal Wedding* (1951), yet another remake of the chestnut *Show Boat* (1951), and the two films considered by many to be the greatest musicals of all, *An American in Paris* (1951) and *Singin' in the Rain* (1952). Both were produced by Arthur Freed, the genius responsible for assembling and inspiring the multitalented people, both on and behind the screen, who created so many great MGM musicals, starting with *The Wizard of Oz*. *An American in Paris* lets loose Gene Kelly (as an ex-G.I. painter) and Leslie Caron to dance on colorful, impressionistic Parisian sets, inspired, in turns, by impressionist works by Dufy, Renoir, Utrillo, Rousseau, and Van Gogh, all gloriously accompanied by the music of George and Ira Gershwin. *Singin' in the Rain* features a plot of the *42nd Street*, "star is born" type, set in Hollywood in the tumultuous days of the conversion from silent to sound pictures. Gene Kelly, Donald O'Connor, and Debbie Reynolds sing and dance to two new songs but the bulk of the tunes—title number, "I've Got a Feelin' You're Foolin'," "You Were Meant for Me," "You Are My Lucky Star," and "Good Morning"—were taken from the earliest MGM musicals, circa 1930. *An American in Paris* won the Academy Award for Best Picture of its year, but later critics and audiences have come to appreciate and prefer *Singin' in the Rain*.

The 1960s and 1970s

In the 1950s and 1960s, besides the enormously successful Elvis Presley vehicles, smaller-budget films exploited the popularity of rock-and-roll music in such series as the beach musicals, starring Frankie Avalon and Annette Funicello (*Beach Party* [1963], *Beach Blanket Bingo* [1965], and so on). By the 1960s, however, the musical's heyday had definitely passed. Despite some blockbusters, fewer and fewer were produced. Musical tastes—and Hollywood itself—were changing. Pop music and rock and roll owed less to Tin Pan Alley and show tunes than to jazz and country music. The musicals that were produced were generally Broadway triumphs, considered to be surefire hits. However, the phenomenal early success of two stars—Julie Andrews and Barbra Streisand—and their films only encouraged the studios to pour ever-greater amounts of cash into one or two big splashy musicals per year, which inevitably lost money. Andrews and Streisand, both hot off Broadway triumphs, proved enormously successful in their film debuts. Not yet proven on the screen, Andrews made *Mary Poppins* (1964) for Disney after being passed over to recreate her Broadway success in the film version of *My Fair Lady*. (The part went to film actress Audrey Hepburn, whose singing was dubbed.) But Andrews won an Academy Award for *Poppins* and her next film, *The Sound of Music* (1965), became the most popular film of its time, due largely to her performance. On the other hand, no one other than Streisand was ever considered to recreate her Broadway success as Fanny Brice in the film version of *Funny Girl* (1968). Like Andrews, she won an Oscar for her film role. Both actresses were immediately pushed into a series of big-budget, overblown musicals—efforts to cash in on their phenomenal initial success. Andrews's musicals were written for the screen: *Thoroughly Modern Millie* (1967) proved slight but enjoyable, but *Star!* (1968) and *Darling Lili* (1970) failed with critics and at the box office, in part because of Andrews's attempt to change her "pure" image but also because of Streisand's arrival on the scene. The late

1960s were simply different from the first half of the decade and these two stars reflect that. While Andrews was sweet and virginal with a voice suitable for operetta, Streisand was loud, brash, and a belter. After *Funny Girl*, she was rushed into two huge period musicals based on the Broadway successes *Hello, Dolly!* (1969; a role for which she was far too young) and *On a Clear Day You Can See Forever* (1970). These did better than Andrews's follow-ups, but are stiffly directed and stifled the young star under layers of costumes and acres of period sets. They never recouped their astronomical production costs.

In the 1960s and early 1970s, Hollywood produced one or two films per year based on Broadway musicals. In addition to those already mentioned, there were *West Side Story* (1961), *The Music Man* (1962), *Gypsy* (1962), *Bye Bye Birdie*, (1963), *A Funny Thing Happened on the Way to the Forum* (1966), *How to Succeed in Business Without Really Trying* (1967), *Camelot* (1967), *Finian's Rainbow* (1968), *Sweet Charity* (1969), *Paint Your Wagon* (1969), *Fiddler on the Roof* (1971), *Cabaret* (1972), *Man of La Mancha* (1972), *Jesus Christ Superstar* (1973), *Godspell* (1973), and *Mame* (1974). Some of these succeeded, owing to an indestructible score, great performances, or a visionary director who saw outside the proscenium arch. *West Side Story* achieved the seemingly impossible task of transforming street thugs into balletic dynamos. The surefire combination of the Romeo and Juliet story, Leonard Bernstein's masterful classical- and Latin-influenced score, Jerome Robbins's athletic choreography, and New York City settings was responsible for the film's success. It was the decade's most awarded film, with Best Picture nods from both the Academy of Motion Picture Arts and Sciences and the *New York Times*'s film critics. However, many of these decades' musicals collapsed under the weight of exorbitant budgets that paid for huge period sets and expensive nonsinging (but dubbable) stars, and by ignoring the script, songs, and public (as well as good) taste. A musical works onstage largely from the frisson and excitement of the live performance. A film musical must recreate this live experience at some level in order to succeed, but far too many of the blockbuster musicals of the 1970s were dead on arrival, killed by their producers' overreaching megalomania and bigger-is-better attitude. Lucille Ball was a comic genius but a terrible singer. Yet, to draw customers, she was cast as the title character in *Mame*. Likewise, Liv Ullmann and Peter Finch are two of the greatest dramatic actors of the 1960s and 1970s—but who in the world agreed to hire them as singers, in the disastrously overproduced musical version of James Hilton's *Lost Horizon* (1973)? Certainly there were plenty of bad musicals made in the thirties, forties, and fifties, but never such staggering wastes of time, money, and talent. Although the big studios had managed to absorb the periodic loss of an unpopular musical, by the late 1970s, with entertainment companies going bankrupt right and left, this was no longer the case. Musicals, which almost invariably cost a great deal to produce, were simply too risky.

The 1980s to the Present

The arrival and success of MTV in the early 1980s triggered a spate of dance musicals whose production numbers—with their exaggerated lighting and colors, fast editing, and high energy—are basically music videos, emerging periodically from plotlines that were stale back when they appeared in the "let's put on a show" MGM musicals starring Judy Garland and Mickey Rooney. The anxious kids enrolled in New York's High School for the Performing Arts in *Fame* (1980), the would-be dancer working as a welder in a Pittsburgh steel mill in *Flashdance* (1983), and the frustrated city kid transplanted to a small town that forbids dancing in *Footloose* (1984) all long for the glitz and glamour—not to mention the sensual excitement—of performing. Under directors such as Adrian Lyne (who began his career working in expensive British commercials), the performers are presented in a slick, extravagant manner. These films were extremely popular, and inspired a string of imitations, thanks in part to best-selling hit singles and soundtrack recordings (which often made more money than the films), as well as to the regular and continuous appearance in video form of their big production numbers on MTV.

In the last few years, a couple of widely popular musicals have been touted as harbingers of a revival of the genre. Australian Baz Luhrmann's *Moulin Rouge* (2001), starring Nicole Kidman and Ewan McGregor, is set in the Belle Epoque Paris of *La Boheme*, peopled by slumming nobility, courtesans, dancehall girls, and starving artists who meet, inspire, plot against, and seduce each other at the famed nightspot of the title. Luhrmann's canvas is an exploding mosaic of colors, sounds, and editing that idiosyncratically mixes late twentieth-century pop songs by Elton John and Madonna into his nineteenth-century milieu. The film polarized audiences, largely along generational lines, as its rapid editing, exaggerated and filled-to-bursting sets, endless movement, and high volume unashamedly utilized the techniques of pop music videos. Most audiences loved the general cacophony and chaos, as well as the high-energy musical numbers, while some viewers longed for some downtime respite and better songs. In *Moulin Rouge*, as in the even more triumphant *Chicago* (2002), all the musical numbers are presented and performed as showstoppers, with no time for musical introspection or reflection. Based on Bob Fosse's dark, cynical stage success, *Chicago* explores America's obsession with celebrity. It is the tale of two desperate women in 1920s Chicago, both driven to commit murders of passion and each using her notoriety (and the public's fascination with sordid sex crimes) to further her singing career. As Fosse did in *Cabaret*—a film whose influence imbues *Chicago* and which shares the same songwriters and dark perspective—director Rob Marshall opted against creating an integrated musical. He instead let the musical numbers spin from the troubled imagination of Roxie Hart, an actual murderess whose trial was followed by the national media. Established stars Richard Gere, Renee Zellweger, Queen Latifah, and Catherine Zeta-Jones (who won an Academy Award) prove accomplished if not tremendous singing and dancing talents. In the case of all but Latifah, the film's rapid editing indicates director Marshall's realization that the camera must both cover and improve his stars' performance abilities. Again like Bob Fosse's *Cabaret*, which exposes the users and the used of Weimar Germany, the *Chicago* of gangster-

and Prohibition-era America indicts an exploitive social system while being simultaneously attracted to its colorful perversity.

Whether the success of these films (*Chicago* won the Academy Award as Best Film of its year) and filmed versions of stage triumphs such as *Hedwig and the Angry Inch* (2001) and *Rent* (2005) will trigger a renaissance in musicals remains to be seen. Just as the musical variety show has vanished from the American television landscape, so movie musicals have been overtaken in popularity by violent special-effects blockbusters that court young male filmgoers. Musicals, on the other hand, have long been associated with female and gay audiences. Perhaps for this reason, the musical has traditionally been slighted by film critics and by some filmgoers who see it as unreal and purely escapist (although such claims could be leveled at all films). In addition to their sheer energy, style, and visual power, as well as their documentation of legendary performances, musicals have showcased technological cinematic innovations and advances in sound, color, and screen size. They have been invaluable social and cultural barometers, revealing and shaping the habits, fears, desires, and frustrations of the American public in the latter three-quarters of the twentieth century.

References and Further Reading

Altman, Rick. *The American Film Musical*. Bloomington and Indianapolis: Indiana University Press, 1987.

Bradley, Edwin M. *The First Hollywood Musicals: A Critical Filmography of 171 Features, from 1927 to 1932*. Jefferson, NC: McFarland, 1996.

Cohan, Steven, ed. *Hollywood Musicals: The Film Reader*. London and New York: Routledge, 2002.

Feuer, Jane. *The Hollywood Musical*. 2nd ed. Bloomington: Indiana University Press, 1993.

Hirschhorn, Clive. *The Hollywood Musical*. New York: Crown, 1981.

Marshall, Bill, and Robynn Stilwell, eds. *Musicals: Hollywood and Beyond*. Exeter, Eng; Portland, OR: Intellect, 2000.

Mordden, Ethan. *The Hollywood Musical*. New York: St. Martin's, 1981.

———. *The Hollywood Studios: House Style in the Golden Age of the Movies*. New York: Knopf, 1988.

Schatz, Thomas. *Hollywood Genres: Formulas, Filmmaking, and the Studio System*. Philadelphia: Temple University Press, 1981. 186–220.

Thomson, David. *A Biographical Dictionary of Film*. 3rd ed. New York: Knopf, 1995.

CHAPTER 8
SCIENCE FICTION AND FANTASY

FROM THE BEGINNING, humanity has speculated on what exists beyond the known world, and for almost a century before the advent of film, science and scientific themes figured heavily in literary works by authors such as Mary Shelley, Nathaniel Hawthorne, Jules Verne, and H. G. Wells. With the invention of the motion picture, what could once only be speculated upon in the imagination might now be brought to vivid life in the new medium. But not until the marriage of science *fiction,* in the truest definition of the term, and the moving image, was a new genre born with the rise of science and technology looming in the background.

DEFINING CHARACTERISTICS

Through an exploration of the unknown, many of the characteristics of science fiction and fantasy films overlap, but discernible elements for each subgenre are present.

Focus on Science and Technology and the Anxieties They Create

The social, philosophical, political, and psychological impact of science and technology and anxieties about their abuse or misuse are at the root of science fiction films. As often presented, scientific and technological knowledge by itself presents no difficulties, as when medical breakthroughs miraculously saves lives or when it can be used as a way of explaining the downfall of a superior species, as numerous alien invasion films, such as *War of the Worlds* (1953 and 2005) or *Independence Day* (1996), demonstrate. But as often depicted in these films, the rapid rise of technological or scientific progress before societal mechanisms can be instituted to control them or before humanity can understand their potential becomes a source of anxiety and sometimes even brittle laughter, as in the case of nuclear annihilation in *Dr. Strangelove: or How I Learned to Stop Worrying and Love the Bomb* (1964).

The presence of science and technology alone, though, does not clearly define science fiction and fantasy films, because science fiction and horror often share similar elements or characteristics (see **Horror**). In his seminal article, "Children of the Id," critic Bruce Kawin concludes that although both genres often include a "bug-eyed monster," as Kawin calls any number of fantastic creatures, the genres differ in their attitudes toward the unknown. As he demonstrates in his comparison of two classics with similar plot elements, the science fiction film *The Day the Earth Stood Still* (1951) and the horror film *The Thing (from Another World)* (1951), both involve alien invasion, how society reacts to the outsiders, and how the military and scientific communities battle each other, sometimes bringing about a dangerous showdown that may mean the end of the world. For Kawin, science fiction films offer the opportunity for new learning and a new understanding of the unknown, which the alien represents, whereas the imperative of horror films is the preservation of the status quo, emphasizing the need to be on guard for future invasion.

Emphasis on the Unknown (Time, Space, and Setting)

Because the possibilities are endless within the realm of science and technology, science fiction films also fall under the category of fantasy films. Reflecting the limitlessness of the unknown, science fiction films often explicitly question the traditional understanding and acceptable limits of time, space, and setting. Time travel and the manipulation of time and its dimensions have become commonplace, as in *The Time Machine* (1960 and 2002), *Time Bandits* (1981), and *Back to the Future* (1985), and the shifting of spaces (both outer and inner) reflect the limitless boundaries of the unknown.

The setting for science fiction and fantasy films vary, however. Laboratories with blinking and buzzing machines, test tubes, and vials full of strangely-colored liquids (*The Fly* [1958]), deserted wilderness regions where alien space craft might land or strange creatures might exist and go undetected (*The Thing* [1951] and *Invaders from Mars* [1953]), and caves or craters that lead deep beneath the earth's surface (*Journey to the Center of the Earth* [1959]) are all iconic earthly settings and images of the classic science fiction and fantasy film. If set in the present, the discovery of new knowledge, new forms of life, or new worlds calls into question the stability of everyday human existence, prompting a reexamination of the status quo (as in *Close Encounters of the Third Kind* [1977] and *Contact* [1997]), sometimes with frightening consequences. Often, settings recognizable enough to qualify as present day take on a dystopic, alienating proportion, with their narratives set a short few years or decades in the future after a scientific or natural catastrophe or social breakdown, as in *The Planet of the Apes* (1968), *Soylent Green* (1973), *Brazil* (1985), *Artificial Intelligence: AI* (2001), and *Minority Report* (2002). Shots of well-known natural and human-made symbolic landmarks and the close chronological proximity of the narrative serve a cautionary function, warning society that some aspect of Earth's culture must change or risk the negative outcomes.

A significant number of science fiction films are set in futuristic landscapes, either in outer space, beneath the sea, or deep within the Earth's crust, and these locations often precipitate the narrative struggle between the known and the unknown, often translated as good versus evil. Space colonies on the outer reaches of galaxies require deep space travel in a variety of space vehicles (*Forbidden Planet* [1956] and *Star Trek: The Wrath of Khan* [1982]), and a quest for what lies beyond the stars supplies many science fiction films with their central themes and narrative devices, a search either by choice or, as in films such as *When Worlds Collide* (1951), out of necessity. Films that journey below the sea, into the Earth's crust, or into humanity's future remind audiences of what they may be sharing the planet with (*20,000 Leagues Under the Sea* [1954]), what they may have to fear in a fight for earth's supremacy (*The Beast from 20,000 Fathoms* [1953]), or where they may have evolved from (*The Planet of the Apes* [1968]). Audiences revel in front of panels of blinking lights in intergalactic space ships or underwater craft, and they marvel at special effects such as lasers and molecular transformers or regenerators in these versions of life in the future.

Fantasy Elements (Nonscientific or Classically Horrific)

Fantasy films which do not include science as a significant component often look back to earth's mythical past for patterns of behavior and codes of chivalry. Locations include kingdoms with a medieval castles and prehistoric misty forests (*Dragonslayer* [1981], *Excalibur* [1981], and *The Princess Bride* [1987]), futuristic landscapes on distant planets with an Arthurian cast (*Dune* [1984]), and other locales where time has stood still or been forgotten (*One Million Years B.C.* [1966] or *The Lord of the Rings: The Fellowship of the Ring* [2001]). Technically, because any film that requires a leap of faith or the suspension of disbelief on the audience's part in terms of the logic of plot, plot elements, setting, or characters can be categorized as a fantasy film, these films may just as easily be set in a suburban neighborhood (for instance, *E.T. the Extra-Terrestrial* [1982]) as in a nondescript wasteland or desert on a distant planet (for instance, *Star Wars* [1977]). A whole spectrum of films, for example, integrates fantasy elements such as magic (*Harry Potter and the Sorcerer's Stone* [2001]), benign supernatural creatures such as angels and fairies (*It's A Wonderful Life* [1946], *The Bishop's Wife* [1947], and *Hook* [1991]), and even God (*The Next Voice You Hear* [1950] and *Oh God!* [1977]) into everyday scenarios.

Plots

Narratively, science fiction films follow several patterns, and any situation might qualify as science fiction by slightly shifting perspective, making the real seem hyperreal, or by exposing a rift or tear in the fabric of accepted reality and stability in a *Twilight Zone* fashion (*Twilight Zone: The Movie* [1983] and *The Matrix* [1999]).

Journeys and quests of all kinds may be the most common motif in science fiction and fantasy films, either literal—such as journeys through space and time (*2001: A Space Odyssey* [1968]), under the ocean (*Voyage to the Bottom of the Sea* [1961]), to the center of the earth (*Journey to the Center of the Earth* [1959]), and into other uncharted territories (such as the human body in *Fantastic Voyage* [1966])—or metaphorical—beyond the boundaries of known science and technology or within the human mind and soul. Arthurian quests or their equivalent figure prominently in fantasy films, as a search for some relic, birthright, or truth lost, as clichéd as the phrase may be, in "the mists of time."

Invasion plots rival journey and quest motifs as the most popular form of science fiction story, particularly in certain eras of cinema history, such as the 1950s. In many films, the invasion of creatures from another world or from within unexplored areas of our own takes on allegorical significance, reflecting on screen the ideological tensions and social and political concerns of an era, such as nuclear apocalypse or the spread of communism (as in *Them!* [1954], *Invaders from Mars* [1953], and *Invasion of the Body Snatchers* [1956]). Films set in space often feature a clash of worlds, battles that also reflect ideological conflicts on present-day Earth. Space invaders visiting Earth, the outbreak of a misunderstood disease (*The Andromeda Strain* [1971] and *Outbreak* [1995]), changes in natural phenomena, the upheaval of the natural order through the intervention of science and technology, or the awakening of creatures from the deepest pockets of the globe often represent forces in society that threaten change. Sometimes, space invaders and other alien entities provide an important critique of the status quo, one that only the most enlightened on the planet are willing to heed, again serving a cautionary function (such as *The Day the Earth Stood Still* [1951]). Invasion films can expose the real conflicting forces in society: enlightenment, understanding, and a community spirit versus authoritarianism, rigidity, and force. These ideas might be represented by an inquiring scientist or intellectual's opposition to a military or political leader. With the rise of computers, cyber invaders may or may not take human or animal form, but they foretell global harm no matter how they appear externally (as in *Tron* [1982] or *The Matrix* [1999]).

Stock Characters

Stock characters in science fiction and fantasy films, both human and nonhuman, overlap with horror films, action-adventure films, thrillers, war films, and even Westerns. As Kawin has suggested, the "bug-eyed monster" and other mutant creatures create terror and sometimes evoke sympathy because they are misunderstood (as in *Starship Troopers* [1997]). Shape-shifters (*The Thing* [1982]) and moving pools of ectoplasm or oozing gelatinous forms (*The Blob* [1958]) raise questions about the line between plant and animal. From the animal world, hitherto relatively benign creatures such as spiders, insects, reptiles, and sea creatures become deadly enemies and predators as a result of radiation exposure, genetic mutation, or some other artificial manipulation of their species (*Them!* [1954], *Attack of the Giant Leeches* [1959], and *Wasp Woman* [1960]).

Other nonhuman figures include space aliens that take on a humanoid form (*The Day the Earth Stood Still* [1951]); robots with remarkable scientific and technical capabilities (like Robbie in *Forbidden Planet* [1956]); androids and cyborgs with flickering implants in their skulls whose machine side either denies them basic humanity and respect (*Westworld* [1973], *Star Wars* [1977], *Blade Runner* [1982], and *Artificial Intelligence: AI* [2001]) or serves as a locus of unhappiness and even violence (*Terminator* [1984], *RoboCop* [1987], or *Total Recall* [1990]). In fantasy films, mythical talking animals, dragons, hydras, flying horses, and unicorns frolic in enchanted medieval forests and woodlands (*The 7th Voyage of Sinbad* [1958] and *Jason and the Argonauts* [1963]). Computers even become significant characters, with HAL from Kubrick's *2001: A Space Odyssey* (1968) as the best example and Mother from *Alien* (1979) another.

Although mutant creatures and extraterrestrials often upstage their human counterparts, science fiction films feature scientists in all varieties, from the most deranged, probing the realms of the science at any cost (*The Thing* [1951] and *Forbidden Planet* [1956]), to the more analytical, sympathetic man (or occasionally woman) of science anxious to understand the phenomena placed before him in hopes of advancing human knowledge (*Them!* [1954] and *Contact* [1997]). Sometimes scientists are of a different generation than the hero or heroine of the science fiction thriller, and they bring a wisdom and experience otherwise lost in the fear and irrationality of the moment. Other intellectuals in science fiction films may include university professors of all kinds—physicists, geologists, botanists, anthropologists, philosophers, archeologists and Egyptologists, to name a few—and other erudite individuals interested in learning rather than killing (such as Jeff Goldblum's character in *Independence Day* [1996]). Public and civilian officials often serve as a moderating force between scientists, whose wish is to explore, and the military, whose instinct is to destroy (as in *The Day the Earth Stood Still* [1951]). Reporters and other members of the media often serve as observers rather than as participants in the advances surrounding science, wishing to save lives by telling the truth about the scientific discovery or otherworldly invaders (*Godzilla, King of the Monsters!* [1956]).

The heroes of science fiction films sometimes find themselves on the margins of society, chosen by authorities in a crisis for the special gifts that made them outlaws. In other cases, the hero is a renegade or free-spirited member of the authoritarian structure who has trouble fitting into it, such as a soldier (*Independence Day* (1996) or police officer (*Blade Runner* [1982]). Typically, science fiction protagonists are male, although prominent female characters played by actresses such as Sigourney Weaver (*Alien* [1979]) and Linda Hamilton (*Terminator* [1984]) are becoming more common. Often, the circumstances he finds himself in are forced upon him, and for reasons that he cannot even explain, he takes on the task of saving the earth, destroying the formula, or defeating the monster (*When Worlds Collide* [1951] and *Armageddon* [1998]). At other times, he serves in what functions as the military, either the conventional army or a space corps, and the dictates of his training send him on an impossible mission that only he can achieve (*Starship Troopers* [1997]). He often succeeds through a mixture of brawn and basic scientific knowledge that proves to be the Achilles heel of his opponent. His heroine and love interest fits all the classic qualifications for a supportive female cohort in classic versions of the science fiction films, and although she reveals a certain amount of courage and spunk, she is rarely his equal, reflecting attitudes toward gender when many of these films were made.

In fantasy films without a scientific premise, the hero is often a knight on a quest or an individual whose gift makes him emerge from the crowd as worthy of a challenge or uniquely qualified for the quest, whether for personal reasons or for his society at large. His world is replete with wizards, sorcerers, and magicians of all kinds, evil and otherwise, knowledgeable authorities on the wisdom of the ages (*The Lord of the Rings: The Fellowship of the Ring* [2001]). Gnomes, midgets, and giants are commonplace in his environment. Black knights, evil warlords, hostile barbaric chieftains, witches, and warlocks become his sworn enemies and stand in the way of the completion of his mission or quest. Fair maids and other women of noble rank or temperament stand by while he battles usurpers, and such a woman often becomes his reward for vanquishing evil and thwarting disorder (*The Princess Bride* [1987] and *King Kong* [1933]).

As science and technology advances and the ethical dilemmas surrounding them increase, the enemies or villains in science fiction films and the means to vanquish them may change, but the basic fear of invasion by an alien entity, animate or inanimate, disruption of the status quo, or journey or quest motives will remain the same, because science fiction films are predicated on the notion of an uneasy peace with the technological environment and a need or desire to understand the unknown.

HISTORY AND INFLUENCES

The Beginning to the 1930s

The pioneering examples of scientific fiction and fantasy filmmaking and cinema in general are often one in the same, as early filmmakers wove narrative features together with stunning visual effects through stop-action photography. Parisian magician Georges Méliès's loose adaptation of the Jules Verne novel *A Trip to the Moon* (1902) best represents this early era in the science fiction film arts, remarkable for advancing the art of filmmaking with its superimposition of images and creative use of dissolves and cuts before D. W. Griffith mastered such techniques. This basic story of a group of astronauts (a term for space voyagers that had not yet been invented) venturing to the moon is the beginning of the journey or quest narrative to come for the next hundred years. Archetypal images and plot points throughout the film include a surprisingly accurate rocket shot from a cannon; the landing of the rocket on the surface, protruding from the eye of the moon's face; and the existence of sprightly moon creatures (portrayed by acrobats from the Folies Bergère). An animated sequence near the end of the fourteen-minute short places the film at the beginning of animation in the twentieth century as well. Audiences originally perceived the film as a comedy, an assessment possibly based upon the entertaining rather than frightening moon creatures and the animated expressions on the face of the moon. The film's influence may be seen in the digitally created Paris nighttime skyline in Baz Luhrmann's *Moulin Rouge* (2001).

Not surprisingly, then, some of the best film explorations of technological anxieties in the emerging science fiction genre appeared in the 1920s, after World War I made all too clear the potential of unrestrained technology to destroy life and create havoc. Perhaps the best expression of postwar angst and technological anxiety is Fritz Lang's 1927 *Metropolis,* a prophetic look at life in the year 2000. Considered a motion picture, not just science fiction, masterpiece, Lang depicts a futuristic "unreal city," to use a reference from Eliot's *The Waste Land*, where humanity exists in two groups: the privileged, leisure classes who frolic in the open air spaces of Metropolis, and the impoverished masses almost literally chained to the machines that keep Metropolis running smoothly. Lang expanded on conventional uses of miniatures to suggest the vast landscape of this sterile, unfeeling city. The angularity of the lines that cross the landscape and Lang's manipulation of perspective to enhance the illusion of distance and size draws on German Expressionist cinema for their inspiration.

The narrative mixes melodrama and socialist polemic in the love story between the son of the master of Metropolis, Freder Fredersen (Gustav Fröhlich), and the beautiful Maria (Brigitte Helm), whom Fredersen spies retreating to the oppressiveness of Underground City. A series of dissolves suggests the demoralizing clock-like efficiency of the worker's lives below, begging the question "Do the workers operate the machines, or do the machines operate the workers?" Meanwhile, Rotwang, a scientist and inventor, creates a state-sponsored robot with the essence of Maria. At one point, the camera cuts to the robot in the guise of Maria preaching upheaval to the workers, convincing them to destroy the very machines that ensure their survival. The resulting flood unleashed by the revolting workers drowns some of their children, and they go in search of Maria to take revenge. Above ground, after the lights of Metropolis go dark, the workers find the robot Maria reveling in her triumph. They burn her at the stake, and Fredersen goes in search of the real Maria. The workers gather in an underground cathedral, realizing Fredersen is the intermediary they need between the privileged class and themselves.

Besides its striking set design, the film is landmark for its stunning, innovative visual effects, such as the subterranean flood and use of dissolves, and veteran German Expressionist cameraman and cinematographer Karl Freund put his mark on Lang's production through the application of light and shadow. The sets themselves are said to have inspired Ridley Scott's presentation of the futuristic and burned out Los Angeles city in *Blade Runner* (1982), and the design of George Lucas's C-3PO in *Star Wars* (1977) pays clear homage to Rotwang's robot Maria.

The 1930s

The 1930s produced a spate of science fiction–horror crossovers including *Doctor X* (1932), shot in the experimental two-strip Technicolor; *The Invisible Man* (1933), with its use of trick photography; and *The Island of Lost Souls* (1932),

The robot Maria in Fritz Lang's *Metropolis* (1927) served as a prototype for all motion picture robots after her, including C-3PO in George Lucas's *Star Wars* series. *Photofest.*

the first sound version of H. G. Wells's *The Island of Dr. Moreau* (1933), with Charles Laughton as a doctor breeding a strange group of animal-human creatures. With the exception of *The Wizard of Oz* (1939), perhaps the best known fantasy film of the 1930s is director Merian C. Cooper's and Ernest B. Schoedsack's *King Kong* (1933). Blonde actress Fay Wray lives up to her reputation as the "Queen of Scream" in this fanciful variation of a Beauty-and-the-Beast tale that involves the capture of a giant ape for exhibition and the actress the creature grows obsessed with. Themes of repressed sexuality, unrequited love, and the conflict between the primitive and the civilized emerge. The film's famous last scene with King Kong high atop the Empire Building swiping at airplanes buzzing around him visually narrates the swallowing up of the natural world by the urban and technological. Shot entirely in the studio, the film's use of miniatures and rear projection contributed significantly to filmmaking at the time, and the film's popularity saved RKO Studios from bankruptcy during the earliest years of the Depression. In contrast to the financial success of *King Kong*, the fantasy, adventure, and romance film *Lost Horizon* (1937) failed dismally in its original release, despite its depiction of sanctuary and repose in an era of circulating "rumors of war," as one of the film's opening title cards reveals. The basic narrative device of the film—a plane crash in a remote region of the Himalayas—transports a diverse group of airline passengers from a war-torn airport to a magnificently landscaped compound in the mythical valley of Shangri-La. Some passengers consider their location a refuge from war, whereas others view it as a prison.

Audiences received prophetic glimpses of another world—this time their own—in films such as the musical *Just Imagine* (1930), with its eerily accurate portrayal of 1980s New York, including automatic doors, test-tube babies, and advanced telecommunications systems. A more serious look into the future can be found in Alexander Korda's *Things to Come* (1936), adapted from another H. G. Wells novel, *The Shape of Things to Come*. Directed by William Cameron Menzies and starring Raymond Massey, the century-long look at an "Everytown" includes the breakdown of society into smaller primitive units brought about by a prolonged world war starting in 1940 and a plague in 1966. Besides predicting accurately the onset of World War II, the film features a helicopter a few years before the first successful models went into widespread production and use. Moreover, released just one month before the outbreak of war in Europe, *The Wizard of Oz* (1939) showed viewers another world as well, this one "over the rainbow" but not totally devoid of evil or obstacles, no matter how colorful it might be. Although it is portrayed in dingy sepia tones in the beginning of the film, Dorothy (Judy Garland) comes to appreciate Kansas and aspires to return home despite the opportunity to remain in the magical land of Oz. Dorothy's mantra "there's no place like home" became a fitting theme for Americans going into uncertain political times (see **Musical**).

To fill out the bill in most motion picture theaters, studios turned out low-budget serials in the 1930s, and two of the most popular featured comic book heroes Flash Gordon and Buck Rogers. Ironically, both are portrayed by athletic actor Buster Crabbe. Really nothing more than action-adventure films or Westerns set in space, common plots found Flash and Buck respectively battling evil in the guise of Emperor Ming the Merciless (Charles Middleton) from the planet Mongo in the *Flash Gordon* series or Killer Kane (Anthony Warde) in the *Buck Rogers* versions. These multiple-part adventures produced by Universal Studios are credited with establishing many recurring stock inventions in science fiction films, such as antigravity belts and guns, high-tech weapons of various kinds, and a variety of space vehicles, the toy versions of which were marketable to the younger populations watching these serials. Sam Jones reprised the role of Flash in *Flash Gordon* (1980), and Gil Gerard appeared as Buck Rogers in a short-lived 1979 television series.

The 1940s and 1950s

During World War II and immediately after, the film industry turned out few, if any, significant contributions to the science fiction genre, occupied instead with contributing to the end of fascism in Europe and then binding up the nation's residual wounds (see **War film**). Films with elements of fantasy from this period, however, include perennial Christmas favorites *It's a Wonderful Life* (1946), which stars Jimmy Stewart and features an angel in corporeal form in a time-honored story of the Golden Rule put into action in a small town, and George Seaton's *Miracle on 34th Street* (1946) which ponders the existence of Santa Claus. An influential carryover from the 1930s, *Death Takes a Holiday* (1934), inspired a whole range of films that feature ghosts, angels, and spirits from other dimensions. Posing as a prince, Death (Fredric March) takes a turn at mortality and causes hearts to flutter at a ducal country party, where the fiancée of his host's son falls in love with him even though she knows his identity. Brad Pitt and Anthony Hopkins star in Martin Brest's 1998 remake, *Meet Joe Black*. Although the Grim Reaper and spirits from another world normally connote horror, when Captain Gregg (Rex Harrison) becomes the constant spectral roommate of strong-willed Lucy Muir in a seaside cottage, the results are instead comedy, fantasy, and romance in Joseph Mankiewicz's *The Ghost and Mrs. Muir* (1947).

Angels also figure prominently in *Here Comes Mr. Jordan* (1941), with Robert Montgomery playing a dual role as a boxer whose soul is taken from his body by an inexperienced angel and placed in the body of a millionaire murdered by his wife. Claude Rains stars as the title character, a sort of heavenly CEO. Similarly, in *Heaven Can Wait* (1943), Don Ameche plays a man who is resigned to going to hell but is surprised when his qualifications for entry are questioned. After reviewing his life, particularly the years of his marriage, he is not so sure anymore. A 1978 remake that combined the plot of *Mr. Jordan* with the title *Heaven Can Wait* starred Warren Beatty. The dead also help the living in Victor Flemings's *A Guy Named Joe* (1943): a dead fighter pilot (Spencer Tracy) watches over another pilot (Van Johnson) as the other goes into battle and romances his own old girlfriend (Irene Dunne). Director Steven Spielberg's 1989 remake, *Always*, featured John Goodman and Richard Dreyfuss. In *Angels in the Outfield* (1951), during a losing streak, the belligerent manager of the Pittsburg Pirates (Paul Douglas) begins to hear the voice of an angel telling him to soften up in exchange for winning games. Danny Glover played the manager in the 1994 remake. God takes to the airwaves to deliver a series of radio broadcasts in *The Next Voice You Hear* (1950), with James Whitmore and future First Lady Nancy Davis (Reagan).

The 1950s

When the World War II era gave way to the nuclear age and the Cold War, international social and political anxiety increased. This tension was reflected in, among other places, the extraordinary number and variety of science fiction and fantasy films and science fiction–horror crossovers released during the 1950s, many of dubious quality. For example, Tim Dirks, in his section on science fiction films, attributes the proliferation of 1950s space travel film to two pioneering features capitalizing on an emerging interest in rocket propulsion and space science. The plot of Irving Pichel's *Destination Moon* (1950) reflects Cold War anxieties about superiority in space: a private businessman sponsors an American mission to the moon before the Russians can, but the astronauts who land may not have adequate fuel to return. Although dated, this Technicolor film is known for its attention to technical detail, with more realistic spaceships, costumes, and representation of the moon's surface than had been seen before, and the film actually won the 1951 Oscar for Best Special Effects. Aware of producer George Pal's promotion of *Destination Moon* as the first space travel film, independent producer Robert Lippert rushed into production *Rocketship X-M* (1950), a story of astronauts en route to the moon but forced to land on a Mars devastated by nuclear war. Producers marketed *it* as the first film about space travel, and it arrived in theaters three weeks before *Destination*, but it should be better known as the first film to examine the effects of nuclear war on an advanced civilization.

A third influential space travel film, Fred Wilcox's *Forbidden Planet,* was made in 1956 when the narrative pendulum of science fiction films had swung past a mere exploration of space travel. The film may be best remembered now for its electronically generated tonal musical score, the first for a mainstream motion picture, and the debut of Robbie the Robot, standing beside Fritz Lang's Maria in *Metropolis* and later George Lucas's C-3PO in *Star Wars* as one of the most recognizable cinematic robots. Writers Irving Block and Allen Adler (story) and Cyril Hume (screenplay) loosely adapt Shakespeare's *The Tempest* in this look at a rescue mission to a distant planet where the secrets of a self-destructive civilization of alien geniuses rests with a lone scientist (Walter Pidgeon) reluctant to divulge them. The film mixes elements of the conventional space travel film—a space colony, a space cruiser, and a journey to the unknown, for example—with Freudian overtones: the mysterious alien entity that killed the other members of the space colony is revealed as the scientist's unconscious, a real "monster from the Id." The pressure is ratcheted up a few jealous notches by the love affair between his daughter (Anne Francis), his constant companion, and the mission's captain (Leslie Nielsen). *Star Trek* creator Gene Roddenberry admitted to modeling the notion of "beaming down" from the Wilcox film. Technically, special effects creators used split-screen photographic techniques to make objects appear to dissolve and reappear. And, in its original release, theaters issued audiences red glasses that made the unseen monster appear during designated scenes.

Perhaps the most prolific group of science fiction films to appear in the 1950s involved alien invasion, many of them either allegorical looks at political and social forces such as communism and the nuclear arms race or cautionary tales of America's destiny if it were to continue on the course it had set. Among the most well-known and most classic is Robert Wise's *The Day The Earth Stood Still* (1951), with Michael Rennie as a messenger sent to warn war-torn Earth about its malevolence and pettiness. Parallels have been drawn between Klaatu, the emissary from outer space, and Christ; Klaatu's adopted Earth name, Carpenter, a reference to Jesus's profession, contributes to this interpretation. Patricia Neal stars as a secretary in a government office who befriends Rennie's Klaatu and saves the Earth from destruction by Gort, an eight-foot robot, when she utters the magical words "Klaatu barada nikto." A victim himself of Earth's violent ways—he is mortally wounded and temporarily revived—Klaatu warns onlookers of Earth's future in the final soliloquy in the film, but not before programming a system-wide interruption or pause in Earth's electrical systems to gain human attention. Theremins, a staple source of otherworldly sound in the form of ghostly humming or vibration, are featured on the sound track.

Space visitor Klaatu (Michael Rennie) and Earthling Helen Benson (Patricia Neal) save the Earth from Gort's death ray in a scene from Robert Wise's *The Day the Earth Stood Still* (1951). *Photofest.*

In addition, director Jack Arnold's 3-D presentation of *It Came from Outer Space* (1953) casts Ray Bradbury's story "The Meteors" as an allegory of McCarthyism in its look at peaceful aliens who must assume human form to repair their spaceship. Steven Spielberg's *Close Encounters of the Third Kind* (1977) presents a similar form of benign alien visitation almost twenty-five years later, as cableman Roy Neary (Richard Dreyfuss) discovers evidence of alien existence, and he and others like him are drawn to a special mountain location for their first contact with extraterrestrial life forms. Moreover, as we establish in the *Defining Characteristics* section, science fiction films and horror films cross over when the invading monster turns malevolent. One of the most cited science fiction–horror crossovers depicting alien invasion is Christian Nyby's *The Thing (From Another World)* (1951). A strange circular area in the permafrost near an arctic outpost renders up a buried frozen space craft, and its half human–half vegetable pilot goes on a rampage in a search of human blood after it thaws. The electrifying clash of two worlds, the human and the alien, illustrates the importance of the film's final warning, delivered in voice-over: "Watch the skies! Keep watching the skies!" Aside from the makeup for actor James Arness playing "The Thing," the fiction aspect of this science fiction classic is rather unimaginative, relying on an isolated arctic setting unfamiliar to audiences in their everyday life as a source of anxiety and suspense. John Carpenter's 1982 remake, *The Thing*, restored from the original short story the shape-shifting monster able to assimilate members of the scientific expedition.

Other space travel and alien invasion films include Bryon Haskin's version of H. G. Wells's *The War of the Worlds* (1953). Hostile Martian invaders arrive in triangular vessels to obliterate Los Angeles and other world cities with their green destro-beams, creating a visual impression of what Orson Welles's Mercury Theater tried to convey through words in his famous 1938 radio broadcast. The green beams might easily be red, because the obvious invader implied in the film is Soviet Communism. Peter Biskind points out how some science fiction films of this era illustrated America's palpable spiritual values and the ending of *The War* bears this out (1993, 116). At one point in the film, as Christians in one church ask for divine delivery from alien invasion, two dead aliens crash through the roof of another. In another episode, a clergyman walks toward a craft reciting the twenty-third psalm, only to be annihilated for his efforts. Eventually, the aliens are destroyed by the equivalent of the common cold, and the film's narrator intones, "After all that men could do had failed, the Martians were defeated by the littlest things that God in His wisdom had put upon the earth."

In an invasion of another sort, a planetoid on a collision course for Earth inspires a desperate plan to evacuate the doomed galaxy in *When Worlds Collide* (1951), with special effects by Oscar-winner George Pal. Scriptures evoking Genesis bookend the narrative, and the montage showing the onset of Earth's destruction still rivals the special effects wizardry today, especially the flooding of a busy metropolitan area by tidal waves. The landscape on the new planet appears right out of a paint-by-number set, a rather fanciful introduction to new worlds years before actual footage of the moon and planets revealed otherwise. William Cameron Menzies's *Invaders from Mars* (1953) reveals the pitfalls of ignoring children's observations, as a young boy tries to tell authorities about the arrival of a Martian space craft, but the horror of, in this case, big green men in costumes with zippers freely visible, proves to be just a dream. Strange ethereal harmonies signal the sinking of another human into a sand pit vortex. And Don Siegel's *Invasion of the Body Snatchers* (1956) provides yet another communist invasion allegory, as the bodies of residents of a small California town are used as the incubators for parasitic alien seedpods and then hatch into soulless, vacant shells of their former selves. Remakes appeared in 1978 and 1994.

The prevalence and variety of mutant monster films to appear in this era—often B movies—reveals fears about controlling science and technology, the unleashing of atomic power in particular. Plots follow a well-defined pattern: mutant creatures exposed to high levels of radiation foretell doom for the whole human race. The names of several films alone paint with a broad brush the extent of the anxiety, as every conceivable mutated menace on the Earth becomes the subject of a low-budget production: *Tarantula* (1955), *The Black Scorpion* (1957), *The Giant Claw* (1957), *The Deadly Mantis* (1957), *The Attack of the Crab Monsters* (1957), *Attack of the Giant Leeches* (1959), *The Killer Shrews* (1959), and *The Wasp Woman* (1959). B-movie status or not, some of the most notable examples of this science fiction–horror subgenre have become cult favorites, including Gordon Douglas's *Them!* (1954), attributed with starting the "giganticism" of the mutant rampaging insect film. Mutant ants zapped by early atomic testing in New Mexico leak into storm drains and start killing innocent citizens in the American Southwest, and the communist overtones and antinuclear message are clear. Like the antinuclear message of *Them!*, Kurt Neumann's *The Fly* (1958) warns against human tampering with what nature never intended: interspecies matter transformation. The classic science fiction tale spawned two sequels (*Return of the Fly* [1959] and *The Curse of the Fly* [1965]) and a well-known remake in 1986 with Jeff Goldblum and Geena Davis.

Sooner or later many B-movie sci-fi monster films made it to late night TV (and sometimes "late, late" night), none more so than the Japanese-inspired

Godzilla series. The cycle began with director Ishiro Honda's *Gojira* (1954), the tale of a giant prehistoric reptilian monster (164 feet tall, not 400 feet tall, as posited in the American version of the film) stirred from its resting place in Tokyo harbor by American underwater nuclear testing. Stop-action techniques and an actor in an unwieldy monster suit stand in for the monster rampaging through a miniature city, and the special effects department employed amazingly simple methods to simulate the monster's destruction, such as constructing the electrical towers that Godzilla melts with his breath out of wax softened by blowing hot air and shining hot studio light on them to simulate a white-hot surface. American director Terry O. Moore edited footage of Raymond Burr, playing a Tokyo-based American reporter, into the 1954 Japanese original to produce *Godzilla, King of the Monsters* (1956). Moore deleted forty minutes of antinuclear and anti-hydrogen bomb sequences and dialogue. Sequels to the film all reinforce the hazards of nuclear radiation, as a spectrum of new mutant monsters, including Rodan and Mothra, joined Godzilla and are often pitted against him. Roland Emmerich's *Godzilla* (1998), the most recent American version to receive widespread release, failed at the box office, nixing plans for future entries in the series.

The 1960s

Fantasy films in the late 1950s, 1960s, and early 1970s drew on mythological and literary themes and relied on an increased used of stop-action photography to create their mystical affects. The special effects artistry of the legendary Ray Harryhausen figures prominently in a significant number of fantasy-related features throughout this period, such as *The 7th Voyage of Sinbad* (1958), with a stop-action Cyclops, a dragon, and the famous dueling and dancing skeleton. A score of dueling skeletons return in *Jason and the Argonauts* (1963) as the title character battles a seven-headed hydra, among other mythical figures, in his search for the golden fleece. Harryhausen's work in the film is painstaking, and the scene with the battling skeletons took four months alone. Of all of the films he designed effects for—including three other mythology-based films, *The Golden Voyage of Sinbad* (1973), *Sinbad and the Eye of the Tiger* (1979), and *Clash of Titans* (1981)—he considered *Jason* his finest achievement. Medusa, bronze giants, Cyclopes, and the winged horse Pegasus number among the many mythological creatures his inventiveness brought to the screen in living detail.

Walt Disney Studios produced a variety of films appealing to families and children in the 1960s, as did other companies in a Disney-esque vein. For example, Julie Andrews won a Best Actress Academy Award for her debut film, the musical *Mary Poppins* (1964), the story of a nanny with magical musical powers who transforms the household of a dour banker. Dick Van Dyke stars as Bert, a chimney sweep and jack-of-all-trades. The film garnered five Oscars total—among them for Best Special Effects—making it Walt Disney Studios' most award-winning film to date. Two other films made by other studios combine a Disney-like mixture of music and fantasy elements. In *Doctor Doolittle* (1967), Rex Harrison stars as an internationally renowned veterinarian with a unique ability to communicate with animals, some more exotic than others. The film won the Oscar for Best Special Effects and Best Song ("Talk to the Animals"). In 1968, actor Dick Van Dyke alienated Disney executives by commenting that "This will out-Disney Disney," a reference to *Chitty Chitty Bang Bang* (1968), in which the actor plays an eccentric and nearly destitute inventor whose specially-equipped, flying automobile becomes the obsession of a fictional foreign government.

Fantasy aside, as explored by pre-1960s science fiction films in a dystopic vein, Earth in the future is not an always desirable place to live. For example, in *Planet of the Apes* (1968), astronaut George Taylor (Charlton Heston) crash-lands with two crew members on an ape-controlled planet and begins to fight for human autonomy with the support of two enlightened chimpanzees, animal psychologist Dr. Zira (Kim Hunter) and archeologist Cornelius (Roddy McDowall). When he utters his memorable first words as a result of assault by an ape guard—"Take your stinking hands off me, you damn dirty ape"—Taylor's obvious intelligence raises fears that apes may have evolved from humans. At the end of the film, a powerful pacifist message comes through as Taylor and a human woman ride a horse up to some wreckage protruding from the sand. With Taylor damning his own civilization for its belligerent tendencies, the camera pulls back from the rear and reveals the catalyst for Taylor's outburst: the head and crown, tablet, and torch of the Statue of Liberty in the sand at the water's edge. In a post-apocalyptic Earth, he and female human Nova (Linda Harris) truly represent the "destiny" of the planet. Technically, the film's music is among the earliest, if not the first, atonal scores for a major motion picture, and John Chamber's Academy Award-winning ape makeup is said to be the most expensive in the history of motion pictures (after adjustment for inflation). The popularity of the film led to four sequels and prequels. Tim Burton's 2001 remake deviated from the original in setting and the means of the ape planet's discovery.

In the history of science fiction filmmaking, 1968 would prove to be a banner year, including the releases of *Planet of the Apes* and Stanley Kubrick's *2001: A Space Odyssey.* Although science fiction films are known for stunning special effects, the Kubrick epic relies almost exclusively on visual imagery, with less than forty total minutes of dialogue in the final film. Scenes include either music or dialogue, but not both. In many shots, there is no sound at all, or only the whirring and clicking of machines. The choreography of special effects with an orchestral score and slow-motion photography also makes the film revolutionary, with Kubrick himself winning the Oscar for special visual effects. The opening fanfare of Richard Strauss's *Thus Spake Zarathustra* peaks at the precise moment when the Earth, Moon, and Sun align perfectly on screen, marking the beginning of life on the planet. The Strauss piece is reprised during the first episode in the film's four-part structure, labeled "The Dawn of Man," as Pleistocene ape-men happen upon the first of three humming monoliths (black, upright stone slabs), signaling man's evolving intelligence. As Strauss's music crescendos in the background, the ape-man discovers the ease of killing an antelope with a bone, and the leap to killing a rival at a watering hole comes quickly. The episode ends with the famous hurling of the bone into the heavens, and a jump cut four million years ahead to the only unlabeled episode in the film (called "The Lunar Journey in the Year 2000" by Dirks) finds the twisting, airborne bone morphing into a lunar transport craft.

This second segment of the film begins with the dance of a circular space station to the tune of Johann Strauss's *Blue Danube Waltz*. Inside, Dr. Heywood R. Floyd (William Sylvester) awaits landing, and a second important image, a pen, floats in the zero gravity of the vehicle retrieved by the attendant. Dirks points to the procreation and reproduction motif throughout the film, citing the docking of the transport vehicle with the space station as a symbolic act of intercourse. The first words of dialogue occur after twenty-five minutes of running time, spoken within the context of Floyd's arrival. The rhythms of the Strauss waltz again mark Floyd's journey to the lunar surface, where Floyd speaks on behalf of the government's desire for caution in keeping secret the existence of the monolith. The visual and the auditory meld again, as a shaft of light signaling the conjunction of the Sun, Moon, and Earth strikes the second monolith and it emits a high-pitched sound.

The mysterious signal to Jupiter emitted by the lunar monolith gives rise to the third segment of the film, labeled "Jupiter Mission, 18 Months Later." This segment introduces another "character" in the film, the advanced, superhuman computer called HAL who serves as the brains of the spacecraft. All but two members of the expedition to find the origins of the subspace sound—Bowman (Keir Dullea) and Poole (Gary Lockwood)—rest in suspended animation chambers, or wombs, throughout the walkways of the ship. This episode of the film reveals true anxieties about technology, as HAL acts on both the worst and the best of human emotions he was programmed to emulate, maintaining an instinct for survival when an error exposes his fallibility and resorting to murder to keep his secret. A sequence that cuts between the two crewmembers inside what they believe to be a soundproof pod and the ominous red eye of HAL in center-screen foreshadows the showdown between man and machine.

The final installment in the film proves to be the most enigmatic. In a repeat of two other episodes in the film, the planet, its moons, the spaceship, and the sun align with the third monolith in the film, sending Bowman in pursuit. In a stunningly colorful sequence, Bowman finds himself sucked down a corridor in the pod with bright lights flashing on each side, symbolizing (for Dirks) the passage through the birth canal. For those interpreting the film as a sign of the times, the parallels might be better made to a drug trip. Extreme close-ups of Bowman's eye symbolize his evolution or rebirth into a new life form. The journey ends at a series of nebulas and surreal planetary surfaces bathed in color. A final vignette finds Bowman looking at himself in a brightly lit French-inspired bedroom as he rapidly ages from youth to old age. The final monolith looms over him as his earthly body decays and dies. To the chords of Strauss's *Thus Spake Zarathustra*, Bowman's face morphs into the face of a translucent fetus, reemerging as the floating "Star Child," traveling throughout the universe toward Earth without benefit of, or threats posed by, technology. The cyclical nature of life in the universe, the basic narrative structure throughout the film, is complete. A reprise of the *Blue Danube Waltz* plays under a blank screen, suggestive of the delicate dance of life and the repetition of the cycle.

The 1970s

The 1970s ushered in the era of the blockbuster science fiction film and witnessed the emergence of the writing, directing, and producing talents of key figures such as George Lucas, Steven Spielberg, and Michael Crichton. Space aliens and the role of technology continue to raise suspicions and create anxiety, but a whole new rash of mysterious phenomena, intruders, and social and political conditions threatens life on Earth. For example, *The Andromeda Strain,* written by Crichton and filmed in 1971 under the helm of legendary director Robert Wise, foreshadows current medical concerns about superhuman viruses in the story of an unmanned space craft that brings back an alien bug from space. Scientists gather in a sequestered laboratory facility to vanquish the germ before it decimates the human race. Crichton's other writing achievements in this era include *Westworld* (1973), the story of an amusement park designed to indulge the fantasies of the wealthy. Shots that allow audiences to see through the eyes of an android gunslinger (Yul Brynner) were the first digital images to appear in a motion picture, taking eight hours to perfect for every ten seconds on screen. Crichton's later writing became the basis of Steven Spielberg's *Jurassic Park* (1993) and *The Lost World: Jurassic Park* (1997), Frank Marshall's *Congo* (1995), and Joe Johnston's *Jurassic Park III* (2001).

Two films from this period relate to ecological disasters, *Silent Running* (1972) and dystopic *Soylent Green* (1973). In an overpopulated New York City of 2022, the assassination of a high-ranking Soylent Corporation official (Joseph Cotten) leads police detective Robert Thorn (Charlton Heston) to make a startling discovery about the origins of the corporation's product, a high-energy vegetable- and plankton-based cracker. When careful analysis of corporation reports by former professor Sol Roth (Edward G. Robinson, in his last role) reveals that the Earth's oceans can no longer sustain plankton, then Thorn must discover what Soylent Green is made from. Examining a similar cautionary theme, Douglas Fuller's 1971 *Silent Running* chronicles one man's fight to preserve the Earth's last forests growing in the artificial environment of space. Lowell Freeman (Bruce Dern) serves on the American Airlines Freighter *Valley Forge* in the eighth year of this ecological mission when word comes from Earth officials that the space freighters are to return to commercial service. As crewmembers jettison and then destroy the living laboratories connected to the freighters, Freeman revolts, accidentally killing crew members who try to stop him. The film was the first-time directorial effort for special effects supervisor Douglas Trumball, who was well-known for his previous work on *2001: A Space Odyssey.*

Other feature-length science fiction and fantasy films from this era resist clear categorization, such as Stanley Kubrick's *A Clockwork Orange* (1974). In the film, ruffian Alex (Malcolm MacDowell) agrees to a new brainwashing treatment to stem his violent behavior in lieu of a long prison sentence, but when the therapy (including the famous forced viewing of violence, or "eye-propping" scene, part of Alex's aversion therapy) threatens his life, the government in a futuristic Britain attempts to undo the experiment. The film's often ear-pleasing classical soundtrack underscores disparate scenes of violence throughout. The violence is also institutionalized in Michael Anderson's *Logan's Run* (1976), which is set in the twenty-third century, when the survivors of a holocaust have sealed themselves in a domed city near Washington, DC. To maintain the population balance, the superhuman computers that operate the city require all individuals to die at thirty, and secret police officers ("sandmen") seek out individuals resisting the policy. Sandman Michael York discovers that life exists outside the dome, and he works to destroy the computer at the heart of it all. Another film that is hard to classify is Australia's futuristic action-adventure film *Mad Max* (1979). It stars Mel Gibson as a police driver who becomes the target of a renegade motorcycle gang anxious for revenge against the man they believed killed their leader. Sequels include *Mad Max 2* (1981; originally released as *The Road Warrior*) and *Mad Max: Beyond Thunderdome* (1985), costarring Tina Turner.

Despite their diversity and timely reflections and examinations of contemporary issues within futuristic scenarios, most science fiction films of the 1970s are overshadowed by the work of George Lucas, beginning with the 1977 science fiction and action-adventure blockbuster *Star Wars, Episode IV: A New Hope* (1977). The film was originally released as *Star Wars* before multiple prequels and sequels necessitated the chronological labeling of films. Made on a modest budget of $11 million, the film ushered in an era of the high-profit science fiction adventure film and introduced to popular culture a host of new characters and catch phrases such as "may the Force be with you." Fundamentally, the story of the rescue of a damsel in distress that draws on medieval romance plots, with light sabers substituting for lances, *Star Wars* was also influenced by the American Western and select examples of Japanese cinema. Its protagonist, Luke Skywalker (Mark Hamill), is a simple farmer brought up in the philosophy of the Force. He allies himself with mercenary smuggler pilot Han Solo (Harrison Ford), a hairy beast named Chewbacca (Peter Mayhew), a former Jedi knight (Alec Guinness), and two lovable robot androids to battle the evil forces of the Empire and rescue the pacifist Rebel Alliance and one of its leaders, Princess Leia (Carrie Fisher). The climax of the film depicts the attack on the flagship of the empire, the Death Star, captained by Darth Vader (played by David Prowse with voice by James Earl Jones).

The film's contribution to the genre rests not only on its special effects innovations and its role in reviving interest in science fiction, but also on its overall motion picture marketing. The broad merchandizing of *Star Wars* figures and products far out-grossed the box office receipts, setting a precedent for blockbusters to come; Lucas's forty percent share in the merchandizing rights earned him far more than his director's fee. With his huge proceeds from the film, Lucas created Industrial Light and Magic, his state-of-the-art special effects laboratory, which has been responsible for innovative special effects ever since, especially computer-generated images. As Tim Dirks notes, critics of the film trace the onslaught of high-tech blockbusters with little plot to the success of Lucas's achievement, but industry recognition of the film resulted in ten Academy Award nominations, with six wins in largely technical categories, including a special award for Benjamin Burtt Jr., who created the alien and robot voices. Lucas drew the idea of filming the opening credits rolling back to a single point in the visual field from *The Phantom Creeps* (1939). The film also is the first film ever screened in Dolby Stereo, now an industry standard. Overall, the legacy of the first *Star Wars* film can be seen in the astounding number and success of its various prequels and sequels extending into the next three decades.

In the wake of the first *Star Wars* film, Gene Rodenberry revived the characters and emblematic Federation starship *USS Enterprise* from his only moderately successful 1960s series *Star Trek* to produce *Star Trek: The Motion Picture* (1979), directed by Robert Wise. The film's special effects compete in the new era ushered in by *Star Wars*, but it may be one of few films in motion history surpassed in viewer memory by its sequel, *Star Trek: The Wrath of Khan* (1982). In this second installment of the series, Kirk's enemy from the "Space Seed" television episode, Khan (played by Ricardo Montalban), captures the top secret Genesis device invented by Kirk's old flame and, as he discovers, the mother of his son. When the *Enterprise*, now a training vessel on a routine cruise, falls prey to Khan's attack, the two old rivals clash. This sequel also featured the much speculated death of Spock (Leonard Nimoy). *Star Trek III: The Search for Spock* (1984) was directed by Nimoy. Kirk's son, Dr. David Marcus (Merritt Butrick) dies in the film, and Nimoy mouths the famous "Space, the final frontier" monologue, changed slightly from the TV series from seeking out "new life forms" to "new life." The success of the *Star Trek IV: The Voyage Home* (1986) installment is said to have inspired the creation of the new television series, *Star Trek: The Next Generation*, in 1987. The *Star Trek: Generations* (1994) film combines the cast of the new television series with the cast from the old show in efforts to stop a madman (Malcolm MacDowell) from killing whole star systems. Additional *Star Trek* films with the new television cast appeared in 1996, 1998, and 2002.

The decade of the big-budget science film concludes with two other entries, *Superman: The Movie* (1978) and *Alien* (1979). *Superman* (1978) features then relatively unknown actor Christopher Reeve as the hero and actress Margot Kidder as his love interest, Lois Lane, in the comic book come to life (see **Action-Adventure**). Sequences that show Superman flying were the result of painstaking experimentation, but a combination of rear projection and special zoom lenses manipulates the eye into believing Reeve is moving and the background is receding. The film is also remembered for including the first computer-generated film titles and the longest end title sequence, which, at about seven minutes, cost more to produce than many films up until that point. Ridley Scott's *Alien* (1979) is one of the more recent science fiction–horror hybrid successes, featuring Sigourney Weaver in a signature and career-boosting role as Ripley, a crew member aboard a deep-space mining vehicle *Nostromo*. The ship answers a distress call from a nearby planet and discovers an abandoned spaceship on its surface full of egg-shaped pods. After responding to the call for help, crew members become infested by a parasite. The film emphasizes the isolation of deep space as the remaining crew members wander the dark industrial corridors of the freighter, attempting to lure the mature creature to the main airlock so it can be jettisoned into space. With the rest of her crew devoured, Ripley leaves the freighter and destroys the ship after her, but she experiences an unpleasant surprise just after detonation. In James Cameron's sequel *Aliens* (1986), Ripley is awakened from her space sleep and returns to earth fifty-seven years after her ordeal to discover the alien planet has been colonized. With significantly more firepower and a new crew, she is sent to discover the fate of the colonists and to destroy the alien menace once and for all.

The 1980s

If the 1970s created a niche for the science fiction and fantasy blockbuster, then the 1980s may be characterized as the dawn of the era of computer-generated imaging (CGI). Exposed film can be scanned into a computer and manipulated by a computer in various ways. Computers can combine images, morph subjects into new shapes, and digitally alter the colors and the quality of the image. Computer manipulation can also correct mistakes by removing or covering up objects whose appearance spoils the effect of a shot (such as protruding wires in stunts), insert fictional characters into footage of real-life events, or superimpose faces on the bodies of others. Critics of computer-generated images often find such techniques distasteful and fake looking, and purists of narrative motion picture making might consider such capabilities as "cheating," but developing public tastes and emerging box-office returns guarantee that computers will be an essential tool in filmmaking for the foreseeable future, particularly in the genre of science fiction and fantasy.

The first shaded three-dimensional computer graphics to appear in film were used to create the virtual characteristics of live action character Cindy (Susan Dey) in Michael Crichton's *Looker* (1981), in which a plastic surgeon discovers a connection between the emergent technologies of a mysterious corporation and the deaths of his patients. Early examples of computer-generated images also include the opening sequence in Disney's 1979 feature *The Black Hole*, detailing the exploration of a black abyss of space, and the one-minute "Genesis" sequence in *Star Trek: Wrath of Khan* (1982). Disney's *Tron* (1982), with its fifteen minutes of combined computer animation and shaded graphics, is considered the first motion picture to have integrated significant computer-generated elements. In his depiction of a computer hacker (Jeff Bridges) entering the cyber world to destroy a master control system, director Steven Lisberger shot all live action sequences against a black screen and later had them "colored" using various photographic techniques. Academy members passed over the film for nominations in the visual effects category because they believed the filmmakers cheated by using a computer, although computer technology was not so advanced at the time to enable shooting both live action figures and computer-generated effects in the same frame. That capability would be demonstrated in *Last Star Fighter* (1984), featuring computer-generated spaceships, planets, and high tech equipment in the context of the story of a video game whiz who enters the game he most excels in and ends up in the position of saving the universe.

Computers begin controlling the future world in *The Terminator* (1984), starring Arnold Schwarzenegger as a cyborg sent from the future to kill a woman (Linda Hamilton) who gives birth to the leader of a human movement resisting cyborg domination, John Connor. Although supposedly soulless and with only sixteen lines in the entire script, one-liners such as "I'll be back," "Stick around," and "Hasta la vista, baby!" give a distinct personality to Schwarzenegger's character. Periodic scenes of the Terminator's vision include computer codes, enhancing his machine-like qualities. Many consider the film's sequel, *Terminator 2: Judgment Day* (1991) better than the original, particularly in terms of the morphing, or shape-shifting, special effects. Time travel once again serves as the subject as an even more superior cyborg (Robert Patrick) sent back from the future to target John Connor (Edward Furlong). Rounding out the series, a female cyborg returns to kill the young adult Connor (Nick Stahl) in *Terminator 3: Rise of the Machines* (2003). Violence, destruction, and general mayhem take the place of a strong storyline, and Schwarzenegger returns in his most memorable role.

As science fiction films advanced in terms of the depiction and uses of technology in the 1980s, fantasy films reverted to a romantic past. In Jeannot Szwarc's *Somewhere in Time* (1980), for example, an old woman accosts a young playwright (Christopher Reeve), entreating him to come back to her. Years later, through a process of self-hypnosis, he returns to 1912 to rekindle a romance with the woman (Jane Seymour), an actress. The most famous time-travel narrative is probably H. G. Wells's *The Time Machine* (1960, 2002), in which a nineteenth-century inventor finds himself transported thousands of years ahead to an Earth divided between two warring factions. Employing a similar device as the Wells scenario, Robert Zemeckis's *Back to the Future* (1985) also examines time travel, as the result of the mysterious invention of Dr. Emmett Brown (Christopher Lloyd) that turns a DeLorean into a time machine at the speed of eighty-eight miles per hour. Michael J. Fox stars as teenager Marty McFly who goes back in time and meets his parents as teenagers, but before he returns to his own era powered by a lightning strike, he must first reunite his parents or he will not even be born. Sequels include *Back to the Future II* (1989) and *Back to the Future III* (1990).

Rends in the fabric of time are also the subject of Terry Gilliam's *Time Bandits*, written by Monty Python alumni Gilliam and Michael Palin, where a young boy (Craig Warnock) ends up joining a bunch of thieves as they traverse time periods in search of valuables to steal. John Cleese, Sean Connery, Shelley Duvall, Katherine Helmond, Ian Holm, and Ralph Richardson make appearances as various historic figures, including Robin Hood, King Agamemnon, Napoleon, and the Supreme Being. David Rappaport joins the cast as Randall, a wise-cracking dwarf. The film begins and ends with the Terry Gilliam trademark map, in contrast with Gilliam's *Brazil* (1985), which opens and concludes with clouds despite its emphasis on the drudgery of an authoritarian bureaucracy in a futuristic society. As one small cog in this bureaucratic machine, civil servant Sam Lowry (Jonathan Pryce) attempts to correct an error amongst mounting paperwork, sending an innocent man to jail instead of the real criminal (Robert De Niro). Dimly lit interior sets suggest the massiveness and oppressiveness of the bureaucracy and Sam's longing for freedom with a fantasy woman (Jill Greist), and the recurrence of the theme song, the Latin-influenced "Brazil," enhance the alienation of this retro-futuristic world.

Darkness and postindustrial urban squalor also permeate Ridley Scott's *Blade Runner* (1982), starring Harrison Ford, Rutger Hauer, Sean Young, and Darryl Hannah. In a futuristic Los Angeles of 2019, overpopulated and polluted, Ford plays a "blade runner," or police officer. He is charged with tracking down and exterminating human-like replicants, in particular, a group of four punk-rockerish creatures who escape from an off-world colony to Earth. The film competes with the best futuristic visions of the world extending back to *Metropolis*—with unusually shaped buildings, the use of flying vehicles, or "spinners," rather than ground-based automobiles, and blimps blaring slogans with digital messages flashing from their bodies—but in mood and setting, it also borrows from the best in the film noir tradition (see **Film Noir**), including the air of menace, the use of voice-over (in the original version only, not the director's cut), an ambiguous hero in Deckard, the contrast of light and dark, the urban grittiness of the city, and the alienation of the cityscape with the exhaust from a chemical plant sending flames shooting in the air. Shots of a model city and painted backdrops were photographed using computer-controlled camera movements designed to enact particular curved motions in certain scenes. Moreover, Rachel's (Sean Young) costumes and styling alone, with a severe silhouette provided by shoulder pads and her tightly knotted chignon, are a futuristic spin on the best in 1940s fashions, particularly the signature style of Joan Crawford. Debate has raged, particularly in light of the release of the director's cut of the film, regarding Deckard's own status as either replicant or human. The tell-tale red light shines in all the known replicant's eyes and in Deckard's at one point, but the director's cut of the film leaves the question open, removing the final sequence with Deckard and Rachel driving down a road in unspoiled nature suggesting his humanity. A unicorn dream sequence was restored to the director's cut, and additional background noise was inserted in place of the removed voice-over.

The medieval era or a pseudo-medieval age is the setting for several fantasy films during this decade, starting with *Dragonslayer* and *Excalibur* in 1981. *Dragonslayer* features Peter MacNichol, Caitlin Clark, and Ralph Richardson in a tale of a king who agrees to provide virgins to a dragon so that beast will leave his kingdom alone. The film garnered an Academy Award nomination for Best Visual Effects for a dragon created in a "go motion" technique, in which shots of a mechanized computer-controlled model blur the image and enhance the dragon's animated qualities. A retelling of Thomas Malory's Arthurian legend, John Boorman's *Excalibur* cast actors relatively unknown to the American audience at that time, including Gabriel Byrne, Patrick Stewart, and Helen Mirren, with extant English estates and castles serving as a backdrop. Similarly, Richard Donner's *Ladyhawke* (1985) evokes a mystical time in a dashing and romantic action-adventure tale of a thief (Matthew Broderick) who escapes from a medieval fortress city and befriends a handsome captain of the guard (Rutger Hauer), enthralled by the beautiful Lady Isabeau d'Anjou (Michelle Pfeiffer). In love with the noblewoman himself, an evil bishop (John Wood) places a curse on the pair and the captain vows to return to the heavily-guarded city to kill the bishop and end the curse. Beautiful landscape shots permeate the film, as well as clever half-lit appearances on screen of the two principals for an ethereal affect, but many believe a Vangelis soundtrack mars the spell cast by this tragic love story.

Perhaps the most enduring of this rash of fairy-tale-inspired fantasy films is Rob Reiner's *The Princess Bride* (1987), the magical adventures of the beautiful Buttercup (Robin Wright) held against her will by the evil Prince Humperdinck (Chris Sarandon) who wishes to marry her, told through the pages of a book that a grandfather reads to his grandchild (played by Peter Falk and Fred Savage, respectively). Meanwhile, her sweetheart Westley (Cary Elwes), in the guise of a pirate, seeks to bring about her rescue. He is supported in his travail by a talented swordsman (Mandy Patinkin) and a giant with superhuman strength (Andre the Giant). Periodic intrusions by the boy and grandfather debating the merits of the story preserve the comedic element, and gigantic rodents keep the tale from pure bathos; the cinematography of Adrian Biddle creates an innocent fairy-tale glow.

As a director, Steven Spielberg made several contributions to the existing genre science fiction–fantasy films in the 1980s, starting with the fantasy adventure film *Raiders of the Lost Ark* (1981), which introduces the Indiana Jones character (played by Harrison Ford) (see **Action-Adventure**). In the same vein as classic adventure films such as *King Solomon's Mines* (1937, 1950, and 1985), globe-trotting archeologist Indiana Jones receives a commission from the U.S. government to find the Ark of the Covenant before Nazi agents do. Set in the exotic locale of 1930s Egypt, the mystical climax of the film when Nazi agents are turned to dust by supernatural elements fittingly ends an adventure filled with mystery, superstition, ancient customs, writhing snakes, and, perhaps most dangerous, Indy's reunion with an old girlfriend (Karen Allen). Like classic movie series, the *Indiana Jones* films hold up remarkably well from installment to installment, but Spielberg's reputation in the minds of new emerging science fiction and fantasy fans of a certain age will almost certainly rest on his 1982 production *E.T. the Extra-Terrestrial*, which made stars of several of its young performers, including Henry Thomas (Elliot) and Drew Barrymore (Gertie). The film—the story of a benign alien creature anxious to return home who befriends a shy ten-year-old boy whose father has abandoned the family—speaks to anyone who has ever felt out of place or alone, no matter what their age. Iconic elements in the film include E.T.'s illuminated finger, his love of Reese's Pieces, one of the most memorable examples of product placement in films, and the magical bike ride as the children escape through a housing allotment and lift off, the image of which became the logo for Spielberg's production company, Amblin Entertainment. A commercial and critical failure, Spielberg's other fantasy film in this era, *Hook* (1991), is an updated version of the Peter Pan stories, starring Robin Williams as Peter, Dustin Hoffman as the kidnapper of Peter's children, Captain Hook, and Julia Roberts as Tinkerbel.

Deep space, or perhaps more aptly put, spaces, again emerges as an important locale for science fiction and fantasy features during the decade. Colonizing space and mining on planetary bodies found there reflect the priorities of Earth's industrialized civilization and compete with the depiction of space as an unclaimed wonderland. In Peter Hyams's *Outland* (1981), for example, Marshal W. T. O'Neil (Sean Connery) investigates the violent and mysterious deaths of miners in a colony on Io, one of Jupiter's moons. When an outside monster and its army attack the planet Krull, as depicted in the 1983 film of the same name, two warring nations unite through the marriage of a rival prince and princess. In possession of a magic multibladed sword, and with the help of a wise man, the prince goes in search of his bride, kidnapped by the invaders. A crash landing on an alien world teaches an Earthling an important lesson about demonizing one's enemies in *Enemy Mine* (1985). And David Lynch's *Dune* (1984), based on the Frank Herbert novels, is set in the distant future, when space travel depends on a particular spice found only on the mysterious sand planet Dune. The emperor sends a duke and his family to rule the planet, knowing that they will not come back alive, but the duke's son (Kyle MacLachlan) survives and lives to learn how to wrest Dune from imperial control and avenge his father's death.

The supernatural serves as the source of the fantasy elements in films such as the anthology film *The Twilight Zone: The Movie* (1983), *Something Wicked This Way Comes* (1983), *Ghostbusters* (1984), and *Field of Dreams* (1989). Taken from four classic Rod Serling tales—three of which were remakes from the 1950s television series—the separate episodes in *Twilight Zone* were directed by established directors John Landis, Steven Spielberg, Joe Dane, and George Miller. The film is unfortunately notorious for the helicopter crash that killed actor Vic Morrow and two children, resulting in the manslaughter indictment and exoneration of director John Landis and three others. Although a rather unusual application of Disney Studios' typical goal of appealing to everyone's fantasies, *Something Wicked This Way Comes* (1983) combines elements of horror, fantasy, and the supernatural in this tale of an early-twentieth-century small town at the mercy of a demonic traveling circus troupe lead by an impresario named Mr. Dark (Jonathan Pryce). In its theme of exposing the longings, miseries, and frustrations of the human heart, the film is an interesting exposé or allegory of the American small town with effective, but now somewhat dated, special effects, such as a carousel with the power to propel occupants forward or backward in their lives.

Ghostly creatures from another dimension take an entirely different form in Ivan Reitman's *Ghost Busters* (1984), as three out-of-work parapsychologists (Bill Murray, Dan Aykroyd, and Harold Ramis) set up a unique extermination service, ridding New York City of assorted ghosts, apparitions, and poltergeists, one paranormal phenomenon at a time. In *Field of Dreams* (1989), the benign ghost of a legendary baseball player, Joe Jackson (Ray Liotta), fills the void in an Iowa farmer's life (Kevin Costner), when he hears a voice among the cornfields urging him to build a baseball field. "If you build it, they will come," he hears rustling in the wind. When he does, six other members of the Chicago White Sox team banned for throwing the 1919 World Series join Jackson, but the farmer must seek out a reclusive author (James Earl Jones) to tell him what it all means. Moreover, in *Beetlejuice* (1988), director Tim Burton creates a rather unique character in the guise of "bio-exorcist" Beetlejuice (Michael Keaton), whose skills are relied upon by a particularly bland couple of new ghosts (Alec Baldwin and Geena Davis) unsuccessful in rooting out a yuppie family from the couple's farm. Burton also brings his atmospheric touch to *Edward Scissorhands* (1990) with Johnny Depp, the saga of a lonely man assembled from spare parts, including scissors for hands. A local woman brings him into her home and into her heart. Sets evoke a fairy-tale air in a suburbia where a haunting castle at the end of a neighborhood block seems perfectly plausible. And Jerry Zucker's *Ghost* (1990), with Demi Moore and Patrick Swayze as two lovers torn apart by a brutal act, demonstrates that true love lasts after death. Whoopi Goldberg won an Oscar for her performance as a medium with soul. Part of the soundtrack, the Righteous Brother's tune "Unchained Melody," enjoyed a brief but strong resurgence in popularity.

1990 to the Present

Longstanding threats to life as we know it and anxieties about the future persist, if the variety of science fiction films produced in the last decade of the twentieth century and the first years of the new millennium are any judge. For example, a carryover from the 1980s, the group of *Batman* films follows a long line of science fiction and fantasy series that started out in another medium, in this case comic books. Director Tim Burton applies his unique vision to a gothic Gotham city, made dark and foreboding by the diverse architectural styles created by production designer Anton Furst and the cinematography of Roger Pratt. Michael Keaton plays a darker Batman than seen in the TV series, with Jack Nicholson as Batman's nemesis, the Joker, whose characterization is enhanced by the permanently affixed ghoulish smile makeup designed by Nick Dudman. The initial film in the series spawned several sequels and a *Catwoman* (2004) spin-off (see **Action-Adventure**). *X-Men* (2000) and *X2* (2003) round out this discussion of comic books come to life, in the tale of mutant children (played as adults by Hugh Jackman, Halle Berry, and Rebecca Romijn-Stamos) born with the "X-factor" that allows them to perform unique and extraordinary feats. Professor Charles Xavier (Patrick Stewart) gathers them together in a "mutant academy" for instruction on how to develop their gifts free from prejudice.

Science fiction and fantasy films based on comic books often depend on the recognizability of the real world for their success, as does the collection of films in this period set on a futuristic Earth not that different from our own. A preoccupation with law and order serves as the foundation of *Timecop* (1994), with Jean-Claude Van Damme as a law-enforcement official assigned to regulate the fair use of time travel pitted against a politician bent on becoming president with the help of the technology. Sylvester Stallone also plays a futuristic cop with instant powers to decide the fate of criminals in the film version of the British comic-book hero *Judge Dredd* (1995). With the aid of a criminal he convicted, Judge Joe Dredd, convicted of a crime he did not commit, works to clear his name, eliminating evil along the way. Three seconds of the flying bike sequence, in which the actor swoops down over a crowd of thugs, are computer-generated images, and transport vehicles remind viewers of the spinners from *Blade Runner.* In the less-futuristic-looking but nonetheless alienating Los Angeles of *Strange Days* (1995), former police officer Lenny Nero (Ralph Fiennes), in the course of his new occupation as a purveyor of data disks containing old memories and emotions, runs across the memories of a murderer killing his friend, a prostitute. His subsequent investigation exposes a police conspiracy that threatens to engulf him. In a similar vein, in *Johnny Mnemonic* (1995), Keanu Reeves plays a data courier carrying a large industrial data package in his head who risks the loss of his life if he doesn't deliver the information within twenty-four hours.

Other science fiction and fantasy films set on a futuristic Earth include Kevin Reynolds's spectacular failure *Waterworld* (1995), starring Kevin Costner as a lone sailor adrift in a trimaran on the oceans covering most of Earth's landmass after the melting of the polar ice caps. He eventually helps a woman (Jeanne Tripplehorn) and her foster daughter escape from pirates anxious to capture a little girl with a map to the "Drylands" supposedly tattooed on her back. Up until *Titanic* (1997), the film cost the most to produce of any motion picture in history, and it has been widely regarded as one of the largest failures in the history of motion pictures, although it actually turned a modest profit. In an era of genetic mapping, Andrew Niccol's *Gattaca* (1997) combines subtle acting and sleek set design reminiscent of film noir's art deco influence in a story of Vincent (Ethan Hawke), whose ambitions to fly in space are doomed from the beginning in a world that discriminates on the basis of genetic flaws. Jude Law, who costars as a genetically superior specimen who enters into an unusual agreement with Vincent, is photographed with a particular feline quality. The film reveals the potential of genetic engineering to run amok, and it raises questions about a new future source of discrimination and prejudice.

The continuing drama of humanity's contact with extraterrestrials became the subject of several films around the turn of the millennium, as alien invaders rear their literally ugly heads once again. For example, critics who consider Roland Emmerich's *Independence Day* (1996) a mixture of 1950s alien invasion saga and a 1970s disaster movie peg the film well, particularly in terms of its large cast. Despite its formula, for fans of both 1950s sci-fi and 1970s disaster epics, there is much to love, from the ominous computer-generated city-sized flying saucers, to the destruction of national and international landmarks such as the Empire State Building and, chillingly, the World Trade Center, to a hip, albeit geeky scientist (Jeff Goldblum) and a wise-cracking pilot (Will Smith) who pair up to defeat the aliens on their own turf. Although the computer-generated images often appear fake, they nonetheless effectively portray the menace from above, particularly in the iconic scene of the aliens zapping the White House, which is shot from a low, tilted angle. The structure explodes from within in a brilliant red-tinged firestorm while the alien behemoth hovers above. When contact with the aliens is made, the creatures look like dishes served on a sushi bar, a consistent pattern since the days of *Alien*. Earth's fate rests on an unlikely alliance between conventional sources of authority (military and government leaders) and more unlikely heroes like an alcoholic pilot played by Randy Quaid and a stripper played by Vivica A. Fox. Conventional and nuclear weapons fail to make a dent, literally, in the alien vessels, suggesting that human survival depends on a universal desire to be free rather than machinery. Consistent with the jingoistic tone established in the film, with deliverance from the alien threat coming, as might be expected, on July 4, the President declares human Independence Day for the world (although the film makes only cursory reference to the alien threat around the globe).

Paul Verhoeven's *Starship Troopers* (1997), an adaptation of a Robert Heinlein novel, borrows from both the war film genre (see **War Film**) in its exploration of male initiation and male bonding borne of combat service and action-adventure films (see **Action-Adventure**) or political satire, in that the "good guys" look like Nazis in a futuristic totalitarian regime. Propaganda that demonstrates what's at stake should any citizen falter motivates Earth's youth to join the ranks despite the insane violence and malevolence of intergalactic bugs in eviscerating human flesh. Yet the creatures have a soft side. Battle sequences with computer-generated mutant insects—landmark for their time—put the film squarely in the realm of both science fiction and fantasy and action-adventure. A story of unrequited high school love carried into the starship ranks somewhat humanizes a film largely dependent on special effects to convey both its antiwar message and its prowar appeal in terms of the nobility of warfare to foster important societal values.

Whereas *Independence Day* and *Starship Troopers* rely on a certain comic-book appeal to succeed, *Contact* (1997), based on the Carl Sagan novel, offers a more cogent examination of the relationship between science and religion and a powerful critique of the political and mercenary motivations that often surround new technology and even matters of faith. Since birth, Ellie Arroway (Jodie Foster) has had a fascination with the farthest reaches of the universe. Her work on the search for extraterrestrial intelligence in Puerto Rico results in a brief relationship with Palmer Joss (Matthew McConaughey), who is researching and writing a book on the impact of technology on civilization. The unexpected detection of a multilayered pulsation in prime numbers emanating from the Vega star system—plans for a transportation device to their dimension—results in revitalized interest in the project many scoffed at. Initially, Ellie is disqualified as the first astronaut chosen to make contact with the alien when she cannot affirm a belief in God, but a terrorist attack on the public model of the craft finds her strapped into the transport pod of a second secret one. Shots of stunning lightning effects whizzing by crosscut with distorted images of Ellie's face convey dramatically the possibilities and dangers of travel across dimensions.

Considering her doubts about God, the world she encounters is about as close to heaven as one might be able to conjure up. Once she returns to her own time and place, doubts surround her experiences, because witnesses saw the pod she was strapped into merely fall through the rings of the transport device without traveling to another dimension. The very principles of science that she has often relied on to support her contention about life in the universe eludes her now, because there is no proof that she experienced anything more than a hallucination. A skeptic about matters of religion, she now adopts the language of faith in describing her experiences, and Palmer, whose description of his spiritual conversion earlier in the film was met with some condescension by Ellie, stands by her side. Beautifully photographed with images that remind viewers of the vastness of the space we occupy, *Contact* raises interesting questions about the interconnection of science and religion and about the capabilities and liabilities of technology to improve our lives, a tenet of science fiction and fantasy films from the beginning.

Besides films focusing on space, the 1990s and the first years of the new millennium saw the production of landmark "techno-thrillers" featuring advanced and innovative uses of computer-generated imaging. Written and directed by Larry and Andy Wachowski, *The Matrix* (1999), starring Keanu Reeves and Laurence Fishburne, is among this group (see **Action-Adventure**). On the surface, the story of a man who discovers the fallibility of his reality is age-old. What makes the film so chilling are the philosophical questions it asks about the nature of reality in a technologically reliant, computer-driven, ecologically eroding planet such as our own. Specifically, computer hacker Neo (Reeves) believes he is living in the present, but he discovers that the world he knows is actually a computer simulation, a "matrix," created by advanced computers with artificial intelligence 200 years in the future to pacify humanity and ensure a ready source of human "fuel" for their elaborate scheme. Convinced that Neo may be the mythical "One" able to defeat the oppressive technology, Morpheus (Fishburne), leader of a group of human rebels, exposes to Neo the rifts in this giant integrated computer matrix. The matrix is often revealed to viewers through a series of numerical sequences, reversed letters, and Japanese ideograms in green lettering trickling down a black computer screen. Neo gradually begins to accept the shocking truth and his role in destroying the elaborate computer simulation. "Agents," life-like matrix-generated figures, seek to destroy Neo before he can destroy them.

Set in the cyber world, the visuals had to be top notch, and they do not disappoint, winning Oscars for the members of the visual effects team. Debate surrounds whether this film should receive credit for independently creating or merely perfecting the incomparable "bullet-time" shots—in which individual frames in sequences are elongated, creating a smearing or time-freezing effect—but the sequences have no doubt proven influential, appearing in several films since then. The sequences were created through the computer combination of live action martial arts movements shot against a green background combined with still photography and footage of model buildings in the background. New computer programs were written to create the desired final visual effect, and sound designer Dane Davis whirled bullets on strings to simulate the sound of slow motion projectiles. Narratively, like others before it, *The Matrix* remains fascinated by the notion of birth and humanity's origins, as Neo is jettisoned at one point from a watery pod and flushed down a sluice into a lake. Philosophical, mythological, and religious questions surrounding origin and belief also abound in the first of two sequels released in 2003, *The Matrix Reloaded*, and digitally created special effects play an important role in the final climatic battle in *The Matrix Revolutions* (2003). *The Matrix* charted new ground in terms the synthesis of story and visual effects, and the critical appeal of the last two films in the sequence suffered as a result.

Based on the metaphysical notion that homicide sends ripples through the fabric of human civilization with the most devastating effects of any crime, Steven Spielberg's *Minority Report* (2002) is among the best and most recent techno-thrillers. In 2054, murder has been eliminated in Washington, DC, thanks to an experimental "pre-crime" program that relies on the predictive abilities of three "pre-cogs," a set of male twins and a young woman (Samantha Morton) born to parents addicted to a particular mind-altering drug. A pre-crime expert, Chief John Anderton (Tom Cruise), has saved the lives of many in the six-year history of the program, but government oversight in the guise of agent Danny Witwer (Colin Farrell) disrupts the franchising of the operation throughout the nation. When the emotionally scarred and drug-abusing Anderton must unravel a murder to clear his own name, the alleged existence of so-called "minority reports," alternative visions of murders offered by the pre-cogs but suppressed, motivates him to find the truth behind the pre-crime program itself.

Spielberg and cinematographer Janusz Kaminiski create a visually interesting film reminiscent of the best films noir or neo-noir to date, complete with faded or muted tones along a limited color spectrum for urban exteriors and interiors and only slightly more saturated color for the countryside. Lucite, chrome, glass, and steel sets evoke a classic, and impersonal, art deco style. Although fashion in 2054 differs little from our contemporary era, the futuristic capital consists of diversely shaped buildings and pod-like cars that drive themselves, conveying their occupants from their apartment living rooms across both horizontal and vertical surfaces. Retinal identification even in the most mundane of locations keeps track of all citizens, and the black market transference of eyes is a viable business. Advertisements scan retinas and personalize promotions, and, in one scene, set at a futuristic Gap, a digital greeter welcomes customers into the store and reminds them of past purchases. Industrial Light and Magic seamlessly integrates special effects into the film, including futuristic helicopters that plant pre-crime officers in any location, and "spyders," automated sensors on spindly legs that seek out signs of human life—at one point, even a small bubble on the surface of bath water. A well-constructed story that makes room for the human factor, amid all the technology and strong performances by Cruise and Samantha Morton as the pre-cog Agatha, enlivens a film whose basic premise addresses the debate at the heart of Judeo-Christian ethics: is true transgression found in the intention behind a criminal act or in the committing of the act itself, and when is redemption granted, if it is possible at all?

Spielberg's other millennial entry into the science fiction and fantasy genre is *Artificial Intelligence: A.I.* (2001), from a concept by Stanley Kubrick. With the melting of the Earth's ice caps flooding many major coastal cities and forcing millions to be displaced or to starve, the government creates mechanized creatures to replace human children. One advanced robotic boy, David (Haley Joel Osment), finds himself abandoned in the woods by his human parents when their own son awakens from cryo-statis and returns home. Elsewhere, love robot Gigolo Joe (Jude Law) becomes implicated in the murder of a client, and he must cut off his registration label and escape the city to avoid detection. Captured by scouts for the exploitative "flesh fairs" and then released, the two go in search of the Blue Fairy (from the Pinocchio story), who can turn David into a real child.

The look of the film, although not entirely dark, nonetheless creates a futuristic atmosphere of alienation and anxiety through muted colors and effective backlighting, as well as a reliance on piercing flashlight beams, spotlights, and other shafts of light. The red-light district where Joe plies his trade is revealed as a sort of neon Emerald City, complete with a mechanized wizard the pair seeks out for the whereabouts of the Blue Fairy. In their search for a professor who may hold the answers to making David real, Spielberg includes an impressive, but nonetheless gratuitous, depiction of a Manhattan under water, complete with the Statue of Liberty's torch protruding from the water, as well as the Empire State Building. Of special note are the special effects applied in depicting the robot "Mechas." Fitting his role as a gigolo, Joe morphs into the ideal of each woman, with his hair changing both color and texture on screen. The porcelain, almost metallic, appearance of actor Jude Law's skin and molded hair conveys an eerie but effectively high-tech quality necessary for his character. At one point, during the flesh fair sequence, blinking circuits and electronic currents are fronted by the barest of human faces to imply a human form. From the same creator as *E.T.*, this film with another child-like creature at its center on a heart-breaking quest fell surprisingly flat with many viewers, despite high-quality special effects, believable futuristic scenarios and set designs, and a poignant story.

The director's most recent venture is an old favorite, H. G. Wells's *War of the Worlds* (2005), starring Tom Cruise as deadbeat dad Ray Ferrier who works on the New Jersey docks. When his ex-wife leaves with her new husband on a trip to Boston to see her parents (played by Gene Barry and Ann Robinson, the performers from the 1953 version of the film), she reluctantly leaves their teenage son Robbie (Justin Chatwin) and young daughter Rachel (Dakota Fanning) with their father. During their stay, unusual electromagnetic activity saps all electric power and stops all mechanical functioning, but unlike typical lightning strikes, the ground is cold and not hot, and the wind in the storm blows toward the clouds and not away from it. Quickly, the inhabitants of Ray's neighborhood understand why, as, in a suspenseful special effects sequence, the ground opens up at the middle of an intersection, and a long arm with three suction-cupped fingers protrudes from the crater. With an eerie roar, a three-legged pod emerges, spewing death rays and eviscerating all in its path.

In series of effectively executed crowd scenes, Spielberg portrays the panic of the human species struggling to survive. A mob pulls Ray from the minivan he has commandeered, and the hijacker himself is shot by the crowd while they all wait to board a ferry across the Hudson River. A riveting sequence involves the detection of a tripod emerging from a vortex forming in the river as the ship's captain of orders the ferry ramps lifted in a desperate attempt to escape. In the eerily lit chaos that emerges, the tripod capsizes the boat, and Ray and his children scramble to a shore patrolled by more tripods. The military wages a futile defense against the creatures from another world—the visuals during their fearless charge up a hill, in combination with the soundtrack, create a stirring moment of pathos—and Ray must choose between being separated from Rachel or keeping Robbie from joining the human forces battling the aliens. With Robbie lost in the chaos, father and daughter eventually are waved to safety by a gun-toting ambulance driver named Harlan (Tim Robbins), who has been driven mad by the slaughter around him. During this sequence, viewers also get a close-up look of the aliens outside the pods: the squiggly, slimy aquatic aliens of the past have been replaced by sinewy upright cricket-like figures with three legs and flat, pod-shaped heads. Eventually, the devouring of human flesh results in the downfall of the alien species, as the microbes that humans have developed immunities to over the centuries bring the supposedly superior beings crashing to the Earth. Believable performances by both Tom Cruise and Dakota Fanning highlight the human element, and if the remake has a flaw, it is the distracting voice-over that bookends the film. Criticisms that the film follows a conventional and well-established pattern of alien invasion films and that it fails to explain why advanced creatures should make elaborate plans over centuries to invade the Earth may also be true, but the voice-over, taken directly from Wells's book, provides no insight.

Among the most heralded of fantasy films in recent memory are the film versions of J. R. R. Tolkien's *Lord of the Rings* trilogy, *The Fellowship of the Ring* (2001), *The Two Towers* (2002), and *The Return of the King* (2003), and the *Harry Potter* series. Epic in scope, the Tolkien trio takes advantage of innovations in computer-generated cinematography to create a magical world of elven princesses, noble knight-like leaders, and evil creatures from the pits of darkness, or "the shadows," as the film defines the netherworld (see **Epic**). Largely true enough to the original texts to satisfy die-hard Tolkien enthusiasts, director Peter Jackson and a team of creative artists capture the scope of the novels through the use of elaborately decorated sets enhanced by computer effects. Like the Tolkien stories, the *Harry Potter* series of books and films have tremendous crossover appeal for children and adults alike, as the popularity and box office receipts of the first of the three films in the series attest, second only to *Titanic* by the third month of its release. The film is known for its almost entirely British cast and principal crew, a contingency of filming placed on the material by author J. K. Rowling. Harry Potter (Daniel Radcliffe) is the son of a witch and wizard of remarkable abilities, but their most important gift may have been their love for their son. When the pair supposedly dies in a car crash, the infant is placed with a neglectful maternal aunt (Fiona Shaw) and uncle (Richard Griffiths) by Professor Dumbledore (Richard Harris) and Professor McGonagall (Maggie Smith) until the boy is old enough to matriculate to Hogwarts, a boarding school for up-and-coming wizards and witches. When the letter arrives securing his admission to the academy, Hagrid (Robbie Coltrane) arrives to personally escort him to the school and acquaint him with his new life. In the process, Harry learns the true fate of his parents and his own legacy: they were killed by a wizard gone bad, Voldemort (voiced by Richard Bremer) and he was the only survivor of the encounter, receiving a lightening-shaped scar on his forehead as a result. As Harry learns, therein lies the secret of his celebrity among the magical class. With all the equipment necessary to begin study as a wizard—a white owl, a magic wand, and a cauldron—Harry's adventures as a first-year student at the secret boarding school begin when he meets two friends on the train, Ron Weasley (Rupert Grint) and Hermione Granger (Emma Watson).

Even in its infancy, the art of filmmaking seemed uniquely suited for exploring the unimaginable and the fantastic because the creature of motion pictures themselves seemed futuristic, if not magical, from the outset. With technological and scientific advancements coinciding with the evolution of motion pictures, the wonders of the unknown world and advancement of computer-generated techniques make the boundaries of motion picture making only as limited as the human imagination.

References and Further Reading

Biskind, Peter. "Pods and Blobs." In *Seeing Is Believing: How Hollywood Taught Us to Stop Worrying and Love the Fifties*, 101–160. New York: Pantheon, 1993.

Dirks, Tim. "Science Fiction Films." *Film Site*. 1996–2005. http://www.filmsite.org/sci-fifilms.html.

Johnson, William, ed. *Focus on the Science Fiction Film*. Englewood Cliffs, NY: Prentice-Hall, 1972.

Kawin, Bruce. "Children of the Light." In *Film Genre Reader III*, edited by Barry Keith Grant. 324–345. Austin: University of Texas Press, 2003.

Shusser, George E., and Eric S. Rabkin, eds. *Shadows of the Magic Lamp: Fantasy and Science Fiction in Film*. Carbondale: Southern Illinois University Press, 1985.

Tarratt, Margaret. "Monsters from the Id." In *Film Genre Reader III*, edited by Barry Keith Grant. 346–365. Austin: University of Texas Press, 2003.

CHAPTER 9

SUSPENSE

WHEREAS SOME FILM GENRES are identifiable by their conventions—the common settings and characters found in westerns or the big song and dance numbers in musicals, for instance—others, like horror or suspense films, are characterized by the emotion they cultivate in a viewer. The success or failure of suspense films is determined by their ability to create and sustain tension. And although most film plots, harkening back to Aristotelian dramatic rules, involve conflict and the mounting of suspense to a climax, some movies are clearly tailored to exploit and exaggerate suspense and tension above all else. Such terms as *nail-biting* and *edge of your seat* characterize the experience of watching a suspense film (also referred to as a *thriller*). It is the storyline, twisting and unlikely as it may be, that primarily produces the requisite audience tension, and therefore these films, even when they are as character-driven and image-aware as those in other genres, place particular importance upon plot and its development. In order to produce the desired climactic payoff, the plotline must be paced carefully, reveal information judiciously, and build and sustain just enough—but not too much—tension and suspense. A character is placed in menacing circumstances or some vital piece of information is withheld from the viewer: a killer's identity, a family secret, a competition's results, political or military outcomes, a momentous decision, and so forth. In order to fully connect with audiences, suspense (unlike horror) films are fully grounded in the familiar. They bring fear and the unthinkable into the most mundane and commonplace of circumstances, producing *frissons* of both recognition and shock in audiences who empathize with people like themselves caught up in almost unbearable situations.

Many suspense films are clearly intra-generic hybrids in the sense that there are suspense westerns (*High Noon*), films noir (*The Maltese Falcon*), and science fiction films (*Alien*). In most cases wherein a film shares obvious roots and conventions with one of the aforementioned genres, we have discussed it in that particular chapter.

DEFINING CHARACTERISTICS AND CATEGORIES

The defining characteristic of all suspense films is the tension that keeps viewers guessing and desirous to know what might happen next. Beyond that, certain plot scenarios and character types lend themselves to suspense films and comprise recognizable subtypes within the genre.

Courtroom Dramas

With their meticulous revelation of facts, built-in connection to misunderstandings and crimes, and inevitable, life-altering decisions, courtroom dramas have been a Hollywood staple from the beginning—and a mainstay in theater before that. Court cases *are* high drama, with a set cast of conflicting characters and roles and a plot arc that leads to a final climactic judgment. Usually the courtroom sequence is the major set piece of a film, coming toward the end and determining the story's conclusion. The viewer might know beforehand the circumstances of the criminal act, and sit in suspense to see whether justice will be served; or the audience might be kept in the dark, waiting for the revelation of truth (often as a result of the theatrical—if unrealistic—emotional breakdown of a witness or the accused upon the stand). Lionel Barrymore won an Academy Award for his performance in *A Free Soul* (1931) as a hard-drinking criminal lawyer who is so impassioned and emotional in addressing the jury in his final defense of his daughter, on trial for murdering a gangster, that he falls dead at its completion. The title of *Twelve Angry Men* (1957) nicely sums up its premise of a lone juror (Henry Fonda) desperately trying to convince his eleven cohorts that they are wrong and must reconsider their hasty conviction of the young man on trial. In *To Kill a Mockingbird* (1962), the fate of Tom Robinson (a black man accused of assaulting a white woman in the Depression-era South), not to mention the coming of age of the Finch children, depends upon the outcome of the rape trial. In *Nuts* (1987), a belligerent call girl (Barbra Streisand) would rather stand trial for manslaughter than, as her family desires, be declared legally insane. Jack Nicholson's fiery commanding officer, crying out, "You can't handle the truth!" at young Naval lawyer Tom Cruise, highlights the emotional courtroom scene at the end of *A Few Good Men* (1992) and sets the scene for a showdown of wills.

Whodunits

The large country house, the dead body, the assembled group of suspects, the prescient, observant detective who methodically reveals the killer—these are the components of the classic whodunit, as created by such English novelists as Agatha Christie and Dorothy Sayers. At some level and form, they appear in any story of multiple criminal suspects who, through the process of elimination ("Where were you on the night of April 12th?"), are narrowed down to one. Christie novels have been adapted for stage and screen, from *And Then There Were None* (1945), remade three times as *Ten Little Indians*, to the all-star-cast versions of *Murder on the Orient Express* (1974), *Death on the Nile* (1978) and *The*

Mirror Crack'd (1980). *Mirror* features Angela Lansbury as Christie's famous elderly sleuth, Miss Marple. Several years earlier, the wonderful comedienne Margaret Rutherford took on the role in four British films: *Murder, She Said* (1961), *Murder at the Gallop* (1963), *Murder Most Foul* (1964), and *Murder Ahoy* (1964).

Christie's oeuvre owes much to the fictional world of mystery created by Sir Arthur Conan Doyle. Sherlock Holmes has appeared in more films (well over 200), and been played by more actors (75), than any other fictional character. Dining on kippers at breakfast, playing his violin, exchanging barbs with his assistant Dr. Watson, and (much less frequently in the films than in the novels) ingesting cocaine, the ultimate sleuth appeared in silent films (John Barrymore played him in *Sherlock Holmes* [1922]), a series of British films in the 1930s and, as part of Hammer Films' sex-and-blood horror movies, *The Hound of the Baskervilles* (1959), starring Peter Cushing and Christopher Lee. Hollywood's, and audiences', favorite Holmes-Watson pairing is that of Basil Rathbone and Nigel Bruce, who appeared in an astonishing fourteen films together. The first two are the best: *The Hound of the Baskervilles* (1939) and *The Adventures of Sherlock Holmes* (1939) are faithful to Doyle's novels, wonderfully atmospheric, and generously budgeted by Twentieth Century-Fox. Rathbone's smooth, slightly menacing Holmes perfectly matches Bruce's chatty, bumbling Watson. The twelve later films, made by Universal between 1942 and 1946, were updated, so that the Victorian Holmes was now taking on Nazis (*Sherlock Holmes and the Voice of Terror*, 1942) or traveling to exotic locales (Canada in *The Scarlet Claw* [1944] and the Mediterranean in *Pursuit to Algiers* [1945]).

Psychos

Particularly potent for audiences are stories of violent, psychotic characters who terrorize the innocent. In horror films, an inhuman monster is on the loose. In suspense-thrillers, the monster is all too human, and a twisted mind, not a deformed physiognomy, is at work. Horror films frighten us but, deep down, we know that they could never really happen; suspense films unnerve us because we realize that such unbalanced predators do exist. No vampire or mummy is as wrenchingly frightening or disturbing as is Ed Gein, the serial killer who was the basis for characters in *Psycho* (1960) and *The Silence of the Lambs* (1991). Over the years there were occasional films about mass murderers, specifically historical figures such as Jack the Ripper and the Boston Strangler. However, only relatively recently have serial killers come to so fascinate the public. Besides *The Silence of the Lambs'* Hannibal Lecter and Buffalo Bill, *Seven* (1995) features a madman who targets perpetrators of the seven deadly sins (doling out sickly appropriate means of death), and *Copycat* (1995) concerns a San Francisco murderer who imitates the crimes of past killers. In other films there are psychopathic sons (*Psycho*), lovers (*Play Misty for Me* [1971], *Fatal Attraction* [1987]), mothers (*Carrie* [1976]), husbands (*The Shining* [1980]), sisters (*Whatever Happened to Baby Jane?* [1962], *Sisters* [1973]), in-laws (*You'll Like My Mother* [1972]), roommates (*Single White Female* [1992]), babysitters (*The Hand*

That Rocks the Cradle [1992]), schoolgirls (*Poison Ivy* [1992], *Swimfan* [2002]), preachers (*The Night of the Hunter* [1955]), drug dealers (*Wait Until Dark* [1967]), fans (*Misery* [1990]), prostitutes' johns (*Klute* [1971]), ex-cons (*Cape Fear* [1962 and 1991]), and urbanites (*Taxi Driver* [1976], *Falling Down* [1993]), among others. The crazies in these movies are usually ingenious and wily, increasing our enjoyment of watching victims, police, or vigilantes ultimately outsmart them and end their dreadful perpetrations.

Men and Women in Peril (Victims)

This category of suspense films obviously overlaps with the preceding section. If a madman is on the loose, there will be terrorized potential victims. Sometimes it is simply a desperate character who takes or holds innocent people hostage, as is the case of the criminals on the lam in *The Petrified Forest* (1936) and *Key Largo* (1948). Hostages are a mixture of young and old, male and female—people who are simply in the wrong place at the wrong time. More frequently, movies have exploited the power in situations wherein apparently defenseless women and children are victimized. The young innocents in *The Night of the Hunter* (1955) are under threat because a murderer is after the money their father stole. The names of films in which women are threatened, held captive, killed, or harmed are, unfortunately, too numerous to list. Our society is both shocked and titillated by the spectacle of the threatened woman, a scenario that taps into all manner of uncomfortable psychosocial phobias and fetishes. Cultural critics have devoted countless pages to exploring the concepts of socophilia (pleasure derived from gazing at objects) and the male gaze, whereby females are objectified and codified for male enjoyment, often in connection to cinematic representations of imperiled women. Upping the stakes are films that place a handicapped woman under threat. She may be blind (*Wait Until Dark* [1967], *See No Evil* [originally released in the UK as *Blind Terror*, 1971]), mute (*The Spiral Staircase* [1946]), or bedridden (*Sorry, Wrong Number* [1948]).

Another branch of this category concerns the wrong men and women—as in, "You've got the wrong man!" These unsuspecting characters, so favored by Alfred Hitchcock, stumble into criminal situations and are immediately and unwittingly drawn into the deadly mechanizations of the mad and the violent. Hitchcock's wrong men are suddenly (and wrongly) suspected of the heinous crimes that they have inadvertently stumbled upon, and the hapless protagonists must disentangle themselves as best they can. They are often on the run from both the criminals and the police, and must risk everything in order to locate and identify the true perpetrator and clear their names.

Political Thrillers

Every era's political tensions and neuroses influence its films; political bogeymen can be either homegrown or foreign. The growing threat of fascism and war during the 1930s resulted in countless espionage films. Sometimes the films feature a doomed secret agent who is impossibly beautiful and glamorous, such as Marlene Dietrich in *Dishonored* (1931), who applies a fresh coat of lipstick as she stands before the firing squad, or Greta Garbo in *Mata Hari* (1932). Hitchcock's British films of the period often deal with spies, and America's entry into the war upped the political urgency in Hollywood; Rick's nightclub in *Casablanca* (1942) is a veritable hive of secret political machinations. Hitchcock came to America and brought espionage storylines with him, in such films as *Foreign Correspondent* (1940), *Saboteur* (1942), *Notorious* (1946), *The Man Who Knew Too Much* (1956), and *North by Northwest* (1959). These latter films were but a few of the many motion pictures produced during the Cold War that tapped into America's obsessive fear of Communist expansion and the threat of nuclear war. Cold War paranoia sometimes found an outlet in humorous, tongue-in-cheek action films, such as the James Bond series, but more often in far more serious and sinister stories, such as the noir *Pickup on South Street* (1953), about a missing strip of microfilm bearing confidential U.S. secrets, and *The Manchurian Candidate* (1962), the ultimate brainwashing story. The social and political turmoil of the 1960s and 1970s resulted in films that sought to expose corruption and plots at all levels of society. Alan J. Pakula directed *The Parallax View* (1974), about a reporter investigating a senator's assassination, before taking on the true story of two *Washington Post* reporters' revelation of the Watergate break-in in *All the President's Men* (1976). More recently, *The Constant Gardener* (2005) depicts a naïve low-level British diplomat in Africa who realizes too late that his wife's emotional accusations regarding a drug company's sinister and deadly intentions are heartbreakingly accurate.

Competitions

One of the reason millions of people tune in to the Olympics on television is the drama inherent in competition. Networks play up behind-the-scenes, "up-close and personal" biographies in order to connect audiences to individual athletes (and their personal setbacks, struggles, and crises) and intensify the suspense of who will emerge victorious. Films have exploited almost all areas of human competition in order to provide suspenseful storylines. Among many other competitions, there have been movies about piano awards (*The Competition,* [1980]), chess matches (*Searching for Bobby Fischer* [1993]), and pool hall habitues (*The Hustler* [1961] and *The Color of Money* [1986]). Most popular, of course, are athletic or sports films. Boxing (*The Champ* [1931], *Somebody Up There Likes Me* [1956], *Cinderella Man* [2005]), cycling (*Breaking Away* [1979], *American Flyers* [1985]), football (*Rudy* [1993], *Friday Night Lights* [2004]), basketball (*Hoosiers* [1986]), baseball (*Bang the Drum Slowly* [1973], *Eight Men Out* [1988]), hockey (*The Deadliest Season* [1977], *Slap Shot* [1977]), and horseracing (*National Velvet* [1944], *Seabiscuit* [2003]) are just some of the sports whose competitions provide the action and suspense of popular films. Audiences love rooting for the underdog or the good guy, and the wait for a competition's outcome provides powerful anticipation.

Erotic Thrillers

Romantic comedies follow the format of boy meets girl, boy loses girl, boy gets girl. When the girl or boy turns out to be crazy, a stalker, on the run from the law, or a ghost, we enter the realm of erotic thrillers. Troubled relationships, whether long-standing marriages or one-night stands, contain the material for a tense, suspenseful movie. In films such as *Suspicion* (1941), *The Two Mrs. Carrolls* (1947) and *Deceived* (1991), a wife comes to realizes she really doesn't know the true nature of her husband, who may be capable of murder. Audiences find a homicidal woman even more titillating—and terrifying, especially when she is unapologetically sexual and independent, as in *Black Widow* (1987) and *Basic Instinct* (1992). Films such as *Play Misty for Me* (1971), *Fatal Attraction* (1987), and *Swimfan* (2002) explore the danger of one-night stands, offering strong messages of monogamy.

HISTORY AND INFLUENCES

The Beginning to 1930

As soon as early films developed from short, straightforward depictions of reality in motion to planned and staged stories, moviemakers incorporated suspense as an essential plot tool. Edwin Porter's *The Great Train Robbery* (1903), a milestone in (among other things) film editing, cut from the train, where bandits are holding up passengers, to the depot, where the telegraph operator is tied up, to a nearby dancehall, where a soon-to-be posse is enjoying itself, temporarily unaware of unfolding events. Unlike stage audiences, who could witness but one scene at a time, cinemagoers were now able to see multiple scenes almost simultaneously. The groundwork for all future film chases and rescues had been laid. In *The Adventures of Dollie* (1908), maverick filmmaker D. W. Griffith's directorial debut, a gypsy steals a child and hides her in a barrel—which falls into a river, goes over a weir, and navigates rapids before finally coming to rest on shore where daughter and frantic father are reunited. A hackneyed story, but Griffith, who didn't necessarily invent new film techniques but first mastered, integrated, and combined them, uses close-ups—essential for drawing in and engaging audiences—and crosscutting to maximum effect. Today we take visual crosscutting and close-ups for granted (indeed, we cannot imagine film suspense without them), but they were exciting new tools to early filmmakers, devices that defined and differentiated the new art form from its predecessors (photography and theater). Griffith's *The Lonely Villa* (1909) cuts from the isolated home of the title, where a mother tries desperately to protect herself and her child from robbers, to the determined husband as he rushes from the city to their rescue. *The Lonedale Operator* (1911) ups the number of locations to three for an exciting sequence of continuous movement that cuts from a frightened telegraph operator to thieves breaking in on her to a train crew hurrying to the rescue. In these films we witness Griffith—and cinema—discovering the importance of early scenes to establish character, relationships, and values, the power of cutting and editing film for maximum interest and tension, and the ability to unfold, intertwine, and sustain plot threads, thereby enriching the overall story.

These scenes of menace and impending danger were soon imitated, and their successors fill suspense films to this day. Early on, filmmakers also saw the potential of suspense in comedies. The films of Harold Lloyd, unlike those of the two other great silent comics, Charlie Chaplin and Buster Keaton, turn more on gags and situation than upon character. And what situations! Lloyd's has been called a "comedy of thrills," purely physical comedy derived from his limber body and daring stunts. His characters must attempt to maintain some shred of human dignity—and try desperately to survive—in the midst of mayhem. Lloyd's most famous sequences are his most breathtaking. *Look Out Below,* the title of his 1919 film, indicates the direction in which the acrobatic actor's career was headed, as the stunts grew even more spectacular. Lloyd traverses high building ledges, careening, slipping, and only *just* managing to hold on in *Safety Last!* (1923) which features the quintessential image of Lloyd: hanging precariously from a public clock many stories above a busy city street as the clock's face slowly gives way. Even as they laughed, audiences held their breath to see how he would survive his latest risky situation.

The 1930s

Suspense films of the early 1930s were often adaptations of popular mystery and detective novels—chatty whodunits that leant themselves well to the new sound medium. Most movies from this period are roughly 80 minutes long, brevity that produced, in the best of them, tightly edited and scripted thrillers, greatly benefiting from this taut economy. The sleuths in these and other suspense films are erudite masters of quiet observation and deduction, doing the odd bit of dirty work but largely inhabiting drawing rooms and society watering holes. Later film detectives would become much more physical and active in solving and preventing crimes, relying as much on brawn as on brains; many of their films fall within the action-adventure genre (see **Action-Adventure**).

Several popular mystery novel series became successful film series, including the detective exploits of Philo Vance, Perry Mason, Bulldog Drummond, and Nancy Drew. These tended to be low-budget programmers that could be produced cheaply and rapidly—a step above serials but certainly not in the A-picture range. Nevertheless, the filmmakers occasionally struck gold. *The Kennel Murder Case* (1933) was the fifth of fourteen Philo Vance films (which were produced over two decades by several studios). It stars William Powell as "the world's champion trouble-shooter," in the words of an admiring policeman. Set amidst the toffs of the Long Island Kennel Club, the film concerns the death of a wealthy, almost universally loathed man. All the circumstances indicate a suicide, but Vance smells a rat ("Do you know anyone who would have reason to kill your uncle?" "Practically everyone he came in contact with.") and the film follows his investigation of several suspects. The usual mystery plot devices are all there—suspects telling their stories in flashbacks, a convoluted explanation of the murder—but the film is nevertheless slick and engaging, its pacing assisted by interesting technical devices such as split screens and quick camera pans to the right or left that blur the picture and provide a transition to the next shot.

The Kennel Murder Case is the best of the Vance series, and marked Powell's last performance in the role. The next year, at MGM, he appeared in the first of six films that differ from most of the other sleuth and mystery series in that the films were leisurely and carefully produced (one every two to three years, as opposed to the usual quick one per year), had large budgets, and featured first-rank stars. *The Thin Man* (1934), adapted from a Dashiell Hammet novel, wasn't planned as part of a series, but audiences went wild for the lead characters: urbane super-sleuth Nick Charles and his dazzling, liberated wife Nora—not to mention their energetic terrier, Asta. Powell and costar Myrna Loy had priceless chemistry in the roles and clearly enjoyed playing the quarrelsome but demonstratively affectionate (and alcoholic) couple who happen upon all manner of nasty murders and proceed to outwit both the crooks and the police in solving them. The first film is the best, filled of sparkling repartee, mixing screwball humor with the macabre, and striking the occasional risqué note ("Who's that man in my drawers?" cries Nora at a nocturnal bedroom intruder). Nick and Nora drink like fish as they hit the swankest New York hotspots, all the while investigating the disappearance of an inventor. In the climax, Nick audaciously strong-arms all the suspects into attending a dinner at the Charles home for a series of accusations before he exposes the murderer. Director Woody Van Dyke (nicknamed "One-Take Woody" for his no-nonsense, rapid moviemaking) shot the film in just two weeks, and its freshness continues to captivate audiences. The film's winning combination of murder, suspense, comedy, and romance (Nick and Nora can't keep their hands off each other) was exploited to huge box office success in *After the Thin Man* (1936), *Another Thin Man* (1939), *Shadow of the Thin Man* (1941), *The Thin Man Goes Home* (1944), and *Song of the Thin Man* (1947). Oddly, the Thin Man was not Nick Charles, but a character in the first film.

The pairing of Powell and Loy proved successful, and the actors made other films together in addition to the Thin Man series. In the years before this success, Loy, decidedly Caucasian, was often cast as an exotic and evil Asian. In *The Mask of Fu Manchu* (1932), based on the Sax Rohmer novel, she plays the sadistic daughter of the maniacal Dr. Fu Manchu who, in order to topple European dominance and conquer the world, is bent upon stealing the sword and mask of Genghis Khan from British archeologists. The film is high camp fun, with lines such as "Should Fu Manchu put that mask across his wicked eyes and take that scimitar into his boney, cruel hands, all Asia rises," and "I will wipe out your whole accursed white race!" The members of the archeological party are captured and subjected to various diabolical but wildly ingenious instruments of torture, from massive, constantly tolling bells to ever-narrowing razor-studded walls to an injected serum, taken from poisonous reptiles, which renders victims "living instruments of my [Manchu's] will." Loy's character is inflamed with passion upon witnessing the flogging of a young Englishman, whereupon she takes and binds him as her personal plaything. Despite Manchu's bid for Asian world dominance, he betrays the story's Eurocentrism when the daughter of the leader of the archeological dig is taken captive by Manchu's Chinese henchmen and becomes the object of their lust. "Would you all have maidens like this for your wives?" asks Manchu. "Then conquer and breed! Kill the white man and take his women!" Manchu is overplayed with exaggerated menace by Englishman Boris Karloff, and the *Frankenstein* connection is further evoked by Manchu's mad scientist laboratory, complete with electric currents, boiling liquids, and flying sparks. At the last minute, these pyrotechnics are turned upon their creator and the whole diabolical plot is foiled, thus saving the West.

In *Thirteen Women* (1932), Loy plays a mixed-race woman who, years after enduring slights and rejection at an exclusive all-girl school, sets about murdering her former classmates one by one. Her mad, pitiless thirst for revenge and a gift for hypnosis are typical of the period's xenophobic portraits of Asian villains. The publicity for Paramount's early talkie *Chinatown Nights* (1929), about a society woman mixing with the wrong crowd, screamed, "The oriental mask stripped from the undercover warfare of the terrorizing tongs. A white woman lost among Chinamen . . ." Since the earliest days of cinema, filmmakers have exploited the prurient suspense wrung from the racist fear of a woman suffering a fate worse than death at the hands of the inflamed Other. In a famous and brilliantly edited chase sequence in D. W. Griffith's *Birth of a Nation* (1915), the virginal little sister is pursued by a free black man to a rocky cliff-edge, from which she throws her innocent self to escape his advances. *The Cheat* was filmed three times (1915, 1923, and 1931), recounting the story of an upper-class woman who sells herself to a wealthy Asian, resists his advances, is sadistically branded by him as his property, and finally dies by his hand.

From 1929 to 1949 the Chinese Hawaiian sleuth Charlie Chan (based on a character by novelist Earl Derr Biggers) proved the rare Asian hero in a series of popular Hollywood films. Nevertheless, many of the villains fit the racist model and other, less hostile Asian stereotypes persist in the films in Chan's inscrutability and awkward, stilted speech patterns. Typical of Hollywood hiring practices, no Chinese actor ever played Chan. In fact, the most famous actor to take on the role was a Swede (!), Warner Oland, who appeared in sixteen Charlie Chan films for Twentieth Century-Fox between 1931 and 1938 and played the title character in *The Mysterious Dr. Fu Manchu* (1939). Four of his earliest Charlie Chan films are lost, but the best are *Charlie Chan in London* (1934), *Charlie Chan in Egypt* (1935), and *Charlie Chan at the Opera* (1936). The relaxed, comic-relief patter, in the vein of Holmes and Watson, is here provided by the interaction between Chan and his thoroughly modern, Americanized "Number One Son," Lee, played by Keye Luke. The other Asian sleuth of the 1930s was the Japanese Mr. Moto, played by a German, Peter Lorre, in eight films churned out between 1937 and 1939.

Also released in 1939 were the two most acclaimed Sherlock Holmes films, *The Hound of the Baskervilles* (the fourth screen version of this often-filmed tale) and *The Adventures of Sherlock Holmes*. These films followed the Doyle novels more closely than would later films and first paired Basil Rathbone and Nigel Bruce as Holmes and Watson. The two actors play brilliantly off each other, and the films are highly atmospheric and visually evocative. They successfully mix thrills with laughs, most of the humor resulting from the main characters' close but prickly relationship. *Baskervilles* ends with the drug-addicted Holmes moaning, "Quick, Watson! The needle!" *Adventures* introduces Holmes' arch-enemy, intellectual equal, and frequent screen villain, the nefarious Professor Moriarty, this time out to steal the Crown Jewels.

Suspense films from the 1930s that contain elements of horror include *The Most Dangerous Game* (1932), with frightened shipwreck victims at the mercy of a lonely island's resident madman who, burnt out and jaded with the thrills offered by the civilized world, now big-game hunts the unfortunate humans who wash upon his shore. Tod Browning's *Freaks* (1932), perhaps the strangest film ever produced by a major studio, is a nightmarish meditation upon beauty and cruelty, chronicling the hideous revenge wrought by a group of carnival "freaks" upon a beautiful woman who mistreats and betrays them. The nocturnal scene, set during a cloudburst, is truly unnerving, as the misshapen, knife-wielding sideshow denizens silently stalk and surround their unsuspecting tormentor. *The Black Cat* (1934) features fantastic sets, an equally fantastic plot (involving necrophilia, human sacrifice, Satanism, and sadism), and the initial screen pairing of horror heavyweights Boris Karloff and Bela Lugosi as a crazed, devil-worshiping architect and a doctor searching for his wife.

The "Master of Suspense," of course, is Alfred Hitchcock, perhaps the most famous of all film directors. Much of his celebrity stems from Hitchcock's love and mastery of publicity. He appeared briefly in cameos in his films, lent his name to a mystery magazine, edited books of suspense stories, filmed and narrated macabre, tongue-in-cheek trailers for many of his movies, and personally introduced short mystery and suspense films in a popular television series in the 1950s and 1960s that bore his name. The "Master of Suspense" sobriquet—well earned by the films themselves—was itself a publicity ploy, bestowed upon Hitchcock in 1940 by New York admen in preparation for an unrealized radio series the director was to host.

Hitchcock's mastery of the film medium resulted directly from his early apprenticeship in Europe. An Englishman, he was hired in 1921, at age 22, by an American-based film company to write and illustrate the explanatory title cards that appeared in silent movies. Within a year he had moved up in the British film industry to set designer and assistant director, before going to work at the legendary UFA studio in Berlin at the height of the golden age of German cinema. There his visual style was influenced by film Expressionists such as G. W. Pabst, Fritz Lang, and F. W. Murnau. His unique style fully flowered upon his return to England. *The Lodger* (1926), his first important film, introduced many of those elements that have come to be labeled *Hitchcockian*: a plotline turning on coincidence, a long chase, and a wrong man—a poor innocent who inadvertently stumbles upon a murder, is falsely accused, hunted, and persecuted, and finally must locate and reveal the actual criminal in order to clear his name. In this case, the young lodger who comes and goes at odd hours is suspected of being a Jack the Ripper–type murderer. He is hunted down and handcuffed but manages to escape, setting off an exciting urban chase sequence. At one point, catching the cuffs on a railing he is scaling, he hangs from his wrists, Christ-like, as the angry mob falls upon him. The moody, evocative angles and lighting in this silent film bespeak Hitchcock's time at UFA. Three years later, he directed Britain's first full-length sound film, *Blackmail* (1929). The wrong man here is in fact a woman, blackmailed after she kills a man attempting to rape her. The film is important in Hitchcock's oeuvre in that it introduces the knife as a weapon of menace (knives would reappear in *Sabotage*, *The 39 Steps*, *Dial M for Murder*, *Psycho*, and *Torn Curtain*) and uses a famous monumental setting as the backdrop for a final confrontation and struggle. In this case it is the cavernous halls and domes of the British Museum; years later, it would be the Statue of Liberty in *Saboteur* and Mount Rushmore in *North by Northwest*.

From his British period, Hitchcock's greatest films—those that opened the door to Hollywood—are *The 39 Steps* (1935) and *The Lady Vanishes* (1938); the latter earned him the best director prize from the New York Film Critics Circle. Based on the novel by John Buchan, *The 39 Steps* is a story of foreign spies and an innocent man who, through a chance encounter with a mysterious woman, is drawn into a web of murder. In typical Hitchcock fashion, the film mixes high drama, comedy and romance, as the wrong man (played by Robert Donat) flees north to Scotland, pursued by both secret agents and the police. En route he chances upon a beautiful blonde (another Hitchcock feature: the beautiful young ally who, initially resistant, comes to believe in the man's innocence and eventually falls in love with him). There is always a high sexual charge to Hitchcock's films. Here, Donat and Madeleine Carroll rush into the Highlands, at times handcuffed together, which of course forces them to sleep together. In one scene, as Carroll removes her stockings, Donat's bound hand appreciatively rubs up and down her naked leg. They stay one night with a poor crofter and his young romantically and sexually starved wife, who helps them escape even though it will bring down her jealous husband's wrath. The film's extended chase leads the hero back to where he (and the film) began, in a vaudeville house. As the police arrive to take him away, he outsmarts the spies and reveals the secret to the 39 steps.

In *The Lady Vanishes*, most of which takes place on a train, a little old lady befriends the female lead (Margaret Lockwood) then suddenly disappears—and, suspiciously, no one else admits to having seen her onboard. Based on a novel by Ethel Lina White, the story again involves international spies and a pair of young and attractive innocents drawn into danger. Lockwood and costar Michael Redgrave must deal with skeptical passengers and crew, an obstructive snowdrift over the train tracks, and a fiery final shootout.

Like many of Hitchcock's films, these were adapted from preexisting material. The director preferred to adapt his films rather than create original material, seeing the task as an interesting exercise in visualization and condensation. Years later in Hollywood, when adapting popular novels and plays, he would also have to jump through the hoop of censorship enforced by the Motion Picture Production Code.

Hitchcock is known for his visual flair, but his 1930s pictures also show an innovative and inventive use of the new medium of sound film. In a famous scene from *Blackmail*, the nervous heroine, listening to friends discuss the recent murder (which, unbeknownst to them, she committed), uneasily slices a loaf of bread. The conversation around her dissolves into a blurred unintelligible drone, punctuated only by the frequently spoken word "knife," which jumps out of the confusion at her. In *The 39 Steps*, a cleaning woman enters a flat, only to discover a dead body. Turning toward the camera, she opens her mouth to scream but the scene cuts immediately to a rushing train (on which the hero flees) as its whistle shrieks. *The Lady Vanishes* features spies exchanging vital information in an idyllic Alpine village by means of rustic folk songs sung in the moonlight.

The 1940s

Hitchcock moved to the United States in 1939, and the following year saw the start of his amazing, prolific American film career. Considered Hollywood's greatest year, 1939 represented the apogee of the studio system. Hitchcock flourished despite, rather than because of, this production system, under which directors—like actors—were simply technicians in a film factory, contributing their talent to the steady output of product under the supervision of studio bosses and producers. Hitchcock demanded much more control than was usually allotted to directors, and it was his misfortune that the man who brought him to Hollywood was producer David O. Selznick, the most hands-on and demanding of bosses. The perfectionist Selznick was then immersed in *Gone With the Wind*, which took most of his energy, but he nevertheless expected to have a hand in Hitchcock's moviemaking. The director took full advantage of his contractual option to work for other producers and studios; he would ultimately make only three films for Selznick.

Hitchcock had already established his unique manner of film preproduction. Long before the cameras started to roll, he would create detailed graphic storyboards, rather like comic books, completely outlining the look, angle, and details of each shot of the film. When filming started, the director didn't bother to get shots from several angles, or covering shots, for later consideration in an editing room. He already knew exactly how a scene should look, and he stuck amazingly close to his initial instincts (and his early visual sketches). This infuriated Selznick, who expected much more footage in the daily rushes—alternate takes and angles from which *he* planned to choose the most effective. Hitchcock employed this method throughout his career. It is fascinating to see how closely his most famous film sequence, the shower scene in *Psycho*—shot twenty years later—follows the storyboard graphics he drew from his mind's eye before filming.

Of his first American film, *Rebecca* (1940), the director said, "Well, it's not a Hitchcock picture" (McGilligan 2003, 260), probably referring to the fact that Selznick had a hand in (and strong opinion regarding) everything from screen tests to script to final shot. Never again would the controlling Hitchcock suffer such external input. Nevertheless, the film was an immediate success and won the Academy Award for Best Picture (though Hitchcock himself, in one of the chief scandals of that award's history, would never win a statuette for his direction). The film, based on the popular novel by Daphne Du Maurier, follows the trials of a timid young woman (Joan Fontaine) married to the wealthy widower Max de Winter (Laurence Olivier). She moves with him to the Cornish estate Manderley, forever haunted by the memory of the *first* Mrs. De Winter, Rebecca. Secret passions, alliances, and misdeeds abound, and the young wife soon butts heads with the mysterious, sinister housekeeper Mrs. Danvers (Judith Anderson), who remains devoted—to a hysterical, sensual degree—to the memory of Rebecca. The exact nature of Max and Rebecca's relationship is withheld until the end of the film, which concludes with a deadly conflagration. To satisfy the Hays Office, Rebecca's death was changed from a murder to a suicide, but the film's power remains—due largely to the menace provided by the Manderley sets and by Anderson's performance. The subject of a wife's agonizing realization that she doesn't really know her husband would reappear in later Hitchcock films.

Hitchcock's more domestic films of the 1940s include *Suspicion* (1941), set in England with Joan Fontaine essentially reprising her *Rebecca* role as an immature wife married to a debonair, urbane husband with a mysterious past. This time around, she is the wealthy partner, who comes to suspect her husband is plotting her murder. It was Cary Grant's first film for the director, and the first to really tap the star's darker side. Grant's aloof, secretive persona, coupled with his impossible charm, beauty, and magnetism, made him the perfect Hitchcock actor. Grant as a dark character was permissible, but only to an extent. The star's (and film's) studio, RKO, would *not* allow him to play a cold-blooded murderer, so the original novel's ending had to be altered. Alternative scenes were shot, but the one finally chosen, in which the wife's suspicions are proved wrong, undeniably weakens the film's impact. Despite this compromise, the film is slick and gripping. A classic scene involves the glass of milk the husband brings his wife in the evenings. In light of evidence she has discovered in the house, she and the audience suspect that it contains poison. Hitchcock placed a small light bulb in the tall glass of milk, so that it glows unnaturally as Grant carries it through the darkened house and up the stairs, bathed in a threatening web of shadows.The 1940s saw eleven more American films from Hitchcock. Some were disappointing (*The Paradine Case* [1947] and *Under Capricorn* [1949], for example) but several were undisputed masterpieces. Stories involving spies and secret agents continued to fascinate the director, particularly as America entered the war. *Foreign Correspondent* (1940), set in England and Holland, concerns an unsuspecting American (Joel McCrae) trapped in the middle of a spy ring posing as a political Peace Party. The film features the obligatory romance with a young woman but also a brilliantly staged sequence of an airplane crashing into the ocean after being hit by a German destroyer. *Saboteur* (1942), during production of which Pearl Harbor was attacked, seizes upon the national fear that fifth columnist Nazi supporters might sabotage American heavy industries. It is yet another of Hitchcock's wrong man stories, as the innocent protagonist, accused of starting a fire at a wartime defense plant, must flee cross-country (with a blond billboard model, no less, in tow) and eventually prove his innocence. The leader of the fascist group that set the fire exclaims inflammatory, antidemocratic lines, calling Americans "the great masses" and "the moron millions," before the hero (Robert Cummings) catches the saboteur on the *torch* of the Statue of Liberty—the fire-starter overcome and destroyed at the flame of democracy and freedom. The film's thrilling chase sequence culminates as the saboteur slips, the hero catches his arm, the coat sleeve slowly rips, and the man falls to his death. Wartime audiences loved it. The third spy story is perhaps Hitchcock's greatest film of the decade, *Notorious* (1946). It features a dream cast: Cary Grant as American intelligence officer Devlin, out to crack a post–war Nazi exile ring in Brazil; Ingrid Bergman as Alicia, guilt-ridden over her executed father's traitorous work for the fascists and now convinced to infiltrate the group of exiles; and Claude Rains as Alex, the cold leader of the Brazilian ring. At Devlin's urging, Alicia agrees to romance and even marry Alex in order to acquire and pass on information, but the growing relationship between the two agents results in Devlin's hurt and heartless condemnation of Alicia's willingness to sell herself to a man she loathes. The movie boasts several spectacular scenes, one of which has been called the longest kiss on film. In another sequence, Alicia has hugged Alex at a large party at their estate in order to steal the key to the wine cellar where, it is suspected, bomb-making material is hidden. The camera performs an amazing crane shot from Devlin's perspective upstairs, high above the grand room, gradually moving down and down to Alicia, whose back is towards us. The camera continues zooming in to a close-up of her hand, where she motions toward the key she has lifted from Alex's jacket.

Inter-familial suspicions also arise in *Shadow of a Doubt* (1943), in which sweet Uncle Charles (Joseph Cotton) arrives for a visit in the placid little town of Santa Rosa, California, to the delight of his niece and namesake, Charlie (Teresa Wright), who idolizes him. Over time, however, she come to the conclusion (already clear to the audience) that he is in fact the "Merry Widow murderer" who has been marrying and killing wealthy women on the East Coast. The film has a noir feel to its exploration of appearance versus reality and its exposure of evil and darkness lurking beneath the wholesome surface of innocent small town life (Thornton Wilder worked on the screenplay). Uncle Charles is disillusioned and bitter about the modern world and tries to contaminate the idealistic, innocent Charlie: "you're just an ordinary girl in an ordinary town. . . . You go through your ordinary little sleep, filled with peaceful, stupid dreams. And I brought you nightmares—or did I? . . . You're a sleepwalker, blind. How do you know what the world is like? Do you know the world is a foul sty? Do you know if you ripped the fronts off houses, you'd find swine? The world's a hell! What does it matter what happens in it?" To varying extremes, this unnerving fact—that evil and violence are all around us, waiting to strike from behind false smiles and apparent normalcy—is reiterated by Hitchcock in film after film and would be explored even further by his cinematic heirs, including

When alter egos collide: Teresa Wright learns the hard way that her beloved Uncle Charles is not the wonderful man she always imagined in *Shadow of a Doubt* (1943), Alfred Hitchcock's study of dark secrets lurking in an all-American town. *Photofest.*

Brian De Palma, David Lynch, and Sam Mendes. The duality of human nature and the existence of evil in us all are explored through the twin imagery that characterizes Charles and Charlie—shared dialogue as well as parallel scenes and shots. *Shadow of a Doubt* ends with a powerful confrontation between niece and uncle on a speeding train, from which one character falls to a horrible death.

Spellbound (1945), dismissed by the director himself as "just another manhunt story, wrapped up in pseudo-psychoanalysis" (Phillips 1984, 116), follows an amnesiac who fears that he has murdered his psychiatrist. The film's treatment of psychoanalysis is blunt and heavy-handed, complete with obvious visual Freudian symbols (closed and open doors, eyes, wayward ski-tracks, etc.). One typically Hitchcockian surprise effect occurs when a man kills himself. We see things from the man's perspective, as the gun is turned and aimed towards the audience. When it goes off with a loud bang, a flash of blood red fills the screen, a vivid shock in an otherwise black and white film.

Hitchcock loved thinking up and pulling off technical stunts, including unique camera angles and movements. Two 1940s films were exercises in technique: *Lifeboat* (1944) and *Rope* (1948) both feature claustrophobic single settings from which the story never strays. *Lifeboat* follows a random group of survivors stranded in a small boat after a German U-boat torpedoes their freighter. They, along with a Nazi who is pulled onboard, are presented as a microcosm of the world. By necessity, the film is very talky, but Hitchcock never lets the story drag, despite the restricted single setting. The film was shot in a huge studio tank and proved a trial for the actors, who were constantly wet and often seasick. In order to concentrate on the story, the director avoided hiring well-known performers. Playing Constance, a successful newspaper reporter, stage actress Tallulah Bankhead is appropriately larger than life in a part specifically written for her. Her character initially views the tragedy simply as a great story, photographing a baby bottle bobbing in the water. "Why don't you wait till the baby floats by and photograph that, too?" snarls a disgusted fellow survivor. Constance's detached, superior air is gradually stripped away, and as she systematically loses her possessions overboard—camera, typewriter, fur coat, and jewels—we witness her blossoming humanity and hatred towards Nazi atrocities. The Office of War Information strongly objected to the fact that the smartest, strongest person in the lifeboat is the German, a doctor. But Hitchcock insisted upon this, and played up the irony by having the doctor inhumanely shove overboard the very man whose life he saved earlier. The cold-hearted German espouses the wonders of the *Übermensch*, the Nietzschean superman figure central to Nazi racial theories. Hitchcock succeeds in sustaining audience interest without ever leaving the small, isolated lifeboat.

Four years later, the director decided to make a film set entirely in a small New York apartment. In addition, he would film the entire picture as if in a single take. *Rope* consists of ten unbroken single takes, each roughly ten minutes in length and ingeniously cut and dissolved together so that one appears to flow seamlessly to the next. The reason for this interval was purely practical: a single reel of film—all that a camera could hold—lasted about ten minutes. This is also the director's first color film and the first to bear the enviable above-the-title billing format the director would enjoy with many of his future pictures: "Alfred Hitchcock's *Rope*." Based upon the famous Leopold-Loeb murder case, the film tells of two brilliant young men—implicitly gay and also enamored of Nietzsche's Superman concept of superior and inferior humans—who decide to commit the perfect, unsolvable murder. They kill a former classmate, stuff his body in a large trunk, and invite family and friends over for dinner—a dinner set and eaten off the trunk.

The 1940s were the decade of the private detective, a jaded loner, fearless and incorruptible, despite his general lack of money. Although not overly talkative, he wisecracks with the best of them, in his cynical, deadpan way. He is experienced with crooks and also with dames, for whom he shows appreciation—but who usually slip through his fingers. The greatest embodiment of the hard-boiled dick is, of course, Humphrey Bogart. Apart from the occasional bright spot, such as *The Petrified Forest* (1936), Bogart spent the 1930s toiling away as a lower-level studio contract player for Warner Brothers. He appeared in twenty-nine films, mostly B-pictures, in the thirties, often portraying a gangster. As the bad guy, Bogart had limitations, appearing stiff and remote. The breakthrough occurred when directors such as Raoul Walsh, John Huston, Michael Curtiz, and Howard Hawks grafted Bogey's cynical, tough-guy persona, honed in all those minor gangster films, to basically good characters. Suddenly the actor's career took off, as audiences identified and felt for this new type of antihero, whose cynicism and rough, loner experience lead him to question and dismiss authority, while living according to a rigid personal code of morality. Some critics have called Bogart the greatest American hero figure in films, as he represents the little guy who is mistreated by the system but retains a belief in individual worth and possibility. The thrillers that Bogart made in the 1940s established this persona, which he would maintain for the rest of his illustrious career.

Bogart portrayed Dashiell Hammett's detective Sam Spade in the third (and best) filmed version of *The Maltese Falcon* (1941). The convoluted plot, the bodies that pile up and the motley crew of desperate and shady characters who gather in San Francisco in search of an enamel bird statuette, filled with priceless jewels, keep the viewer guessing about who shot Spade's partner and whose version of events is true. The supporting cast is outstanding: Peter Lorre plays the evasive Joel Cairo, with a thinly veiled homosexuality, Sydney Greenstreet portrays the notorious Fat Man, and Mary Astor plays Brigid O'Shaughnessy, Spade's client, whose lies and desperation almost fool the detective. In his directorial debut, John Huston (who also wrote the script) keeps things moving to the surprise ending and allows Bogey to snarl out classic lines such as "When you're slapped, you'll take it and *like* it," and, foreshadowing the sort of part that he would play throughout the next decade, "Don't be too sure I'm as crooked as I'm supposed to be. That sort of reputation might be good business, bringing high priced jobs and making it easier to deal with the enemy."

The classic *Casablanca* (1942) and *To Have and Have Not* (1944), thrillers set in French seaports during Nazi occupation, follow the plotting and maneuverings of French Resistance fighters, harsh Gestapo authorities, and the varied human flotsam that has washed into the seedy bars and hotels of this corner of war-torn Europe. In the first film, Bogart plays Rick, owner of an American bar in French North Africa where everyone—high and low, rich and poor, French and German and every other nationality—hangs around, some waiting for forged visas with which to leave Europe, escaping the war and the past, others just drinking the time away. In *To Have and Have Not*, Bogart plays Harry Morgan, captain of a sea-fishing boat hired by wealthy tourists to Martinique. In both films, the apolitical protagonist is dragged unwillingly into the affairs of resistance fighters and forced to take a stand regarding human rights and dignity. And then there are the women. *Casablanca* features a resplendent Ingrid Bergman as Ilsa, Rick's old flame, now married to the leader of the underground. The second film was Lauren Bacall's debut; her pairing with Bogey fit so well that they would marry the next year and make three more films together. Bogart and Bergman are a hyper-romantic coupling, her dewy fragility enveloped by his bruised masculinity. Bogart and Bacall, on the other hand, are equally cool, cynical and independent. The suspense in these films is threefold: Will Bogart and the woman get together and stay together? Will the hounded, outnumbered resistance fighters escape and continue their struggle for freedom? And will Bogart's character come to see that sometimes a guy's gotta go out on a limb for something bigger than himself? The answer, at least to the third question, is a resounding *yes*. Rick realizes that the problems of a few people "don't amount to a hill of beans" in relation to what is happening in Europe, and a character comments tellingly on Harry by stating that "This is not his fight . . . yet. Someday I hope it may be, because we could use him."

The pairing of Bogart and Bacall proved so potent that they were cast in *The Big Sleep* (1946), a legendary filming of Raymond Chandler's first novel, featuring Bogey as the hard-boiled shamus Philip Marlow, hired by an ailing millionaire to help get his wild young daughters out of trouble. The picture was filmed in 1944 and 1945 but, unhappy with newcomer Bacall's performance and bowled over by the success of *To Have and Have Not*, the studio had director Howard Hawks reshoot some scenes and create several new ones in early 1946 to play up both Bacall's sultry independence and the heated romance between the two stars. The plot is notoriously convoluted (to the extent that one of the many murders is never even explained), with extensive characters and subplots. Nevertheless, the noirish atmosphere of rain-soaked nocturnal streets and impending menace is potent. In order to ensure that audiences are as confused as Marlow as he attempts to figure out murders, disappearances, and the extent to which the millionaire's daughters are involved in it all, Hawks puts Bogart in every scene; we see things entirely through his eyes.

By 1947, Bogart's success was such that he was the highest paid man in America. The following year, the actor made two suspense films in which his characters undergo behavioral change, one towards goodness and the other towards evil. *Key Largo* is the penultimate pairing of Bogart and Bacall, in a story about a group of gangsters who take hostage the elderly owner of a Florida Keys hotel and his widowed daughter Nora, as well as the ex-GI who happens to have wandered in. Edward G. Robinson plays the gangster, Johnny Rocco, with relish, chewing up the scenery and preening about menacingly. Claire Trevor won an Academy Award as Rocco's boozing, neurotic moll. Lionel Barrymore and Bacall play the hotelier and his daughter, respectively, and Bogart is Major McCloud, who fought alongside Bacall's husband and now drifts from place to place and job to job. McCloud is a typical Bogart hero: he is selfish and opportunistic but, when faced with true evil and pushed to the extreme, he finally takes a stand. Early on, he passes up the chance to shoot the gangster, explaining, "What do I care about Johnny Rocco, whether he lives or dies? I only care about me and mine." McCloud doesn't give a damn: "I fight no battles but my own." Nora is disgusted by his outlook, but realizes there is more to the man than even he realizes. "Maybe it is a rotten world," she says, "but a cause isn't lost as long as someone is willing to go on fighting." And McCloud is that someone: "You may not want to be but you can't help yourself." After a few more of Rocco's acts of wanton violence and cruelty, the Major (in a post-Hitlerian message that wasn't lost on audiences) comes to realize the necessity of fighting evil. "I've got to," he says.

Like his earlier film *The Maltese Falcon*, director John Huston's *The Treasure of the Sierra Madre* (1948) is a parable about greed, specifically its corrupting effects on human nature. Inspired by one of Chaucer's *Canterbury Tales* and based on a novel written by the mysterious B. Traven, the film recounts the gradual descent of three prospectors into murder and madness after they strike gold, as greed and paranoid distrust consume them. The film was one of the first to be shot on location, and its stark, inevitable storyline perfectly matches the remote, arid Mexican countryside (shot in beautiful black-and-white). Like the Chaucer tale, the film is an allegory, pitting Bogart's viciously evil character, Dobbs, against the naïve, compassionate Curtin (Tim Holt) and the sage and experienced (albeit somewhat crazy) old prospector Howard (played by the director's father, Walter Huston). Of course, it is the alliance of greed and death that wins in the end, tantalizing and taunting the men to acts of murder and self destruction. Although the film seems appropriate to the dark, cynical post–WWII world that begat film noir, contemporary audiences were not ready for such a grim revelation of human nature and, despite the film's glowing critical reviews and awards (Huston won two Academy Awards, for his direction and his screenplay adaptation, and his father won in the supporting actor category), audiences largely stayed away.

Despite the power of his complicated anti-heroes, Bogart did take on the occasional purely evil character, though not to much success. Twice he played wife-murderers. In *Conflict* (1945), after he falls in love with his wife's sister, he kills his spouse, then sets it up to look like a car accident. The audience simply awaits the inevitable revelation of the husband's true character. In *The Two Mrs. Carrolls* (1947), Bogart plays a deranged artist who, as viewers and the current Mrs. Carroll (the increasingly panicked Barbara Stanwyck) come to discover, paints his wives as the Angel of Death before murdering them. Despite the presence of its two stars, the film's heavy-handed direction, under Peter Godfrey, noticeably lacks the stylish and subtle treatment that Hitchcock could bring to a similar story. The film even shares *Suspicion*'s poisoned glass of milk as the husband's weapon, but what Hitchcock can do with such a simple prop sets him apart from most other directors.

Another important suspense film of the decade is Otto Preminger's *Laura* (1944), featuring the stunningly beautiful Gene Tierney in the title role, Vincent Price as a smarmy fortune hunter, Dana Andrews as the puzzled detective falling in love with the portrait of a dead girl, and Clifton Webb in a delightfully witty and campy performance as a cynical newspaper columnist—and Laura's Pygmalion. The identity of a corpse suddenly changes and Andrews must figure out how, why, and by whom a bizarre murder was committed. *Gaslight* (1944) is director George Cukor's remake of the 1940 English film of the same title, based upon a play about a killer trying to drive his wife insane in order to get his hands on a cache of jewels. Ingrid Bergman won an Academy Award for her bravura performance as the frantic, hysterical wife, trying desperately to believe—and convince others—that she has not lost her mind. Charles Boyer is suavely sinister as the scheming husband, and, in an impressive film debut, Angela Lansbury shines as the slatternly housemaid who captures Boyer's attention.

The Spiral Staircase (1946) and *Sorry, Wrong Number* (1948) are classic woman-in-peril films, compounded here by the heroines' disabilities. The former, set early in the twentieth century, features Dorothy MacGuire as a mute servant girl in a large spooky house. A madman has been killing local women who suffer physical disabilities and imperfections, and he may be hiding out inside the house. Dark corridors, the unsteady staircase of the title, and deafening nocturnal thunderstorms help set the scene for a hair-raising finale. *Sorry, Wrong Number* is based on a successful radio drama and stars Barbara Stanwyck as a bedridden virago who pesters and berates everyone around her. The telephone is her lifeline to the outer world and the means by which she overhears the plotting of a murder—only to realize that she is the planned victim and that no one believes her story. Stanwyck's bravura performance overcomes the stagy scene restrictions, and the film builds to a nightmarish climax as the murderer slowly enters the house, ascends the stairs, and approaches the hysterical woman's bedroom. . . .

The 1950s

Despite the many classic films he made up to this point, many people consider the 1950s to be Hitchcock's greatest period. Certainly, his films from this decade (which number eleven, one less than the dozen produced in the 1940s) enjoy the assurance of an artist working at his peak, coupling visual richness (the majority are in brilliant color and feature exotic location shooting) with a sly, sometimes macabre sense of humor. Amazingly, this particularly fertile period (six films between 1954 and 1956) also witnessed the inauguration of his television series, which he supervised and hosted for the next decade.

Strangers on a Train (1951), based on the novel by Patricia Highsmith, is another Hitchcock examination of our mixed human nature and the propensity for evil in us all. Two men on a train meet by chance: manipulative and highly-coded gay Bruno (Robert Walker) and golden boy tennis champion Guy (Farley Granger). Bruno corners the celebrity and, in the course of their conversation, we learn that both men suffer painful relationships. Bruno, devoted to his scatterbrained mother, despises his father, while Guy has fallen for a girl but is trapped in a loveless marriage. Bruno unveils his plan for the perfect crime: they will exchange murders, each killing the other's nemesis and thus producing apparently motiveless crimes that will be almost impossible to trace. Despite his wish to be free of his wife Miriam, Guy nonetheless is horrified by Bruno's apparent seriousness about such an undertaking and is glad to disembark the train. All semblance of normalcy is shattered when Bruno proceeds to kill Miriam and then harangue and pester Guy about fulfilling his part of the bargain. Much of the film takes place in Washington, and, in one scene, Hitchcock illustrates his theme of evil lurking just beneath a placid, innocent surface by placing Bruno's dark shadowy figure before the gleaming white of the Jefferson Memorial. From a distance, Guy notices this ominous silhouette, nightmarishly watching and waiting for the younger man to do his part in a devil's pact. To the dismay of some of his screenwriters, Hitchcock was always more interested in striking visual effects and in scenes or sequences that generate extreme tension than in stories or characters that are completely plausible or logical. At one point, as Guy plays a tennis match, all of the spectators' heads swivel back and forth simultaneously, watching the ball move from end of the court to the other. But we notice that one head is *not* moving; Bruno keeps his eyes fastened upon Guy the entire time. The two most memorable scenes in *Strangers on a Train* occur in a fairground—violence and death in the midst of pleasure and innocent fun. Bruno follows the bespectacled Miriam to the dark and deserted edge of the amusement park to murder her. After her glasses are knocked to the ground, we witness the death as reflected and slightly distorted in their lenses. The film's climax takes place on an out-of-control carousel, where Guy confronts and struggles with Bruno. The carousel turns faster and faster, and children and parents are thrown around and off, until the entire thing crashes and splinters in a deadly finale. *Dial M for Murder* (1954) also features a spouse plotting murder, as Ray Milland hires someone to strangle his wealthy wife (Grace Kelly). The film was shot in that short-lived technological craze, 3-D, but is now available in its "flat" version.

Returning to the circumscribed confinement of *Lifeboat* and *Rope*, Hitchcock set his next film entirely in a small New York apartment. In *Rear Window* (1954) press photographer Jeff Jeffries (James Stewart) is laid up, immobile in a full leg cast, spending his long hot days observing (through his cameras' zoom lenses) the behavior of the inhabitants of the apartment across the courtyard. As in *Lifeboat*, we have the world in microcosm: lives playing out stories of hope, betrayal, love, loneliness, creation, and, apparently, murder. Jeff's nosiness replicates our own as, in Hitchcock biographer Patrick McGilligan's words, the film is about "a voyeur—as filmed by a voyeur director, and watched by a voyeur audience." (2003, 481–482). Rather than looking closely at his *own* troubled life, which calls for decisions and action, Jeff becomes a peeping Tom. In her second Hitchcock film, Grace Kelly plays fashion model Lisa, the photographer's girlfriend, initially put off by his snooping but eventually convinced that a murder has taken place across the way. The actress is stunningly gorgeous (Hitchcock gives her a breathtaking entrance) and chicly outfitted by legendary Hollywood costumier Edith Head. Kelly was the perfect Hitchcock heroine: a cool, remote blonde who nevertheless suggests raging sexuality just below the surface. Hitchcock realized that film suspense turns upon the audience knowing some vital piece of information (a bomb placed under a table, a body in the kitchen, etc.) of which the character onscreen is ignorant. More specifically, our tension increases in those excruciating, drawn-out moments, as we wait for the character to realize that vital piece of information. At one point in *Rear Window,* Lisa goes to the building next door, breaks into the apartment of the man they suspect has murdered his invalid wife, and searches for evidence. The entire process is seen from Jeff's removed point of view, and we and the photographer watch helplessly from a distance as the murderer returns home unexpectedly, crossing the street, climbing the steps, entering the apartment, and coming upon the unsuspecting Lisa.

Kelly is paired with Hitchcock's other favorite leading man, Cary Grant, in *To Catch a Thief* (1955). The film, set on the French Riviera, tells the story of notorious but retired jewel thief and Resistance hero Johnny Robie (Grant) who must catch a copycat burglar in order to prove his own innocence. The film is lighter and funnier than most Hitchcock thrillers, as much light comedy as suspense, with beautiful people (Kelly plays a rich Texan heiress, stunning in jewels and designer clothing), beautiful settings, and a script that pulses with sexual double entendres. It features the much-imitated sequence in which, as Kelly seduces Grant and they start to make love in a hotel suite, the camera cuts to the night sky and an orgasmic explosion of fireworks. Figurative pyrotechnics follow in a breathtaking car chase along the precipitously winding roads high above the Mediterranean (roads upon which, thirty years later, as Princess Grace of Monaco, Kelly would die in a car accident) and in Grant's final and precarious confrontation with the copycat burglar, high on the rooftops. Hitchcock's last important film of the decade is the dreamlike *Vertigo* (1958), with James Stewart as a retired police detective falling in love with the woman (Kim Novak) he was hired to shadow. The film's convoluted plot and surprise twists, not to mention its unsettling explorations of gender, identity, phobia, and obsession, hindered the film's initial appeal, but these very features have gradually won over fans and critics alike, making it perhaps the most discussed and analyzed of Hitchcock's films. Bernard Hermann's much-imitated score perfectly fits the tortured path down which the unsuspecting protagonist travels.

Film noir flourished after the war, filling cinema screens with nightmarish urban worlds of chiaroscuro suspense and mystery (see **Film Noir**). Samuel Fuller's noirish Cold War thriller *Pickup on South Street* (1953) follows pickpocket Skip McCoy (Richard Widmark), who is plying his trade on the New York subway when the wallet he lifts from a woman's purse turns out to contain top secret microfilm intended for Communist agents. Police and crooks alike embark on a frantic and deadly search for the film, enlisting the aid of pitiful professional stool pigeon Moe (Thelma Ritter, in her best performance). The script (which Fuller wrote) is tough and fast, packing a wallop in a mere eighty minutes. As it moves towards its climax, the film mixes harsh violence with a softer portrait of honor, and even love, among thieves.

Susan Hayward won an Academy Award for her unrestrained (and unsubtle) performance as a prostitute and petty crook who is framed for murder and sent to the gas chamber in *I Want to Live!* (1958). We see her hard-knocks life and the unfortunate twist of fate that leads to her imprisonment on death row. The latter part of the film is a nerve-wracking series of postponements and dashed hopes as the date for her execution is set, changed, and set again, leading up to a harrowing wait for a possible last-minute telephone pardon from the governor, even as the gas chamber is being prepared.

The 1960s

Hitchcock's output after *North by Northwest* suffered a general decline in both quantity and quality. The decade began with a bang—or a scream—with the 1960 release of *Psycho*. After the lushness of his 1950s color travelogue extravaganzas, *Psycho* was a brilliant experiment in stark simplicity, influenced no doubt by the cheap but successful black-and-white shocker films of the time as well as by Hitchcock's own television series. Although Hitchcock may have borrowed the stark immediacy of B-pictures, his thriller was as meticulously planned out and produced as ever. Telling the story of a series of murders at a lonely roadside motel, the film broke all the rules by killing off its one star early in the picture—and what a killing it was. Janet Leigh steps into a shower at the Bates Motel and, in what is perhaps the most famous sequence in all of film, endures several agonizing seconds of horror in footage that has been pored over, discussed, and analyzed by film scholars and critics ever since. True to form, Hitchcock had carefully broken down the angles and shots (there are more than sixty) in advance. Everything works toward creating a scene of sheer terror and surprise: the slicing knife, wielded by an unseen assailant, the naked, defenseless woman with whom we all identity (is one ever more exposed and vulnerable than when in the shower?), the rapid editing of various perspective shots, and, most unforgettable, the shrieking, jabbing violins in Bernard Hermann's legendary score. With this shocking plot twist, the film's story takes an unexpected lurch in a new direction, as the audience no longer cares about stolen money but only wants to know about that crazy mother living in the remote, eerie house on the hill. Yet again Hitchcock sought to expose a dark underside to sunny American normalcy.

Hitchcock had one more great film up his sleeve. Based on a short story by Daphne Du Maurier (who wrote *Rebecca*), *The Birds* (1963) depicts—but never explains—a series of increasingly deadly attacks by flocks of birds upon the idyllic seaside village of Bodega Bay, California. The film explores some of the director's favorite topics: sudden, unsuspected violence from a normally benign and pleasant source, and the different ways that humans react to a crisis. Flighty socialite Melanie (Tippi Hedren, one of the last of Hitchcock's cool blondes) arrives in the village just as the dangerous birds do, and the various attacks she experiences have a definite humanizing effect upon her, rather like the experience of Tallulah Bankhead's character in *Lifeboat*. Whereas Bernard Hermann's score is an inseparable part of *Psycho*'s power, this film is strengthened by a soundtrack utterly devoid of music; the title sequence is accompanied only by the sounds of birds. Visually, despite some obvious special effects, the film is striking. In one memorable sequence Melanie waits impatiently outside the village school for the children to break for recess. As she casually smokes a cigarette, the audience sees a bird descend upon the jungle gym behind her. In a series of shots, more and more birds arrive until, finally, Melanie follows a flying bird with her eyes—only to see it join hundreds of others now completely covering the bars and swings in the playground. Later, Melanie is trapped in a telephone booth as kamikaze seagulls swoop down and shatter the glass walls in an attempt to reach her.

Hedren also appeared in Hitchcock's next film, *Marnie* (1964), about a beautiful kleptomaniac, and the director made four more films before his death, but his glory days were behind him. *Frenzy* (1972), about a necktie murderer and a wrongful suspect in London, was something of a return to form, with wicked black humor and some stylishly suspenseful camera work (it was also the director's return to filming in England), but some viewers objected to an increased level of overt, graphic violence, only hinted at in the director's earlier works.

As seen, Hitchcock's films—both before and after the war—often revolve around spies and secret agents. Many other films exploited post–war paranoia to the extent that 1950s and early 1960s movies, across almost all genres, evidence Cold War suspicions and fears (in particular, see **Action-Adventure**, **Film Noir**, **Science Fiction**, **Western**). There were tongue-in-cheek action films featuring such sexy and suave defenders of democracy as James Bond. On a more serious note, many suspense films conjured frightening scenarios in which Communist or resurgent fascist groups threatened America's welfare. John Frankenheimer's *The Manchurian Candidate* (1962) follows the tribulations of a group of Korean War veterans, unwittingly brainwashed and conditioned by the enemy to kill upon command. A decorated war hero becomes an unsuspecting assassin, and the story unfolds with a series of shocking revelations as to who is involved in the diabolical plot to kill a Presidential candidate. Loyalty to comrades-in-arms, McCarthyism, Oedipal complexes, and the nature of nightmares highlight the intriguing if outrageous story, which builds to a surprising climax. A remake appeared in 2004, updated to concern Gulf War soldiers in Iraq.

Sidney Lumet's *Fail-Safe* (1964), based on a best-selling novel, explores the harrowing possibility of an American pilot mistakenly receiving orders to bomb Moscow and the international crisis of finger-pointing, grudge-venting and face-saving that ensues. Other films that tapped into the country's paranoia over internal and external political threats include *Seven Days in May* (1964), about a military plot to overthrow the government, and *Mirage* (1966), another nightmarish tale of brainwashing, wherein an accountant suffers amnesia after an urban blackout and desperately tries to discover why people around him are being murdered.

Producer/director Robert Aldrich staged a sort of comeback for Bette Davis in his Grand Guignol exercises *What Ever Happened to Baby Jane?* (1962) and *Hush . . . Hush, Sweet Charlotte* (1964). The former picture disturbingly mirrored life by pairing Davis with fellow Golden Age star and lifelong antagonist Joan Crawford as embattled sisters and has-been stars who make life hell for each other in their faded Los Angeles home. Crawford is confined to a wheelchair and suffers the physical and emotional abuse doled out by her caregiver, the sadistic, crazed Davis. The latter plays the titular Jane, once a child star but now a crazy old lady who dresses in the frills and ringlets of childhood, her face excessively plastered with creased and flaking white makeup. As much as to discover the sisters' dark secrets and see who will survive, audiences flocked to the film to witness the ravages of time and lost glory upon the two legendary actresses, who acted out personal frustrations and jealousies on the screen. At the last minute, Crawford pulled out of a planned re-pairing in *Hush . . . Hush, Sweet Charlotte*; Olivia de Havilland stepped in as the conniving cousin Miriam determined to run mad, reclusive Charlotte (Davis) out of her stately Louisiana mansion and pocket the money offered by the highway commission, which plans to bulldoze the estate. Charlotte lost her mind years before when, as a demure young girl, her lover was beheaded and mutilated and she was wrongly blamed for the murder. A series of gruesome deaths and apparitions are arranged in an attempt to push Charlotte over the edge, but it's a huge cement flowerpot that is finally and literally pushed over the edge—by Charlotte on Miriam and her co-conspirator.

The success of these films started a brief craze for movies starring older actresses as madwomen either victimizing or victimized by family and friends: Bette Davis in *The Nanny* (1965), Joan Crawford in *Strait-Jacket* (1964) and *Berserk!* (1968), Geraldine Page in *Whatever Happened to Aunt Alice?* (1969), Shelley Winters in *Who Slew Auntie Roo?* (1971) and, with Debbie Reynolds, in *What's the Matter with Helen?* (1971). *Baby Jane* apparently set a pattern not only for thrillers starring has-been actresses but for film titles worded as questions and including a female character's name. These films, especially Davis's, are appreciated today primarily for their high camp value.

Like *I Want to Live!* (1958), *In Cold Blood* (1967) also ends with an execution, but its story is presented in a stark, semi-documentary style, compared to the loud emotional melodrama of the earlier film. Based on the book by Truman Capote, *In Cold Blood* tells the true story of two young drifters who slaughter an entire Kansas farm family. The haunting, black-and-white photography and Richard Brooks's powerful direction sustain the unsettling mood from the time of the dispassionate murders to the eventual capture and execution of the perpetrators. Like the book, the film particularly follows Robert Blake's character as he recounts his empty, loveless youth and suffers the hopeless final hours. The research and writing of the book are dramatized in Bennett Miller's fascinating *Capote* (2005), for which Philip Seymour Hoffman won an Academy Award for his portrayal of Truman Capote.

Wait Until Dark (1967), based on the hit Broadway play by Frederick Knott, returns to the scenario of a handicapped woman in peril that worked such nail-biting wonders years before in *The Spiral Staircase* (1946) and *Sorry, Wrong Number* (1948) and would be tried again in 1971 in *See No Evil*. In *Wait Until Dark*, Audrey Hepburn plays a blind woman terrorized by thugs after her husband unwittingly accepts a heroin-stuffed doll at the airport. He brings home the doll—and the trio of unforgiving dealers in pursuit of it. The pacing is a bit slow by today's standards, but the tension builds relentlessly as the protagonist gradually comes to realize that the various harmless men coming in and out of her Greenwich Village apartment are in fact the same three men—criminals who are out to harm her. Alan Arkin, as the sadistic, switchblade-wielding drug dealer, has a field day, as does Hepburn, playing the ingenious and resourceful Suzy in what would be her last film before a self-imposed retirement that lasted nine years. In the powerful finale, when the knife comes out and Suzy is trapped inside the apartment with the homicidal dealer (and a corpse or two), she comes up with a plan to use her disadvantage to her advantage, smashing all the light bulbs and thus gaining the upper hand. As a promotional gimmick for the film's initial release, all the lights were extinguished in cinemas at this point so that the few minutes of total screen darkness, as the two characters scream and thrash about in pitch black, would prove even more shattering to audiences.

The 1970s

The social turbulence of the 1960s carried over into the next decade, and political thrillers continued to address the concerns and hot topics of the day. Francis Ford Coppola's brilliant but often overlooked *The Conversation* (1974) explores our loss of privacy at the hands of powerful corporations and ever more sophisticated technology. Highly regarded professional surveillance expert Harry Caul ("the best bugger on the West Coast"), played by Gene Hackman, is paid to follow the wife of a wealthy businessman as she meets her lover. Several years earlier, Harry's revelatory work led to the murder of a family and, upon listening to his new tapes, he starts to fear that the husband who has hired him might be planning to kill his rival. As befits its subject matter, the film layers and uses sound—both recorded and live—most impressively, and it raises questions about human communication and trust. As the film builds to its climax and Harry tries to prevent a murder, several plot twists leave us wondering just who is listening in on whom.

Seizing upon the fears of the day and, after Watergate, the realization of the immense power of the whistle-blower, many of the political thrillers of the decade pit an individual against corrupt and sinister organizations. *The Parallax View* (1974) explores conspiracy territory, specifically a powerful corporation involved with the assassination, witnessed by an investigative reporter (Warren Beatty), of a US senator running for President. In *Three Days of the Condor* (1975), an intelligence researcher (Robert Redford) is stalked by a professional assassin. *Marathon Man* (1976) plays upon our fears of the dentist by staging nightmarish scenes of torture between a former concentration camp Nazi dentist (Laurence Olivier) and a poor, unsuspecting man (Dustin Hoffman) whose brother is suspected of having stolen a fortune in diamonds. Finally, *The China Syndrome* (1979), about an attempted cover-up of a nuclear plant accident and the dogged reporters attempting to expose it, received undreamed-of publicity when just such an accident occurred at Three Mile Island around the time of the film's release.

Jane Fonda, then at the height of her career, portrays the reporter whose cameraman captures the power plant crisis on tape in *The China Syndrome*. A decade earlier, Fonda threw off her sex-kitten screen persona and proved herself a gifted actor in the melodramatic, simplistically psychoanalytical *They Shoot Horses, Don't They?* (1969). Fonda starred as one of a group of desperate down-and-outers struggling to retain their stamina and some shred of dignity during an endless (and rigged) Depression-era dance marathon. Even more impressive was Fonda's performance as call girl Bree Daniels in *Klute* (1971), for which she won the Best Actress Academy Award. Donald Sutherland plays the titular character, who comes to New York City to locate a friend who went missing and is soon caught up in a world of drugs, pimps, and prostitutes. A sadistic killer has murdered one woman and begins stalking Bree, making ominous phone calls and following her. In sessions with her analyst, Bree is self-assured and angry, particularly over her difficulties in finding work as an actress. But the city around her is frightening and controlled by exacting men who wrestle away her convictions. The film, complete with an eerie score and dark, claustrophobic interiors, builds to a terrifying climax in which the killer, a former john, reveals himself to Bree but, before killing her, taunts her and prolongs the agony by playing a recording he made of her brash, practiced bravado from their earlier sexual encounter. Even though the film is a definite step forward in terms of its presentation of a strong, independent female character, it nevertheless gives Bree the job of prostitute and lets male characters both capture and rescue her.

John Boorman's harrowing *Deliverance* (1972), based on the James Dickey bestseller, follows four Atlanta businessmen on a weekend white-water canoeing trip along a river slated to be dammed up. The film presents a variety of culture clashes—urban and rural, civilized and natural, peaceful and violent—just as the river comes to symbolize things beyond a simple physical test: life itself and a return to a primitive state. The trip was arranged by Lewis (Burt Reynolds), a risk-taking survivalist determined to prove his masculinity by escaping the nine-to-five drudgery and taking on nature and her challenges before the city swallows up the wilderness. What the men haven't bargained for is the hostile brutality of some of the wilderness's inhabitants. Early on, the urbanites make fun of the slow, apparently inbred hill-folk they encounter; later, two rogue mountain men take a couple of the canoeing party hostage, threatening them with knives and sexually assaulting Bobby (Ned Beatty). Lewis kills one of the rapists with an arrow, and the escapist weekend trip becomes a debate over what to do with the body. Stripped of all their possessions and comforts and facing the death of one of their number, the men are forced to reevaluate their strongest beliefs. The film is beautifully shot in north Georgia and features Reynolds's best performance, as well as the debuts of Beatty and Ronny Cox. The "Dueling Banjos" bluegrass number (actually played by banjo and guitar) became a hit record.

The 1970s saw the arrival of Steven Spielberg, who made his name with taut, suspenseful films that tapped into filmgoers' fears and phobias. His first big splash was the television Movie of the Week *Duel* (1971), starring Dennis Weaver as a man in a rental car on a lonely stretch of Southwest highway who encounters a marauding and vengeful (and, all the more frightening, never seen) trucker. The tension builds as the man realizes that the initially irritating truck driver is, in fact, out for blood, initiating circumstances likely to produce accidents and, eventually, actually trying to run down the rental car. Spielberg's first theatrical film was *The Sugarland Express* (1974), a highly entertaining and perfectly paced true story of a woman who helps her husband break out of prison, take a policeman hostage, and drive across Texas in order to retrieve their young son, taken from them by social services. The director ensures that audience members, like the Texans along the route, sympathize and totally identify with the misguided parents, as the ill-fated journey becomes increasingly dangerous. With *Jaws* (1975), Universal Studios ushered in the concept of the heretofore unheard-of summer blockbuster, featuring massive publicity and blanket simultaneous release in hundreds of cinemas. Based on the shark attack novel by Peter Benchley, the film is a masterpiece of suspense, combining brilliant editing, John Williams's unforgettably ominous musical score (probably the second most famous film score, after *Psycho*), a scenario that plays upon our most primal fears, and Spielberg's cinematic genius for straightforward albeit gripping storytelling. The *Enemy of the People*–style plot concerns a small New England resort town whose livelihood is threatened when a rogue shark starts attacking swimmers. Concerned and cautious local police chief (Roy Scheider) butts heads with the city fathers who, fearing financial catastrophe at the loss of tourists, attempt to cover up the attacks and keep the beaches open. With terrifying shots of unsuspecting swimmers from the shark's point of view, scenes of mass hysteria on the beaches, and a final showdown between man and shark, Spielberg plays on our emotions and never lets the tension drop. *Jaws* became one of the highest-grossing films in history and spawned three sequels, none directed by Spielberg and nowhere near as good as the original.

Much of the police chief's anxiety in *Jaws* stems from his fear for his own son's safety. Spielberg's films repeatedly fixate upon threatened, orphaned, and (literally or psychologically) fatherless boys. In this respect, he is the heir to D. W. Griffith and his imperiled young women. *Close Encounters of the Third Kind* (1977), *E.T.* (1982), *Empire of the Sun* (1987), and *Artificial Intelligence: A.I.* (2001) all generate suspense and tension through the travails and adventures of a young innocent thrown into contact with an unfathomable, uncaring world of adults. As much as in *The Wizard of Oz*, home, family, and reunion are the ultimate goals in so many Spielberg films.

Clint Eastwood made his impressive directorial debut with *Play Misty For Me* (1971), in which he plays the womanizing late-night DJ for a Monterrey cool jazz radio station who goes to bed with a fan and wakes up next to an obsessed, dangerous stalker who won't take no for an answer (brilliantly and frighteningly played by Jessica Walter). The gorgeous Big Sur scenery and sultry, world-weary music (two of Eastwood's own obsessions) are effectively woven into a cautionary tale whose violence and tension build to a powerful nocturnal climax high above the crashing waves.

Director Brian De Palma has made a career of film homage. *Blow Out* (1980), wherein a sound-effects man records a car wreck only to discover that he has uncovered a political murder, directly references Antonioni's *Blowup* (1966), about a photographer who accidentally captures a murder on film. De Palma's *The Untouchables* (1987) is based on the television series about the exploits of federal agent Eliot Ness, out to stop rum-runners and gangsters in 1930s Chicago. The film made a star of Kevin Costner, as Ness, and it features an operatic performance by Robert De Niro as Al Capone. A tour de force sequence set on the grand staircase of Chicago's main train terminal is an homage to the classic Odessa Steps sequence in Sergei Eisenstein's silent classic *Battleship Potemkin*. De Palma audaciously choreographs the long, suspenseful scene (in which Ness and his men foil an attempt by Capone to secret away his witness) on a grand scale and utilizes slow-motion, one of several camera techniques that (along with split-screen) appear in many of his films. It is Hitchcock, however, whom De Palma most frequently and lovingly imitates, in appropriate stories of obsession, voyeurism, and unexpected violence. *Sisters* (1973) tells of Siamese twins—one normal, one homicidal—and the reporter who, *Rear Window*–style, thinks she witnessed one of the murders through a window. *Carrie* (1976) and *The Fury* (1978) explore the phenomenon of telekinesis, the ability to effect physical movement or destruction through mental concentration. The former film is a delicious exercise in revenge, as a nerdy, lumpish high school girl suffers insults and attacks at the hands of her schoolmates. The cruel treatment reaches a crescendo at the prom, where (in a wonderful sequence involving close-ups, slow-motion, and split screens) she unleashes the violent fury of her telekinetic powers upon her tormentors. *Obsession* (1976) echoes *Vertigo* not only with a Bernard Hermann score (he also scored *Sisters*) but in its story of a lost loved one and the desire to remake a woman into the person of a dead wife. *Dressed to Kill* (1980) is a frightening and suspenseful story of a killer stalking two women in New York City. As in *Psycho*, one star is killed early on; the film is also Hitchcockian in its emphasis on slick visual style and tension over plot logic. *Body Double* (1984) again revisits *Rear Window* territory, as a Los Angeles man spies on his neighbors through a telescope, only to witness the gruesome murder of the beautiful woman who has been performing a strip tease in front of her window at night.

Moving from old movies to contemporary headlines as inspiration, Sidney Lumet's *Dog Day Afternoon* (1975) is a stunning crime thriller based on an actual Brooklyn bank robbery that went horribly wrong. In a brilliant, mercurial performance, Al Pacino plays a married father who undertakes the hold-up in order to fund his boyfriend's sex change operation. The ineptitude of the robbers swings from slapstick farce to violent rage to pitiful bewilderment as the long, hot summer day progresses into night and the police and growing crowds (and media) outside the bank become increasingly uncontrollable. Strange bonds form between robbers and hostages and between Pacino and the policeman in charge, and the movie ultimately ends in tragedy. Over two hours and ten minutes, director Lumet masterfully choreographs a large cast in restricted settings, in a film that makes interesting statements about homophobia, urban desperation and animosity, and the cult of celebrity.

The 1980s

Echoing Hitchcock, writer and director David Lynch seeks to expose the dark, evil, and twisted elements hiding behind the sunny façade of wholesome, bourgeois America. His *Blue Velvet* (1987), outrageously perverse and extreme, polarized audiences and critics. Its opening shots reveal his intent: colorful vignettes of stereotypical small-town felicity—waving firemen with Dalmatians, white picket fences, protective crosswalk tenders, homeowners watering the lawn—give way to a man suffering a heart attack and, as the camera reveals when it zooms in to a manicured, grassy lawn, aggressive and repulsive insects battling one another just below the surface. Bugs aren't the only thing lurking beneath the surface of this logging town, as young, clean-cut Jeffrey Beaumont (Kyle MacLachlan) soon discovers. After coming across a human ear in a field, Jeffrey becomes entangled with the organ's back story, which involves a terrified, masochistic nightclub singer (Isabella Rossellini) and the twisted, drugged-up psychopath (Dennis Hopper) who has trapped her in an abusive, sexually perverse relationship. "I'm seeing something that was always hidden," the naïve young man realizes. Jeffrey's innocent, adolescent friendship with the lovely young Sandy (Laura Dern) is a marked contrast to the older couple's violent and destructive relationship but, as Jeffrey becomes involved with the singer, Lynch points out the darker side in us all, creating something of a parable about adolescents' corruption and initiation into the irrational, sexual, and cruel adult world. "Why is there so much trouble in this world?" asks Jeffrey and, as the film races towards its climax, we witness a struggle between depravity and what Sandy calls "the blinding light of love"—"the only thing that would make any difference."

Fatal Attraction (1987), a revisit to *Play Misty For Me*'s knife-wielding, outraged scorned woman territory, proved a huge box office success. Michael Douglas plays the hapless happily married man who betrays his perfect wife and home by sleeping with a bold, independent businesswoman (Glenn Close), only to be terrorized and threatened when he tries to break things off. The primal potency of the story made it ripe for various interpretations: AIDS-era cautionary tale and defense of monogamy; demonization and punishment of an independent, sexually autonomous woman; empowerment of the traditional used and abandoned woman as sex object ("I won't be *ignored*, Dan"); and so on. Former commercial director Adrian Lyne brings a visual slickness and urgency to the proceedings, particularly a sprawling sex scene that travels from a slowly ascending freight elevator, through the woman's loft-like apartment, and onto the kitchen sink, water and body parts splashing about photogenically. Equally effective is Close's quicksilver ability to transform effortlessly from sexy lover in haloed golden ringlets to scary, psycho Medusa, lashing out with sharp knives and even sharper words. The film's ending (altered from the original, which proved unsuccessful with test audiences) features shocks and surprises, and its rollercoaster of false endings inspired countless suspense and slasher film endings through the 90s and beyond.

The 1990s to the Present

The most lauded and successful thriller of the decade is Jonathan Demme's harrowing *The Silence of the Lambs* (1991), one of only three films in history to have won the Academy Awards for Best Picture, Director, Actor, and Actress (the others are *It Happened One Night* and *One Flew Over the Cuckoo's Nest*). Demme's award is unique in that no other director has won for a thriller. The film, based on Ted Tally's bestseller, exploits our fascination with serial killers in a story about the FBI utilizing an imprisoned killer, brilliant psychiatrist-turned-psychopath Hannibal Lecter (Anthony Hopkins), to try to figure out the identity and whereabouts of a killer on the loose. Young FBI trainee Clarice Starling (Jodie Foster) is sent to interview and draw out "Hannibal the Cannibal," and much of the film's strength comes from their four sequences together: two gifted actors in wonderful scenes of cat-and-mouse, as their characters bargain back and forth as to who will divulge information—and how much. As the movie progresses, we learn not only about Lecter's twisted and gruesome past but also Starling's troubled childhood and her search for a father figure. Running parallel, but eventually intersecting the FBI storyline, is that of the serial killer presently capturing the headlines: Buffalo Bill, who, we gradually come to realize, kidnaps overweight women, starves them so that their skin becomes loose, and then skins them, in the crazed belief that he can then stitch together and wear their skin to become a woman himself. Lecter's brilliance does in fact pinpoint Buffalo Bill's identity and the film ends with a terrifying sequence in which frightened Clarice stalks a hiding (and armed) Bill in his dark basement, while the latest kidnapped girl screams from a pit in the ground. In a final darkly humorous coda, Clarice receives a phone call from the escaped Lecter, who is now out for revenge from the doctor who imprisoned him. "I do wish we could chat longer," purrs the Cannibal over the telephone line, "but I'm having an old friend for dinner." Hopkins's is one of the most unforgettable performances in film; his Lecter is apparently passive in demeanor, but with demonic eyes—his only spark of life other than a cruelly sadistic mind, all too capable of manipulating people. For the bulk of the film he is heavily guarded and straitjacketed, imprisoned within windowless cells. However, the sense of menace and threat is palpable, as we identify with a terrified Starling, come face-to-face with our most terrifying nightmare.

The year before *The Silence of the Lambs*, Kathy Bates won an Academy Award for her performance as the crazy fan in *Misery* (1990), the film version of Stephen King's novel. After a car accident on a deserted snowy road, a successful romance novelist (James Caan) is nursed back to health by a lonely woman who claims to be his number one fan. Everything goes well until she learns that he has killed off her favorite character, Misery Chastain, in his most recent book. Determined to rectify the situation, she turns on the man, cutting him off from the outside world and keeping him bedridden (with drugs and a swift blow with a sledgehammer to the kneecaps) until he rewrites the book, allowing Misery to live. Bates's transformation from dumpy, kindly spinster to ferocious, psychotic avenger is truly amazing. In the same year as Bates's success, Whoopi Goldberg won the Supporting Actress Academy Award for her uproarious performance, in *Ghost* (1990), as a fake clairvoyant unwillingly roped into assisting ghost Patrick Swayze (who can communicate only with her) convince his distraught girlfriend (Demi Moore) that the man who killed him is a danger to her as well. The film's hyper-romanticism and message that love is stronger than death made it a huge box office success (particularly with aging baby-boomers), and Goldberg helps things immeasurably with her raucous humor. Swayze and Moore are limited as actors, but their romantic scenes together and Moore's luminescent beauty sustain the film between scenes involving the outrageous Whoopi or the girlfriend's encounters with the killer.

Michael Mann, creator of the stylish and successful 1980s police television series *Miami Vice*, has directed several action thrillers. He followed *Thief* (1981) with *Manhunter* (1986), about a troubled FBI agent forced to think like a madman in order to track a serial killer. Hannibal Lecter even makes a short appearance, five years before *The Silence of the Lambs*. *Heat* (1991) is overlong, but offers Al Pacino and Robert De Niro together (they never shared screen time in *The Godfather: Part II*) as an L.A. detective and the robber gang leader he is out to locate, respectively. Good guy and bad guy turn out to have more in common than either would like to admit. Mann's *Collateral* (2004) again sets up a battle of wills, as cold-blooded hit man Vincent (Tom Cruise) commandeers L.A. taxi driver Max (Jamie Foxx) and his vehicle in order to kill five witnesses in a drug case over the next couple of hours. The action sequences are impressively staged (including a shoot out in a crowded Korean nightclub), and the two charismatic stars play well off each other. Unfortunately, there's a bit too much stagy philosophizing from the characters about childhood, life, and dreams, and the last half hour ventures into all-too-familiar "the killer is *in* the house with you!" territory.

While Brian De Palma lovingly imitates Hitchcock, one of the oddest films of recent years sought slavishly to redo *Psycho*. The 1998 remake was precisely that: an exact, scene-by-scene replica of the original, this time in color. Director Gus Van Sant's exercise in unoriginality, which seemed more like a film school project than a film, was trashed by critics and audiences alike. Starting in the late 1990s there was a vogue for suspense films with convoluted plots and twist endings. After sitting through so many mindless, derivative recent films, audiences enjoyed the novelty of actually having to think about what they watched; studios appreciated the fact that viewers returned to see the films repeatedly or bought the DVD in order to more closely observe plot twists or watch for hidden clues to the surprise ending. One might argue that the trend began with *The Crying Game* (1992), about an IRA volunteer who, after killing an English soldier, allows his guilty conscious to lead him to startling redemptive actions. The film features a plot that repeatedly lurches in unexpected directions and discloses a shocking revelation about one of the main characters. *The Usual Suspects* (1995) gathers several disparate criminals, held for a crime they didn't commit, who agree to pull off a caper only to discover someone else may be pulling all the strings. The ultimate film in terms of surprise ending—one that became a surprise box-office blockbuster and inspired countless discussions—is M. Night Shyamalan's *The Sixth Sense* (1999), about a little boy (Haley Joel Osment) who sees dead people and the psychologist (Bruce Willis) he enlists for help. The film masterfully builds suspense, combining shocking, frightening moments with tear-jerking scenes while subtly dropping enough clues that the undeniably surprising twist at the end makes complete sense and, even more importantly, is completely satisfying. Shyamalan revisited the tense eeriness of the film in his next work, *Signs* (2002), a financial but not overwhelming critical success about a disillusioned minister (Mel Gibson) and his family, trying to make sense of inexplicable crop circles. The director's third effort in the genre is *The Village*

They see dead people: Bruce Willis and Haley Joel Osment appear as unsettled as were audience members, shocked both by corpses and by spectacular plot twists in M. Night Shyamalan's *The Sixth Sense* (1999). *Photofest.*

(2004), about a breakdown in the ancient pact of nonaggression between the inhabitants of a tiny village and the dreadful creatures that inhabit the dark surrounding forest.

Writer-director Christopher Nolan's *Memento* (2000) concerns a man (Guy Pearce) suffering from short-term memory loss due to head trauma who must rely upon post-it notes, Polaroids, and tattoos in an attempt to discover what has been done to him and by whom. From this bizarre but fascinating premise, the film goes one step further, telling its story *backwards*, as we move back in time to the critical event, searching for clues alongside the bewildered protagonist. Reminiscent of *The Sixth Sense*, *The Others* (2001), set in a dark and mysterious haunted Channel Island mansion at the end of World War II, hits viewers with a twist ending, forcing them to rethink scenes and connections and conclude that, yes, everything has led to this point, surprising and unsuspected as it may seem. Of course, sometimes a film's convoluted plotting only serves to outrage viewers: as many people hated *Mulholland Drive* (2001) as enjoyed its confusing, twisting (and twisted) story about amnesia and ambition in Los Angeles.

References and Further Reading

Cocchiarelli, Joseph J. *Screen Sleuths: A Filmography.* Hamden, CT: Garland, 1991.
Davis, Brian. *The Thriller.* New York: Dutton, 1973.
Derry, Charles. *The Suspense Thriller.* Jefferson, NC: McFarland, 1988.
Everson, William K. *The Detective in Film.* Secaucus, NJ: Citadel, 1972.

Gow, Gordon. *Suspense in the Cinema*. Cranbury, NJ: A.S. Barnes, 1968.
McGilligan, Patrick. *Alfred Hitchcock: A Life in Darkness and Light*. New York: Harper Collins, 2003.
Parish, James Robert. *The Great Cop Pictures*. Metuchen, NJ: Scarecrow, 1990.
Parish James, Robert, and Michael R. Pitts. *The Great Detective Pictures*. Metuchen, NJ: Scarecrow, 1990.
Phillips, Gene D. *Alfred Hitchcock*. Boston: Twayne, 1984.

CHAPTER 10

WAR FILM

EVOLVING DURING ONE of the bloodiest centuries in recorded history, film became an influential medium in documenting war, gaining the power to shape public opinions about political issues, to record the miseries of the fighting man (and woman), and to peer into the homes of those on the home front. As the wealth of World War II films alone suggests, film became so influential by the mid-twentieth century that Allied governments quickly enlisted the help of filmmakers to remind the public of the virtues for which they were sacrificing. Just a few decades later, however, film would be, just as successfully, a powerful method of protest when political unrest and moral ambiguity surrounded international events.

DEFINING CHARACTERISTICS

War films may address a number of issues, from political ideology or the origins of the war (as embodied in the phrase "Why We Fight") to the trials of the home front and the war's aftermath. Films about specific wars have evolved to include motifs and episodes that add to the conventions of the broader war film genre overall. For example, the antiwar films of the era after World War I, such as *All Quiet on the Western Front* (1930), would depict different experiences specific to combat or politics in that war, but comparable motifs or scenes of slaughter, sacrifice, vulnerability, and the futility of armed aggression proved to be easily translatable and were duplicated in post-Vietnam-era antiwar films such as *Born on the Fourth of July* (1989). Although the specific language of conflict might change, war films still often share similar visual and narrative motifs:

Depictions of Combat

Conventionally, the war film is most epitomized or categorized by the degree, type, and amount of combat or direct warfare portrayed. Quite often, if history looks favorably upon the war, combat experience is presented as ennobling participants, teaching them the value of teamwork and new lessons about themselves applicable to civilian life. If public opinion does not favor the war historically, combat is shown as a process of grinding down the individual against his will, often forcing the soldier to make decisions that compromise his ethics. In still other cases, particularly in World War II films, men who profess to have no stake in the outcome of the experience risk their lives in combat to preserve values that had been abstract to them before the war, but that they now understand for having served. The transformational experiences of these men (and until recently, always men) serve, then, as an example to men in civilian life who would put personal interests ahead of national concerns. At other times, combat experience preaches the importance of faith in the face of adversity, faith in national and military leaders, faith in the cause worth fighting for, and faith in one another. Combat also becomes a time of initiation for some, as filmmakers depict young men "growing up" in the trenches or in a foxhole as they learn the importance of tenacity, loyalty, and getting the job done. Sometimes the loss of a loved one stirs such determination in the individual soldier that he single-handedly tries to take on the enemy, taking unnecessary risks that sometimes end in his demise.

Camaraderie

The bonding of fighting men often serves as the structuring principle in war films, with the struggles and hardships of a small squadron of men speaking for the collective experience and brotherhood of all soldiers in the specific war. The squad members often come from different racial, ethnic, social, political, and religious backgrounds, representing the impact of the combat experience on the nation as a whole. Frequently, conflicts exist between the men within the squad as a result of these differences, threatening the cohesiveness of the unit, but by the climactic battle in the film, these differences become secondary to the success of the larger mission. The loss of a squad member often erases individual concerns in favor of the broader ideological cause at stake, spurring comrades of the fallen soldier to fight even harder.

Political Slant

Depending upon the historical perceptions of the war in question, war films have a tendency to support either the announced and prevailing reasoning offered for the war or to show the falsity and futility of the experience. Rarely are war films purely documentary in approach and politically neutral. The moods and political philosophies presented tend to emphasize justifications for the war despite the sacrifices required; to reveal the futility and martyrdom many experience in the combat zone itself; or to prompt outright disgust for the ideologies leading to armed conflict or the ineptitude of officers. Often filmmakers depict wars according to the point of view prevailing when the film is made, not the perspectives of the war's era itself, particularly in the case of Vietnam. Public perception of a war cannot be underestimated as an influence on the evolution and creation of significant war films. American wars that have not captured the public's imagination or that have not been seen (at least in the Hollywood community) as making significant differences in America's political or social life, such as the Mexican-American War, the Spanish-American War, and even the first Gulf War, have sparked few, if any, significant filmic depictions.

Stock Figures

Although social and cultural conflicts may call into question the effectiveness of the group as a whole, experiential differences may threaten the lives of the men overall. This concept is often explored through the use of stock figure such as the *green kid* who comes of age in battle. What he lacks in prudence and knowledge, he makes up for in sheer instinct and bravado, sometimes to his detriment. Like the greenhorn, the *tough street fighter* operates on an instinct and resourcefulness borne out of life surviving on American urban streets, regarded as another form of war itself. The wisdom of an *intellectual*—sometimes a minister, teacher, or doctor in civilian life—tempers the bravado of these younger character types, for, although frustrated by the futility and waste of armed conflict, he values the male bonding that often results as a byproduct of the carnage. Other character types include the mature middle-class *businessman* in civilian life who applies his organizational skills to a new type of project. A savvy businessman, a loving father, and a faithful husband, he serves as a role model for the younger men and represents the best of the American home and American capitalist values, often reflected in the steady stream of letters he receives from his wife and children. This mature middle-class citizen soldier is what the disaffected *combat-hardened veteran* with a death wish or the older *squadron commander* might have become had some mysterious event or emotional wound not festered unacknowledged. The squadron commander—the stereotypical character played by John Wayne in *The Sands of Iwo Jima* (1949)—risks the mutiny of his squadron under his harsh command as long as he does what it takes to make sure they stay alive.

Romantic Entanglements and Representations of the Home Front

War-related conflicts often play themselves out in the context of romance, where two soldiers vie for the same woman and attempt to win her love. With the possibility of death around every corner, traditional morality often breaks down for the soldiers, the women who love them, and the support staff. Romances are often deep, fast, but short-lived. Women permit liberties for "the boys" they might not otherwise tolerate in more stable times. The plight of these women, both at home as wives, mothers, daughters, and girlfriends and (in limited roles) in the war theater as nurses, "hostesses," USO workers, refugees, and bombing victims expand the understanding of war's influences, as depicted in motion pictures.

HISTORY AND INFLUENCES

The Beginning to 1940

The first moving images of war were grainy depictions of troop movements and historic recreations of actual battles of the Spanish-American War and Philippine Revolution shot by Edison Manufacturing Company camera operator William Daly Paley and by the American Mutoscope and Biography Company from 1898 until 1901. Not until closer to the World War I era did motion pictures play a significant role in documenting or narrating stories about warfare, with D. W. Griffith's *Birth of a Nation* (1915) [see **Epic**] and *Hearts of the World* (1918) breaking new ground. Griffith pulled out all the stops for *Birth,* and film critics and historians know Griffith's film today for its innovative use of narrative crosscutting, its panoramic battle scenes, and, unfortunately, its highly stereotypical and racist portrayals of African Americans, played by white actors in blackface. Griffith's filming of wide-angle battle scenes, along with the use of smoke bombs (which largely obscured the live action) to simulate the confusion of the battlefield, have served as a model for filmmakers such as Steven Spielberg (*Saving Private Ryan* [1998]) and Anthony Mighella (*Cold Mountain* [2003]). The incredible popularity of the film also revealed both the profitability of motion pictures as an entertainment medium and war films as well. Commissioned by the British government and filmed with the cooperation of the British, French, and Belgian governments on actual fields of battle, *Hearts of the World,* Griffith's tale of French youth under German occupation, makes a decidedly antiwar statement, although it was intended to convince the United States to aid the Allies. British and French versions of the film include prologues by Griffith and Prime Minister David Lloyd George and archival footage of British Foreign Secretary Sir Edward Grey and French Premier Rene Viviani.

Many films depicting World War I balanced propaganda with entertainment appeal. President Wilson appointed newspaperman George Creel to head the Committee on Public Information (CPI), created to ensure truth in reporting about enemy combatants and to maximize support for the war effort in documentaries such as *Pershing's Crusaders* (1918) and in documentary-style narrative films such as *Lest We Forget* (1918), with its depiction of the sinking of the *Lusitania* as a reminder of German militarism. Moreover, Cecil DeMille's *The Little American* (1917) contained a message of America's civilizing influence on Old World stock, as the German-American Karl (Walter Long) and the Franco-American Jules (Raymond Hatton) return to Europe when war breaks out and both fall in love with the gentle Angela (Mary Pickford) on her way to France. The German invasion of France coincides with Angela's near rape at the hands of Karl, who, with the help of Jules, redeems himself by successfully defending Angela against German charges of espionage. Similarly, in *The Kaiser: The Beast of Berlin* (1918), the greed of the Kaiser in Germany contrasts with the fears of a simple Belgian family for the neutrality of their country. Scenes of the Kaiser ripping up the treaty of neutrality with Belgium are juxtaposed against the declaration of war by the President of the United States. By film's end, the Belgian, wishfully but fictitiously, captures the Kaiser.

After the armistice, filmmakers offered more serious and more balanced assessments of World War I than the propaganda of the period created. Rex Ingram's *The Four Horsemen of the Apocalypse* (1921) casts the outbreak of the war as a warning sign of humanity's impending doom. To an Argentinian cattle baron whose daughters marry French and German men, the possibility of a European war presents a serious rift. Rudolph Valentino, in a star-making performance, portrays Julio, the wastrel French grandson who changes his ways in the wake of meeting his cousin in battle and a visit from the Four Horsemen of the title, taken from the Biblical book of Revelation: War, Pestilence, Famine, and Death. As a sacrifice for his married lover (Alice Terry), whose own husband has been blinded in the war, Julio dies at the hand of his German officer cousin. Aside from its imagery of the Four Horsemen themselves, the film is best known for Valentino's sultry tango inside a smoky Argentinian cantina. Raoul Walsh's *What Price Glory?* (1926) presents a mix of comedy and drama in the story of two Marines whose romantic rivalry gradually turns to camaraderie once service in wartime France interrupts their romantic endeavors.

Director King Vidor received cooperation from actual army units in filming *The Big Parade* (1925), known for its realism in portraying trench warfare. Realistic scenes in the second half of the film make it a model for later filmmakers by dramatizing the larger experience of war through a select but diverse group of three soldiers' experiences. Vidor gives some indication of the scope and magnitude of the war through a long shot showing the serpentine progression of men and military trucks down a road to the front. A similar long shot depicts a wounded Jim Apperson (John Gilbert), a rich man's son, in another "big parade," this time a Red Cross caravan taking him to a field hospital. A second wound results in the amputation of his leg and a ticket home, and Vidor transposes scenes of his mother's welcoming hug with memories of young Jim frolicking as a child on two good legs. At the urging of his mother, he returns to France to find his love (Renée Adorée) slaving in the fields. He feverishly quickens his pace to meet her, though hampered by the injuries he received in the war; the two embrace, symbolically suggesting the salvation of the Old World in the arms of the New.

In a similar vein, *Wings* (1927), the first Oscar winner for Best Picture and the only silent to win, features a much duplicated scenario in war films: the love enacted between a man and a woman and the love between a man and his comrades-in-arms, in this case in the clear blue skies. With none of these earthly rivalries resolved, high in the skies over Europe, Jack and David develop a comradeship stronger than anything they ever experienced with women. Viewers should remember the film most for its aerial photography rather than its melodramatic plot, because the performers, Charles "Buddy" Rogers and Richard Arlen, actually shot the up-close aerial photography themselves while simultaneously flying their planes.

Three years later, another World War I film, Lewis Milestone's *All Quiet on the Western Front* (1930), won an Oscar for Best Picture. Shot on studio sets and on acres of California ranch land converted into a recreated No Man's Land, the film follows men from a young German squadron led by Paul Baumer (Lew Ayres) as they get caught up in the jingoism surrounding the Great War, endure hardship, grow disillusioned, and finally meet their end after debunking patriotic myths that led to the war in the first place. Mindful of viewers' emotional wounds still unhealed from the Great War, director Milestone and writers Erich Maria Remarque (author of the novel), Maxwell Anderson, and George Abbott offer a prologue to the film that politically sanitizes all events depicted, a statement of regret lifted from the pages of the novel itself. The film's notable battle scenes place viewers below ground level in trenches, watching the charge of soldiers as they go over the top. The bombardment of a dugout, causing soldiers to lose emotional control, as well as the passing of a pair of boots from one comrade to another as each man falls, details the human toll that armed combat takes.

Like many archetypal characters depicted in war films, Paul finds himself more comfortable with his brothers-in-arms than at home on furlough. The death of Katczinsky (Louis Wolheim), Paul's surrogate father and his spiritual guide in the trenches, numbs him completely and symbolizes the loss of Paul's last hope for a palatable resolution to his own private war. Cinematically invoking the pathos of the novel's last episode—a simple dispatch reporting both "all quiet on the Western front" and Paul's death—presented a problem for director Milestone. The actual last action scene in the film, crosscutting Milestone's own hand reaching into no man's land for a butterfly against the aiming of a sniper, with the sound of a harmonica in the background, was actually suggested by Czech cinematographer Karl Freund, uncredited for his work on the film. In the film's last silent minutes, the director superimposes a younger Paul's image looking backward out of the ranks over a long shot of row upon row of stark white crosses.

Although the 1930s saw political turbulence break out into armed conflict in the Spanish Civil War, the dominant message in Depression-era war films was one of preparedness. A few films, such as *Operator 13* (1934) and *So Red the Rose* (1935), attempted to revive interest in the Civil War, but with the exception of the saccharine Shirley Temple film *The Littlest Rebel* (1935) and David O. Selznick's lush production of *Gone with the Wind* (see **Epic**), such subject matter became box office poison. Relevant to political issues of the time, British and American films such as *The Man I Married* (1938), *Night Train to Munich* (1940), *Foreign Correspondent* (1940), and *Four Sons* (1940) detailed the insidious Nazi threat as Hitler's influence and then army swept through Europe. As early as *Navy Secrets* (1939), American films began warning, perhaps hysterically, against Nazi infiltration of the American armed forces. *A Yank in the RAF* (1941), starring future pinup favorite Betty Grable and Tyrone Power, the latter as an American already fighting Nazis, joined a small group of early films preaching patriotic messages about much-needed American sacrifice and solidarity with Great Britain. Filmmakers looked to heroism in the previous war in *Sergeant York* (1941), starring Gary Cooper in an Oscar-winning role as backwoods pacifist turned decorated war hero Alvin York. The film balances York's Christian conversion, hatred of killing, and love of home with his belief in duty and honor once he is drafted into the American armed forces—the moral dilemmas many American might have to resolve in the upcoming war.

World War II Films of the 1940s

During the World War II era, the "golden age" of Hollywood's American war film, American filmmakers enjoyed unprecedented assistance from the armed forces and the Office of War Information in producing films favorable to the Allied cause, many of them shot in pseudo-documentary style mere weeks after the events depicted took place. A case in point is MGM's *A Yank on the Burma Road* (1942), with Barry Nelson as a taxi driver whose renown earns him an offer to lead a convoy for the Chinese government on the Burma Road, hit theaters a mere seven weeks after American entrance in the war. Similarly, Paramount had started production on *Wake Island* (1942) before the outcome of that battle in the Pacific was even certain. Starring Brian Donlevy as the fictional commander of a diverse group of Marines and civilian workers shoring up defenses on Wake Island, the film establishes the basic narrative and thematic paradigm indicative of World War II features to come, opening with an epigram saluting the small group of men who "bravely," but "futilely," fought to hold the outpost. Once the Japanese begin their assault, montages in the form of newspaper headlines provide status reports on the men pinned down on Wake Island. Director John Farrow intersperses these slides with episodes dramatizing the actions described to the outside world through the press. Although the actual defenders of the island eventually surrendered to the enemy, the film's stoic fight-to-the-last-man Hollywood ending more effectively stirs civilian contempt for the enemy than the truth.

Similar to *Wake Island* in its episodic quality, *Guadalcanal Diary* (1943) may be most notable for its visual "dispatches" by a fictional war correspondent/narrator (in voice-over by Reed Hadley), pre-invasion sequence depicting black troops standing in readiness alongside their white colleagues (a visual image of America's united resolve), and vignette detailing the creation and distribution of "dog tags" (a quintessential element of war film *mise en scène*). Actual archival footage taken under combat conditions blends with a series of fictional episodes, including a soliloquy by a hunkered-down private (William Bendix) who speaks for beleaguered servicemen as a whole: "I'm no hero. I'm just a guy. I just came out here because someone had to come. I don't want no medals. I just want to get this thing over with and go back home." Moreover, what *Guadalcanal Diary* did for the Marines, *Wing and a Prayer* (1944) attempted for the Navy air corps. With the newspapers and the public clamoring for an answer to the post–Pearl Harbor question "Where is our Navy?", a torpedo squadron flies daily reconnaissance missions from the an unnamed carrier off Midway Island, resisting the temptation to fire on the enemy until given the order. Once American forces go on the offensive, in a particularly effective sequence in the film, the men back on the carrier (and the audience) hear over the radio, but never view, the squadron's successful engagement with the enemy during the battle of Midway.

The prevalence and popularity of American World War II-era combat films such as those already mentioned guaranteed that by the time peace came, every branch of the military had been lauded and practically every theater of war, major engagement, or battle had received a serious cinematic treatment. Representative titles tell the story: *Bataan* (1943), *Back to Bataan* (1945), and *Corregidor* (1943), about the Philippines; *Objective Burma!* (1945); *Destination Tokyo* (1943); *Thirty Seconds Over Tokyo* (1944); *Action in the North Atlantic* (1943), concerning the Merchant Marine; *Sahara* (1943); *Commandos Strike at Dawn* (1942); *Stand By for Action* (1942), about the Navy; the Technicolor *Crash Dive* (1943), about submariners; *The Purple Heart* (1944) and *God Is My Co-Pilot* (1945), both about the Air Corps; *Fighting Seabees* (1944), about military construction workers; and *They Were Expendable* (1945), telling the story of PT boat operators.

Combing patriotism with entertainment, other more lightweight vehicles such as *To the Shores of Tripoli* (1942), with such lines as "I bet I'm the first leatherneck in history to ever kiss a lieutenant," fell short as serious analyses of wartime experience, as did the spate of home front melodramas and musicals produced by the major studios during the war years. In their defense, the makers of these films were pursuing other objectives, principally to bolster morale, promote unity, and provide entertainment. Home front melodramas such as *Mrs. Miniver* (1942), *Tender Comrade* (1943), and *Since You Went Away* (1944), and depictions of women under fire in films such as *So Proudly We Hail!* (1943) and *Cry Havoc!* (1943), provided an outlet for women experiencing emotional and economic hardships with their loved ones abroad and detailed women's direct contributions in the war theater (see **Woman's Film**). Wartime musicals such as *Pin Up Girl* (1944), *Hollywood Canteen* (1944), *Four Jills in a Jeep* (1944), *This Is the Army* (1943), and *Thank Your Lucky Stars* (1943) combined the barest of plots with elaborate production numbers and star performers, many playing themselves, to provide audiences with a wholesome diversion from their everyday responsibilities and a stable source of funding for veterans' organizations (see **Musical**). It would take a new rash of films, appearing near the last stages of the war and after, to begin critically interpreting wartime involvement.

A sterling example includes William Wyler's *The Best Years of Our Lives* (1946). With perhaps Oliver Stone's *Born on the Fourth of July* (1989) and Hal Ashby's *Coming Home* (1978) as exceptions, no film has more eloquently and poignantly portrayed the uncertainty and anxiety of postwar reintegration better than *The Best Years of Our Lives*, which won Oscars for Best Picture, Best Director (Wyler), Best Actor (Fredric March), Best Supporting Actor (Harold Russell), and a special award (also to Russell). The title of Robert Sherwood's Academy

Award-winning screenplay is meant to be ironic. The men who successfully defeated Fascism should have a bright future, but instead, they find themselves separated from the prewar world and their prewar selves, their "best years" perhaps behind them. Wyler's film combines elements of both the war film and the home front melodrama in depicting the (re)adjustment of three representative veterans to peacetime. Middle-aged Al Stephenson (Fredric March) reunites with a loyal wife (Myrna Loy) accustomed to fending for herself and their two now-grown children. Bomber pilot Fred Derry (Dana Andrews) returns to a wife (Virginia Mayo) who eventually deserts him once his nest egg runs out, and his service to his country earns him only a degrading job behind the soda fountain of a chain drugstore. Besides its courageous treatment of American postwar anxieties, *Best Years* is also known as the first film to feature a disabled actor in a prominent role, in this case Harold Russell as former football hero Homer Parish. Although he is as adept with hooks as most men are with hands, Homer's homecoming and civilian reintegration is not an easy one, particularly with reference to his prewar fiancée Wilma (Cathy O'Donnell). In a touching variation on a love scene, Wilma helps Homer to bed one night and learns what her intimate life with Homer would be like. The film concludes with the wedding of Wilma and Homer, and the vows they repeat take on individual significance for the couples, or titular couples, looking on. The film foreshadows the restoration of a changed postwar world.

Three years after *The Best Years of Our Lives,* films such as Henry King's *Twelve O'Clock High* (1949), William Wellman's *Battleground* (1949), Mark Robson's *Home of the Brave* (1949), and Allan Dwan's *The Sands of Iwo Jima* (1949) provided additional commentary on the war just fought, but they also began the mythologizing as well, ending the war decade on a banner note as America transitioned into the Cold War period. *Twelve O'Clock High,* for example, depicts the pressure placed on the only Americans fighting in Europe during 1942, a bomber squadron led by commanders (Garry Merrill and Gregory Peck) whose attachment to their men and the stress of their missions begin jeopardizing the success of the war effort. The aerial battles depicted were actually photographed by the United States Air Force and the German Luftwaffe during combat, adding a compelling element to the narrative. In *Battleground,* a squadron of men from the 101st Airborne is sent to protect a French village at the beginning of the Battle of the Bulge, eventually ending up pinned down by the enemy with little hope for rescue. Mark Robson's psychological drama *Home of the Brave* (1949) suggests that not all the conflicts soldiers experienced occurred on the battleground. And finally, with the exception of its ending, Allan Dwan's *The Sands of Iwo Jima* (1949) seems a throwback to the kind of patriotic, morale-boosting film produced during the early World War II period, with John Wayne garnering an Academy Award nomination for his portrayal of an embittered Marine drill instructor with a history. Stryker (Wayne) battles with the squad under his charge who accuse him of brutal training tactics, but he earns their respect when he knocks out a Japanese bunker that has been mercilessly pummeling trapped Marines. With Stryker's training methods seemingly validated, the ending of the film catches audiences off guard. The modestly sized Republic Studios scored a major hit in *The Sands of Iwo Jima,* which earned three times its production costs and contributed to Marine Corps legend.

World War II Films of the 1950s and After

The Second World War continued to be fought in films throughout the 1950s and well beyond, but never in as much concentration as during the war era itself. For example, *Go For Broke!* (1951) showed just how varied and complicated American attitudes about World War II had become a scant six years after Japanese surrender and nine years after Japanese internment. In the film, the racial prejudices of a reluctant training officer are exposed as false as his platoon of Japanese-American soldiers, or "Buddhaheads," as they call themselves, win high accolades from the men alongside whom they fight. Two innovations—vivid color and widescreen filming techniques such as CinemaScope (see **Epic**)—come together in *Battle Cry* (1955), directed by Raoul Walsh, in the story of a major (Van Heflin) who is training groups of new Marine recruits (played by Tab Hunter and a cast of unknowns) to ensure the successful execution of the war after devastating Marine defeats at places such as Guadalcanal. The film adopts a typical convention of older war films such as *Guadalcanal Diary*—namely, voice-over narration by a seasoned member of the squad (James Whitmore) or observer—but female costumes and hairstyles right out of the 1950s and relatively romanticized battle scenes somewhat mar the presentation.

In *From the Halls of Montezuma* (1951), veteran war film director Lewis Milestone cast Richard Widmark as a Reservist Marine Corps lieutenant commanding a platoon of seven Marines charged with knocking out a Japanese rocket-launching site on a heavily guarded Pacific island. War catches up to former chemistry teacher Carl Anderson (Widmark), who suffers from "psychological migraines," a psychosomatic manifestation of command pressures. The Technicolor presentation includes some of the best integration of actual color combat footage and flashbacks of the unit's history together. Particularly noteworthy is the relationship depicted between Anderson and Corporal Conroy (Richard Hylton). Conroy's assurances to Anderson on board ship that he can be counted on introduces a flashback to three years before, when, as a stutterer, Conroy feared speaking up on the first day of Anderson's chemistry class. His successful speech at graduation after the ministrations of Anderson illustrates the fortitude and courage of both men.

Submarines spring into action in *The Enemy Below* (1957), where U.S. destroyer captain Robert Mitchum and German submarine commander Curt Jurgens engage to the death during the Battle of the Atlantic. Conflict emerges within the close confines of an American Navy sub between Clark Gable's Commander Richardson and Burt Lancaster's Lieutenant Bledsoe, in Robert Wise's *Run Silent, Run Deep* (1958), a likely forefather of Tony Scott's *Crimson Tide* (1995) and Jonathan Mostow's *U-517* (2000) in its use of underwater effects and camera angles that emphasize a submarine's claustrophobic interiors. *Torpedo Run,* also produced in 1958, combines an eye towards realism in submarine terminology, operation, and setting, with a rather contrived story of an American submarine commander seeking out the Japanese aircraft carrier that launched the attack on Pearl Harbor. Much later, German director Wolfgang Petersen's *Das Boot* (1981) presents a much grittier expose of the claustrophobic life below the seas in a film sympathetic to the plight of the average German serviceman grappling with the ideology of the nation to whom they profess their loyalty.

Color photography brought to vivid life *To Hell and Back* (1955), the story of Audie Murphy, the most decorated soldier in World War II, who plays himself in the film. Included on many critics' list as one of the top 10 World War II films, the film would also hold the record as Universal's top grossing film for 20 years. Murphy also starred in an adaptation of Stephen Crane's novel *The Red Badge of Courage* (1951), directed by John Huston and also starring the rather unlikely Bill Mauldin, best known for his cartoon soldiers Willie and Joe appearing regularly in *Stars and Stripes*. The Murphy biopic finds itself among an august list of cinematic portraits of military or war-related figures, such as General George Custer in *They Died With Their Boots On* (1941), Ernie Pyle in *The Story of GI Joe* (1945), Field Marshal Erwin Rommel in *The Desert Fox* (1951), Admiral William "Bull" Halsey in *The Gallant Hours* (1960), General George S. Patton in *Patton* (1970), and General Douglas MacArthur in *MacArthur* (1977), to name a few.

In a year that boasted Best Actor nominations for both Montgomery Clift and Burt Lancaster in Fred Zinnemann's *From Here to Eternity* (1953), William Holden's Oscar for a relatively insubstantial leading part as a prison camp "scrounge" in Billy Wilder's *Stalag 17* can be best explained in terms of the likely split in Academy votes for the two other actors. An uneven mix of comedy and drama muddles the thrust of the film, and audience interest and sympathy often rests more with the captors (film director Otto Preminger is prominently featured as a stereotypical version of a German colonel) than the captured. Unfortunately, Wilder's production may be best known as the alleged progenitor of TV's *Hogan's Heroes* (set in Stalag 13 and, like the film, featuring a Sgt. Schultz; the producers of the film sued the producers of the series unsuccessfully). The far more important war film of that year, Zinnemann's adaptation of James Jones's novel *From Here to Eternity,* ranked behind only *The Robe* (1953) as the most profitable film of the year, and it won Academy Awards for Best Picture, Best Supporting Actress (Donna Reed), and Best Supporting Actor (Frank Sinatra), among others. Set in Hawaii in the days leading up to the attack on Pearl Harbor, the novel's strong language, violence, criticism of the military establishment, and bold sexual content defied Hollywood's motion picture production codes, still in force at the time of production, and Zinnemann added to the production's drama by casting performers against type, including Donna Reed as a hostess (a euphemism for prostitute), the accomplished British actress Deborah Kerr as an adulterous wife, and the effete Montgomery Clift as a former boxer and recalcitrant soldier refusing to buckle under the abuse of his commanding officer. Sinatra's appearance in his best role to date as Private Angelo Maggio and the accompanying Oscar boosted his film career as a result. Shot on location in a realistic style of black-and-white cinematography, the film

Kirk Douglas charges across No Man's Land in one of director Stanley Kubrick's classic tracking shots in the anti-war *Paths of Glory* (1957). *Photofest.*

was rivaled only by *Gone With the Wind* for its eight Oscar wins, and the result is evident in the final product. Zinnemann's production set a new standard for war-making in motion pictures, often reflected in the epic war films to come.

Stanley Kubrick's *Paths of Glory* (1957) makes a far more overt criticism of military incompetence and abuses of power than even Zinnemann's drama. Based upon a 1935 Humphrey Cobb novel, the story reveals the gulf between the officer who make command decisions out of harm's way behind the line and the men forced to carry them out. The French failure to capture a disputed hill in No Man's Land leads to plenty of finger pointing up through the ranks of the French command, eventually resulting in the scapegoating of three soldiers supposedly chosen at random for execution to ward off mutinies. Kubrick photographs the disastrous grab for the hill in a gripping extended sequence of almost eight minutes, combining a mixture of wide angle, tracking, and medium shots that portray the lunacy of the mission in the first place. A lawyer in civilian life, the colonel (Kirk Douglas) who cautioned against the advance attempts to defend the prisoners, but the fate of the men has already been determined despite appeals to the general who planted the seed for the suicidal attack in the first place. At the moment of execution, the prisoners march between rows of soldiers, drums roaring in the background, and a series of medium and low-angle point of view shots of the posts where they will die, with dignitaries in the background looking on.

Although critics consider *Paths of Glory* to be an important anti-war film, making a trilogy of sorts with Kubrick's *Dr. Strangelove, Or How I Learned to Stop*

Worrying and Love the Bomb (1964) and *Full Metal Jacket* (1987), it earned little at the box office. One reason was that it premiered one week after David Lean's blockbuster *The Bridge on the River Kwai* (1957), which would become the highest grossing film of the year. The story of British prisoners of war who build a railroad bridge in the Burmese jungle, only to see it blown up by American-led British commandos, began a trend toward epic war films still recognizable today. As is discussed elsewhere in this book (see **Epic**), epic films often defy minute analysis by virtue of their running time, plot complication, and multiple characters and settings. References to a few representative war epics through time, however, will demonstrate the prevalence of these multidimensional cinematic landmarks that expand the boundaries of the medium. Producer Darryl F. Zanuck's three-hour, black-and-white, documentary-style retelling of the D-Day invasion of Europe, *The Longest Day* (1962), cost a record eight million dollars, the most expensive black-and-white production until Steven Spielberg's *Schindler's List* (1993). Really a series of four separate productions by four different directors, this cinematic depiction of European liberation is also known as one of the first films to tell the story of the four principal nations launching the invasion in their own languages, accompanied by subtitles. Beaches on Corsica stand in as beachheads on the Normandy coast, and ships from America's Sixth Fleet on maneuvers off Corsica double as the invasion fleet in the film. The successful filming of the script required over forty major speaking parts and twenty-three thousand extras, but the film maintains its particular intimate appeal by portraying the invasion as a series of discrete, but combined, actions by individuals. Red Buttons's performance as a paratrooper snagged on the spires of a French church at the beginning of the invasion provides humor, but also a sense of the vulnerability most soldiers must have experienced in an operation of that magnitude. Obvious comparisons to Steven Spielberg's *Saving Private Ryan* (1998) seem unfair, considering that relaxed production standards enabled Spielberg to portray more extensively and more graphically the real threats American servicemen faced as they stormed up heavily fortified beachheads on France's northern coast. For its elaborate chronicling of events as they unfolded, the Zanuck film remains a classic.

Other World War II epics include Franklin Schaffner's biography of "Old Blood and Guts" General George S. Patton in *Patton* (1970), which presents a complicated portrait of the military genius some considered half mad. Scott won an Oscar for Best Actor, an award he refused, and Karl Malden heads up the supporting cast, portraying General Omar Bradley. With a nod towards the storytelling technique applied in *The Longest Day,* the joint Japanese-American production *Tora! Tora! Tora!* (1970) recounts the attack on Pearl Harbor from the perspective of both combatants. Jack Smight's *Midway* (1976) applies the same dual-narrative strategy in detailing the events surrounding America's surprise victory in the Pacific, with Charlton Heston, Henry Fonda, Robert Mitchum, and Toshiro Mifume leading an all-star cast.

Stephen Spielberg has directed three epic films that examine cross sections of the World War II experience directly. His *Empire of the Sun* (1987) recounts the

Japanese invasion of Shanghai in 1941 through the eyes of a British youth. *Schindler's List* (1993), winner of Oscars for both Best Picture and Best Director, brings to the screen the biography of Oskar Schindler (Liam Neeson), a German businessman who, at first, exploited the cheap Jewish labor in Poland and then ended up saving approximately a thousand Jews from extermination by employing them. Spielberg shot the film in black-and-white both to emphasize the documentary feeling of his story and to evoke the cruelty of Jewish life under the harsh Nazi regime. Three episodes in the film use color for maximum purpose. In the beginning, the vibrant warmth of a Sabbath candle dissolves into the filmy gray mist of history about to be recounted. The turning point for Schindler comes during the "liquidation" of the Jewish ghetto in Poland when he spies a young Jewish girl wearing a faded red coat dodge Nazi bullets, a literal "red flag" marking the magnitude of Nazi atrocities. Moreover, at the end of the film, characters whose lives Spielberg have followed in the film accompany real-life Schindler survivors to place a fragment of stone on Schindler's Jerusalem grave in remembrance. Banners on the screen remind us of Schindler's failure as both a husband and a businessman before his death in 1974, but visually, the scene reminds audiences of his human success story sheltering those left so vulnerable in a world gone mad with the excesses of the Third Reich.

Spielberg's more classic war epic, *Saving Private Ryan* (1998), centers around the question asked by the anguished, and now elderly, Private Ryan (Harrison Young in the present, Matt Damon in the flashbacks) standing in a military cemetery, roughly paraphrased, "Was the goodness of my life worth the sacrifice expended to save it?" With a nod to the earlier film *The Fighting Sullivans* (1944), Spielberg tells the tale of eight soldiers sent into enemy territory to rescue the sole surviving son of the Ryan family. A point-of-view shot of a dark car moving down a winding rural road, shot over a nondescript woman's shoulder and through her kitchen window, harbingers news of the death of the Ryan brothers. The anonymity of the woman stands in for the legion of other women who received similar tragic news, for she sinks to the porch floor as two government officials approach the house with a telegram. Such episodes in the film reveal Spielberg's agility in storytelling, but certainly the chaotic, visceral, and raw first twenty-minute sequence depicting the treacherous advance on Normandy beaches during D-Day will go down in cinema history as one of the most evocative portrayals of warfare ever. Scenes of men vomiting in troop transports and taking bullets under water and the overall carnage, photographed in all its bloody details, bring home the real risks and sacrifices endured by "the Greatest Generation," not the typical Hollywood ones. Tom Hanks, as Captain Miller, the resolute yet sympathetic squad leader, feels the weight of command greatly, but he performs his duty without question as the men battle the enemy in a series of engagements that stand between them and the successful fulfillment of the mission. The mystery behind Captain Miller's civilian identity fuels speculation about his leadership style. Viewers later discover anticlimactically that he's an English teacher—hardly as unlikely a fit for military leadership as membership in the clergy, for example—but such a minor flaw does nothing to minimize the panoramic quality of the film.

Saving Private Ryan unfortunately overshadowed Terence Malick's *The Thin Red Line* (1998), adapted from James Jones's fictional account of the bloody battle for Guadalcanal. Nick Nolte, as a "tough-as-nails" commander determined to get the job done, and Jim Caviezel, representing a morally conflicted soldier during wartime, shine in a cast including George Clooney, Adrien Brody, and Woody Harrelson. Admirers of a more traditional narrative structure will find *Saving Private Ryan* more to their taste, but Malick's poetic and lyrical style adds new dimension to making a war story. Returning to the events surrounding the Japanese attack on Hawaii on December 7, 1941, Michael Bay's *Pearl Harbor* (2001) follows two boyfriends as they serve in the Army Air Corps. After friend Rafe (Ben Affleck) is shot down and presumed dead, Danny (Josh Harnett) comforts Rafe's love interest (Kate Beckinsale), which makes the two men enemies once Rafe returns from the dead. The two attempt to mend their relationship amidst the chaos of the Japanese attack and its aftermath.

Films of the Korean War

As many epics revealed, World War II inspired an unprecedented social cohesiveness, united behind the cause of freedom. Yet, as history revealed in the 1950s, new enemies had appeared on the horizon after the Second World War and during the first years of the Cold War, and films such as Dick Powell's Korean War drama *The Hunters* (1958) reflected the threats they presented. Major Cleve Saville (Robert Mitchum), his wingman, Carl Abbott (Lee Philips), and Saville's rival, Lieutenant Pell (Robert Wagner), face an uncertain future behind enemy lines until they are sheltered by a Christian Korean family and have to fight off a Chinese search party. Stunning aerial photography demonstrates the awesome speed and firepower of both the American and Chinese air forces at odds during the Korean War. More antiwar in tone than *The Hunters* (1958), Lewis Milestone's *Pork Chop Hill* (1959) portrays men as pawns in the larger international power game surrounding the peace talks at Panmunjom, Korea, during the last days of the Korean War in 1953. When word comes down from command that his unit must participate in a counterattack on the barren, Chinese-held Pork Chop Hill, a mere seventy miles from the peace table, Lieutenant Joe Clemmons (Gregory Peck) cannot convince himself of the merits of the operation. Indeed, his unit sustains heavy casualties fighting for control of the hill. As the minutes run out before a threatened Chinese assault brings the men certain death, Milestone cuts to the peace talks, where American negotiators attempt to reason with the Chinese delegates. In a back room, an American official admits that the hill has no value except as a bargaining chip with a Chinese government willing to waste lives in a show of force. Are the Americans willing to make the same sacrifices? In the insistence that American troops remain in place despite their presumed destruction, stubbornness and pride unfortunately win out.

Compared with World War II—"The Good War"—which has continued to be the preoccupation of filmmakers and audiences since the event, the Korean War sparked fewer films of more varied quality. In *The Bridges at Toko-Ri* (1955), William Holden plays a Navy pilot questioning the nature of warfare itself and particularly uncertain about a bombing mission against a set of highly defended bridges. A U.S. Marine battalion in *Retreat, Hell!* (1952) battle both the weather and the Chinese army as they fight their way out of a frozen Korean mountain pass. The film is notable for its sympathetic and multidimensional portrayal of Asians, which puts it in contrast with Lewis Seiler's *The Bamboo Bed* (1954), a Korean prisoner-of-war drama about an American intelligence officer, undercover in a detainment camp, whose reputation as a traitor to the allied cause helps him discover atrocities perpetrated there. E. G. Marshall stars as a Communist posing as a priest for similar purposes, and the stereotyping of Asians is laughable. Director Samuel Fuller provided two films to the canon of Korean War dramas: *The Steel Helmet* (1951), where a group of misfit infantry soldiers led by a curmudgeonly sergeant fights to save a Buddhist temple with the help of a Korean orphan during a Chinese offensive, and *Fixed Bayonets!* (1951), with a stand-out performance by Richard Basehart as a corporal whose fast thinking and heroic action under fire reveals his courage to his comrades in the wake of advancing Red Chinese troops.

A tragicomic vein permeates perhaps the most famous movie about the Korean War in recent memory, Robert Altman's *M*A*S*H* (1970), starring a cast of relative unknowns as surgeons, nurses, and support personnel who cope with the daily hellishness of war a laugh at a time. Originally intended as a comment on the Vietnam War—Altman stripped the Ring Lardner Jr., script of all references to Korea initially—it comprises a series of episodes rather than a cohesive plot structure, but moments throughout the film convey the obvious absurdity of war. The "suicide" ritual of the dentist, blood-themed with the performers cloaked in red, evokes Da Vinci's *Last Supper* and makes for a particularly effective contrast to the hilarity throughout, paired with film's memorable theme song, "Suicide Is Painless." After filming was completed, Altman dubbed in announcements on the medical unit's public address system as a transitional device. The film inspired a long-running television series of the same name.

Films of the Vietnam War Era and Beyond

International attention again focused on Asia in the 1960s as America found itself embroiled in an anti-Communist conflict on the Vietnamese peninsula. With one exception, John Wayne's *The Green Berets* (1968), American films lagged behind in commenting on these events, largely explainable in terms of the turmoil the Vietnam War wrought in American society. The Wayne vehicle remains unquestionably the best known and most controversial film made during the war, offering what Wayne, co-director Ray Kellog, and screenwriters James Lee Barrett and Colonel Kenneth B. Facy saw as a necessary corrective to negative attitudes about intervention in Indo-China. The first sequences in the film, for example, are clearly designed to dispel doubts about American involvement in Southeast Asia, as reporter George Beckworth (David Janssen), among others, questions highly skilled Marines about American involvement in the "Vietnamese civil war." Dared by Colonel Mike Kirby (John Wayne) to visit Vietnam for himself, Beckworth arrives in Da Nang, a city full of American military installations named after dead American soldiers, and a series of encounters with the South Vietnamese throughout the rest of the film argue for the merits of American intervention. After promising to escort local villagers to a remote outpost at dawn, for example, Kirby and his band arrive to find the chieftain and his men murdered and the women terrorized and abused—episodes clearly intended to sway American doubters. Scenes show the Viet Cong in a feeding frenzy after the Americans and South Vietnamese defenders temporarily abandon the outpost, plundering the bodies of dead American soldiers and raising the Viet Cong flag. After Americans recapture the base, Beckworth vows to write truthfully about the challenges the South Vietnamese face.

The next sequence of the film dissolves into a more typical action-adventure mode as Kirby and his unit successfully capture an influential North Vietnamese general deep in the heart of enemy territory with the help of a Vietnamese model, Lin (Irene Tsu). Lin's seduction of the General—committed to vindicate her father and younger brother's death at the hands of the Viet Cong—comes at the price of her virtue, another nod to the sacrifice of the Vietnamese people and another justification for American involvement. The episode ends tragically, as the scrounger Petersen (Jim Hutton), who has added some comic relief, steps into a booby trap and ends up skewered, upside down, on a bed of bamboo spikes. Back in Da Nang, Kirby must tell Petersen's Vietnamese sidekick, a boy named Hamchunk, of his surrogate father's death. With Petersen's beret on his head, the wide-eyed boy asks, "What will happen to me now?" "You let me worry about that, Green Beret. You're what this is all about," Kirby reminds him, as the two walk into the sunset and "The Ballad of the Green Berets" thundering on the soundtrack, ratcheting up the sentiment for audience members still in doubt about what's at stake in Vietnam.

Warner Brothers studios took a tremendous gamble in agreeing to distribute *The Green Berets*—jingoistic in its approach, as war films of its type must almost certainly become—given the unrest surrounding the Vietnam conflict. No film about the Vietnam War filmed and released in the years just following the fall of the South Vietnamese capital could possibly have thought of presenting such a simplistic and patriotic call to arms, but John Wayne's appearance in a spate of patriotic films throughout his career and his support of conservative political ideals perfectly coincided with the values espoused in this most lauded and excoriated of war films. Thirty-five years would lapse before another politically conservative actor would involve himself in the subject of Vietnam minus the cynicism or bitterness. Randall Wallace's *We Were Soldiers* (2002), starring Mel Gibson, details in documentary fashion the first major battle between American forces and battle-hardened North Vietnam regulars in the Ia Drang Valley in the central highlands of Vietnam, where four hundred American men clashed with an enemy division. The film's narrative focus cuts back and forth between American forces on the ground and the North Vietnamese command post embedded in a nearby mountain, and Wallace's script sensitively portrays the North Vietnamese as world-weary, battle-scarred combatants defending their homes. Episodes of resourcefulness, efficiency, and heroism occur on both sides throughout the engagement, as do moments of sorrow and reflection once the battle ends. At home, telegrams informing survivors of the death of their loved ones arrive by taxi because "the Army wasn't ready" for casualties, and a montage of shots framing each woman's face as she receives news of her husband's death tells the story of the battle being waged ten thousand miles away.

Wallace's achievement goes where most Vietnam War films in the postwar era never ventured. In fact, most significant filmic treatments of the Vietnam War after the 1975 cessation of hostilities fall into two categories: dark, often violent, antiwar combat or combat-related narratives with a psychological bent, and equally somber, harshly critical probing exposés of the war's aftermath, sometimes with vengeance as a byproduct. For example, Michael Cimino's *The Deer Hunter* (1978), alongside Francis Ford Coppola's *Apocalypse Now* (1979), remains among the most controversial and critically debated films of this era, receiving five Academy Awards out of nine nominations. Epic and excessive in length (which many critics consider an unnecessary liability), the story opens on the last hunting trip of three Russian-American steelworkers in 1968, Michael (Robert De Niro), Nick (Christopher Walken), and Steven (John Savage), before Steven's marriage and their impending service in Vietnam changes their lives forever. Michael's "one shot" code—according to which a hunter fells an animal with one shot to prevent cruelty—reveals his true reverence for the hunt, as well as the masculine codes of honor in place in the film. After Steven's wedding, Nick makes Michael promise to get him back to this town no matter what, and the next morning, in the sanctity of nature—this scene is played for all its ritualistic and sacred effect—Michael downs a buck deer in a single shot, the camera momentarily focusing on the fear in the eyes of the animal.

The sound of helicopter blades transitions viewers into the next segment of the film, two years later, as Michael, Nick, and Steven rot in a North Vietnamese prison. In the most controversial and terrifying sequence in the film, each prisoner is forced to play Russian roulette, but luckily the lone bullet only grazes Steven's temple. Michael's plan to save them all depends on the remaining two friends playing against one another, and Michael and Nick escape injury in the first two clicks of the trigger before Michael shoots the captor leader in the middle of the forehead on the third. A copter pulls Nick to safety downriver, but a weakened Steven falls back into the river, smashing his legs. Although no evidence exists that the North Vietnamese ever engaged in that particular tactic against prisoners of war, the episode nonetheless effectively illustrates the depravity and violence of the Vietnam War.

The third segment of the film focuses on Michael's difficult reintegration into civilian life. Through Steven's ailing wife, Michael learns that Steven is an embittered amputee in a veteran's hospital, but he cannot bring himself to call him, nor can he find comfort with the woman he loves, the absent Nick's girlfriend Linda (Meryl Streep). In a return to prior rituals, Michael and other friends go into the wilderness in the second ritualistic hunt depicted in the film. Aiming at a beautiful buck, he fires above the animal's head, shouting, "Okay?" as if to ask the universe whether the score has been settled. Michael learns that Steven has been receiving parcels of hundred-dollar bills, probably from Nick, and he returns to Vietnam to find his friend heroin-addicted, mentally paralyzed, and getting money by playing Russian roulette for high stakes. Buying into one of the games, Michael risks his own life bringing his friend temporarily out of his war-induced daze, but the next pull of the trigger sends a bullet into Nick's head. A news report about the ending of the Vietnam War dissolves into the ringing church bells of Nick's funeral. Michael has, indeed, brought Nick home, all the principal characters reunited as the survivors lift glasses to Nick.

In *The Deer Hunter,* the men exchange roles as both the hunter and the hunted. Many war films, and Vietnam War films in particular, explore human transition, sometimes portrayed as a journey from innocence to experience for the servicemen involved in combat and the nations at war as a whole. *Apocalypse Now* exploits this journey motif, as Captain Benjamin Willard (Martin Sheen) ventures upriver to Cambodia "to terminate the command" of renegade Green Beret Colonel Kurtz (Marlon Brando). Based on Joseph Conrad's *Heart of Darkness,* with the poetry of T. S. Eliot as an influence as well, the film explores, metaphorically, a journey inward to the darkest reaches of the human soul, a place of unspeakable horror for some, depending upon what they may find there. The film is epic in scope—even more so after previously deleted footage added to the original was released under the name *Apocalypse Now Redux* (2001)—but Willard barely notices the surrealistic landscape he encounters on his trek up the Nung River as his journey to terminate Kurtz becomes linked to his own soul searching. As mishap after mishap on the river reveals the futility of subduing an unidentifiable enemy, one as much internal as external, Willard begins to sympathize with Kurtz because at least the renegade colonel is winning the war his way. Kurtz welcomes Willard to his domain by a barrage of arrows but spares his life, Willard supposes, to use him to explain why evil must be confronted.

Kurtz's end, when it comes, occurs during a festival involving the actual on-camera slaughter of a cow. Willard arises slowly from the water, in a much excerpted scene from the film, and he finds Kurtz reading another of his diatribes aloud, almost waiting. The camera cuts back and forth between the natives hacking off the head of the cow, with drums beating in an orgiastic ritual, and Willard wielding a machete on the target he was sent to terminate. At the climax of the scene the camera freezes on Kurtz lying prone, muttering, "The horror, the horror"—a quote from Conrad's novel. As Kurtz's followers bow down to their new god, Willard, muddy and splattered in blood, throws down his machete as he wades through the crowd and escapes back down the river in the boat. With Kurtz's voice echoing "the horror, the horror," on the sound track, Willard's face is superimposed over the face of a stone

To the blare of the music of Wagner, Huey helicopters strike terror in the Viet Cong in Francis Ford Coppola's *Apocalypse Now* (1979). *Photofest.*

statue carved into one of the ancient compound buildings, with versions of the ending varying from here. The 35 mm version of the film shows the destruction of the compound in flames as the credits role, but the 70 mm version merely runs a copyright marker across the bottom of the screen. At 153 minutes (and 202 minutes for *Redux*), *Apocalypse Now* can be best described as an experience rather than a film, and words can't adequately describe the mysticism of Vittorio Storaro's cinematography, for which he won an Academy Award, or the symbolic motifs of John Milius's and Coppola's screenplay. The lone acting nomination went to Robert Duvall's performance as Colonel Kilgore, whose line, "I love the smell of napalm in the morning. . . . It smells like victory," has become synonymous with a particular kind of win-at-any-cost mentality.

In many respects, Sergeant Barnes (Tom Berenger) in Oliver Stone's *Platoon* is the logical successor to Colonel Kilgore, at least in the evolving subgenre of the Vietnam War film. Perhaps the most provocative and outspoken director/writer/producer of his era, Stone puts forth a powerful antiwar message in his Vietnam trilogy, *Platoon* (1986), *Born on the Fourth of July* (1988), and *Heaven & Earth* (1993), making a clear distinction between criticizing the men and women affected by the war—on both the American and Vietnamese side—and criticizing the military or political apparatus with an investment in armed conflict overall. Based on his own experience, Stone structures *Platoon*'s narrative around the loss of innocence of Chris Taylor (Charlie Sheen), a college dropout who arrives in Vietnam disillusioned from the beginning and seeking something he can be proud of without being fake. In the film, Stone presents the clash of two American military ideologies, represented by the idealistic "crusader" Sergeant Elias (Willem Dafoe) and the hardened, sadistic Sergeant Barnes (Tom Berenger), as Barnes eventually kills or tacitly sanctions the deaths of villagers. Barnes eventually shoots Elias for reporting the incident in the village, their eyes locking and a slight grin of primal recognition crossing Elias's face before the bullets rip into his chest. Left for dead, Elias runs out of the jungle in slow motion, throwing his hands in the air before he falls in a Christ-like gesture of resignation. A shot-reverse-shot sequence between Barnes and Taylor foretells of the grudge that will result in the death of one of them. The film ends with Taylor's call "to teach to others what we knew and to try with what's left of our lives to find a goodness and meaning to our life." As the critical and financial success of *Platoon* revealed—it won an Academy Award for Best Picture and Best Director and earned more than $125 million—audiences were very much ready to learn new lessons.

In Stone's second Vietnam film, *Born on the Fourth of July* (1989), Ron Kovic's experience takes audiences one step further in chronicling the aftermath of a life spent believing in the "old lie," *dulce et decorum est pro patria mori* ("it is sweet and fitting to die for one's country"). In patriotic 1950s and 1960s Massapequa, Long Island, Kovic's parents rear him to excel and to love his country, so much so that when a Marine recruiter (in a cameo by Tom Berenger) speaks to the young men in Kovic's class, Ron enlists. He almost gets his wish to die in Vietnam if the cause calls for it, as the film's setting changes to Ron's second tour of duty in 1967, where, while crossing grasslands, Kovic "shakes off" a foot wound and stands up to continue firing when bullets rip into his chest, photographed in a particularly effective reddish slow-motion sequence. Stone shoots scenes in red, white, or blue throughout the film depending upon their thematic content. Kovic is airlifted to a field hospital, and the screen fades to black after a priest administers last rites. Kovic's experience in Vietnam is over, but his real fight has just begun as he convalesces in a rat-infested, underfunded veteran's hospital stateside.

Gradually, Ron begins to see his life in a wheelchair as a testament to the foolishness of the heroic codes he accepted while growing up and as penance for accidentally shooting a squad mate a year before his own wounding. Hitting bottom after finding himself lying along a Mexican road, he seeks absolution for what he sees as his war crimes and begins healing by protesting the war.

Nominated for Best Picture, Best Actor (Cruise), and for its adapted screenplay, and winner of Best Director and Best Film Editing, *Born on the Fourth of July* carries the Vietnam saga to the next level where *Platoon* leaves off, chronicling the aftershocks that rumbled throughout America as citizens saw up-close the legacy of the war when veterans returned. American reaction was not always an entirely welcoming one, although the nation still managed to salvage its reputation as a homeland for millions seeking a better life, even former enemies such as Le Ly Hayslip in Stone's third film *Heaven & Earth* (1993). A Viet Cong guerrilla fighter, Hayslip struggles to survive through any means necessary, including prostitution, until she finally marries an American serviceman and emigrates to the very nation she once fought to defeat. Although *Born on the Fourth of July* and *Heaven & Earth* would not enjoy the financial success of *Platoon*, the three films as a group examine different, if not complementary, facets of the Vietnam War.

Some viewers and critics consider Stanley Kubrick's *Full Metal Jacket* the best of the rash of antiwar films centered on Vietnam. Near the film's beginning, a characteristic Kubrick tracking shot between the rows of bunks introduces audiences to Gunnery Sergeant Hartman (R. Lee Ermey, an actual former drill sergeant), inaugurating the eight weeks of physical and emotional duress a new group of recruits will endure as they develop into trained killers. Members of the platoon find their own way of coping with the constant battering: Private J. T. "Joker" Davis (Matthew Modine) "cuts up," while the overweight Private Leonard "Gomer Pyle" Lawrence (Vincent D'Onofrio) descends into a psychotic rage on their last night in training, loading his automatic rifle with live ammunition. "Seven point six two millimeter. Full . . . metal . . . jacket," he recites, and commences ceremonial gun-handling maneuvers before pumping a round in Hartman's chest and blowing his own head off.

With training concluded, the film turns towards the men's service in Vietnam, although *Full Metal Jacket* focuses on comparatively few episodes of combat in comparison to other films like it. Sent to cover the Tet offensive, Joker and fellow journalist Rafterman (Kevin Major Howard) experience the devastating influence of combat on the psyche immediately, as they witness a gleeful American soldier shoot at Vietnamese civilians from a chopper. Joker and Rafterman rendezvous with Joker's "bro" from basic training, Cowboy (Arliss Howard), and the two join his squad as they root out the enemy from the battle-scarred Hue City. Their lieutenant and another squad member die in the engagement, and the camera, positioned from the point of view of the corpses lying on the ground looking up, follows each member around a circle as they reflect upon the death of the men. In the final episode in the film, Kubrick crosscuts between the squad, lost and unable to rescue members of the unit "wasted" by sniper fire, and the sniper's point of view. In a hellish setting with flames casting a red glow over the scene the female sniper, once felled, asks in English to be shot, but Joker hesitates. Screwing up his anger—his face takes on the mask of the unthinking killer viewers recognize from boot camp—he fires the bullet that ends her life. As the city burns behind them, the men reverse "hump" to the Perfume River, singing the theme from the Mickey Mouse Club, a reference to the "Mickey Mouse" war they're fighting. "I am so happy I am alive," Joker declares. "I'm in a world of sh--. Yes, but I am alive and I am not afraid." Kubrick forces viewers to wonder whether he intends the end to be read as a triumph over the enemy or as a celebration of the survival of the self, confusion caused by Modine's surprisingly flat, almost monotone delivery.

Full Metal Jacket captures well the dehumanization of the American soldier. Other films meriting comment in the combat narrative or training category include John Irvin's *Hamburger Hill* (1987), a day-by-day telling of the ten-day battle to capture Hill 937, a North Vietnamese Army fortress in the A Shau Valley. Alienation from home (the film refers to civilian attitudes about Vietnam fighters in more detail than others in its subgenre), racial tensions, and the elements compound the effort to meet the military objective day after day and heighten the men's frustrations. Lionel Chetwynd's *Hanoi Hilton* (1987) details the suffering of American prisoners of war in Hanoi's infamous Hoa Lo Prison, with

Michael Moriarty as their leader. Francis Ford Coppola's *Gardens of Stone* (1987) casts James Caan as an aging veteran responsible for burying fatalities from the Vietnam War in Arlington National Cemetery, one "garden of stone" from the title. His transfer to Fort Bragg enables him to do what he can to ensure the survival of the young men he trains for service in Vietnam, particularly the son of an old army colleague (played by D. B. Sweeney). Moreover, Brian De Palma's *Casualties of War* (1990) begins with a Vietnam veteran named Ericksson (Michael Fox) propelled back to Vietnam when a young Vietnamese girl leaves a scarf on board a commuter train, reminding him of a painful episode when five American soldiers kidnapped a Vietnamese girl and four of them brutally raped her. Ericksson ruffles more than a few military feathers when he reports the incident and risks his own life out in the bush when he insists that the men responsible be brought to justice, principally squadron commander Sergeant Tony Meserve (Sean Penn).

Although the brutally realistic combat narrative describes the majority of the films about Vietnam, a second group of films adds to the cinematic understanding of America's most prolonged war by examining its aftermath. In addition to *Born on the Fourth of July*—a hybrid of the two categories of Vietnam War film—Hal Ashby's *Coming Home* (1978) remains the most critically acclaimed example of this second category in the Vietnam subgenre. Not since *The Best Years of Our Lives* has a film presented a more touching portrayal of men who serve their country, only to find themselves struggling and largely forgotten once they return home. Nominated for Best Picture but losing the award to *The Deer Hunter*, this film brought Oscars to Jon Voight (Best Actor, over Robert De Niro's performance in *The Deer Hunter*) and the controversial Jane Fonda (Best Actress), well-known for her antiwar activism.

Like Coppola's *Gardens of Stone*, *Coming Home* explores the Vietnam War experience stateside. Left to her own devices by her officer husband Bob (Bruce Dern), who gets his wish to fight in Vietnam, Sally Hyde (Fonda) volunteers at a local veteran's hospital, and her first visit leaves her splashed with urine and witness to the outburst of Luke Martin (Jon Voight), complaining about his neglect at the hands of the staff. Her continued service at the hospital educates her about the deplorable conditions of veterans and encourages her to break out of her passive, submissive officer's wife mode, reflected by changes in her hair and costuming throughout the film. When Sally bails Luke out of jail after he is arrested for a one-man war protest, the night they spend together teaches Sally more about physical passion than all the years spent married to her husband. Their relationship is brought to a standstill when Bob returns to a hero's welcome he admits he does not deserve. Bob learns of his wife's relationship with a war protestor from FBI agents who followed the pair, and he confronts Sally and Luke, gun in hand. As war films have demonstrated time and time again, only a veteran can understand another soldier's experience, and Luke attempts to provide comfort for Bob. Pacified for the time being, Bob pleads, "I want to be a hero, that's all. . . . I want to go out a hero. That way I've done something that was mine."

Ashby's last sequence reminds viewers of the legacy of the Vietnam War for those fighting it. Humiliated, Bob stands in full dress uniform listening to a litany of heroic acts committed by another veteran at the decoration ceremony. Ashby crosscuts to Luke rebutting the "sales pitch" of a Marine recruiter at a high school, as he discloses, "I have killed for my county, and I don't feel good about it." The film cuts back to Bob walking to the beach, removing his dress uniform piece by piece, and stripped bare, running into the ocean until he vanishes. Sally and a friend enter a grocery store, the camera lingering on the "Out" from the opposing door, and the Rolling Stones' anthem "Out of Time" starts pulsing on the soundtrack to end the film as it began. The symbolism of the sign and the song, of course, reflects the outsider status of many Vietnam veterans. Many Vietnam War films make strong use of contemporary music to create the mood of the era (the Rolling Stones' "Paint It Black" and the Jefferson Airplane's "White Rabbit" appear on more than one soundtrack), and the choices from *Coming Home*—the Beatles' "Hey Jude," "Time" by the Chambers Brothers, and "Once I Was" by Tim Buckley, in particular—propel the narrative.

Vietnam's legacy can be seem in the most recent crop of war films to arise out of American involvement in the invasion of Grenada, the first Gulf War, Bosnia, and Somalia, while historical themes take precedence in others. For example, in *Heartbreak Ridge* (1986), Korean and Vietnam veteran Sergeant Tom Highway (Clint Eastwood) has a reputation among his superiors for irreverence and disrespect, only useful when in times of war. Seeking one last hurrah before retirement, Highway is assigned to train a reconnaissance unit made up of underachievers, and Highway's methods are tested, as is the mettle of the recruits, during America's invasion of Grenada in 1993. The desire to award a Medal of Honor to a woman for the first time overshadows the truth in Edward Zwick's *Courage Under Fire* (1996), or so Lieutenant Colonel Nat Serling (Denzel Washington) discovers. A friendly fire incident in Desert Storm wracks Serling with guilt, but he accepts a job at the Pentagon to recover after his exoneration. His superiors assign him the task of assessing the eligibility for the Medal of Honor of Captain Karen Taylor (Meg Ryan), a helicopter pilot who is believed to have rescued another chopper crew and, after her own chopper crashed, held her crew together during a firefight in which she was killed. Serling, however, finds that the accounts told by each individual present during the crash do not exactly match up. Told in flashback, the film boasts an impressive cast, including Matt Damon and Lou Diamond Philips, but it does little to examine the complex international issues involved in the war itself. The same might be said about John Moore's *Behind Enemy Lines* (2002), with Owen Wilson as fighter navigator Chris Burnett, shot down while on a diversionary Christmas Day mission over war-torn Bosnia. Politics get in the way of his rescue, and Burnett has to make a daring trek over an icy lake amid gunfire to escape.

David O. Russell's satirical *Three Kings* (1999) offers a more thoughtful analysis of American involvement in the Gulf War. In Russell's examination of Iraq after Desert Storm, four American soldiers go on a mission to steal Kuwaiti gold from Saddam Hussein at the end of Desert Storm. When Archie

Gates (George Clooney) refuses to cooperate with the press and his commanding officer reminds him, "This is a media war and you better get on board," Gates admits, perhaps only half in earnest, "I don't know what we did here." Therein lies the question at the center of the film: Was the Gulf War nothing more than a photo opportunity for American politicians and American military might? After the surrender and stripping of Iraqi soldiers results in the discovery of a map of Saddam's bunkers, Troy Barlow (Mark Wahlberg), Chef Elgin (Ice Cube), and Conrad Vig (Spike Jones) join Archie in hatching a plan that sends them on a joyride of sorts for gold through the Iraqi desert. Along the way, the three witness firsthand Hussein's violent campaign of repression and America's betrayal of the people. "Bush told people to rise up against Saddam," Gates explains, "They thought they had our support, but they don't. Now they're getting slaughtered." Iraqi soldiers capture Troy, and his Iraqi captor expresses a similar sentiment when he tells Troy of his family's death and insists Americans only want oil. Two sequences throughout the film follow the path of a bullet through the human body in an unexpected anatomy lesson, and Russell shoots the film in faded color and makes creative use of slow motion at moments, enhancing the irreverent nature of its subject matter.

Ridley Scott's *Black Hawk Down* (2001) recreates the actual events of October 1993, when a select group of American forces slipped into Mogadishu to capture a warlord who was prolonging the Somalian civil war. Nineteen American soldiers died in the assault that quickly turned to chaos after two Black Hawk helicopters took fire and crashed. The script establishes the politics of American involvement in the Somalian civil war early on in the film. "This is our war, not yours," a captured Somalian leader and militia member insists to the commanding American general, Major General William F. Garrison (Sam Shepard). Among the men themselves, Sergeant Matt Eversmann's (Josh Hartnett) idealism turns to guilt when several members of the squad he leads during the mission have been hurt or killed. Accused beforehand of liking the "skinnies," as the American refer to the Somalian people, Eversmann clarifies, "I just figure we have two things we can do. We can either help or sit back and watch the country destroy itself on CNN. . . . I think I was trained to make a difference." The actual helicopter crashes are dramatic, with some of the most vivid scenes shown from overhead and at a distance as the helicopter spins out of control. Overhead shots show marauding bands of Somalians like swarms of hornets in the streets of the city parading the bodies of the American dead amongst themselves. Scott adopts a particular monochrome cinematography throughout much of the film—sometimes in a greenish cast to simulate military night vision—and the blood, sweat, and dirt of war comes across vividly against such a backdrop. Moreover, the pacing of the film simulates the chaos and urgency of the mission, as the men find themselves literally surrounded by an entire city ready to attack and kill any American they see.

Despite the diversity and historical specificity of war films such as *The Patriot* (2000), set during the American Revolution, and the Civil War film *Gettysburg* (1993) and its prequel *Gods and Generals* (2003), many examples can fundamentally be boiled down do the often poignant, sometimes initially antagonistic, but always present bonding between men who find themselves fighting side by side for a shared cause. *Jarhead* (2005) seems to bear that conclusion out once again. American filmmakers take seriously the role they play in boosting morale or otherwise shaping public opinion, and the films they produce are often either churned out to meet demand in times of national emergency or lovingly and carefully crafted over a period of years, reflecting their creators' objectives to present a multidimensional perspective on an unfortunate constant in human society, warfare. With women entering the combat arena and new weapon systems changing the face of combat, it remains to be seen how the conventional narrative pattern and symbolic motifs of the war film may change to accommodate societal shifts and technological advances.

References and Further Reading

Anderegg, Michael, ed. *Inventing Vietnam: The War in Film and Television*. Philadelphia: Temple University Press, 1991.

Basinger, Jeanine. *The World War II Combat Film: Anatomy of a Genre*. New York: Columbia University Press, 1986.

Chung, Hye Seung. "From Saviors to Rapists: G.I.s, Women, and Children in Korean War Films." *Asian Cinema* 12.1 (Spring-Summer 2001): 103–116.

Cullen, Jim. *The Civil War in Popular Culture: A Reusable Past*. Washington, D.C.: Smithsonian Institute Press, 1995.

Davenport, Robert Ralsey. *The Encyclopedia of War Movies: The Authoritative Guide to Movies About Wars of the Twentieth Century.* New York: Facts on File, 2004.

DeBauche, Leslie Midkiff. *Reel Patriotism: The Movies and World War I*. Madison: University of Wisconsin Press, 1997.

Dick, Bernard. *The Star-Spangled Screen: The American World War II Film*. Lexington: University of Kentucky Press, 1985.

Dittmar, Linda, and Gene Michaud, eds. *From Hanoi to Hollywood: the Vietnam War in American Film*. New Brunswick, NJ: Rutgers University Press, 1990.

Doherty, Thomas. *Projections of War: Hollywood, American Culture, and World War II*. New York: Columbia University Press, 1993.

Koppes, Clayton R., and Gregory D. Black. *Hollywood Goes to War: How Politics, Profits, and Propaganda Shaped World War II Films*. New York: Free Press; London: Collier-Macmillan, 1987.

McAdams, Frank. *The American War Film: History and Hollywood*. Westport, CT: Praeger, 2002.

Paris, Michael, ed. *The First World War and Popular Cinema, 1914 to the Present*. New Brunswick, NJ: Rutgers University Press, 2000.

Schatz, Thomas. "World War II and the Hollywood 'War Film'." In *Refiguring American Film Genres: Theory and History*, edited by Nick Browne, 89-128. Berkeley: University of California Press, 1998.

Solomon, Stanley J. "Wars: Hot and Cold." In *Beyond Formula: American Film Genres*, 242–295. New York: Harcourt, Brace, Jovanovich, Ind., 1976.

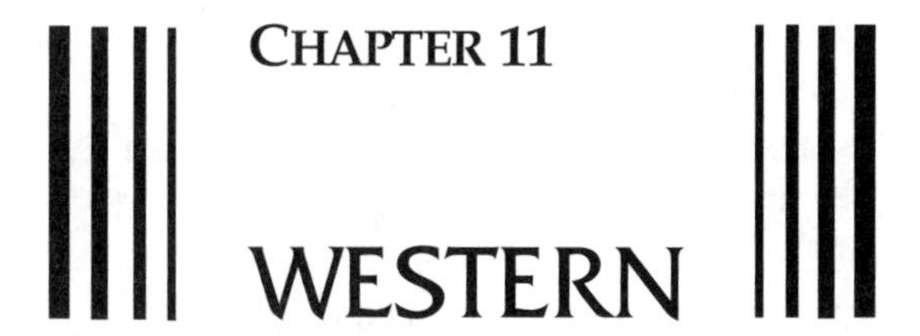

CHAPTER 11
WESTERN

IN HIS SEMINAL ESSAY "Movie Chronicle: The Western," Robert Warshow argues that the two most successful American creations in motion pictures have been the Western and the gangster movie, in both of which guns figure as the "visual and emotional centers" of the films (1999, 654). The Western is, indeed, a most uniquely American creation, arising out of deeply held and embedded cultural and mythical traditions about the frontier as well as evolving forms of American popular culture. Although the American frontier had closed by 1890, as historian Frederick Jackson Turner argued in his famous 1893 essay "The Significance of the Frontier in American History," filmmakers and audiences around the world have never quite gotten over their love affair with the wide open spaces of the American West, at least as portrayed mythically in the Western film. This genre has been so popular for audiences around the world and such a moneymaker for filmmakers that some believe more films in this genre have been produced than in any other. Yet at the center of the history of the genre is an irony. Andrew Sarris writes that "the western is one genre that has become richer in feeling and more profound in form as it rode ever closer to utter extinction" (1998, 104).

DEFINING CHARACTERISTICS

Although no two films are exactly alike, perhaps Westerns are the most identical of any films within a genre, with formulaic plot lines, standard settings, clearly drawn conflicts, and stock characters. The easy recognition of these features should not suggest, however, that variations do not occur in the films or that Westerns are simplistic in theme and content. To the contrary, for Westerns examine topical issues, the structure and function of myth, the stratification of gender roles, environmental issues, and deeply held beliefs about human nature and human experience, particularly violence. They also probe beneath the surface of and provide new insight into traditional definitions or assessments of history and culture, most notably the concept of Manifest Destiny in the United States.

Elemental Conflicts

Throughout, these films often portray the fundamental clash between the wilderness and forces of civilization, sometimes broken down into conflicts between the individual and the community, nature versus culture, the West versus the East, and good versus evil—the latter often being reflected, literally, in a squaring off of the "white hat" versus the "black hat." George Stevens's *Shane* (1953) serves as a prominent example in the gunfight between buckskin-clad Shane and the hired gunman Wilson (Jack Palance), for example. In the conflict between the restriction represented by the East and the rugged open spaces of the West, male Easterners are often viewed with suspicion if not outright ridicule because, until they adapt (if they do), they often appear unsuited to life in a rugged hinterlands. Often, Eastern women come to represent refinement—sometimes admirably and sometimes in terms of their displacement—in comparison to some Western women, whose moral reputation is somehow questioned as a result of the extended influence of lawlessness and moral excesses. In John Ford's *Stagecoach* (1939), for example, Lucy Mallory (Louise Platt), an expectant mother en route to her calvaryman husband, is accorded a degree of chivalry by a professional gambler (John Carradine) who fought with her father on the side of the Confederacy, whereas saloon girl Dallas (Claire Trevor) finds herself on the stagecoach, literally driven out of town by the morals league. Only another "outlaw," the Ringo Kid (John Wayne), treats her with finesse and care.

Typical Plots and Subvariations

Not surprisingly, the forces in conflict dictate the ritualistic plot variations seen across the genre. In *Sixguns & Society: A Structural Study of the Western*, a study of the mythical underpinnings of the Western's structure, author Will Wright provides four useful categorizations for Western plots. In the first category—the classic plot structure—vulnerable farmers and unsuspecting townspeople are saved from purveyors of evil, corruption, control, and vice, such as gamblers and big ranch bosses, by the lone male gunslinger or hero who swoops down to rescue the community but often cannot become one of them (illustrated in *Shane* and its virtual remake, Clint Eastwood's *Pale Rider* [1985], Anthony Mann's *The Bend in the River* [1952] and The *Far Country* [1954], and Eastwood's *High Plains Drifter* [1973]). The second category represents the first plot type in reverse, featuring an alienated or disaffected individual who becomes an outlaw dedicated to wreaking vengeance. He must leave the community because those same capabilities that brought him to the notice of the group in the first place might be, or are, used against it. Films that explore this shift in the relationship between the hero and society include *Stagecoach*, *Red River* [1949], *The Man from Laramie* [1955], *The Searchers* [1956], and *The Quick and the Dead* [1995].

In the classical narrative pattern and the vengeance pattern, changes in the relationships between hero and society have evolved. The vengeance pattern, Wright demonstrates, emerges or mutates relative to the position of the hero in the classical pattern. With the third narrative plot—a transitional phase—elements of the Western myth began shifting dramatically, so that the arrangement of traditional images and plot structures results in new meaning, straining the boundaries of the classic Western structure (1977, 74). The hero starts out as a part of society and becomes an outsider while maintaining his strength, but the society or community itself has grown strong and stable enough to fight both villains and heroes. In *High Noon* (1952), *Broken Arrow* (1950), and *Johnny Guitar* (1954), the opposition between good and bad inherent in Westerns is assigned to the hero and the society or community respectively, presenting more of an internal imbalance that is a threat, rather than a menace from the outside (1977, 75).

In the last narrative category, questions of motivation come into play. Westerns that can be classified as following the "professional" plot include protagonists who become guns for hire. The conflict between heroes and villains takes center stage as social values such as truth, justice, and love, which the community or society espouse or represent, become irrelevant. Neither hero nor villain fights for ideological reasons; both are professionals of equal abilities whose confrontation occurs for its own sake. What becomes pivotal is how the professionals clash, because out of that scenario emerges a new set of values replacing the old (Wright 1977, 86). According to Wright, several later John Wayne films fit this profile, such as *Rio Bravo* (1959), *The Alamo* (1960), *True Grit* (1969), *Big Jake* (1971), and *The Cowboys* (1972), as do *The Wild Bunch* (1969), *Butch Cassidy and the Sundance Kid* (1969), and *Unforgiven* (1992).

Obviously, each of the four categories contains subvariations, and many films fit more than one descriptive category and include features not described in Wright's formulations. For example, several Westerns tell their stories from the perspective of a child or youth, such as *Shane* and *The Shootist* (1976), where the youth learns from the mistakes of an elder but absorbs positive aspects of his legacy. Similarly, Westerns also often feature journey motifs, which function literally (as in *Stagecoach* or *Bend of the River*), when travelers and settlers battle the elements, outlaws, and hostile natives, or symbolically as a representation of the evolution of characters and change in mindsets, as in *Red River*. Moreover, shootout sequences occur in most variations of the Western plot, to the degree that they are often foreshadowed and highly anticipated from the beginning. This tangible clashing of abstract forces throughout the film may actually serve as the structuring principle of the plot, with all scenes included only as they add to the suspense of the final moments and follow the "code" of the Western. These well-established rules demand that the hero refrain from running away from the challenge presented by the threat, and they dictate the hero's use of his gun. Throughout the genre, never is a Western hero permitted to draw and fire preemptively. To do so is to compromise and contaminate the moral high ground he has chosen to occupy through his social sacrifice.

Settings and Features

As made explicit in the name of the genre, these sagas are, with few exceptions, set in the American West, defined literally as the area from the Great Plains westward, but also mythically as environments where victory in the struggle for law and order had not materialized. In some cases, the notion of a "frontier" shifts from America to some other lawless or frontier region, such as revolutionary Mexico in Sam Peckinpah's *The Wild Bunch* (1969). Also, some historians and critics use the term *Pennsylvania Westerns* for films set in the colonial west—defined roughly as upstate New York, western Pennsylvania, Ohio, and Kentucky—and other regions east of the Mississippi that changed from colonial wilderness to well-established civilized locales as settlement continued to occur west of the Mississippi.

Overall, as a result of the elemental conflicts played out in the Western, the landscape becomes a character as much as the humans often struggling against it, so much so that the setting is often duplicated from film to film. Canyons, lonesome sun-dried communities rising up out of the arid grasslands or deserts, sheer rock faces, and broad mesas abound in Westerns. Recognizable locales such as Monument Valley, Utah, appear over and over again in the films of John

Monument Valley, Utah, an often recognizable setting in several classic Westerns, is pictured here in a long shot from John Ford's *Stagecoach* (1939). *Photofest.*

Ford, for example. Dirt trails and railroad tracks leading beyond the horizon supply the only routes to and from the Western community.

The smoke from the train engine's smokestack and its mournful whistle often both serve as the catalyst for and signal the conclusion of the action. The train brings in outlaws (as in *3:10 to Yuma* [1957]), naïve Easterners, and lawmen; it carries bodies away for burial back East, victims not strong enough to survive in the alienating Western wasteland; and it marks the departure of outcasts or misfits thrown out of a community that has adopted "civilized" ways. Standard fixtures in small Western towns, typically having a single street of clay or dirt, include a saloon, from which tinny piano music and raucous laughter emanates; a sheriff's office and jail, where drunken rowdies can "sleep it off"; a livery stable and forge, essential to any community dependent upon horsepower for transportation; a general store, surrounded by buckboard wagons as farmers stock up on supplies after a long haul into town; a doctor's office, where an often grizzled figure patches up the wounds sustained in a barroom brawl or gunfight; and, when the town becomes more civilized, a newspaper and telegraph office, quaint churches, schools, boardinghouses, and hotels. Plank sidewalks, hitching posts, and watering troughs line the dust-covered streets.

Stock Characters

Perhaps more than in any other genre, stock characters abound in the Western. Western historian Kathryn Esselman argues that one proposed cultural influence on the development of the Western, a form of melodrama associated with the fictional works of Bret Harte, presented stock characters, such as the gruff miner with a tender heart or the saloon girl redeemed by the virtues of marriage, with more emotionally complex, if not less sentimental, dilemmas (1974, 16–17). As the most significant stock figure in the genre, the Western hero predominates, but several other figures or character types appear in Western after Western. Schoolmarms and other transplanted Easterners, dance hall or saloon girls, farm and merchant wives, and Native American women cover the spectrum of femininity on the Western frontier. Cowboys and cow hands, cattle barons, bank robbers, prospectors, saloon keepers and bartenders, Native chiefs and warriors, sheriffs, marshals, army officers, preachers, undertakers, blacksmiths, and merchants all populate the farms, ranches, mining communities, cattle towns, stockades, Indian encampments, and cattle drives found in the filmic Old West.

The Western hero (up until recently, exclusively male) himself is often portrayed as fiercely independent, with no more than tangential or temporary ties to the community. Women, in particular, often present complications. He shuns marriage and traditional domestic situations, and if he does form a union, it is often with a woman of his own breed, a social outcast who must live outside the boundaries of polite society. In contrast, Eastern women serve as civilizing but stifling influences, which explains why his interaction with them is limited rather than continuous: They may remind him of his moral obligations to the community that ostracized him, or they may fail to understand what keeps him committed to a lost cause with likely tragic outcomes. His costuming often reveals his literal and emotional marginal status. In the most formulaic renderings of his character type, the color of his hat and his clothing may reveal important information about his moral leanings in the most archetypical sense. The angle of his gun belt may indicate something about his ease with a weapon and his preferred methods to end conflicts. The Western hero often wears clothing and adopts a posture that sets him apart from the community he enters, as in the buckskin of Shane in the film of the same name or the Confederate cavalry cape of Ethan Edwards in *The Searchers*. Like Natty Bumppo in James Fenimore Cooper's *Leatherstocking Tales* and even Captain Ahab in Herman Melville's *Moby Dick*, he is another in a long line of lone male figures battling the forces of the wild.

HISTORY AND INFLUENCES

The Beginning to 1930

As Kathryn Esselman shows, historically, the classic American screen Western emerges from divergent literary and cultural conditions, including a particular American fascination with the Wild West, with its origins in the novels of Sir Walter Scott, Arthurian legends, the idylls of Tennyson, and perhaps the fall of the Confederacy and the migration of some former Southerners, raised on tales of such honor and gallantry, to the West (1974, 10–11). Most immediately, the tradition of nineteenth-century American stage melodrama, which merged the figure of the knight with the Western hero; the emerging showmanship of American "Wild West" shows such as Buffalo Bill Cody's, with precision shooting exhibitions and exotic animals on display; and dime novels and other popular literary influences probably account most for the convergence and codification of themes and motifs seen in the classic American Western (1974, 12).

Aided by the nineteenth-century melodramatic tradition, the cowboy or Western hero was firmly ensconced in the American literary tradition by the beginning of the twentieth century. Dime novels, or pulp novels, which began to appear during the Civil War, took advantage of the mounting interest in the West and created a number of memorable Western figures such as Deadwood Dick and Buffalo Bill, bringing the cowboy hero from the periphery to center stage. When an awareness that the West was rapidly becoming civilized prompted more tourism in the region in the period from 1880 through 1900, more and more established literary publications anxiously printed the accounts of these tourist exploits to feed the mounting interest of their readership. As the era of American imperialism and international influence, the 1890s privileged a new style of masculine vigor in writing produced by Theodore Roosevelt, Jack London, and others indicative of this "strenuous age," as it came to be called. Interest in the one-dimensional, cardboard Western protagonist and his sensationalistic exploits quickly gave way to a desire for a more robust figure, and the Western hero filled the bill (Etulain 1974, 20–21).

The earliest film Westerns capitalized on the popularity and spirit of Wild West shows and dime-novel heroes. The early Western hero Broncho Billy got his start when actor Gilbert M. Anderson purchased the rights to the character from the writer of a *Saturday Evening Post* story in 1909. Anderson's foray into the Western genre, playing three extra roles in Edwin S. Porter's successful one-reeler *The Great Train Robbery* (1903), proved to be a landmark in the history of both cinema and the Western. Porter's one-reeler not only established the archetypal Western pattern, which George Fenin and William Everson have called "crime, pursuit, and retribution" (1962, 47), but also used narrative film techniques now taken for granted: smooth cuts from interior to exterior shots, balanced frame composition, and suspense built carefully through the ordering of scenes. Mostly filmed on a railroad track near Dover, New Jersey, the film lays claim as perhaps the first to use the close-up, in this case of actor George Barnes as an outlaw pointing his gun directly at the audience. Officials from the Edison Company, Porter's employers, never specified when to insert the scene, either at the beginning or the end of the film, calling into question its effectiveness and the deliberation of the director in filming it. Anderson, in his Broncho Billy persona, created the archetype of the Western hero well before the star system emerged (Fenin and Everson 1962, 50).

Fenin and Everson cite evidence that, as early as 1910, Westerns were being taken seriously by film critics and that repeating narrative threads were emerging, but the genre had yet to develop aesthetically until the works of directors Thomas Ince and D. W. Griffith. Perhaps the only important trend generalizable to these early films was contrasting attitudes toward Native Americans. One perspective cast Native Americans as vicious bloodletting savages, whereas the other, more dominant, one depicted sympathetic warriors forced to give their lives—often at their own hands—to preserve their honor against white encroachment (1962, 58). Films that depicted, among other plots, the civilization of the West by the whites suffered from an overall a lack of consistent direction, a lapse made up for in among other ways in the cross-cutting techniques of D. W. Griffith in his earlier two-reelers, some of which featured perennial Western character actor Harry Carey Sr. Although Griffith's Western films transcended the typical "horse opera" formula, he would earn his place in film history exploring other subjects.

What Griffith's films provided in terms of the buildup of dramatic suspense, Thomas Ince's Westerns accomplished in scope and drama, often epitomized by unhappy endings used for their melodramatic effect. Collectively, Griffith and Ince offered filmgoers far more realistic settings than had been used previously, with films shot in the West itself. Although they offered better stories and displayed increased technical achievement, box office receipts for Westerns waned by the mid-1910s, a trend that the Western would experience again in more recent times.

As directors, Ince and Griffith contributed much to the development of the Western. The next individuals crucial to its evolution were William S. Hart, who both acted and directed in a series of Western films over a ten-year period, and Tom Mix, himself a former cowboy, Wild West show performer, and law enforcement official. Living for a time in his youth next to a Sioux reservation in the Dakotas and working as a real-life cowboy in Kansas, Hart acted early on in a series of successful Ince Westerns, which eventually lead to directing and starring in his own popular features. Hart's most memorable films and one of the most significant Westerns of this era, *Hell's Hinges* (1916), combined a strong screenplay with a "near-evangelistic" promotion of Western codes of honor in a tale of an outlaw hired by a saloon owner to drive away a minister and his daughter only to find himself redeemed by the young woman's influence (Fenin and Everson 1962, 90). Roughly paralleling Hart's emergence on the scene, Tom Mix replaced G. M. "Broncho Billy" Anderson as the most prominent Western star, rapidly eclipsing Hart as well. Among the highest paid stars in his era—$17,000 per week in 1925—Mix is credited with Fox Studios' rise to prominence through his lightweight Westerns, which cast him as an idealized Western character who takes on the town's troubles and may win the girl at the end but receives no other rewards, with no efforts to achieve historical realism other than their real-life location (Fenin and Everson 1962, 116). Among other accomplishments, Mix reportedly hired a youthful John Wayne as a prop boy.

Extending into the 1920s, the era of the Tom Mix Western saw the standardization of Western serials and programmers and produced perhaps the first two Western epic films. The popularity of Westerns had actually waned by the time James Cruze directed *The Covered Wagon* (1923), important for establishing the journey as a standard Western plot. Fundamentally a chronicle of a wagon train trekking to California, the film's notable panoramic cinematography and scope enhances several archetypical rituals often repeated in Westerns since then (the crossing of a river, a burial in the wilderness, and the struggle against savage natural elements, to name a few). Perhaps more important, it served as the inspiration for other epics to come, including *The Iron Horse* (1924), a fictionalized treatment of the building of the Transcontinental Railroad, directed by John Ford, who would go on to direct perhaps the best known and most critically acclaimed films in this genre. The film runs some two hours and forty minutes with 1280 separate scenes, and in it Ford created many archetypal scenes and techniques that became staple Western fare, such as a long shot of Native Americans edging a ridge, riders sauntering into the sunset, and the use of a moving camera (Fenin and Everson 1962, 136). More and more critically regarded as the years have progressed, though not as commercially popular as *The Covered Wagon* in its own time, *The Iron Horse*'s importance can perhaps be best recognized as the prototypical Western narrative involving the harnessing of the West by the railroad track and the telegraph wire, illustrated in film through *Union Pacific* (1939) and *Western Union* (1941), respectively.

The mid 1920s saw the emergence of new Western performers such as Buck Jones, Hoot Gibson, and Ken Maynard, whose B-movie Westerns evoked the

Tom Mix era more than the William S. Hart style. Gibson and Maynard offered an immaculately dressed protagonist whose comic antics and showy riding tricks respectively moved the Western away from its realistic underpinnings. Harry Carey, a veteran Western performer since 1910, starred in more traditional Westerns of the Hart variety, with a strong emphasis on protecting female virtue as a plot line. Buck Jones's contribution to the Western encompassed both the traditional gritty Western of Hart and the "slicker" and more lightweight comedic varieties popularized by Gibson and Maynard. The popular Fred Thomson, a minister before his acting career began, is attributed with bringing audiences back to the Western, in high-quality, high-action films with vivid stunt work, including a biography of outlaw Jesse James in 1927 that would be remade with Tyrone Power in 1939. Not to be outdone by their human counterparts, canine stars such as Warner-First National's Rin Tin Tin were presented in enjoyable and popular Western fare on a budget, films so successful in relation to their production costs that they offset studio losses on more prestigious productions (Fenin and Everson 1962, 160). The proliferation of Westerns in this era peaked between 1925 and 1927, but not before directors such as Ford and William Wyler had cut their directorial teeth, making a variety of Western films during this decade in which many staple features of Western films emerged and evolved and several stars who would make bigger splashes in films during the sound era learned their craft.

The 1930s

Other than Victor Fleming's *The Virginian* (1929), the first couple of years of the sound era produced no significant films in the Western genre, with many studios even suspending production of their B-movie serials. Based on Owen Wister's perennially favorite 1902 novel of a ranch foreman who captures and sees hanged a group of cattle rustlers, including his best friend and rival for his beloved, *The Virginian* marked Gary Cooper's entrance into sound features. The film's trademark ending of a gunfight between Cooper and gang leader Walter Huston followed the vintage Western pattern of slow build-up of conflict to codified climatic conclusion. The film is generally agreed to be the best of the filmed versions of the story (which had previously been filmed in 1914 and 1923 and would be remade in 1946 and for TV in 2000), with beautiful photography and fine acting, although the pacing almost grinds the narrative to a halt in an effort to minimize the dialogue and increase the action.

Among other early treatments of the West, *In Old Arizona* (1929), *The Big Trail* (1930), and *Cimarron* (1931) proved that sound techniques and speech could be used to solid effect in the Western. *In Old Arizona* is perhaps only notable as the first sound installment in the Cisco Kid saga and for Warner Baxter's Best Actor Academy Award. Today, the film is a horribly dated treatment of Mexican-American relations along the border. *The Big Trail* is a saga that reinforces the paradigm of Europe civilization of the West versus Native American savagery in Westerns in years to come (Garfield 1982, 115). Twenty-year-old John Wayne's performance (not too long after his name change), in combination with a sluggish script, led to the failure of this film, although Wayne would go on to great popular success as a Western star. The failure of the film may also be attributed to experiments in widescreen photography, which would not be completely worked out technically or economically until the 1950s. Its panoramic scenes of wagon trains migrating westward on the Oregon Trail, shot on actual locations, represented film making in epic proportions (see **Epic**), with several hundred cast members and several animal performers for director Raoul Walsh to coordinate in a ten-week shooting schedule. Wesley Ruggles's *Cimarron*, based on Edna Ferber's novel of the same name, survives from this period as the far more successful Western epic, chronicling the opening of frontier Oklahoma for white settlement. Ruggles's staging and Edward Cronjager's cinematography in filming the first-day Oklahoma land rush sequence have influenced Western filmmakers ever since. *Cimarron* held the record for almost sixty years as the only Western to win the Best Picture Oscar.

From the production of *The Big Trail* and *Cimarron* until *Stagecoach*, few notable big-budget Western epics were made. Independent production companies and B-units of larger studios making the conversion to sound turned out Western films and serials of various qualities, including the introduction of the "singing cowboy" pictures, originating with Ken Maynard, but made popular later by Gene Autry, who regularly appeared on Hollywood's top-ten moneymakers list. Other early cowboy serial stars of this era included Roy Rogers with his trademark horse Trigger, his sidekick Gabby Hayes, and his co-star and wife Dale Evans in a series of low budget films for Republic Studios. Rogers replaced Autry in the 1940s as the "King of the Cowboys" and later migrated to television. Geared toward younger audiences, the highly popular B-movie Hopalong Cassidy series, starring Paramount's William Boyd, stood as the only rival to the Autry vehicles. Individuals from the silent days of the screen Western such as Hoot Gibson, Ken Maynard, Harry Carey, and William Desmond extended their careers into the sound era by acting in often quickly produced and modestly budgeted programmers and serials. Others who starred in quickly made and economical Westerns at their respective studios include Tim McCoy, Charles Starrett, George O'Brien, Tex Ritter, Rex Bell, Bob Steele, Johnny Mack Brown, and Al "Lash" LaRue. Western films of higher quality that fell neither into the epic nor the serial category in this era include *Viva Villa!* (1934) with Wallace Beery as the Mexican outlaw, Barbara Stanwyck in the title role as a Wild West performer in *Annie Oakley* (1935), Gary Cooper as Wild Bill Hickok and Jean Arthur as Calamity Jane in *The Plainsman* (1936), and Pennsylvania Westerns depicting life in the then West of colonial America (*The Last of the Mohicans* [1936]; *Allegheny Uprising* [1939]; and *Drums Along the Mohawk* [1939]).

The year 1939 has been called a high point in motion picture production, with the release of films such as *The Wizard of Oz* and *Gone With the Wind*. That year is also notable for producing Westerns of unique quality, including *Dodge City, Union Pacific, Jesse James,* and *Destry Rides Again*, the last with a most unlikely Western "heroine," Marlene Dietrich, in a near parody of the genre. Considered by many the most important Western of that year and possibly any year, John Ford's *Stagecoach* almost single-handedly established the basic archetypes of the modern Western film to follow for the next several decades. Along with other Westerns of that year, it contributed considerably to elevating the genre from B-movie or serial status to a serious art form through its richer narrative texture and more complex characterizations. Foreshadowing later psychological or sociological Westerns such as *The Ox-Bow Incident* (1943), the film documents a social experiment in the guise of a stagecoach journey through hostile Indian country as soon-to-be stock Western character types are forced to depend upon one another for survival. In the fashion of Bret Harte's fiction, socially undesirable individuals rise above their ignominy to demonstrate their real noble characters. As Tim Dirks has pointed out, Dudley Nichols's screenplay, from Ernest Halcox's 1937 *Collier's Magazine* short story "Stage to Lordsburg," is divided into eight perfect segments, alternating between episodes of action and moments of character development. The film marks John Ford's return to Westerns after a thirteen-year hiatus, and it became his first sound film in the genre and the first featuring Monument Valley, a setting he would return to again and again in later Westerns such as *My Darling Clementine* (1946) and *The Searchers*. Ford's direction remains remarkably interesting, such as an episode in which Dallas (played by Claire Trevor) is silhouetted and framed in a doorway with light forming a trapezoid around her, a technique he would use later in *The Searchers* in reverse to highlight Ethan Edwards (played by John Wayne). The film elevated the career of many individuals who were involved in it, including Ford and Wayne, saved from B serial martyrdom, and Thomas Mitchell, who won a Best Supporting Actor Oscar for his portrayal of the alcoholic Dr. Boone. In reference to the importance of the film in the history of the genre, Joseph McBride writes, "Before *Stagecoach*, the Western seemed to be dying; after *Stagecoach*, it became the one permanently popular film genre" (1975, 53).

The 1940s

Studios took Westerns much more seriously after *Stagecoach* and launched many A-level productions. Not surprisingly, with the advent of World War II and an emphasis on American democratic values and sacrifice, many Westerns produced during the war years harkened back to historical incidents and figures from the past, on both sides of the law, and broadened the scope of the Western to examine social and psychological issues. Fenin and Everson call this collection of films, which glamorize outlaw figures, "badman" Westerns, a group that begins with director Henry King's *Jesse James*, starring Tyrone Power in the title role and Henry Fonda as brother Frank (1962, 241). Others in the group include *The Return of Frank James* (1940), directed by Fritz Lang and starring Henry Fonda again, and *Billy the Kid* (1941), the first color Western shot in Monument Valley, with romantic leading man Robert Taylor in the title role. Worthy of note for less enviable reasons, Howard Hughes's *The Outlaw* (1943) also examined episodes in the life of the same famous criminal figure, but the film's better claim to fame might be the censorship controversy surrounding Jane Russell's wardrobe, including a bra specially designed by Hughes. Newcomer

Jack Buetel portrays Billy perhaps most accurately as a confused, uncertain youth, but the acting is often stiff and the film wavers uncertainly from a biography of a legendary outlaw figure to an erotic thriller to a love story. The score, borrowing from Tchaikovsky's *Symphonie Pathétique,* sends the film into the realm of kitsch.

Generally, the effect of these films portraying outlaws and others was to humanize and explain the antisocial behavior of many of the figures and those involved in bringing them to justice. William Wyler's *The Westerner* (1940) pits outlaw Cole Hardin (Gary Cooper) against the legendary Judge Roy Bean (Walter Brennan in his third Oscar-winning performance), demonstrating that filmmakers could treat issues of law and order and human longing and aspiration seriously while at the same time entertaining audiences.

As a counterpoint to films with outlaws as central characters worthy of sympathy, historical films that focused on other kinds of figures populating the West and the dilemmas and pitfalls of civilizing it included *Santa Fe Trail* (1940), with Errol Flynn as cavalry man J.E.B. (Jeb) Stuart and Ronald Reagan as George Custer on the eve of the Civil War, and the fictionalized biography of Custer *They Died With Their Boots On* (1941), in which Flynn played the flamboyant general. Flynn first replaced the sword of the swashbuckling hero for the sixgun of the Western protagonist in *Dodge City* and *Virginia City* (1940), both set in the post–Civil War West. The most notable Western of this group is likely William Wellman's somber look at mob justice, *The Ox-Bow Incident*, starring Henry Fonda as a cowhand and Dana Andrews as an unlucky settler come to Nevada to ranch. When a local rancher is allegedly killed by cattle rustlers, various members of a stagnant community representing stock Western types take the law into their own hands to see that "justice" is done and personal property is preserved. With the sheriff out of town and the admonitions of the local judge ignored, townspeople, led by a mayor of dubious background, "string up" three unsuspecting homesteaders nearby over the protest of Fonda and companion Harry Morgan. The magnitude of what they have done hits many of the townspeople hard, although not hard enough, as the sheriff returns to report that the rancher is not dead after all but only wounded, with the men responsible already in custody. Rather than accept personal blame, the culpable townspeople scapegoat the mayor instead, who commits suicide as a result. As this brief recounting of the story suggests, the film is dark both in tone and in appearance, with the menacing theme of injustice reflected in gradient lighting. Daylight often appears as dark as night, and the hanging of the three innocents invokes Christ's crucifixion and points to the greater social message of the film as an allegory against fascism ("the mob") abounding in Europe.

The influence of the international social and political situation on Westerns during World War II continued in films made after the war. As Thomas Schatz demonstrates about *Stagecoach*, the marriage of scarlet woman Dallas (Claire Trevor) and the outlaw Ringo Kid (John Wayne), sanctioned by officialdom in the guise of Sheriff Wilcox (George Bancroft), symbolized the optimism and opportunity of America's wide open spaces. Of subsequent films, Schatz writes,

"The gradual fading of this optimistic vision, more than anything else characterizes the evolution of the Western genre. As the formula was refined through repetition both the frontier community and its moralist standard-bearers are depicted in increasingly complex, ambiguous, and unflattering terms" (1981, 50–51). As with the impulse toward alienation, doom, and moral ambiguity found in film noir (see **Film Noir**) of the postwar era, Westerns such as *The Westerner, The Gunfighter* (1950), *Blood on the Moon* (1948), and the later *3:10 to Yuma* all share a sense of menace, tension, moral complexity, and sexuality. Notable as well for bringing back an epic quality to the Western genre, King Vidor's *Duel in the Sun* (1946), like Hughes's *The Outlaw*, introduced overtly sexual themes in this story of a half-breed woman (Jennifer Jones) who is taken in by a rancher (Lionel Barrymore) but seduces his two sons (Joseph Cotten and Gregory Peck), causing strife and upheaval in both his home and the community at large. Critics dubbed the film "Lust in the Dust," and the film was one of the top moneymakers in its era despite its hefty price tag of $6 million to produce—ranking it the most expensive film made until that time—and its production of over 250 hours of unedited film (Garfield 1982, 152). The fundamentally soap-opera plot is offset by quality production values, fine performances (by Peck in particular, in one of his first starring roles), and artistically staged and framed scenes. Producer David O. Selznick had high hopes for the film as the epic follow-up to *Gone With the Wind*, but the film never quite lived up to its artistic and critical potential.

Two films and one director are particularly worthy of note as embodying and projecting respectively an increased narrative and cultural complexity in the immediate postwar Western. Part *Mutiny on the Bounty* and part *Oedipus Rex*, Howard Hawks's *Red River* (1948) chronicles a cattle drive as it blazes through hostile Indian country to establish a new route from Texas to the railroad and the commercial markets of the East—the route that later became known as the Chisholm Trail. More important, the film documents the personal journey of two men of different generations and the shift in ways of thinking about commerce, propriety, and progress in post–Civil War Texas in particular and the American West in general. Tom Dunson (John Wayne) is a man used to getting what he wants even if he has to take it. Fourteen years earlier his pivotal decision to leave a wagon train and the woman he loved resulted in her death in an Indian ambush, the beginning of his cattle empire on land stolen by a Mexican landowner from the natives, and the discovery of his surrogate son Matthew Garth (Montgomery Clift in his first film role). The South's loss in the Civil War dries up the cattle markets, so Dunson decides to drive his herd to Missouri despite risks to himself and his men. Hard times on the range and rumors of a shorter route to the railroad encourage Matt to take control and drive the herd to Kansas against Dunson's wishes, and Dunson vows to kill Matt for his insubordination. After the two men and the values they represent collide in a climactic fight and gunfighter Cherry Valance (John Ireland) is killed in the process, a new way of life bursts forth—one borne out of compromise and not violence, with an eye toward the potential of the future and not the hardships or wounds of the past.

As in war films, guns often serve an important mediating function in Westerns, particularly among men. In an early scene in *Red River*, Cherry Valance admires and caresses Matt's gun lovingly, which some take as a suggestion of homoeroticism. Cherry remarks, "You know, there are only two things more beautiful than a good gun: a Swiss watch or a woman from anywhere. Ever had a good . . . Swiss watch?" Later, Dunson chides Matt for allowing Cherry to take his gun away from him, a sign to Dunson that Matt is not yet worthy of the addition of his initial to the Red River D brand and not yet heir to the cattle ranching tradition Dunson carved out of the wilderness. Although Hawks clearly centers the story on the next generation rather than the previous, Matt must not only challenge but topple Dunson's authority in order to inherit the West in the new post–Civil War era. Cinematically, the ideological and Oedipal link between Dunson and Matt and a foreshadowing of their conflict as a result is made most clear in Hawks' sequence set on the morning of the cattle drive. As Tim Dirks describes it, Dunson's point of view is portrayed through the camera's eye, as the lens slowly surveys in 180 degrees the landscape dotted with cattle and the men who risk the unknown to drive them to market. With the half arc complete, the camera rests on Dunson from Matt's point of view, cementing the fate of the two characters together, one as progenitor and one as inheritor. With the call to begin the drive, a new Western perspective is established.

Similar in scope and mythical appeal, in *My Darling Clementine*, director John Ford returns to Monument Valley, casting Henry Fonda as Wyatt Earp, held back from exacting revenge by an abiding belief in the law. Moral complexity or ambiguity comes in the form of Doc Holliday (Victor Mature), whose cultured Eastern education and background should be aligned with community values, but whose fits of drunkenness (to forget a failed career and a failed romance) and violent outbursts suggest more elemental Western origins (like Earp) and primitive reactions. In that sense, social mores and social roles are reversed in this film, and Earp and Holliday, as "doubles," come to blows. Other central oppositional figures in the narrative include Clementine Carter (Cathy Downs), who has tracked Holliday to Tombstone and battles her rival, Chihuahua (Linda Darnell), a dancehall girl of questionable virtue, for Holliday's soul. The four characters provide a strong counterbalance to the Clantons, who prove to represent external evil in the Arizona garden of Eden that Ford creates in Tombstone. With Holliday doomed to die through either tuberculosis or a gunfight, a death at the OK Corral that seems to redeem him for his earlier contribution to the demise of Chihuahua, Clementine becomes the pivotal figure in altering Earp's mythic character. Her function in the film thus defies the typical role of the Easterner as a stagnating force. Visually, the famous square dance scene at the church raising juxtaposes the civilizing influence of the East against the rugged individualism of the West, with Earp and Clementine as mediators. Ford casts the entire mythic drama of good versus evil against one of the last vestiges of the frontier, represented by the heroic and iconic landscape of Monument Valley, sealing Wyatt Earp's fate as one of the principal players in an American West that existed only in the imagination.

Without question, John Ford's contribution to the Western cannot be underestimated, nor is it entirely based on *Stagecoach* and *My Darling Clementine* alone. Out of 137 films directed in a fifty-seven-year career, some fifty-four were Westerns (McBride and Wilmington 1975, 45). Although he was not the only director to offer iconic versions of the American Western frontier saga—Howard Hawks, Delmer Davies, Nicholas Ray, Henry King, and Anthony Mann would do the same in lesser form—he undoubtedly presented a cinematic mythical Western language that audiences could easily understand. In *Wagon Master* (1950), said to be Ford's favorite of all his Westerns, the director uses a group of Mormons on their Western trek to represent all American settlers and the challenges that threaten to separate them. The central conflicts of his Cavalry trilogy—*Fort Apache* (1948), *She Wore a Yellow Ribbon* (1949), and *Rio Grande* (1950)—involve a crisis in leadership intensified by the threat of Indian attack, once again staged against the monoliths of Monument Valley (McBride and Wilmington 1975, 97). To phrase it another way, this collection of films is "a family tragedy about the birth of a nation, with the Indians as estranged brothers and the Cavalry as the better part of white culture—the people, not the government" (McBride and Wilmington 1975, 99).

The 1950s

With *Stagecoach* and *My Darling Clementine, The Searchers* cements Ford's legacy as a masterful filmmaker and Western auteur. Rarely have story, director, and star been so dramatically suited to one project. Ford returns to his favorite location, Monument Valley, in a story of former Confederate veteran and mercenary Ethan Edwards (John Wayne), who searches for the niece captured by sadistic Indian chief Scar (Henry Brandon)—first to rescue her and, as the search continues through the years, to ensure that the blood of his family does not mix with the blood of the Native peoples he despises. Edwards follows in a long line of antiheroes who cannot function within the boundaries of civilized society and yet who is inextricably linked to what it has to offer, in this case unrequited love for his brother's wife and the children she bears him. His rudeness to an adopted nephew (Jeffery Hunter) with Indian blood makes his discomfort with family life and Native society that much more apparent. What makes Edwards so complex and compelling as a Western figure are, as Joseph McBride notes, parallels between Ethan Edwards and the epitome of all he despises, Scar, who are both motivated by the loss of family members to violence perpetrated by each other's societies (1975, 152).

Ford emphasizes Edwards's isolation and alienation from the human community in the two scenes that bookend the film, both shot through the open door of a cabin framing the gaze of the audience. In the first, sister-in-law Martha (Dorothy Jordan) swings the door open to frame Ethan emerging from the wilderness with the potential for reintegration into civilization, but held back by a refusal to steal his brother's wife. The last finds Ethan, after vowing to kill niece Debbie (Natalie Wood), instead returning her to the comfort of home on the threshold of another cabin. Although this act again hints at his redemption for misdeeds only implied by his background, he still cannot enter. Instead, he remains framed in the doorway, caught in some sort of no man's land, rejecting the pitiless wilderness code that had fueled his bloodlust in the first place, but not able to accept what settlement on the frontier may mean either. He has been turned out again. In the history of Western filmmaking, this final scene carries additional meaning, as John Wayne crosses his left hand over to grab his right arm in the characteristic gesture of veteran Western actor Harry Carey Sr., a figure both Ford and Wayne admired.

Visually, the film is also remarkable for both the vivid color cinematography of Winton C. Hoch and the number of high-angle shots Ford makes of the individuals dwarfed by the landscape. At one point, a shot of Scar's band of renegade Indians riding along the high ground parallel to a search party below led by captain of the local militia Samuel Johnson Clayton (Ward Bond) not only adds to the menace of the men who find themselves in the vise-like grip of the "savages" but also hints at the precariousness of life in the Texas wilderness of the late 1860s. In the scene leading up to the massacre itself, Ford creates tension by understatement, as much as in atmospherics and what is not said as in what is. Against the backdrop of an angry, funereal orange sky, mother and father attempt to behave as if nothing is wrong. Knowing glances between characters tell the story. Only the scream of daughter Lucy (Pippa Scott) breaks the silence. The scene ends with Debbie clutching her rag doll, crouched down against the tombstone of her grandmother (massacred by Indians) with Scar's shadow falling over her. The camera frames Scar as he blows the whistle to begin the massacre. The savagery occurs by implication and not by overt depiction, allowing audiences to fill in the blanks for themselves.

The Searchers was far from the only film in this genre to examine the role of the lone male in the Western wilderness whose contact with civilization brings about remarkable change. Throughout that period in the evolution of the Western, predominantly male figures, although not all marginalized from civilization, had responsibilities thrust on them or took up the mantle of social change, which often set them apart from the individuals in their communities. The most famous example of a 1950s Western to portray the figure was George Stevens's 1953 mythic *Shane*, one of the most financially successful Westerns ever. In this quintessential story of two warring factions in the West colliding—farmer and rancher—a mysterious stranger rides into the Starrett homestead moments before rancher Ryker's men trample through the garden, carefully maintained by the Starrett wife (played by Jean Arthur in her last film role). Their message is clear: Leave or be carried out in a coffin. The appearance of buckskin-clad Shane (Alan Ladd) will not make dislodging homesteaders so easy, as he becomes a fierce ally of the farmers as a path to redemption for and surrender to his former gunfighter ways. A combination of facets in the film lend an allegorical and mythical quality to the story, including Shane's lone ride into the valley at the opening of the film and a series of low-angled shots silhouetting his image against the majesty of the Wyoming sky. The most memorable is an episode which clearly marks the alliance between Shane and Joe Starrett (Van Heflin):

The two successfully battle a stubborn tree stump together, symbolic of not only their alliance and the struggles that must be endured on the frontier, but also the evil and obstruction that must be removed for values of home and hearth to flourish safely in the Western wilderness.

The inevitable clash between good and evil foreshadowed by Shane's arrival occurs as Ryker hires rival gunman Jack Wilson (Jack Palance) to even the odds. Although it is not his job to protect the farmer's way of life, Shane knows that no one in the community is better suited to settling the matter for good than he and that no one has so little to sacrifice for the greater good. Partly for this reason, and partly because his fondness for Joe Starrett's wife and his interest in preserving young Joey Starrett's (Brandon de Wilde) image of his father compel him to, Shane straps on his gun and heads for town. The shoot-out, witnessed by little Joey, ends in Shane stopping Wilson with two bullets and taking one himself from a gunman to whom Joey must alert him—a sign that men like Shane and the Western way of life he represents are not as sharp as they used to be and will soon become a dying breed. As a story told from the perspective of an emerging youth, *Shane* presents viewers with an alternative between two conflicting ways of life, the life of the gun and the life of the plow, but the history of the West's civilizing already made the choice clear. "There's no living . . . with a killing. There's no going back from it. It's a brand that sticks," Shane utters. As a sacrificial lamb to the code of the West who cannot escape his past—indeed, Shane is portrayed as a Christ figure or rescuing angel throughout—Shane rides out of the valley as mysteriously as he rode in, wounded and perhaps dying. In one of the most poignant endings in motion picture history, Joey cries, "Shane. Shane! Come back! 'Bye, Shane," a haunting longing for the mysterious wild way of life Shane represents, which cannot coexist harmoniously with values of home and family.

In Fred Zinneman's *High Noon*, Will Kane (Gary Cooper), who, unlike Shane, is a man well integrated into his community, discovers how alone he is when crisis strikes. Although townspeople admit their debt of gratitude to him for making Hadleyville, New Mexico, a secure place for decent women and a safe environment to raise children, no man wishes to take up arms along with Kane when word comes that a pardoned outlaw, Frank Miller (Ian MacDonald), is on the noon train to wreak havoc on the sheriff and the community who put him away. The judge who presided over the trial and Kane's wedding (Otto Kruger) packs up his law books, removes his American flag from the wall, and hightails it out of town. A Mexican woman with romantic attachments to both Miller and Kane (Katy Guardo) quickly sells her store and leaves town on the same train bringing Miller in. Kane himself is urged by townspeople to leave on his honeymoon with his Quaker wife (Grace Kelly) while he has a chance, but duty to his principles and a commitment to finish what he started in the past keep him there. She herself promises to have nothing to do with the violence about to occur.

In terms of cinema history, the film's depiction of real time makes it notable, as the eighty-five-minute running time of the film parallels the period from roughly 10:30 in the morning until noon on a Sunday as Will Kane tries to round up a posse. Frequent shots of clocks in various locations extenuate the tenseness of the drama as the stakes are raised on Will Kane while minutes pass. A long crane shot of Kane walking through the abandoned streets of the community emphasizes his isolation. Given the era in which it was made, the film's ideological and allegorical significance have not gone unnoticed. In this last screenplay by Carl Foreman before his blacklisting, some read Will Kane's plight as symbolic of the position of the Hollywood Ten, denied employment as a result of their alleged political activities. As Tim Dirks points out, others see in Will Kane's commitment and Amy Kane's pacifism a morality play depicting America's foreign policy in the Korean War era. As an aging hero, Kane stands for certain qualities crucial to the preservation of American values taxed by years of struggle during World War II (as represented by the townspeople) against outside forces that threaten them (seen in Frank Miller and his gang). Kane's Quaker wife, who saw both her father and brother gunned down, represents U.S. isolationists. Regardless of audiences' political affiliations, the film examines themes of collective responsibility and conformity, made in an era portrayed to be one of the most outwardly homogenized in the twentieth century.

In his study *Seeing Is Believing: How Hollywood Taught Us to Stop Worrying and Love the Fifties*, author Peter Biskind argues that, although many 1950s films clearly lauded conformity, convention, and domesticity, another look at several motion pictures from this period reveals an era of contradiction and conflict. The prevalence of 1950s and early 1960s films made in the uniquely American genre of the Western seems to support Biskind's observations about the emphasis on conformity and the known. As a genre with an almost forty-year, time-honored history of decline and revival by 1950, Westerns perhaps more than any other type of film provided audiences with both a sense of national identity, albeit often a fictionalized one, and a guarantee of enjoyable entertainment. Although conformity may have reigned during the era when many of the best remembered examples of the Western were made, and although Westerns had an investment in particular attitudes about the shaping of the wilderness, the genre began developing a social consciousness in reference to race also. What John Stahl's *Imitation of Life* (1934) began and Elia Kazan and John Ford's *Pinky* (1949) continued for African Americans, and what Edward Dymtryk's *Crossfire* (1947) and Elia Kazan's *Gentleman's Agreement* (1947) did for Jews, Delmer Daves's *Broken Arrow* (1950) began for Native Americans. Ted Jojola writes, "The Hollywood Indian is a mythological being who exists nowhere but within the fertile imagination of its movie actors, producers, and directors. The preponderance of such movie images have reduced native people to ignoble stereotypes" (1998, 12). Thematically, Hollywood often portrayed Native Americans as either savages to be exterminated for civilization to flourish or children who were often easy to fool with shiny objects or, worse, whiskey. Rarely were actors from Native groups cast in such roles, and Native languages, if portrayed on screen at all, amounted to a series of indecipherable grunts and hand gestures. Although not entirely innocent of such tactics, *Broken Arrow* marks one of the first attempts by the Hollywood establishment to portray Native peoples as members of peace-loving societies with elaborately ordered social rituals and codes of honor. Other films that attempted to broaden understanding and question stereotypes in this era include *Tomahawk* (1951), *Broken Lance* (1954), *Apache Woman* (1955), *The Flaming Star* (1960), and *The Unforgiven* (1960).

Broken Arrow chronicles the subtle changes that take place in white and Apache culture as scout Tom Jeffords (Jimmy Stewart) and Apache chief Cochise (Jeff Chandler) alter their perspectives and grow to trust one another as a road map to future peace between the two groups. For example, concern for the recovery of a young Native American whom he runs across on the trail forces Tom to realize, "It never struck me that an Apache woman would cry over her son like any other woman. Apaches are wild animals, we all said." In return, Apache warriors intent upon killing Tom discover that some whites do fight with a sense of honor, and they spare his life for the concern he showed the youth. But once he reports to the local stockade commander in Tucson, he learns that the Cavalry plans to wipe out Cochise and his band through a show of force. "Who asked us out here in the first place?" Jeffords asks in response to this plan for harsh reprisals against the Apaches. "I know the white men aren't always right, but we're bringing civilization out here," businessman Lowrie (Robert Griffin) offers—with "civilization" amounting to cheaply sold carpets, hats, and whiskey—if Cochise would stop sending out raiding parties.

Angered by the propensity toward killing, Tom begins learning Indian ways, a task that ennobles him to Cochise. However, the film somewhat lapses into bathos when it offers a bridge for understanding between the two groups in the pairing of Tom and Apache maiden Sonseeahray (Debra Paget). Both characters believe that the divisions that exist between their two peoples can be overcome in their union, but Cochise wonders. Still, Tom's commitment to the woman he loves despite the obstacles cements the trust between Tom and Cochise. Further, the film demonstrates that the path of real understanding and trust develops in stages. Cochise's agreement to allow the mail to go through enables Tom to convince others that Apaches may live up to an agreement for a three-month truce. Elements on the fringe of both societies—renegade bands of Apaches under Geronimo and an outraged rancher (played by Will Geer) driven to irrationality at the loss of his wife—strain the tenuous ties between the two peoples to the breaking point, ultimately resulting in the death of Sonseeahray in an ambush. In his loss, Tom comes to accept that "the death of Sonseeahray put a seal on the peace."

Fenin and Everson point out that the increased emphasis on Native American characters and performers ironically had a negative impact on the appearance of black characters, possibly attributable to racial tensions involving desegregation of the South during this period (1962, 282–283). The faithful "Negro" retainer character, such as Pompey (Woodey Strode) in Ford's *The Man Who Shot Liberty Valance* (1962) and other films with a post–Civil War setting, began to disappear. Other casualties in the genre were serials and B-movie Westerns, which also fell victim to attempts by studios to compete with the emerging medium of television by the development of widescreen filming and projection techniques. Cowboy stars such as Roy Rogers and Gene Autry turned to television to reach audiences, and films such as *Broken Arrow* became the basis for series on the little screen.

Among the best widescreen Westerns produced in the 1950s and early 1960s include Howard Hawks's *The Big Sky* (1952), John Farrow's *Hondo* (1953), Robert Aldrich's *Vera Cruz* (1954), George Stevens's *Giant* (1956), William Wyler's *The Big Country* (1958), John Wayne's *The Alamo* (1960), and *How the West Was Won* (1962), an epic directed in segments by John Ford, Henry Hathway, and George Marshall. Westerns were so popular that almost every star of any renown tried to get in on the action, running the spectrum of quality from *Bad Day at Black Rock* (1955), with Spencer Tracy and a contemporary Western setting, to *Johnny Guitar* (1954), with Joan Crawford in a deeply neurotic and kitschy drama with suppressed erotic overtones. *The Misfits* (1961) proved to be the last completed film for both Clark Gable and Marilyn Monroe, a contemporary story that brings the curtain down on a lost Western way of life. A particularly emblematic scene of an aging cowboy (Gable) in a battered truck struggling to lasso wild horses racing across desert flats harbingers the breakdown of both the Western archetypical hero—he no longer relies on brute strength and ingenuity—but also the "civilizing" of the wild by the mechanical.

In *The Man Who Shot Liberty Valance* (1962), in which some critics see a direct line of descent from *My Darling Clementine*, John Ford shows in flashback a senator (James Stewart) whose political reputation ironically rests on an act he did not commit when another man's real sacrifice goes unnoticed. The dialogue in the film could serve as telling commentary about the West itself, both the real one and the mythic region portrayed in motion pictures. When he hears the story of Tom Doniphon (John Wayne), who actually shot the outlaw of the title (Lee Marvin) and saved yet-to-be-Senator Stoddard's life, the local newspaper editor utters, "This is the West, sir. When the legend becomes fact, print the legend." Of the land itself, for example, the senator's wife (Vera Miles) remarks, "It was once a wilderness. Now it's a garden." Later, on the train back to Washington once Senator Stoddard has promised his wife that he will leave politics after the passage of an irrigation bill that benefits the small farmers he started out protecting, the irony of Doniphon's obscurity and sacrifice and that of men like him becomes clear. The railroad company has agreed to hold the express train back to Washington, D.C., until his arrival because "Nothing's too good for the man who shot Liberty Valance."

John Ford's last Western, *Cheyenne Autumn* (1964), returns to the conflict between Native Americans and the Cavalry, this time with Richard Widmark in the role of an officer hoping to guarantee fair treatment of the Cheyenne despite the policies of the Bureau of Indian Affairs and an indifferent East Coast bureaucracy. In a departure from classic Hollywood fare, native peoples are humanized, and Ford uses Native American languages and customs to great effect. Most criticisms see the film as damaged by gratuitous episodes that feature mythical Western characters such as Wyatt Earp and Doc Holliday and too many diffuse storylines all colliding rather than harmonizing. Despite its shortcomings in the minds of some critics, as revealed in a biography written by his grandson, Ford is said to have made the film in part to restore the reputation of the native peoples often portrayed negatively in his previous projects, cultures for whom he had great respect.

The 1960s to the Present

Whereas the 1950s saw both the decline of the B-movie Western and the production of some of the best known A-level examples of the genre, the era beginning in the mid- to late 1960s marked a decline in the number of Westerns produced and an increased cynicism and violence in those that were. In altering the conventional pattern of the Western, directors placed an individual stamp on the genre just as it was emerging internationally. As Bernard Dick has pointed out, polarizing attitudes towards the Vietnam War were often played out not in direct filmic representations of the war when it was occurring, but rather in the Western genre. He writes "[T]he western performed a double function: "it became a metaphor for an ugly war as well as a mirror of an America that the civil rights movement had made more sensitive to the portrayal of minorities" (2002, 132). The only major feature film portrayal of the Vietnam War while it was occurring was John Wayne's *The Green Berets* (1968; see **War Film**), which depicted the events in the film in a manner reminiscent of the classic Western plot and conflicts; the mythic West that Wayne, Ford, and others came to represent was thus called into serious question along with the war itself. The violence and cynicism of a demythologized West, then, could not compare to media coverage of the real-life events occurring on the Vietnamese peninsula (Dick 2002, 132–133).

In "Riding Shotgun: The Scattered Formula in Contemporary Western Movies," Jack Nachbar provides a useful method for categorizing the Westerns produced in this era into four types. The first encompassed the standard or classic Western plot easily identifiable to audiences with the traditional conflicts between good and evil, civilization and wilderness, West and East. More contemporary examples include *The Man Who Shot Liberty Valance*; David Miller's *Lonely Are the Brave* (1962); Mark Rydell's *The Cowboys* (1972); Henry Hathaway's *True Grit* (1969), which won Wayne his only Oscar as Best Actor; its follow-up *Rooster Cogburn* (1975), directed by Stuart Hill; and Don Siegel's *The Shootist*. A second type emerges as the "anti-Western," a film that ironically questions and cynically critiques the classic Western. These films look to the past to films such as *The Ox-Bow Incident* and *High Noon* with their emphasis on social drama, casting the West allegorically as it relates to the East. In Martin Ritt's *Hombre* (1967), for example, the director doubts the merits of the traditional Western with its emphasis on helping the community in a story of a man (Paul Newman) reared by Indians and later killed for trying to rescue a woman from cutthroats, who survive the ordeal (Nachbar 1974, 104). As a vehicle for exposing the gulf between the historical West and the fantasy of the history West, anti-Westerns *Soldier Blue* (1970), *Little Big Man* (1971), and others rely on actual historical events for their subject matter.

Whereas the "anti-Western" turns the conventional Western on itself as a means of social critique, the "new Western" discards the formula of that convention altogether to portray a more realistic West without the extremes of good and evil. Two films that fit into this category are Tom Gries's *Will Penny* (1968) and William Fraker's *Monte Walsh* (1970), both of which depict aging cowboy figures and suggest the maturing and decline of the aging Western hero in the genre overall. "Personal" Westerns—which Nachbar defines as films that represent a subjective vision of the Western by a director—resemble "new Westerns" in their emphasis on alternative motivations and themes not previously examined in the Western genre, but they are "constructed around the epic moment and violent-but-honorable hero of the traditional-Western" (1974, 105).

It is in this experimental category that most Westerns have evolved in recent times. Among the most innovative, Sam Peckinpah's *The Wild Bunch* (1969) uses stop-action photography in a story of a gang of aging outlaws whose last botched great bank job forces them to flee to Mexico to prevent capture. The geographic and temporal relocation of the clash between law and order in the chaos of the Mexican revolution in the months leading up to the First World War signals the end of the traditional American West made famous in lore, normally conceived of as the decade between the 1870s and 1880s in the American Southwest. Now, a particular kind of political lawlessness found among dissidents in the Mexican hills suggests that the civilizing forces of Europe and the East have firmly taken hold. Similarly, the gradual demise of the gang of bank robbers marks the end of a particular type of iconic Western figure also prominent in the myth—a swan song Peckinpah also depicted in his first feature, *Ride the High Country* (1962). And the appearance of the machine gun and the automobile alongside the six-shooter and saddle horse announces the disappearance of mythical Western features altogether. *The Wild Bunch*'s seven-minute climactic shootout at the stronghold of a Mexican warlord is certainly the bloodiest and most violent to date of any episode in the Western genre.

American Westerns had always found an international audience, but not until the 1960s did the genre begin showing up in the canon of international filmmakers in ways rivaling American productions, most memorably in Italian director Sergio Leone's "spaghetti Westerns" starring then-TV star Clint Eastwood. The noticeably more violent tone and darker, grittier portrayal of the American West in these films served as a marked contrast to the mythical West of American filmmakers up until the early 1960s. The "Man With No Name" trilogy—*A Fistful of Dollars* (1964), *For a Few Dollars More* (1965), and *The Good, the Bad, and the Ugly* (1966)—cast Eastwood as an enigmatic gunfighter turned bounty hunter. Like John Ford and John Wayne before him, Eastwood made remarkable contributions to revitalizing the genre right until the 1990s, both as star and director. *Hang 'Em High* (1968) finds Eastwood as Jed Cooper, almost hanged for a crime he did not commit and determined to bring the men responsible to justice. In *High Plains Drifter* (1973)—the second film he directed and the first Western—Eastwood returns to his enigmatic portrayal of the Man With No Name as a gunfighter riding into a town hiding a secret and in need of the kind of protection

Sam Peckinpah's *The Wild Bunch* (1969) is often credited with ushering in a new realism and violent explicitness in the American Western. *Photofest.*

he could offer. Directed by Eastwood and with a whistleable musical theme by Jerry Fielding, *The Outlaw Josey Wales* (1976) stars Eastwood as an ex-Confederate bent on revenge who manages to come to life again. *Pale Rider* (1985) pays direct homage to *Shane,* making explicit the Christian overtones only alluded to in the earlier film. Eastwood's greatest acclaim within the motion picture industry came with *Unforgiven* (1992), which became only the third Western in history to win the Oscar for Best Picture (*Cimarron* [1931] and *Dances with Wolves* [1990] were the others). Nominated for Best Actor and winning the Best Directing statuette, the veteran Western performer draws an engaging portrait of a retired outlaw driven by economic necessity and the well-being of his children to kill two men, who deserve it, for the reward. Although released in an era when Westerns had been largely forgotten as viable box office vehicles, the Eastwood film demonstrated the enduring appeal of the genre.

Other Westerns in the contemporary era are worthy of note for a variety of reasons. George Roy Hill's *Butch Cassidy and the Sundance Kid* (1969) took a new and generally humorous look at bank robbers from the Hole-in-the-Wall Gang, garnering four Academy Awards and box office receipts making it the highest-grossing Western up until that point. *McCabe and Mrs. Miller* (1971) offered a frank portrayal of the world's oldest profession from director Robert Altman. John Wayne's notable output in the 1970s—*Rio Lobo* (1970), *The Cowboys* (1972), and *The Shootist* (1976)—harkened back to an earlier era in Western filmmaking.

The story of a dying gunfighter who chooses to leave this world the way he lived eerily paralleled that of Wayne himself, who died of stomach cancer three years after making *The Shootist*, bringing to a close a significant chapter in the Western genre.

The cataclysmic failure of Michael Cimino's disastrously expensive *Heaven's Gate* (1980) contributed to the downturn of the Western genre in the 1980s as interest in adventure stories about the distant Western past sank to an all-time low. Moreover, despite an all-star cast, including Kevin Costner, and a budget of over $30 million, Lawrence Kasdan's *Silverado* (1985), about four men who overcome obstacles and outlaws to bring justice to a town, did nothing to revive interest in the genre. In an effort to lure younger viewers into theaters, directors Christopher Cain and Geoff Murphy showcased a troupe of younger actors (including brothers Charlie Sheen and Emilio Estevez, Kiefer Sutherland, Lou Diamond Phillips, and Dermot Mulroney) and added a rock music score in *Young Guns* (1988) and *Young Guns II* (with a slightly different cast), reworkings of the Billy the Kid story.

Although featured in *Silverado*, Kevin Costner brought respectability and new cultural sensitivity to the Western with his *Dances with Wolves* (1990), for which he was rewarded with an Oscar for Best Picture and Best Director for his debut behind the camera as producer and director. In casting the film, Costner chose actual Native Americans to play roles in this story of a Union Army officer who learns about the ways of the West firsthand, from the first peoples who settled it. The panoramic scope of the cinematography in scenes such as the buffalo hunt and the battle with a hostile tribe pays respects to the trailblazing Western filmmakers of the past, such as Griffith, James Cruze, and Ford. The film uses Lakota Sioux subtitles and views Native Americans sympathetically, winning the endorsement of the Sioux Nation, but not that of all Native groups. Costner would also play the title character in *Wyatt Earp* (1994), retracing the footsteps of Henry Fonda (in Ford's *My Darling Clementine*), Burt Lancaster (in John Sturges's *Gunfight at the OK Corral* [1957]), and Kurt Russell (in George Cosmatos's *Tombstone* [1993]). Sam Raimi's *The Quick and the Dead* (1995) offered a feminist perspective on the Old West in the story of a mysterious gunslinger—this time played by Sharon Stone—who enters a gunfighting competition in a desolate prairie town.

Comic appropriation of traditional Western conventions appeared as early as Westerns became identifiable as a genre. Films such as Fatty Arbuckle's *The Round Up* (1921) and Buster Keaton's *Go West* (1925) spoofed Western settings and characters early on. George Marshall's *Destry Rides Again* offered Marlene Dietrich as a saloon singer—a character lampooned much later in Mel Brooks's *Blazing Saddles* (1974), itself a send-up of Westerns in which a small town is threatened with takeover and destruction. Bob Hope starred in *Paleface* (1948) and its sequel *Son of Paleface* (1952), opposite Jane Russell, bringing comic timing and deadpan delivery to ridiculous tales of the Old West. In an Oscar-winning performance, Lee Marvin co-starred opposite Jane Fonda in the successful *Cat Ballou* (1965), directed by Elliot Silverstein. Burt Kennedy's *Support Your Local*

Sheriff! (1969) offered a comic retelling of a gunfight similar to the events at the OK Corral with James Garner as a reluctant sheriff; the cast returned in *Support Your Local Gunfighter* (1971). Paul Bartel's *Lust in the Dust* (1985) featured a saloon girl with a heart of gold in this parody of a town threatened by outlaws searching for gold. Hugh Wilson's *Rustler's Rhapsody* (1985) turns self-reflexive, as a singing cowboy star finds himself lifted from the black-and-white screen into a town in living color and riddled with every Western cliché. Ron Underwood's *City Slickers* (1991) brought Jack Palance a Best Supporting Actor Oscar almost fifty years after his last and only other Oscar nomination for *Shane*. And big-screen versions of TV shows *Maverick* (1994) and *The Wild, Wild West* (1999) starred Mel Gibson and the pairing of Will Smith and Kevin Kline, respectively.

With the release of Kevin Costner's *Open Range* (2003), it is clear that the genre is among the most enduring, although Costner's saga of four misfit free-spirited range rovers who must resist the extortion of a maniacal cattle baron and a corrupt sheriff advances the genre very little. A far more likely candidate for Western innovation might be Ang Lee's *Brokeback Mountain* (2005), with a screenplay by veteran Western chronicler Larry McMurtry and a story of love between two men on a Wyoming sheep farm in 1963.

Innovative or not, perhaps part of the enduring appeal of the Western is a result of the medium of film itself, with its potential to carry myth through a combination of the visual, the musical, and the ritualistic. As Will Wright has noted, "Although Western novels reach a large and faithful audience, it is through the movies that the myth has become part of the cultural language by which American understands itself" (1977, 12).

References and Further Reading

Biskind, Peter. *Seeing Is Believing: How Hollywood Taught Us to Stop Worrying and Love the Fifties*. New York: Owl Book-Henry Holt, 2000.

Dick, Bernard. *Anatomy of Film*. 4th ed. Boston: Bedford-St. Martin's, 2002.

Dirks, Tim, "High Noon." *The Greatest Films*. 1996-2002. 19 Aug. 2003 www.filmsite.org/high.html.

———. "Red River." *The Greatest Films*. 1996-2003. 26 July 2003 www.filmsite.org/redr.html.

———. "Stagecoach." *The Greatest Films*. 1996-2002. 27 July 2003 www.filmsite.org/stagec.html.

Esselman, Kathryn C. "From Camelot to Monument Valley: Dramatic Origins of the Western Film." In *Focus on the Western*, edited by Jack Nachbar, 9–18. Englewood Cliffs, NJ: Prentice-Hall, Inc., 1974.

Etulain, Richard W. "Cultural Origins of the Western." In *Focus on the Western*, edited by Jack Nachbar, 19–24. Englewood Cliffs, NJ: Prentice-Hall, Inc., 1974.

Fenin, George N. and William K. Everson. *The Western: From Silents to Cinerama*. New York: Orion, 1962.

Garfield, Brian. *Western Films: A Complete Guide*. New York: Rawson Assoc., 1982.

Jojola, Ted. "Absurd Reality II: Hollywood Goes to the Indians." In *Hollywood's Indian: The Portrayal of the Native American in Film*, edited by Peter C. Rollins and John E. O'Connor. Lexington: University of Kentucky Press, 1998.

McBride, Joseph and Michael Wilmington. *John Ford*. New York: Da Capo Press, 1975.

Nachbar, Jack, ed. *Focus on the Western*. Englewood Cliffs, NJ: Prentice-Hall, Inc., 1974.

———. "Riding Shotgun: The Scattered Formula in Contemporary Western Movies." In *Focus on the Western*, edited by Jack Nachbar, 101–112. Englewood Cliffs, NJ: Prentice-Hall, Inc., 1974.

Sarris, Andrew. *"You Ain't Heard Nothing Yet": The American Talking Film History and Memory, 1927–1949*. New York: Oxford University Press, 1998.

Schatz, Thomas. "The Western." In *Hollywood Genres: Formulas, Filmmaking, and the Studio System*, 45–80. Philadelphia: Temple University Press, 1981.

Warshow, Robert. "Movie Chronicle: The Western." In *Film Theory and Criticism: Introductory Readings*, edited by Leo Braudy and Marshall Cohen, 654–657. New York: Oxford University Press, 1999.

Wright, Will. *Sixguns & Society: A Structural Study of the Western*. Berkeley: University of California Press, 1977.

CHAPTER 12

WOMAN'S FILM

BY THE 1930S, MILLIONS OF AMERICANS, many of them women, packed movie theaters weekly to escape the miseries of everyday Depression life. In response to this increasingly untapped market, movie studios began producing films specifically directed toward these women. Although Hollywood had been producing melodramatic, sentimentalized, and sensationalized stories since the beginning of the medium itself, the "woman's film," as these were called, became a permanent fixture and reliable commodity by the 1940s, aided by the sheer number of women going to theaters on the home front during World War II. Not everyone views the isolation of feminine traits and themes in these films in positive terms, however. In her foundational study *From Reverence to Rape: The Treatment of Women in the Movies,* Molly Haskell alludes to a critical controversy surrounding this emerging genre when she writes, "What more damning comment on the relations between men and women in America than the very notion of something called the 'woman's film'? And what more telling sign of critical and sexual priorities than the low cast it has among the highbrows?" (1987, 153).

DEFINING CHARACTERISTICS

A Focus on Women's Concerns

No matter what precise conditions historians, critics, or moviegoers place on definitions of the woman's film, all examples emphasize the female and traditional female concerns, such as emotions, romance and other personal connections, and the home. Haskell's 1973 study of the feminine role in film anticipates the critical difficulties involved in defining the conventions for the domestic melodramas the woman's film typically encompasses and their location in the history of film criticism. *Domestic*, of course, refers to one of the few areas where, traditionally, females could dominate—the home. In eras when traditional women's tasks and domain were not valued in the marketplace as highly as male endeavors, the art forms that supposedly spoke to traditional domestic concerns—such as women's magazine fiction, soap operas, and other melodramatic serials—were treated with the same level of disregard. Literally translated, *melodrama* means "drama with music," suggesting such maudlin emotional devices as the heavy organ music of radio and silent film serials or the freeze-frame photography of television soap operas that heightens emotions. To define the genre, however, film historians would present an unsatisfying picture of the films in this genre by simply combining the terms, for the woman's film presents a much more complex portrait of women's lives and concerns. Similarly, as the classification of the genre implies, the woman's film explores the concerns of being a woman in various environments with a female audience in mind. Such a definition, however, expands the categorization ludicrously to include any depiction of any event involving women. For this reason, not every film focusing on a woman may be called a woman's film without other elements being present.

Sacrifice, Hardship, and Escapism

In helping to define the genre, Molly Haskell places the woman's films into three categories based on the degree and nature of women's sacrifice depicted. Specifically, she divides this spectrum of sacrifice into three categories. Haskell's first category, "extraordinary women," resist victimization. These are characters like Jezebel (*Jezebel* [1938]) and Scarlett O'Hara (*Gone With the Wind* [1939]) and roles played by actresses like Bette Davis and Katharine Hepburn. "Ordinary women," the typical woman's film character type, endure financial deprivation and traditional marital woe, defining themselves negatively and instructing audience members to accept their own limitations rather than rebel. Finally, Haskell identifies a third variation, the "ordinary woman who becomes extraordinary," often depicted by screenwriters and directors with conviction and respect.

In contrast, in *A Woman's View: How Hollywood Spoke to Women: 1930–1960,* Jeanine Basinger places films into this genre according to the film's purpose: (1) to place women at the center of the story; (2) to confirm and reaffirm that a woman's job is to be a woman, kept in her place under the guise of love; and (3) to provide the woman with "visual liberation," no matter how small, or to encourage her to consider, "Is this all life offers?" (1993, 13). Central to her understanding of the traditional woman's film is the contradiction inherent in the films themselves: while they demonstrate ways in which women could rebel and feel liberated on screen, they also instruct women on the acceptable limits of that liberation. As she puts it, "[The woman's film] both held women in social bondage and released them into a dream of potency and freedom. It drew women in with images of what was lacking in their own lives and sent them home reassured that their own lives were the right thing after all" (1993, 6).

Whereas movie studios' marketing provides some insight into the evolution of the woman's film as a genre, at least in its earlier years, the link between the escapism of women's magazine fiction and motion pictures should not be underestimated. Christine Geraghty divides the genre into two categories deriving from women's utopian vision, carried over from woman's romantic fiction. Stories and novels by such authors as Olive Higgins Prouty, Fannie Hurst, and Edna Lee often turned into these important films. The first embodies the traditional narrative of the woman who endures hardships and setbacks. The second combines melodrama and suspense in the saga of the paranoid woman, where the breach between the public/male and domestic/female spheres allows worldly fears and anxieties to invade her home. The woman's voluntary suffering for the man she loves becomes a fragile victory achieved through his recovery (2000, 104).

Sentimental and Romantic Plots

In times of national struggle, the movies have served as an inexpensive distraction from everyday turmoil. The films' rapid circulation in and out of theaters and promotions such as reduced ticket prices, double features, and giveaways of china and other domestic goods made movie-going an even more attractive escape. Little wonder that the woman's film as a genre evolved during the Great Depression and gained preeminence during World War II, when a ready population of women alone at home flocked to movie theaters to get their minds off their men at the front and to commiserate with others. The woman's film varies narratively to address the changing concerns of women during these periods. The era depicted in each individual woman's film and the era during which it was produced, released, and viewed by audiences also explain these narrative variations. The scenario of the woman's film of the 1930s is much different from that of the 1950s, but two basic thematic threads remain intact: sacrifice (for a spouse or a child) and hardship (physical or emotional).

Molly Haskell is a good place to start in categorizing the sometimes diffuse, sometimes repetitious, but always poignant plots that typify the woman's film. She has categorized the various narratives of the woman's film into four basic storylines that often borrow from one another or appear with subtle variations. Following are examples, some of which are cited by Haskell: In the sacrifice film, women sacrifice themselves for the happiness and well-being of their children (*Mildred Pierce* [1945], *Stella Dallas* [1937], *The Old Maid* [1939], and *Imitation of Life* [1934, 1959]); to preserve the status position, or piece of mind of a husband, lover, or married lover (*Back Street* [1932, 1941, and 1961], *Now, Voyager* [1942]); her career for love (*Lady in the Dark* [1944], *June Bride* [1948]); and her love for a career (*Morning Glory* [1933]). An additional form of sacrifice Haskell omits is the woman left alone to manage at home during wartime (*Tender Comrade* [1943], *Since You Went Away* [1944]), a subgenre that overlaps with the war film. In what Haskell calls "the affliction film," a woman keeps her devastating illness or debilitating injury altogether secret from the man she loves or hides how it affects their relationship and future (*Dark Victory* [1939], *Love Affair* [1939]). The "choice" film details the struggles of a woman caught between the love of two men and the decision she must make that will alter all their lives (*Daisy Kenyon* [1947]). Finally, the "competition" plot involves two rivals for the love of a man who resolve their differences with the best interests of the man in mind (*In Name Only* [1939], *The Great Lie* [1941], *When Ladies Meet* [1941]).

Of course, subvariations of each plot exist and films that fall into one category may also deal with other subjects. For example, an often reworked variation of the sacrifice-for-husband-or-lover theme also depicts lovers torn by social responsibility and morality who cannot deny their passion for one another (*If I Were Free* [1933], *Brief Encounter* [1945]). Similarly, while one variation of the woman's film explores her abject sacrifice for love, another variation depicts the tragedy that ensues when the woman, her lover, or both resort to violence or self-destruction as a result of that sacrifice (*Humoresque* [1946], *Deception* [1946]). A subject for the woman's film sometimes overlooked is the biopic, or biography, of a true-life woman dramatized—and often romanticized—for the screen (Florence Nightingale in *The White Angel* [1936], Marie Curie in *Madame Curie* [1943], singer Jane Froman in *With a Song in My Heart* [1952]).

In defining the woman's film, an additional complication occurs when considering the history of women's lives and roles during the twentieth century, specifically the rise of feminism. Although films such as *The Best of Everything* (1959) and *Peyton Place* (1957) began to present social changes affecting women, no precise markers exist to define exactly when motion pictures began to consistently reflect these changes as the norm, not the exception. For this reason, films made to appeal to women may be divided into two or three separate categories: (1) the classic woman's film, appearing from roughly the early 1930s through the early 1960s; (2) the feminist or post-feminist woman's film, depicting the concerns of women making their way outside the traditional domestic sphere; and (3) harkening back to the golden age, the "chick flick," a largely lightweight romantic exploration of such traditional female concerns as love and romance within a world of broader female choices. Although many classic woman's films have recently undergone feminist analysis, core examples of this genre were not intended to question patriarchy in significant ways. Instead, they convinced women of the importance of their traditional roles, however limited, and their drama often existed in women trying to balance social roles with personal concerns.

HISTORY AND INFLUENCES

From the Beginning to 1940

Hollywood has always been known for both melodramatic films and significant films featuring women in prominent roles, such as D. W. Griffith's *Broken Blossoms* (1919), *Way Down East* (1920), and *Orphans of the Storm* (1921) with Lillian Gish, all of which self-consciously veered toward pathos and emotional excess. Greta Garbo became an international star, exuding exotic foreign appeal in films such as *The Torrent* (1926), *The Temptress* (1928), *Flesh and the Devil* (1926), and *Love* (1927), in which she played Tolstoy's Anna Karenina. In addition, when the Academy of Motion Picture Arts and Sciences was formed, the first Academy Award for Best Actress went to Janet Gaynor for her performances in the silent woman's films *Seventh Heaven* (1927), *The Street Angel* (1928), and *Sunrise* (1927).

The narrative frankness and sexual permissiveness that led to adoption of the first motion picture production codes would carry over into the earliest woman's films of the sound era. These early examples were surprisingly frank portrayals of the broad spectrum of roles that women assumed in desperate economic times. Every major female star at every major studio built her career in this emerging genre; some even won major awards in the process. Two stars awarded Oscars for their portrayals of women who violate traditional social norms were Norma Shearer, for *The Divorcee* (1930), and Helen Hayes, for *The Sin of Madelon Claudet* (1932). Starring in films with such provocative titles as *Play-Girl* (1932), *They Call It Sin* (1932), *Midnight Mary*, and *She Had to Say Yes* (1933), Loretta Young became one of the earliest queens of the woman's film genre. Although she would later develop an on-screen persona that ranged from cultured, elegant lady to simple immigrant farm girl, she portrayed a wide variety of suffering females. These down-and-out roles included a woman in love with her roommate's boyfriend, who she must help to beat a murder rap (*Three Girls Lost* [1931]); a working girl who returns to the job when her husband's career falters, straining their marriage (*Week-end Marriage* [1932]); a woman committed to making a squatters'-camp shack into a home, only to find herself pregnant and alone when her lover is shot trying to rob a toy store before he skips town without her (*Man's Castle* [1933]); another unwed mother, who teaches her child to lie, cheat, and steal until she realizes that her schemes put her child in jeopardy (*Born to Be Bad* [1934]); and a student nurse who endures the arduous trials of medical training and finds love on the side (*White Parade* [1934]).

The range of predicaments in which Young's women found themselves may seem too extreme to be believed by contemporary audiences, but the characters she played were rivaled in variety and plausibility by those brought to the screen by Kay Francis, Barbara Stanwyck, and others. Starting work as a contract player at Paramount, Francis was a veteran performer in the earliest woman's films, so much so that her career peaked and fell into decline all within the first few years of the sound eras. Her voluminous output for Paramount and Warner Brothers included a wide variety of roles in films with such titles as *Virtuous Sin* (1930), where she seduces a Russian general to save the life of her scientist husband and ends up working in a brothel for her trouble; *False Madonna* (1931), where she plays a woman who poses as the mother of a blind boy who backs out of a criminal caper when the entire charade hurts too much; *One Way Passage* (1932), where Francis's terminally ill socialite falls in love with William Powell's fugitive convict as he is transported back to San Quentin Prison during her ocean cruise; and *Mary Stevens, M.D.* (1933) and *Dr. Monica* (1934), in which she plays medical doctors—in the first, impregnated by a former medical school classmate married to an heiress, and in the second, married to a man who impregnates her best friend, whose baby (fruit of the adulterous union) she delivers. Despite a career that continued into the 1940s, largely sustained by appearances in B movies, Kay Francis is all but forgotten now, a casualty of changing tastes.

Barbara Stanwyck started her film career at Paramount within a few years of Francis, but their professional destinies took entirely different paths. In films such as *Forbidden* (1932), in which Stanwyck finds herself pregnant by a married politician, and *Baby Face* (1933), in which a woman uses her feminine powers to climb the social ladder, Stanwyck's reputation as consummate professional actress grew. One film in particular seals her fate as seminal performer in the woman's film genre, King Vidor's 1937 version of Olive Higgins Prouty's novel, *Stella Dallas* (1937), opposite perennial lightweight leading man John Boles with Ann Shirley in a supporting role. Stanwyck's skillful performance raises the story above maudlin sentimentality, heightening her depiction of maternal sacrifice to an emotional level almost unbearable for audiences. From the very beginning when archetypical girl-from-the-wrong-side-of-the-tracks Stella Martin and suave Stephen Dallas enter into a whirlwind romance and marriage, class differences get in the way. No woman's film on this theme would be complete without attempts to bridge differences through the birth of a child. However, the couple's divergent priorities emerge as he longs for home nights with their child and she longs for the nightlife. Eventually, the couple separates after Stephen takes a job in New York. Despite his absence, daughter Laurel takes after the good taste and breeding of her father. The mother-daughter bond grows strong, however, borne of Stella's well meaning but often skewed understanding of her child's best interests. Stella's heartbreaking recognition that her own excess and ostentation embarrass her daughter leads to the ultimate mother's sacrifice: Stella agrees to grant Stephen a divorce so he can marry the more tasteful Helen Morrison and people will think this refined lady is Laurel's mother, "Mrs. Dallas." "In a little while, she'll forget all about me," Stella utters haltingly at this point in the film. "It won't be anytime 'til she'll love you just like her real mother."

Stella Dallas forces viewers to wonder whether Stella should be condemned for her social errors or whether society is to blame for its failure to acknowledge what's really important, her devotion to her daughter. The final, and what should be the deciding, scene in the film makes for great catharsis in melodramatic fashion, but provides few answers. The camera centers on Laurel in her wedding finery looking out into the dark night as if in search of her absent mother. This scene is what all of Stella's sacrifices have been for. A reverse shot from the outside finds a rain-drenched Stella silhouetted against a window watching daughter Laurel walk down the aisle. Shooed away by a police officer for loitering, a seemingly triumphant Stanwyck, smiling through tears, quickens her pace as she walks toward the camera and out of the frame.

John Stahl's 1934 version of Fannie Hurst's novel *Imitation of Life* presents a similar story of woe, this time with race a factor in this story of two mothers, one white and one black, who must sacrifice for the well-being of their children. (The film would be remade under the direction of classic melodrama director Douglas Sirk.) Widow Bea Pullman (Claudette Colbert) has a spare room but no money to pay a domestic servant; Delilah Johnson (Louise Beavers) and her daughter need a roof over their heads. The two combine households. Over the years, both have endured their share of domestic sacrifice—Delilah, in marriage to a man who fought against the limitations of his skin and a daughter following in his footsteps; Bea, in marriage to an older man she did not love. Bea becomes the successful marketer of Delilah's pancake flour. She still denies herself love, although she has begun seeing ichthyologist Stephen Archer (Warren Williams), now that daughter Jessie (Rochelle Hudson) is away at school. Delilah's daughter Peola (Fredi Washington) struggles to reconcile the white face she sees in the mirror with her forced identity as a black woman. When Peola leaves her mother and their background for good, Delilah knows "I lost my baby. She won't ever come back."

Stahl's film is remarkably poignant in its exploration of a subject controversial at the time—racial identity—but less so in its conventional rendering of the white mother's sacrifice. Peola's leaving wears on Delilah, eventually killing her and forcing Bea to a decision of her own. Having vowed to allow nothing to come between her daughter and herself, Bea sacrifices plans to marry Stephen once she realizes her daughter's feelings for him and pulls out of a deal to sell managing interest in the pancake flour company. At Delilah's funeral—the grandeur of which the black mother worked her entire life to guarantee—Peola emerges from the crowd to throw herself on her mother's coffin wracked with guilt and remorse: "She worked for me . . . always thinking of me first, never herself." In the last scene, with Peola back in school, Bea and Jessie reconcile, with a flashing advertisement of Delilah's smiling face sanctioning the reunion from above. If split into two separate films, both would be successful in the woman's film genre, but the black version would be by far the most compelling.

The 1940s

Sacrifice took on new meaning as the woman's film evolved into the 1940s and wartime. The history of the genre in the 1940s begins with Ginger Roger's surprise Oscar for Best Actress in *Kitty Foyle*, the story of a romance between a lower-class woman and upper-class man. By the early 1940s, Kay Francis had performed the best of the roles of her career, but Loretta Young would continue to enjoy a rich and varied career, winning the Best Actress Oscar in 1948 for her role in *The Farmer's Daughter*, where she played a Swedish farm girl who propels her duties as a congressman's housekeeper into a seat in Congress. Stanwyck capitalized on the film noir trend in *Double Indemnity* (1944), *The Strange Love of Martha Ivers* (1946), *Sorry, Wrong Number* (1948), and *Clash by Night* (1952) (see **Film Noir**), but she continued to make woman's films throughout the 1940s and 1950s, including *My Reputation* (1946), the story of a lonely widow who incites gossip as a result of time spent with a military man; *The Other Love* (1947), about a terminally ill concert pianist who sacrifices her remaining energies to the high life despite her attraction to the doctor who warns against it; *All I Desire* (1953), playing a woman in 1910 who abandons her family to go on the stage; and *There's Always Tomorrow* (1956), directed by Douglas Sirk, where Stanwyck's character is an old flame who threatens to break up the home of a successful toy manufacturer.

For a cross section of 1940s woman's films not involving World War II, viewers need look no further than the work of actresses Bette Davis and Joan Crawford, who competed for many of the same roles at Warner Brothers studios throughout most of the 1940s. Starting her career playing the second woman to female stars she would transcend in roles ranging from gun molls to secretaries to the girlfriends of more established male stars, Davis's second Best Actress Oscar, for *Jezebel*, secured her status as Warners' most critically acclaimed and successful actresses to date. *Jezebel* is the story of a headstrong Southern belle who alienates the only man she ever loved (Henry Fonda) when she wears a red dress to a ball where unmarried women wear white. To redeem herself for a series of misdeeds, she accompanies her now-married lover, stricken with yellow fever, into quarantine on a deserted island off New Orleans. The original star of the stage version of *Jezebel*, Miriam Hopkins, would be Davis's costar in two other woman's films, *The Old Maid* (1939), where Davis plays an unwed mother who watches her child grow up thinking Hopkins is the child's real mother, and *Old Acquaintance* (1943), with Davis and Hopkins playing childhood "friends" and rival authors who become entwined in marital breakup and romantic sacrifice over the ten-year span of the film.

Before the release of *Gone With the Wind*, starring Vivien Leigh in the lead role (see **Epic**), Davis was thought to be a shoo-in for a third Oscar for her performance as a twenty-three-year-old heiress dying from a brain tumor in *Dark Victory* (1939). After her doctor (George Brent) risks his scientific objectivity by operating on the woman he loves, the pathology report returns with ominous news that a "glioma" will return to kill the patient within ten months. Mercifully, only a few noticeable hours of interrupted vision will mark the onset of death. Best friend Anne (Geraldine Fitzgerald) and the doctor conspire to keep the news from the patient, but Judith learns the truth by mistake. Her brief, happy months of marriage end when, as her eyesight fails, Judith manages to fool her husband into believing nothing is wrong, a ruse only possible in a woman's film. Dying with his assurance that she's been a good wife, she urges her husband to consider the good life they've created. "What we have can't be destroyed," she assures him. "That's our victory, our victory over the dark." The camera freezes on Davis lying prone on her marriage bed. She sends everyone away, dying the way she lived—independently—and then goes out of focus to simulate her waning life.

Whereas *Dark Victory* makes a significant contribution to the woman's film genre, Davis's tour de force performance and skillful directing by Irving Rapper in *Now, Voyager* (1942) provide the quintessential woman's film experience. Davis plays Charlotte Vale, a prematurely aging, troubled woman under the domination of a shrewish mother (Gladys Cooper, in her Oscar-nominated

The sharing of cigarettes takes on erotic significance in Irving Rapper's *Now, Voyager* (1942), starring Bette Davis and Paul Henreid. *Photofest.*

role), first glimpsed as the camera pans from her sensible black shoes upward to the top of her hair, tortured into a bun. Charlotte's successful treatment by eminent psychiatrist Dr. Jacquith (Claude Rains) finds her the mystery woman on a South American cruise, emerging from her cabin in one of the most memorable scenes in woman's film history. The camera focuses on a woman's foot in stylish two-tone spectator pumps as she takes a step down the gangplank. The camera scans up the slim torso of this fashionably dressed woman, her head partially hidden by the brim of a hat. Slowly, the new and improved Charlotte tilts her head upward and the emergence of the butterfly—a motif in the film—is complete.

Charlotte soon falls in love with the unhappily married J.D. "Jerry" Durrance (Paul Henreid), but after an unforgettable night of love, the two agree they must part. Charlotte returns to Boston unafraid of her mother's threats, signifying the completeness of her transformation. Later, a retreat to Dr. Jacquith's sanitarium after her mother's death brings her in contact with Jerry's emotionally troubled daughter, Tina, an example of a contrivance often found in woman's films. In caring for Tina, Charlotte soothes her own emotional wounds and the child flourishes as a result, but Jerry cannot accept more sacrifice and kindness from Charlotte. As if speaking for all heroines of her kind, Charlotte implores him: "You *will* be giving. Don't you know that 'to take' is a way 'to give' sometimes—the most beautiful way in the world if two people love each other." In a memorable gesture suggesting sexual comingling, Jerry lights two cigarettes and hands her one. The scene ends on a note of self-sacrifice many women may be unable to accept, but would understand. Jerry murmurs, "And will you be happy, Charlotte? Will it be enough?" She replies, "Oh, don't let's ask for the moon! We have the stars." The camera pans through the window to rest on the moon and stars above, a perfectly fitting ending to this reworking of a sort of fairytale that only the movies could make plausible.

Davis enjoyed a long career, and her films meant to appeal specifically to women endure best. Besides *Dark Victory* and *Now, Voyager,* other worthy examples include *All This, and Heaven Too* (1940), where Davis plays a governess accused of falling in love with her employer and murdering his wife; *Mr. Skeffington* (1944), with Davis as the once fabulously beautiful, but soon hideously scarred Fannie Trellis; *A Stolen Life* (1946), casting Davis as a retiring twin who assumes the life of her more vivacious sister when the other mysteriously dies; *Deception* (1946), placing music teacher Davis between the man she gave up for dead and the conductor and composer who has been her benefactor; and *Winter Meeting* (1948), showcasing Davis as an emotionally closed poet burdened by family guilt who falls in love with a much younger naval hero. Aside from *All About Eve* (1950) and roles in other minor films, Davis's feature film career basically dwindled to low-budget clones of one of her most enduring successes, *What Ever Happened to Baby Jane?* (1962).

The later career of her rival, Joan Crawford, suffered much the same fate. Few actresses had worked as hard at being a star as Crawford, who remade herself from Jazz Age flapper into a 1940s and 1950s woman of maturing sophistication and vulnerability, with years playing bored society girls and cultivating the shop girl-who-makes-good image sandwiched in between. As much as Davis's, Crawford's career could be a living chronicle of the evolution of the woman's film. In *Our Blushing Brides* (1930), for example, Crawford is the only one of a trio of shop girls to marry the man she loves. Crawford's Ivy Stevens, a small-town coffee shop entertainer, becomes one of the "laughing sinners" in the film of the same name (1931) once she abandons her love for a traveling salesman and is redeemed by a Salvation Army officer (played by Clark Gable in an early role). In *I Live My Life* (1935), Crawford's bored society-girl ways nearly end up destroying her chances for happiness with a young archeologist who initially misunderstands her intentions. The 1938 feature *Mannequin* casts Crawford in the perennial role of working girl who marries her small-town sweetheart and ends up catching the eye of a shipping magnate (played by Spencer Tracy).

When the type of character Crawford perfected went out of style, she crusaded for the role of the gold-digging shop girl Crystal Allen in *The Women* (1939), opposite society matron Norma Shearer in her last important role. Director George Cukor—known as a "woman's director" for his prowess in shaping female performances and soothing the female artistic temperament in films such as *Little Women* (1933), *Camille* (1936), and *A Woman's Life* (1941)—assembled an all-female cast, including Rosalind Russell, Paulette Goddard, Marjorie Main, and Joan Fontaine (see **Comedy**). *The Women* combines elements of the woman's film (the story chronicles the breakup of a marriage and a family) and drawing room comedy/farce, as a group of friends in upper-middle-class New York dig to "get the dirt" on one another. The inclusion of a fashion show, the only sequence in color, can only be explained as an appeal to female consumers, given the influence of studio designers on American fashion.

After calling MGM home for eighteen years, Crawford left the studio for Warner Brothers where, after a two-year absence from the screen, she earned an Oscar for Best Actress for her role in her first Warner project, *Mildred Pierce,* based on a James M. Cain novella. The use of flashback, voice-over narration, creative black-and-white cinematography, and a prevailing mood of cynicism and alienation place the film squarely within film noir, although narratively the film is pure domestic melodrama. Mildred Pierce (Crawford) bakes and sells pies and cakes to afford for her children the niceties *she* never had. Her single-minded devotion to spoiling oldest daughter Veda (Ann Blyth) causes a rift that leads to the Pierces' divorce. Determined to survive on her own and to meet Veda's ever-increasing demands, Mildred opens a restaurant with the help of a family friend (Jack Carson) who secures a sweet real estate deal with the owner of the site, suave Monty Beragon (Zachary Scott). As the single restaurant grows into a chain, Mildred bribes Monte to break off his evolving relationship with the now-adult Veda, whose amoral and petty ways drive her from her mother's life. Mildred eventually finds Veda working in a gin joint. Mother and daughter are reunited after Mildred marries Monty upon his condition of receiving a one-third interest in her expanding empire. On the eve of losing her business as a result of Monty's chicanery, Mildred learns of his and Veda's rekindled relationship and confronts them, to no avail. Fleeing the scene, Mildred hears a shot ring out, and all their lives change forever.

Crawford went on to make several other woman's films before her career dissolved into low-budget, campy horror films. In *Humoresque* (1945), she plays a dilettante who sponsors and manipulates the career and love life of a violinist, played by John Garfield. In *Daisy Kenyon* (1947), Crawford in the title role is a commercial artist torn between two loves, a married man with whom she has had a clandestine affair and a stalwart gentleman whose love she cannot return. The potboiler *Flamingo Road* (1949) casts Crawford as a carnival singer whose marriage to a political party boss shakes up the political structure of a small Florida town. In the sensationally titled *The Damned Don't Cry* (1950), Crawford metamorphoses from dowdy, fed-up housewife of humble beginnings to mysterious socialite at the center of a crime syndicate. She plays a similar role in *This Woman Is Dangerous* two years later. As Harriet Craig, in the film of the same name (1950), Crawford's maniacal housekeeping leaves her alone in the house she so obsessively controlled. Her role as a lonely older woman married to a mentally unstable younger man (Cliff Robertson) in *Autumn Leaves* (1956) remains her most identifiable performance in a classic woman's film in the 1950s.

Although Crawford and Davis would each make a film set during World War II—*Reunion in France* (1942) and *Watch on the Rhine* (1943), respectively—

neither one particularly memorializes the home-front sacrifices American women endured during World War II. That mission would be better addressed by the Hollywood studios that pumped out some highly fictionalized cinematic accounts of major military campaigns and A-level features depicting the ordeal of the everyday woman adjusting to war work, rationing, and the absence of the men in her life (see **War Film**). These "home-front melodramas," such as *Mrs. Miniver* (1942) and David O. Selznick's *Since You Went Away* (1944), clearly intend to bolster public sentiment for the sacrifices World War II would require of civilian women. In addition, they demonstrate the importance of strong family connections and community spirit and forecast post-war social changes.

William Wyler's *Mrs. Miniver* was one of the most critically acclaimed and most popular war-related films of the 1940s, winning multiple Academy Awards, including Best Picture. The solid life of the upper-middle-class Britons Kay (Greer Garson), Clem (Walter Pidgeon), and son Vin Miniver (Richard Ney) reveals what is at risk if England succumbs to the Third Reich. The local community is home to a cross section of English character types—a curmudgeonly aging aristocrat, Lady Beldon, who finds progress difficult to accept (Dame May Witty); her granddaughter Carol (Teresa Wright); a kindly stationmaster and bell-ringer with a penchant for tending roses (Henry Travers); and a wise, taciturn vicar (Henry Wilcoxon). Although the war comes to this bucolic corner of England in the form of nightly air raids, the annual Beldon flower show establishes a sense of village normalcy until it, too, is cut short by air raid warnings. The next morning, the community gathers in the village church, severely damaged by an overnight air raid, and the vicar reminds the congregation (and moviegoers) of the sacrifices necessary to win the war—sacrifices that hit close to home for the Minivers. In the final scene, the camera pans up through the hole in the ceiling as Royal Air Force fighters fly in formation overhead and "The Land of Hope and Glory" thunders in the background, affirming the film's message of endurance and hope.

What *Mrs. Miniver* revealed about the virtues of British sacrifice more sentimentally, David O. Selznick's *Since You Went Away* examined more ominously for Americans in 1944. The opening sequence establishes the theme of home-front anxiety and sacrifice, with the camera panning through the Hilton home, littered with family memorabilia. The family bulldog watches through a window as Anne Hilton (Claudette Colbert) returns from seeing her soldier-husband off to the war. The film chronicles life without him as the family of three women—Anne and daughters Jane (Jennifer Jones) and Bridget (Shirley Temple)—struggle to survive on allotment checks and rationing. To supplement their income, they take in a boarder (Monty Woolley) whose grandson Bill (Robert Walker) ships out to war himself after he has fallen in love with Jane. Temptation presents itself in the person of an old family friend (Joseph Cotton) who carries a flame for Anne, although her fidelity to her husband remains constant even when he is classified as missing in action. Virtuous Anne poses a marked contrast to one of her acquaintances, the socialite divorcée Emily Hawkins (Agnes Moorhead), whose hoarding Anne finds reprehensible.

Three episodes in the film deserve praise for their dramatic and foreboding effect. Divorcée Emily, in an ostensible attempt to support the troops, organizes a dance at a fictional hangar "for those poor boys who are going off to die." Here the budding romance of Jane and Bill begins, against the backdrop of frenetic jitterbugging on the dance floor. Couples are silhouetted on the dance floor by search lights on either side of the hangar as the camera pulls back to a long shot of the hangar's vaulted ceiling supported by two massive wings, a five-pointed star suspended below. Lighting is similarly used to suggest alienation and loneliness at the train station when Jane declares her love for Bill as his train departs. She runs along with the train, keeping him in sight as long as she can, but ending up alone on the platform, casting an elongated shadow created by the dramatic backlighting. Finally, to emphasize both a mother's sacrifice and the nobility of American virtues, Anne's shipyard coworker (Alla Nazimova) tells of the death of her child at the hands of the Nazis. With the two women at a lunch counter and framed against a circular window through which streams of war workers are seen emerging from the plant, Anne's friend describes poignantly the significance to her of the Statue of Liberty and its inscription. "You are what I thought America was," she tells Anne, who listens intently. The final episode of the film strikes an anticlimatic note. At Christmas, with Anne now resigned to living with the unknowns of her husband's fate and what the future will hold, the phone rings, with news that he is safe and coming home. The film ends just as it began, with a simple message about faith and hope.

Other war-related woman's films fall into the typical home-front subgenre, some tangentially through flashbacks to earlier wars, others depicting the lives of women on the battlefront or in other ways actively involved in the war. *Tender Comrade* (1943) offered RKO Studios a substantial wartime profit in a film about a group of women living under one roof, sharing household and emotional burdens while the war wages abroad. Ginger Rogers heads the cast as Jo, an aircraft worker whose voice narrates the events in each woman's life, in particular the story of her courtship and concerns for her husband Chris (Robert Ryan), who eventually dies in battle, leaving her alone with an infant son. In her only purely dramatic role, Judy Garland as office worker Alice in *The Clock* (1945) meets Robert Walker's Sergeant Joe Allen in New York. The two see the sights together, fall in love, and decide to marry during his two-day furlough. In *Waterloo Bridge* (1940), Roy Cronin (Robert Taylor) crosses London's Waterloo Bridge on the eve of World War II, remembering poignantly where he met the love of his life, beautiful ballerina Myra (Vivien Leigh) and what led to her death during the last war. Similarly, in MGM's *The White Cliffs of Dover* (1944) American Susan Dunn (Irene Dunne) loses her husband in the trenches of World War I, but soldiers on through the years rearing their son, who eventually volunteers for service in World War II. Finally, the milieu of World War II London becomes the frame through which the events of the interwar years are narrated in *To Each His Own* (1946). Middle-aged Jody Norris (Olivia de Havilland in an Oscar-winning role) tells of the circumstances that initially brought her to wartime London. With her scheme to adopt her own illegitimate son falling through, Jody throws herself into life as a cosmetics mogul. A wily English lord (Roland Culver) eventually helps Jody's son learn the truth of his parentage.

Although many wartime melodramas provide sentimental depictions of wives, mothers, daughters, and sweethearts enduring on the home front, some films actually depict the experiences of women themselves in combat or combat-related activities. In *So Proudly We Hail!* (1943), nurses Claudette Colbert, Paulette Goddard, and Veronica Lake recount their adventures during the fall of the Philippines just after the attack on Pearl Harbor. As island after island falls to the enemy, the living and nursing conditions and the fighting worsen with successive evacuations. Opportunities for romance become as treacherous and short-lived as fighting the enemy. Examining a variation of the same plot and locale, *Cry "Havoc"* (1943) depicts battle-hardened nurses in Bataan who are joined by unlikely reinforcements from several walks and classes of civilian life.

When World War II ended and veterans returned to their civilian roles, women also returned home in droves, voluntarily or through subtle pressure. These conditions proved ideal for the continuation of the woman's film, with conventional stories of romantic conflict, domestic anxiety, and maternal and filial sacrifice, and sometimes with the harder-edged, grittier, more psychologically influenced, postwar impulse characteristic of film noir (see **Film Noir**). Although not exclusive to film noir or any other film genre, voice-over and flashback are two techniques that proved useful in these grittier woman's films. *Letter from an Unknown Woman* (1948), directed by Max Ophüls, is a case in point. Here, concert pianist Stefan Brand (Louis Jourdan) rushes away from turn-of-the-century Vienna with a letter in his hands from a dying woman (Joan Fontaine) he cannot remember. Flashbacks and voice-over reveal her lifelong passion for him that culminated in the birth of his child. Ophüls would work in Hollywood for a short ten years and largely build his American reputation on crime dramas and films noir. *Letter from an Unknown Woman* is often cited as among the best of women's films for the director's careful telling of a melodramatic plot without losing the story to fatal sentimentality, for his attention to detail and camera angle, and for the careful performances of both Jourdan and Fontaine. Listed with George Cukor, Vincente Minelli, Mitchell Leisen, Irving Rapper, William Wyler, John M. Stahl, and Douglas Sirk as select directors able to present melodramatic plots with nuance, Ophüls's reputation as a woman's film director rests largely on *Letter*, and is enhanced by *The Reckless Moment* (1949), a study of murder, maternal sacrifice, and unforeseen love.

Other notable examples of the use of voice-over and flashback in the woman's film in this period include Joseph Mankiewicz's *A Letter to Three Wives* (1949) and David Lean's *Brief Encounter* (1946). Actress Celeste Holm provides the voice-over for Addie Ross, the catalyst in Mankiewicz's day-in-the-life story of three women (Jeanne Craine, Linda Darnel, and Ann Sothern) who receive a collective letter from Holm's character notifying them that she has run off with one of their husbands. Examining a related theme of marital restlessness and infidelity, David Lean's *Brief Encounter* opens in a train station when middle-aged doctor Alex Harvey (Trevor Howard) and housewife Laura Jesson (Celia

Johnson) exchange polite, restrained good-byes, marking the end of their extramarital life-giving romance—unconsummated, it would seem. Photographed in inky black voids and through icy gray steam and smoke, the arriving and departing trains symbolize the routine of both characters' lives and the passing of each "briefly" through the existence of the other. Rather than with grand passionate gestures, audiences perceive the relationship's meaning and intensity through glances, voices, and small gestures of each character. Passages from Rachmaninoff's undulating and lyrical Second Piano Concerto waft and then take over as the dominant musical motif of the opening credits, establishing a mood of melancholy and poignancy. At other times throughout the film, the melody permeates and then brings to a close Laura's particularly evocative monologues about her home and family and her "brief encounters" with Alec.

The 1950s

The decade of the 1950s saw its share of melodramas and biopics, with the production of woman's films meriting bigger budgets, more big-name stars, higher production values, more exotic settings, and vivid color—all in attempts to rival the competition offered by television. Lana Turner, Susan Hayward, Jennifer Jones, and Jane Wyman, among others, joined woman's film perennials Bette Davis and Joan Crawford as the stars of these upscale vehicles. For example, Katharine Hepburn's wide-ranging appeal is showcased nicely in David Lean's *Summertime* (1955), a story about a middle-aged, self-sufficient spinster from Akron, Ohio, who unexpectedly falls in love with a married man while on a once-in-a-lifetime vacation in Venice, Italy. Set in the similarly exotic location of Hong Kong, *Love Is a Many-Splendored Thing* (1955) chronicles the story of a Eurasian doctor (Jennifer Jones) who falls in love with an American reporter (William Holden) during the Korean War. Mounting pressures from friends and family cause conflict in the relationship. A score by Alfred Newman and Sammy Fain (with Oscar-winning song by Sammy Fain and lyricist Paul Francis Webster) add to the pathos of this story of doomed love.

Susan Hayward's performances in biopics would eventually result in an Oscar for *I Want to Live!* (1958), the real-life story of convicted murderer and party girl Barbara Graham, who was scapegoated, according to the film, for a murder she did not commit. The last fifteen minutes of the film are a harrowing emotional roller coaster ride as Graham's on-again, off-again sentence of execution is finally carried out in San Quentin's gas chamber. Earlier in the decade, Hayward played song plugger Jane Froman (whose records she lip-synched) in *With a Song in My Heart* (1952). Froman answers the USO call to entertain troops, but her plane crashes off Lisbon, leaving plucky Froman crippled, but soldiering through. Hayward returned to the musical arena in *I'll Cry Tomorrow* (1955), portraying yet another actual person, entertainer Lillian Roth, whose descent into alcoholism began after the death of her childhood sweetheart. Although a talented Broadway and film star by age twenty, Roth struggled through two failed marriages and a suicide attempt during the next sixteen years of steady drinking. With the help of a sympathetic Alcoholics Anonymous sponsor (Eddie Albert), Roth fought her way back.

As several of these films from the 1950s and since demonstrate, America in this era was preoccupied with family relationships and the violation of social mores. At the same time, films were pushing the limits of the production codes, bringing increasingly provocative material to the screen in films intended to appeal to women. Nowhere was this break with the past more apparent than in films that dealt with the woman of questionable moral virtue, living on the margins of social order. Susan Hayward, for example, starred as "the other woman" in the third and final version of *Back Street* (1961), an updated adaptation of Fannie Hurst's 1930 novel. The Hayward version finds Rae Smith as a fashion designer who falls in love with married man John Saxon (John Gavin). The trouble is, his alcoholic wife (Vera Miles) will not grant him a divorce. In what seems like an implausible choice, even by 1960s standards, Rae remains faithful to him on a "back street" in his life even as she achieves success in her own career. A related film with a harder and less "sudsy" edge is *BUtterfield 8* (1960), for which Elizabeth Taylor won a Best Actress Oscar for her portrayal of call girl and model Gloria Wandrous. Gloria's dates with Weston Liggott (Laurence Harvey), a poor boy who rises in the world to marry into a blue-blooded family, turn into something more than the dalliances for which she is well known. The often-misspelled title refers to the answering service and telephone exchange where Gloria receives her messages, often a harbinger of the loneliness and alienation in her life. In true melodramatic fashion, events turn tragic as Gloria and Weston find themselves on a collision course with destiny. Moreover, Constance McKenzie, Lana Turner's character in *Peyton Place* (1957), lives in strict adherence to a rigid façade of middle-class respectability, compensating for past sins but alienating her daughter in the process. The story became popular because of the social class strife, suppressed desires, and small-town secrets—something clearly unsavory—that were lurking beneath the surface of 1950s America. The film would spawn a sequel, *Return to Peyton Place* (1961), and an early 1960s television series starring Dorothy Malone in the Turner role.

However, films like the aforementioned did more than merely depict the lives of women living outside the mainstream in this era. As Thomas Schatz points out, whereas the 1950s' melodramas provided emotional outlets for women in suburbia, they also reveal themselves as some of the most "socially self-conscious" and "covertly 'anti-American'" films produced by mainstream Hollywood studios (1981, 224–225). Varied critical opinion, some appearing as early as the release of his last Hollywood feature of director Douglas Sirk, consider his films to be among the most stylistic and the most scathing critiques of dominant middle-class values in this period. Sirk's earliest American films were formulaic potboilers, but when he turned to lush, richly photographed melodramas in the 1950s, he established himself as a stylist and profitable filmmaker. Urbane, accomplished, and aesthetically aware, Sirk raises style above subject matter. He highlights the artificiality of melodrama through lighting, uses contrasting images for thematic purposes, and applies color to enhance theme. As a director under studio contract, Sirk filmed whatever material he was assigned, no matter how far it stretched the realm of plausibility. In the process, he adapted studio resources into a small stock company of performers and technicians, and achieved a style duplicable from film to film as a result.

One of his first "stock company" ventures—a remake of John M. Stahl's 1935 "weepie," *Magnificent Obsession* (1954)—struck gold. Rock Hudson had been languishing for five years in nondescript roles before being cast opposite Jane Wyman in this soap opera about a ne'er do-well playboy, Bob Merrick (Hudson). When Merrick's speedboat crashes, the only resuscitating equipment in the vicinity is rushed to the accident. Meanwhile, a beloved doctor and humanitarian suffers a heart attack. Without access to a resuscitator, he dies. When Merrick discovers what his foolishness has caused, he attempts to make amends by following the doctor's example of generosity and compassion. He blends expiation of his sins with falling in love with the doctor's widow, Helen (Wyman), whose eyesight he eventually saves. Despite its maudlin sentimentality, the film earned $8 million and ranked seventh among all Hollywood releases in 1954. To capitalize on the success of the Wyman-Hudson pairing, Sirk again cast them opposite one another in *All that Heaven Allows* (1956), shot in vivid but saturated hues to suggest the fairy-tale world of comfortable middle-class existence in New England. The progression of the seasons from June to December serves as the colorful backdrop for the May-December romance of the two characters, widow Cary Scott (Wyman), settling into comfortable middle age, and nurseryman and nature enthusiast Ron Kirby (Hudson). With the responsibilities of childrearing out of the way, Cary expects to be satisfied for the rest of her life, watching the world go by through the frame of her window or the television screen—framing devices Sirk uses throughout the film to suggest both narrowed perspective and altered vision. Class expectations would have her settled down with faithful family friend Harvey (Conrad Nagel), but Cary knows something is missing under the surface. Ron's tumble off a snow-covered outcropping eventually brings her to her senses: she has been allowing others to make her decisions. She rushes to his bedside with the news that she's ready to join his world and "come home." Outside, a lone deer framed by a large window symbolizes the resolution of their differences and the approval of nature.

Sirk cinched his reputation at Universal-International as a successful house director with *Imitation of Life* (1959), both his last American film and his biggest moneymaker for the studio. Ranking fourth out of all Hollywood releases for 1959, the film was the highest-grossing feature to date for the studio. In this reworking of the 1933 Fannie Hurst novel, Lora Meredith (Lana Turner) is a single parent and actress entering the profession late, who shares a sparse apartment with Annie Johnson (Juanita Moore) and her daughter, Sarah Jane. Lora's career eventually takes off, to the detriment of her daughter Susie's upbringing and putting at risk a romantic relationship with photographer Steven Archer (John Gavin). She has her pick of stage and film roles. "Below stairs," roommate Annie has faithfully remained by "Miss Lora's" side, while Annie's daughter Sarah Jane (played as an adult by Susan Kohner) has grown angrier at the second-class status to which she is relegated by race. Sirk repeats the poignant scene from the 1934 original when Annie delivers Sarah Jane's boots to her school only to have the child hide from her mother to avoid being recognized as black. That episode, along with one involving Sarah Jane's preference for a white doll of Susie's, foreshadows the turmoil of the growing child. "I want to have a chance in life. I don't want to have to come through back doors or feel lower than other people," the adult Sarah Jane utters. "She can't help her color, but I can." As a young woman, her efforts to "pass" have grown more adventurous until one episode with a boy (Troy Donahue) who claims to love her ends in violence. Eventually, Sarah Jane breaks from her racial identity by running, and Annie makes the ultimate maternal sacrifice by leaving her daughter alone.

Lora has her own problems with daughter Susie, played as a young woman by perennial ingénue Sandra Dee. With photographer Steven Archer back in the picture, Lora still chooses acting roles over rekindling her prior relationship with him. When Steve agrees to look after Lora's daughter while her mother makes a film in Italy, the daughter mistakes his attentions for romance. Meanwhile, hard work and the rejection of her by Sarah Jane take a physical toll on Annie, who finds solace in planning her own funeral. Self-absorbed to the end, Lora realizes at Annie's deathbed that Annie's life encompassed far more than the confines of Lora's kitchen. At Annie's funeral, with the rousing voice of Mahalia Jackson wailing the soulful "Trouble of the World" in the background, Sarah Jane bursts from the crowd of mourners and hurls herself on her mother's casket, sobbing with remorse over what she put her mother through. The prophecy of the song Nat King Cole croons over the opening crystal-strewn credits ("What is love, without the giving/Without love, you're only living an imitation, an imitation of life") comes true. The formula of maternal error and maternal sacrifice, combined with beautiful production values and melodramatic acting, proved successful once again, with Susan Kohner and newcomer Juanita Moore earning Oscar nominations for Best Supporting Actress.

If one film in this era rivaled *Imitation of Life* for its sentimentality, it may be Leo McCarey's story of love with fate intervening, *An Affair to Remember* (1957), which closely follows McCarey's 1939 version, *Love Affair,* with Irene Dunne and Charles Boyer. When Nickie Ferrante (Cary Grant) and Terry McKay (Deborah Kerr) meet on a cruise, both seem ready to change their lives. Nickie's love of the finer things without the resources to purchase them links him with amiable but often tedious wealthy women, and former nightclub singer Terry finds her relationship as the companion of a wealthy man pleasant and convenient, compared to having to make her own living. What both lack, however, is passion—until they meet one another aboard ship and fall in love. Willing to sacrifice whatever is necessary to be together, they agree to meet in exactly six months on the observation deck of the Empire State Building.

Terry and Nickie would realize the claim of Lysander, from Shakespeare's *A Midsummer Night's Dream:* "the course of true love never did run smooth." Fate intervenes and Terry is hit by a car on her way to their rendezvous, her attention on the impressive edifice where her beloved waits—"the nearest thing to heaven" because Nickie is there. Nickie waits for hours high above Manhattan, unaware that his beloved has been rushed to the hospital, calling for him in delirium. Only by chance six months later does he discover that Terry was crippled in the accident, but had intended to meet him all along. The plot would receive another makeover in 1994 under the original title, with soon-to-be real-life lovers Warren Beatty and Annette Bening in the lead parts. Nora Ephron's *Sleepless in Seattle* (1993) pays homage to the 1957 version, particularly in the device of the New Year's Eve assignation at the top of the Empire State Building.

The 1960s and 1970s

As women's roles changed with the rise of feminism in the 1960s, the days of the classic woman's film depicting redeeming female sacrifice and suffering were numbered. An example of how women's roles had already begun shifting is seen in *The Best of Everything* (1959), featuring Hope Lange, Suzy Parker, Martha Hyer, and Diane Baker as young women trying to decide between finding success in a career and finding a man. Joan Crawford, as Amanda Farrow, presents one end of that spectrum—the hard-nosed career woman. While examining options for women, the film ultimately reinforces traditional notions of what a woman's choice should be. Another film that marks the conclusion of the classic phase of the woman's film is *A Summer Place* (1959), telling parallel stories of young love that take place twenty years apart on an island off the coast of Maine. Lovers reunited as adults (played by Richard Egan and Dorothy McGuire) engage in an adulterous affair that draws together in disgust at their parents' behavior the son (Troy Donahue) and daughter (Sandra Dee) of each marriage. Susan Hayward treads the well-worn path of the affliction film in *Stolen Hours* (1963), basically a reworking of the earlier *Dark Victory.* And in the often-filmed *Madame X* (1966) (earlier versions of which were made in 1929 and 1937), Lana Turner plays a woman innocently caught up in an indiscretion, who is forced out of her family by a meddling mother-in-law to save the reputation of her husband and son. Twenty years later, identifying herself only as "Madame X" to save his reputation, she is on trial for murder, represented by her own son, the public defender.

No one film clearly demarcates changing depictions of women's lives, because traditional woman's films such as *The Stolen Hours* and *Madame X* continued to be produced alongside more progressive and gritty films such as *Darling* (1965) and *Georgy Girl* (1966). British actress Julie Christie won an Oscar for her performance in *Darling* as Diana Scott, a rising model who parlays into fame and fortune her relationships with a well-known television reporter and an advertising executive. *Darling* Director John Schlesinger structures the film like a magazine interview in flashback, shooting in a more realistic black and white. Drawing upon the "kitchen sink" style of British cinema with its unflattering, naturalistic look—narratively and cinematically—at British life, *Georgy Girl* stars Lynn Redgrave as a homely, overweight girl grappling with complicated relationships against the backdrop of the 1960s' sexual revolution. Both British imports, these films marked a new sexual frankness in the woman's film that would soon be reflected in American cinema as well, hastened by the implementation in 1968 of the Motion Picture Production Code. The Code offered producers and audiences the opportunity to depict and view more adult themes on screen—with the appropriate rating, of course.

Rachel, Rachel (1968), the story of the sexual and emotional awakening of a lonely spinster schoolteacher in small-town Connecticut, is one example. The film is memorable not only as Paul Newman's directorial debut, but also for the repressed sexuality portrayed in Joanne Woodward's restrained performance and in a lesbian kiss between Rachel and equally repressed Calla Mackie, played by Estelle Parsons. Rachel is the daughter of a former funeral director and still lives above the funeral home with her mother. She sees her one opportunity for fulfillment in a sexual affair with a former high school acquaintance (James Olson) who briefly returns to the Connecticut village. After a harsh rebuke from her mother, who suspects Rachel's activities, and fearing she may be pregnant, Rachel makes a final break from the community and seeks hope and fulfillment on the West Coast. Woodward was nominated for Best Actress for her performance as Rachel, but the award went to Barbra Streisand in *Funny Girl* (1968), a biopic–woman's film–musical hybrid that highlights the career of vaudevillian and Ziegfeld headliner Fanny Brice. The sequel *Funny Lady* would follow in 1975.

The 1960s' mix of the traditional woman's film with the rise of the feminist depiction of women's lives would end on a high note with *The Prime of Miss Jean Brodie* (1969). Maggie Smith plays a supposedly progressive Edinburgh schoolteacher "in her prime" during the years between the wars. Her rather unorthodox teaching methods and emphasis on "truth, beauty, and romantic history" take precedence over a more practical view of living and contemporary politics. "Safety does not come first. Goodness, truth, and beauty come first," she pronounces. Her claim, "I am a teacher, first, last, and always," comes with some rather disastrous consequences, as she freely admits to shaping young minds in her image. Her misguided admiration of fascists Franco and Mussolini results in the death of one of her more impressionable pupils, who has taken to heart Miss Brodie's call for devotion to a cause. "You're a dangerous woman, Miss Brodie," one of her more earnest pupils asserts—and she may well be just that, in Smith's subtly shaded portrayal of an intricate character type.

By the 1970s, women's roles on screen were clearly keeping up with changes in society at large, combining issues found in traditional woman's films with a feminist slant and often examining the conflicts or hardships involved in women's traditional roles as wives, mothers (sometimes raising children alone), and helpmates, with opportunities for personal fulfillment. In *Alice Doesn't Live Here Anymore* (1974), Best Actress winner Ellen Burstyn plays a widow with one son who sets out to begin life anew as a singer. The pair's journey from California to Phoenix parallels Alice's stunted career as a singer when she takes a waitress job to support her child and meets a man with whom she may find a future. The feminist elements of the film are offset somewhat by the suggestion that women's destiny lies in traditional heterosexual pairing rather than in the attainment of personal success, while themes of sacrifice and domestic stability prevail. *Claudine* (1974), starring Diahann Carroll, presents a similar picture of the struggles of single motherhood, this time adding the element of race and socio-economic hardship to the mix. Nominated for an Oscar alongside Burstyn,

Carroll portrays a black maid in a wealthy white household. She tries to support her six children in Harlem while involved in a romantic relationship with a commitment-phobic garbage man (James Earl Jones). Paul Mazursky's *An Unmarried Woman* (1978) chronicles the recovery process of a woman (Jill Clayburgh) who is abandoned by her husband for another woman. With the support of friends and a sympathetic therapist—the best friend of the contemporary woman's film heroine—she begins putting her life back together again, and even contemplates another romantic relationship.

Female performers known to excel in other entertainment media turned in memorable filmic performances in this period. When Barbra Streisand brushes the hair from Robert Redford's forehead in the last moments of *The Way We Were* (1973), she reveals the lingering tenderness that exists between them long after their life together has ended. Katie Morosky (Streisand) and Hubbell Gardner (Redford) come from two different worlds when they meet in college in the 1930s. She is drawn to political activism; he coasts through a life of relative privilege. After the embers of romance kindle into a marriage, their differences begin to tear the two apart during an era of government censorship. Soon all they share are some beautiful memories and one of the most memorable of all motion picture theme songs, "The Way We Were." Two years later, Streisand reprised the role made famous by both Janet Gaynor and Judy Garland, as Esther in *A Star Is Born* (1976), recast in the music industry. Sharing both acting and directing credits, in *The Mirror Has Two Faces* (1996), Streisand plays frumpy English literature professor Rose Morgan who meets her husband (Jeff Bridges) through personals ads. He has been burned by too many relationships and swears off sexual consummation, but the two marry anyway. His new wife, however, misunderstands his vow of celibacy, so she works to transform herself into a goddess in hopes of jump-starting their amorous relationship.

Like Susan Hayward's roles from the 1950s, Diana Ross's Oscar-nominated performance as Billie Holiday in *Lady Sings the Blues* (1972) helped to sustain the woman's biopic–music hybrid. She followed that performance with *Mahogany* (1975), playing a woman from the ghetto whose aspirations as a fashion designer succumb to the ambitions and desires of others. Another example of the contemporary woman's film–musical–biopic hybrid is *Sweet Dreams* (1985), with Jessica Lange garnering an Oscar nomination for her portrayal of country music pioneer Patsy Cline. Lange would be Oscar-nominated for the on-screen biography of actress Frances Farmer in the self-titled *Frances* (1982), as well. Sissy Spacek would win an Oscar for her portrayal of country music superstar Loretta Lynn in *Coal Miner's Daughter* (1980). Moreover, Bette Midler scored a success with *Beaches* (1988), opposite Barbara Hershey, in the story of two childhood friends from two different worlds who share a lifetime of memories together, eventually both falling in love with the same man. Midler attempted to step into Barbara Stanwyck's shoes in the less-than-sterling remake of *Stella Dallas*, simply titled *Stella* (1990). Finally, perennial television favorite Sally Field was an unlikely choice to play a single mother, textile worker, and union organizer in Martin Ritt's *Norma Rae* (1979), for which she won an Academy Award.

The 1980s

Several films of the 1970s, 1980s, and 1990s deal with the complicated relationships among women. Although not a hitherto unknown subgenre in American motion picture making, this subgenre drew top-name stars and directors, and its films became marketable commodities at the box office. In *Julia* (1977), for example, Jane Fonda as real-life playwright Lillian Hellman embarks on a dangerous mission at the behest of lifelong friend Julia (Vanessa Redgrave) to smuggle money out of Nazi Germany to support the anti-Fascist cause. When Hellman learns her friend has been murdered, she begins a search in England to find Julia's daughter Lily, her own namesake. Somewhat a mixture of the two Bette Davis films *The Old Maid* (1937) and *Old Acquaintance* (1943), *The Turning Point* (1977) casts Shirley MacLaine as Deedee, who left a career as a dancer to become a wife, mother, and dancing teacher in Oklahoma, and Anne Bancroft as Emma, who continued with their company and became its star performer. When Deedee's daughter joins the dance company, both women reflect on the choices they made and find them difficult to live with years later. In *Rich and Famous* (1981), clearly a remake of *Old Acquaintance* and the last movie made by legendary woman's film director George Cukor, Southern belle and hack novelist Merry Noel Blake (Candace Bergen) is pit in professional and personal competition with serious writer Liz Hamilton (Jacqueline Bissett). The film chronicles the history of their friendship from college through middle age as both suffer the ups and downs of personal and romantic successes and hardships that women often experience.

Proving that her acting abilities in the woman's film genre were no fluke and that a market and critical interest in domestic melodrama still existed, Sally Field earned a second Oscar for Best Actress for her role in *Places in the Heart* (1984), playing a Depression-era Texas widow struggling to hold together a cotton farm and a family with the assistance of a ragtag group of social misfits. Finally, *Not Without My Daughter* (1991) cast Field as a the wife of an Iranian doctor living in the United States who dupes his wife into a visit to his homeland, and then refuses to allow her to leave Iran with their daughter.

Shirley MacLaine returned to the woman's film genre in her Oscar-winning performance as Aurora in *Terms of Endearment* (1983), combining the "maternal sacrifice" and "affliction" themes. The montage of the classic woman's film depicting marital bliss and woman's successful transformation for the better is replaced here by prissy Aurora's raucous ride on the beach in a Corvette driven by scamp ex-astronaut Garrett Breedlove (Jack Nicholson). Although costar Debra Winger, as Aurora's terminally ill daughter Emma, should have been the more traditional favorite for the Oscar, MacLaine likely won the prize for discrete scenes such as her twenty–second, increasingly hysterical insistence that nurses administer Emma's pain medication on time, and her unexpected yet carefully nuanced collapse at Emma's eventual death.

The reverse scenario occurs in *One True Thing* (1998), as career woman Ellen Gulden (Renée Zellweger), who has always identified more with the intellectual pursuits of her father than with what she considers the limited domesticity of her mother (Meryl Streep), is met with news of her mother's cancer. When her mother's illness in its advanced stages requires around-the-clock nursing, Zellweger's character reluctantly returns home to nurse her. In the process, she discovers remarkable truths about both her mother's strength and adaptability and her father's shortcomings. Despite Ellen's perception that disappointments in her parents' marriage explain her father's infidelity, he admits to his daughter, "I loved your mother. She was my one true thing." Adding insult to injury, the police are investigating her mother's death as a potential mercy killing. As this film and others attest, Meryl Streep joins a small number of actresses to enjoy critical acclaim for a career making films geared toward women. These include *Out of Africa* (1985), *A Cry in the Dark* (1988), *Postcards from the Edge* (1990), *The Bridges of Madison County* (1995), *Music of the Heart* (1996), and *Marvin's Room* (1996). In *Sophie's Choice* (1982), Streep's painfully beautiful portrayal of a former concentration camp prisoner forced to choose between her two children earned a much deserved Oscar for Best Actress, establishing her as one of the foremost film actresses of the contemporary era. With thirteen Oscar nominations, Streep is the most nominated performer in the history of the Academy Awards

In *Postcards from the Edge* (1990), Streep and MacLaine team up in the story of the difficult relationship between a mother and daughter in the entertainment field. MacLaine had earlier been cast with a varied female ensemble that included Olympia Dukakis, Dolly Parton, Darryl Hannah, Julia Roberts, and Sally Field in the tearjerker *Steel Magnolias* (1989). The wedding of Shelby Eaton (Roberts) is overshadowed by her mother's fear that her diabetes may dangerously complicate future childbirth for the bride. Despite the fears of her mother (Fields), Shelby's desire for "thirty minutes of something wonderful" outshines "a lifetime of nothing special." When Shelby's pregnancy does, indeed, contribute to her premature death, her mother's rage proves an ironic commentary on the strength of men versus women in a film all about the virtues and hardships of life as a woman.

Steven Spielberg's 1985 adaptation of Alice Walker's *The Color Purple* continues the trend toward examination of female bonding. Two black sisters separated in adolescence lead very different lives in a story of African American women joining together to fight sexual and racial oppression. Similarly, four black women cynical about love find hope in one another's company in *Waiting to Exhale* (1995). The title refers to that moment when a woman can finally stop holding her breath and relax into a trusting relationship with a man. Demonstrating that relationships between women are complicated regardless of age, in *The Whales of August* (1987), screen veterans Bette Davis and Lillian Gish play sisters who face how worldly changes and their age intrude on the idyllic Maine island where they have summered for the past 50 years. And *Fried Green Tomatoes* (1990) portrays how a bored housewife, Evelyn Couch (Kathy Bates), learns assertiveness from an octogenarian with an adventurous past (Jessica Tandy) while the elder makes a much-needed friend.

Geena Davis and Susan Sarandon take an empowering trek through the American Southwest in Ridley Scott's *Thelma and Louise* (1991), a new take on the traditionally male-oriented "buddy" picture. *Photofest.*

Perhaps no discussion of something called a "woman's film" in the last twenty-five years would be complete without comment on Ridley Scott's "buddy picture" *Thelma and Louise* (1991), starring Susan Sarandon and Geena Davis as an Arkansas waitress and a dissatisfied housewife whose two-day vacation to the mountains ends up in a "manhunt" through the American Southwest. "In the future, when a woman's crying like that, she isn't having any fun," Louise (Sarandon) reminds a good 'ole boy outside an Arkansas bar right after she stops him from brutally raping her friend Thelma (Davis). Whether Louise intentionally pulls the trigger, or fear and adrenaline cause an involuntary muscular reaction, the gun she holds goes off, lodging a bullet in the man's chest and killing him. Certain that Thelma's story of attempted rape and self-defense will not be taken seriously in a man's world—a conclusion heavily influenced by some mysterious event Louise experienced in Texas—the two make their getaway. Hailed by feminist critics for its depiction of female empowerment and liberation, the film actually raises questions about the relationship between feminism and the woman's film proper, questions that do not seem entirely resolved by the evolution of the genre after this production. The emphasis on the concerns of women place the film within the woman's film genre, as does the ambiguous ending with its message that freedom and escape are only possible in death. However, the more traditionally masculine behavior of the two characters (e.g., their tendency to solve problems in traditionally male ways, as through violence) casts doubt on the feminist implications of the film overall.

From the 1990s to the Present

Since the 1990s, a new generation of actresses has arrived, starring in films that focus on universal female issues, but meant to appeal to men as well. This most recent revamping of the woman's film combines the influences of feminism, now taken for granted, with the traditional emphasis on love, romance, heartache, and sacrifice. It may best be labeled "the chick flick," suggesting not only a lighter approach to the stereotypic feminine concerns, but also an appeal to younger audiences, even to teenagers. Many of these films deal with young adult romance, more appealing to a Generation X or post–Baby Boom market than are the traditional portrayals of the long-suffering heroine caught in sometimes implausible domestic situations. The chick flick may also blur the boundaries that separate comedy, romance, and drama, making distinctions between genres even more difficult (see **Comedy**). Representative examples spanning an extended period include *Ice Castles* (1978), *Pretty in Pink* (1986), and *13 Going on 30* (2004). Sandra Bullock has contributed significantly to the genre with *Hope Floats* (1998), in which she plays a young divorcée who crawls back to her small Texas hometown to start life over as a single mother, and *The Divine Secrets of the Ya-Ya Sisterhood* (2003), an ensemble piece with Bullock cast as a successful playwright kidnapped by friends from her mother's childhood destined to reunite mother (Burstyn) and daughter and explain secrets from the mother's past that influenced events in the daughter's childhood.

Contributing to the woman's film in *Steel Magnolias* early in her career, Julia Roberts has appeared in a long line of films depicting the complicated roles women fill in contemporary society. Her portrayal of a prostitute who finds love with Richard Gere in the highly implausible Cinderella story *Pretty Woman* (1990) should serve as a lightning rod for discussions of women's roles in a patriarchal society for years to come. In *Something To Talk About* (1995), Roberts's Grace Bichon begins to question everything she was brought up to believe when she faces strong family and community pressure to take back her cheating husband. Moreover, *Stepmom* (1998) casts Susan Sarandon opposite Roberts as a terminally ill divorced mother with grave concerns about her ex-husband's new romantic partner (Roberts) stepping in as a full-time mom. *The Runaway Bride* (1999) reteams Roberts with Richard Gere as a woman unable to make the ultimate commitment until she finds the right man. In her Oscar-winning role in *Erin Brockovich* (2000), she plays a real-life crusader against a powerful public utility that is polluting the water supply. *Mona Lisa Smile* (2003) casts Roberts as a free-thinking art professor at a women's college in the 1950s whose most important lesson to her students is to question the conventional roles society would cast for them.

Before concluding our discussion of the woman's film, a word or two ought to be said about a collection of films that might be labeled "male weepies"—domestic melodramas fitting many of the characteristics of the woman's film genre but with a male in the lead role. An essential characteristic of the woman's film is the depiction of how women endure their culturally limited feminine roles while being temporarily freed from them on screen. The male weepie demonstrates how the forces of female restriction could catch the logical inheritors of that patriarchal tradition in their snare. As Thomas Schatz points out, one variation of the male melodrama is the portrayal of the "tormented son" who cannot or will not assume the responsibilities of middle-class male adulthood because of inadequate father figures—films such as *Rebel Without a Cause* (1955) and *East of Eden* (1955), starring James Dean, and *Tea and Sympathy* (1956), with John Kerr as a college boy who has no interest in pursuits that could test his manhood. Often considered his masterpiece, Douglas Sirk's *Written on the Wind* (1956), although not set in the middle class, clearly fits this variation as well. In an attempt to put his debauched life behind him, Kyle marries Lucy (Lauren Bacall), an executive secretary who was loved first by family stalwart Mitch (Rock Hudson). When Kyle and Lucy attempt to have a baby and the couple's infertility proves to rest with Kyle, sexually precocious sister Marilee (Dorothy Malone) encourages her brother's paranoia by suggesting the child Lucy eventually conceives is Mitch's. The disastrous shoot-out that ensues changes the destiny of everyone involved. Moreover, Nick Nolte's character in Barbra Streisand's adaptation of the Pat Conroy novel *The Prince of Tides* (1991) has been dominated his entire life by a controlling mother (played by Kate Nelligan). Only when his sister attempts suicide can he bring into focus the horrible secrets of his childhood.

Love Story (1970) presents a new twist on the affliction film. Instead of the woman being left by the death or abandonment of a man, in this story, preppy, privileged Oliver Barrett learns from his working-class wife, "Love means never having to say you're sorry." Bucking the disapproval of his wealthy father and the family set, Oliver marries Jenny anyway and the two enjoy a short but happy period as husband and wife, struggling to make ends meet until leukemia takes her away. A final and more contemporary example, *Kramer vs. Kramer* (1979), demonstrates how much the gender tables have been turned. In an Oscar-winning role, Dustin Hoffman plays Ted Kramer, a professional man left to rear his young son after his wife *inexplicably* abandons them. When the child's mother (played by Meryl Streep, who won her own Oscar for Best Supporting Actress for this performance) returns asking for custody, Ted learns about the rewards of family life and goes to court to fight for his child.

In Woody Allen's *The Purple Rose of Cairo* (1985), Cecilia (Mia Farrow) finds escape from her marriage to an abusive husband through the magic of 1930s movies. "You like sitting through that junk," her husband Monk (Danny Aiello) hurls at her, refusing to spend even one night with his wife in a darkened theater. Yet, for Cecilia, the flickering image on the big screen both figuratively and literally comes to life for her. For women like Allen's Cecilia, films directed at a female audience may have started out as a marketing vehicle to encourage more women to purchase theater tickets, but the genre became a mainstay of motion picture production, providing not only a means of escape for women from their everyday lives, but also strong examples of how to survive and endure the hardship and struggles of being a woman. Moreover, the popularity of these films has provided their principal actresses opportunities to showcase and sustain their careers, offering them some control over their own destiny within the studio system. Perhaps because of the profit potential of these films and the high-caliber talent they feature, many directors who earned their reputation in other genres eventually made important examples of this sometimes questioned, but nonetheless perennial, genre in motion picture production.

References and Further Reading

Basinger, Jeanine. *A Woman's View: How Hollywood Spoke to Women* 1930–1960. Hanover, NH and London: Wesleyan University Press, 1993.

Doane, Mary Ann. *The Desire to Desire: The Woman's Film of the 1940s*. Bloomington and Indianapolis: Indiana University Press, 1987.

Geraghty, Christine. "The Woman's Film." In *The Film Studies Reader*, edited by Joanne Hollows, Peter Hutchings, and Mark Jancovich, 102–105. New York and London: Oxford University Press; Arnold, 2000.

Gledhill, Christina. *Home Is Where the Heart Is: Studies in Melodrama and the Woman's Film.* London: BFI Publishing, 1987.

Haskell, Molly. *From Reverence to Rape: The Treatment of Women in the Movies*. 2nd ed. Chicago and London: University of Chicago Press, 1987.

Landy, Marcia. *Imitations of Life: A Reader on Film & Television Melodrama*. Detroit: Wayne State University Press, 1991.

Leobowitz, Flo. "Apt Feelings, or Why 'Women's Films' Aren't Trivial." In *Post-Theory: Reconstructing Film Studies*, edited by David Bordwell and Noël Carroll, 219–229. Madison: University of Wisconsin Press, 1996.

Schatz, Thomas. "The Family Melodrama." In *Hollywood Genres: Formulas, Filmmaking, and the Studio System*, 221–260. Philadelphia: Temple University Press, 1981.

Williams, Linda. "Melodrama Revisited." In *Reconfiguring American Film Genres: Theory and History*, edited by Nick Browne, 42–88. Berkeley: University of California Press, 1998.

SELECTED BIBLIOGRAPHY

The following print and electronic sources provide general histories of film, film production, film as an industry, genre, film, criticism, and film viewing in general.

Academy of Motion Picture Arts and Sciences. www.oscars.org.

Ballo, Tino, ed. *The American Film Industry.* Madison, WI: The University of Wisconsin Press, 1976.

Belton, John. *American Cinema/American Culture.* 2nd ed. Boston: McGraw-Hill, 2005.

Bergan, Ronald. *The United Artists Story.* New York: Crown, 1986.

Bergman, Andrew. *We're In the Money: Depression America and Its Films.* New York: New York University Press, 1971.

Biskind, Peter. *Down and Dirty Pictures: Miramax, Sundance, and the Rise of the Independent Film.* New York: Simon & Schuster, 2004.

———. *Seeing Is Believing: How Hollywood Taught Us to Stop Worrying and Love the Fifties.* New York: Henry Holt, 2000.

Bordwell, David, Janet Staiger, and Kristin Thompson. *The Classical Hollywood Cinema: Film Style & Mode of Production to 1960.* New York: Columbia University Press, 1985.

The British Film Institute. www.bfi.org.uk.

Browne, Nick, ed. *Refiguring American Film Genres: Theory and History.* Berkeley: University of California Press, 1998.

Cook, Donald A. *A History of Narrative Film.* New York: Norton, 1981.

Cowie, Peter, ed. *Concise History of the Cinema.* 2 vols. London: A Zwemmer; New York: A. S. Barnes, 1971.

Crafton, Donald. *Talkies: American Cinema's Transition to Sound, 1926–1931.* New York: Scribner, 1997.

Dick, Bernard F. *Columbia Pictures: Pictures of a Studio.* Lexington: University of Kentucky Press, 1992.

Dirks, Tim. "The Greatest Films." *Filmsite.* www.filmsite.org.

Eames, John Douglas. *The Paramount Story.* New York: Crown, 1985.

Ellis, Jack. *A History of Film.* Englewood Cliffs, NJ: Prentice-Hall, 1985.
Grant, Barry Keith, ed. *The Film Genre Reader III.* Austin: University of Texas Press, 2003.
Haberski, Raymond J., Jr. *"It's Only a Movie": Films and Critics in American Culture.* Lexington: University of Kentucky Press, 2001.
Halliwell, Leslie, and John Walker. *Halliwell's Who's Who in the Movies.* 15th rev. ed. New York: Harper Resources, 2003.
Hampton, Benjamin Bowles. *The History of the American Film Industry from Its Beginnings to 1931.* New York: Dover, 1970.
Hay, Peter. *MGM—When the Lion Roars.* Atlanta, GA: Turner Pub., 1991.
Hill, John, and Pamela Church Gibson, eds. *The Oxford Guide to Film Studies.* Oxford; New York: Oxford University Press, 1998.
Hirschborn, Clive. *The Columbia Story.* New York: Crown, 1990.
———. *The Universal Story.* New York: Crown, 1983.
———. *The Warner Bros. Story.* New York: Crown, 1979.
The Internet Movie Database. www.imdb.com.
Jewell, Richard B., and Vernon Harbin. *The RKO Story.* New York: Arlington House, 1982.
Kaminsky, Stuart. *American Film Genres.* 2nd ed. Chicago: Nelson-Hall, 1985.
Karney, Robyn. *Cinema Year By Year: 1894–2000.* London; New York: Dorling Kindersley, 2000.
Kashner, Sam, and Jennifer MacNair. *The Bad and the Beautiful: Hollywood in the Fifties.* New York: W.W. Norton & Co., 2002.
Neale, Stephen. *Genre and Hollywood.* London; New York: Routledge, 2000.
Norman, Barry. *The Story of Hollywood.* New York: New American Library, 1988.
Osborne, Robert. *75 Years of the Oscar: The Official History of the Academy Awards.* New York: Abbeville Press, 2003.
Prince, Stephen. *A New Pot of Gold: Hollywood Under the Electronic Rainbow, 1980–1989.* New York: Charles Scribners', 1999.
Ray, Robert B. *A Certain Tendency of the Hollywood Cinema, 1930–1980.* Princeton: Princeton University Press, 1985.
Sarris, Andrew. *"You Ain't Heard Nothin' Yet': The American Talking Film, History and Memory, 1927–1949.* New York: Oxford University Press, 1998.
Schatz, Thomas. *Boom and Bust: The American Cinema in the 1940s.* New York: Scribners, 1997.
———. *The Genius of the System: Hollywood Filmmaking in the Studio Era.* New York: Henry Holt and Co., 1988.
———. *Hollywood Genres: Formulas, Filmmaking, and the Studio System.* Philadephia: Temple University Press, 1981.
Solomon, Stanley J. *Beyond Formula: American Film Genres.* New York: Harcourt, Brace, Jovanovich, Inc., 1976.
Stanley, Robert Hay. *The Celluloid Empire: A History of the American Movie Industry.* New York: Hastings House, 1978.
Stempel, Tom. *American Audiences on Movies and Moviegoing.* Lexington: University of Kentucky Press, 2001.
Thomas, Tony, and Aubrey Solomon. *The Films of 20th Century-Fox: A Pictorial History.* Rev. ed. Secaucus, NJ: Citadel Press, 1985.
Thomson, David. *The New Biographical Dictionary of Film.* New York: Knopf, 2002.
———. *The Whole Equation: A History of Hollywood.* New York: Knopf, 2004.
Wood, Robin. *Hollywood from Vietnam to Reagan—and Beyond.* New York: Columbia University Press, 2003.

INDEX

About the Authors

MARK A. GRAVES is an assistant professor in the Department of English, Foreign Languages, and Philosophy, Morehead State University (KY), where he teaches courses in American literature, Southern literature, and film.

F. BRUCE ENGLE is an instructor in the Department of English, Foreign Languages, and Philosophy, Morehead State University (KY), where he teaches courses in composition, English and world literature, film, and women's studies.